GLOBAL COMMUNICATION IN THE TWENTY-FIRST CENTURY

GLOBAL COMMUNICATION IN THE TWENTY-FIRST CENTURY

R O B E R T   L .   S T E V E N S O N
University of North Carolina at Chapel Hill

Longman
New York & London

**Global Communication in the
Twenty-first Century**

Longman, 10 Bank Street, White Plains, N.Y. 10606

Associated companies:
Longman Group Ltd., London
Longman Cheshire Pty., Melbourne
Longman Paul Pty., Auckland
Copp Clark Pitman, Toronto

Acquisitions editor: Kathleen M. Schurawich
Sponsoring editor: Gordon T. R. Anderson
Production editor: Professional Book Center
Cover design: David Levy
Cover photo: Reprinted with permission of AT&T Bell Laboratories Archives
Production supervisor: Richard Bretan

Library of Congress Cataloging-in-Publication Data

Stevenson, Robert L.
      Global communication in the 21st century / Robert L. Stevenson.
            p.   cm.
      Includes bibliographical references and index.
      ISBN 0-8013-0403-2
      1. Communication, International.   2. Intercultural communication.
I. Title.
P96.I5S75   1994
302.2—dc20   93-27339
                                                         CIP

1 2 3 4 5 6 7 8 9 10-MA-97969594

Contents

CHAPTER 3 **COMMUNICATING ACROSS CULTURES**   55

Introduction

The study of global communication is as exciting, diverse, and disjointed as the field itself. My own course, which was the inspiration for this book, is taught in the School of Journalism and Mass Communication, but it is cross-listed in the Department of Radio, Television, and Motion Pictures and in the Department of Political Science. It also meets a "social science perspective" requirement in the College of Arts and Sciences. Courses that overlap mine are found in both of these departments, plus the Department of Speech Communication and probably one or two others I haven't yet discovered.

In a recent overview, I suggested semi-seriously that international communication as an academic field is defined by neither substance nor research method, only geography.[1] Even that is confusing because the root word *communication* must be combined with *inter, cross,* or *comparative* and then with *national, cultural,* or *global* to complete the phrase. Courses, textbooks, and research interests are formed around every possible combination.

You will note how I switched from "global communication," which is the focus of the book, in the first paragraph to "international communication," which is the area of *Journalism Quarterly (JQ)* for which I was responsible for five years, in the second. The rule of thumb at *JQ* was that if the research took place outside the United States, the manuscript was my responsibility. As a result, studies of just about every aspect of culture and mass media in countries outside the United States came across my desk. In this book, I aim for some greater coherence in a field noted more for diversity of interest, method of scholarship, and departmental affiliation. It is aimed at two specific audiences.

---

[1] Robert L. Stevenson, "Defining International Communication as a Field," *Journalism Quarterly,* vol. 69, no. 3 (Fall 1992), pp. 543–553.

The first is students in the traditional course taught in almost all schools and departments of journalism. My own contact goes back to an undergraduate course at the University of Wisconsin that included something new and exciting called the "four theories of the press," which was the first effort to compare various national media systems systematically. The content has changed dramatically since then, but the focus of such courses is still on mass media, news flow, and problems of international journalism.

The second audience is more likely to be found in a department of speech communication where the basic undergraduate course emphasizes culture (rather than media institutions) and usually focuses on an interpersonal level (rather than national or global media systems). The journalism course is usually called "International Communication"; the speech communication version is frequently "Cross-cultural Communication." The thoughtful undergrad scanning the course listings at preregistration might reasonably ask, "What's the difference?"

It's a good question. When I started teaching the course, I didn't think culture was very important. People seemed pretty much alike around the world, and global communication was blurring cultural differences. Over the years, I changed my mind. The speed with which old cultural conflicts resurfaced in the wreckage of communism is the latest dramatic demonstration of the persistence of culture—and of its likely importance in the twenty-first century. I gradually came to the conclusion that you could not understand international communication—foreign media, news flow, and all of the political issues swirling around them—in the 1990s without understanding something about culture. At the same time, issues of culture—global Western influence, cultural autonomy, real multiculturalism—are so linked to mass media that some understanding of international journalism is required. Hence, this book.

The book is intended for students studying in any of the permutations of courses and departments that share an interest in global communication now and in the next century: inter/cross/comparative/foreign—cultural/national/global—communication/journalism/media. I would like to think that the book will be useful in courses in journalism, mass communication, speech communication, plain old communication, maybe occasionally even in political science, international studies, and international relations.

The first chapters emphasize culture and provide a context for the study of media systems that comes in the following chapters. In selecting only certain aspects of culture, I have tried to highlight those that are pertinent to the study of mass media around the world at the end of the twentieth century. In examining media around the world, I have tried both to avoid too much mind-numbing detail and to see mass media embedded in their cultural framework. A handful of countries get special attention because of their size, importance, or usefulness as examples of broader themes. Basic statistics about most of the others and starting points for research follow each chapter. The final chapters examine current issues pertinent to both culture and journalism and, I hope, build on the earlier chapters to explain some of today's headlines and to anticipate tomorrow's controversies. These chapters are especially vulnerable to being overtaken by current events. The four global trends that are developed in the first chapter and serve as common threads throughout the rest of the book are about evenly balanced between culture and mass media. I hope they help bind the two fields together.

Generalization inevitably means simplification and omission. Interpretation is always personal. Students using early drafts in class and professional colleagues reviewing the manuscript at various stages have pointed out errors and occasionally raised questions about my choice of material or interpretation of it. I've tried to catch most of the mistakes, and I acknowledge that others, better qualified than I am, would organize a course, a book, or the field itself differently. I hope the materials in the data bases and suggestions for discussion and reading will inspire challenges and alternative explanations to my generalizations and lead to further investigation of all manner of interesting and important questions about which honest people can disagree. I still like British broadcasting and dislike English coffee.

This book is a product of personal experience in about 50 countries and the knowledge I have gleaned from contacts with several hundred scholars, journalists, and students from around the world in the decade-plus that I have taught, researched, and thought about the subject of global communication. I have met these people in their own homes, classrooms, and offices as well as in mine. Sometimes we agreed; sometimes we didn't. With remarkably few exceptions, discussions have been cordial and useful. I have used these occasions to try out my ideas on others and to solicit alternatives. In more cases than I can document, my thinking has been influenced—and certainly enriched—by people I have met along the way. Their views are reflected on every page. Also, I am grateful to the following individuals who reviewed the manuscript and provided many helpful suggestions:

Stuart Bullion, University of Maine

John Rider, Southern Illinois University

Huber Ellingsworth, University of Tulsa

Zho He, San Jose State University

Lucila Vargas, Bowling Green State University

Nishan Havandjian, California Polytechnic State University at San Luis Obispo

Louise Montgomery, University of Arkansas

Robert Buckman, University of Southwest Louisiana

Shirley Peroutka, Goucher College

Festus Eribo, East Carolina University

The extended metaphor of the book is that of an armchair tour of global communication. Students come to the study of other cultures and media systems with a variety of backgrounds. Almost every class has students from other countries. These students are an invaluable resource who can shed light on their own countries and help us see ourselves from the outside. Homegrown students, too, range from "jet-setters" at home in any culture to those who rarely have been outside the state. I hope the former will use their experiences to refine, complement, or challenge what they read in the book. I hope the latter will use the book as a guidebook to the extraordinary diversity of the rest of the world that is open to them—if they seek it out—without ever leaving home. In the best of all worlds, the armchair tour in the following pages will be a spark that ignites an interest in global communication and inspires a few "stay-at-homes" to explore the world at close range.

But a word of warning: We Americans, unique among the peoples of the world, can travel the globe surrounded by a bubble of our own media and culture. Although I don't accept this as evidence of "cultural imperialism," we ought to be sensitive to the unique advantages and disadvantages it gives us: advantages of Big Macs and Cokes, familiar news media and pop culture, and somebody who can speak English just about anywhere we go; disadvantages of the temptation to leave cross-cultural communication one-sided and to stay inside the bubble of our own experience. That's all right for accidental tourists, but it would defeat the purpose of this book.

CHAPTER 1

The Context of Global Communication

ABOUT THIS CHAPTER

Global communication at the end of the twentieth century is in the midst of a revolution. You hear a lot about revolutions—political revolutions, social revolutions, fashion revolutions—but global communication really is going through the total upheaval that has happened only twice before in history. Evidence of the revolution is all around you. You see it every day on TV news, a global pop culture, and phone calls from friends halfway around the world.

In this chapter, we consider what this revolution includes and why it came about. Then we look at four trends in global communication that are a product of the current explosive change in communication, trends that will shape global communication well into the twenty-first century. These four trends—Anglo-American[1] dominance of all aspects of global communication, a resurgence of cultural identity as the basis for conflict, the beginnings of a global culture, and the triumph of independent journalism—are themes that recur throughout this book and provide a framework for our study of global communication.

INTRODUCTION

Think ahead a few years to the arrival of the twenty-first century. In the United States alone, 100,000 people will be 100 years old. You probably will know several of them. These centenarians will have seen more social change in their

---

[1] By Anglo-American dominance, we mean dominance by English-speaking countries including Britain, Australia, Canada, New Zealand, and the United States.

lifetimes than any of their ancestors did; in fact, they may have lived through more change than most of their ancestors combined. Most of that change has been or will be a direct product of communication.

A Century of Change

At the beginning of the twentieth century, people must have marveled at the innovations the previous century had witnessed: electricity, telephone, telegraph, trains, a few ungainly machines propelled along dusty roads by internal combustion engines. The idea that a human being might be able to fly through the air was regarded as a fantasy. Probably a good number would have agreed with the short-sighted congressman who, in the middle of the nineteenth century, had proposed closing the Patent Office because he thought everything that could be invented had been. No more change seemed possible.

He was wrong, of course, as prophets often are. Few people understood that all elements of communication were approaching the takeoff point on an accelerating curve that would reach an explosive vertical climb at the end of the twentieth century. Consider a few of the changes during the lifetimes of our hypothetical centenarians:

- In 1900, no one except a few hot-air balloonists had risen off the earth. Now by the millions every day, we jet around the world. Almost every week, satellites are shot into space, adding more or less permanently to the web of communication that covers the globe. One remarkable spacecraft, *Voyager I,* actually flew out of our solar system with a message on board in anticipation of the possibility that someone or something out there would receive the message.

- In 1900, a few people had traveled up to about 100 kilometers per hour (kph) on a train. Most travel was still done at the speed of a walking horse, as it had been for centuries. By midcentury, travel up to 100 kph in a car or train was common, and air travel was the luxury of a few. Now, of course, millions of us jet around the world every day at 1,000 kph. The privileged elite travel about 2.5 times as fast in the Concorde, but few expect to reach the 30,000 kph speeds that took the *Apollo* astronauts to the moon. You might, however, and your children probably will regard such speeds and distances with little more attention than we give the hourly New York–Washington shuttle or a routine vacation flight between North America and Europe.

- In 1900, telephones were still a rarity, and the telegraph was limited to the speed with which the operator could tap out a simple message. For most people, contact with either of them was rare. Now your home telephone can connect you with virtually any other telephone, fax machine, or computer on the planet. Ordinary telephone conversations, fax messages, and data transmissions are all translated into streams of binary digits and sent around the globe more quickly and reliably than your grandparents could call the next city. Satellite telephones packed in a suitcase and satellite-based systems that locate your position within a few meters came into use during the 1991 Gulf War and are now available commercially. Pocket versions available to all of us are on the horizon.

The global communication web embraces us all and exposes everything. We expect TV news to bring us pictures—live and in color, of course—from even the most isolated "hot spot." In the 1977 movie *Black and White in Color,* French and German colonists in Africa lived together peacefully for six months after the declaration of World War I, until a mail boat brought word that made them enemies. In 1989, television viewers around the world watched while the Chinese Army crushed student demonstrators in Tiananmen Square, communism in Eastern Europe collapsed, and U.S. forces invaded Panama. It is hard to imagine any important event anywhere in the world that is not reported instantly around the world.

The Information Revolution

In short, the end of the twentieth century is the start of a new information age. It is the product of a communication revolution that includes three elements Chapter 13 discusses in detail. The three elements are computers, satellites, and digitization. The revolution came about when all three new technologies converged to produce a global communication web that covers the earth as completely as the atmosphere.

All three technologies are so common that we can forget how new and how important they are. Big mainframe computers go back to the 1950s, but the personal computers (PCs) that most of us use to plug into the global information network go back only to the late 1970s. The first communication satellite was launched in 1964, but the cheap, reliable telephone circuits that make global communication possible date from the following decade. Digitization—the conversion of any form of text, sound, or picture into a simple binary language represented by zeroes and ones—is really a product of the 1980s. You know the technology through compact discs (CDs) that reproduce music with startling fidelity and are rapidly replacing hard-copy reference works in the library. You may not know that most long-distance telephone calls are also transmitted the same way. Computers, which themselves operate internally in this binary language, can convert any combination of text, sound, or pictures into packets of data that can be sent by satellite to any spot on earth. Most satellite circuits are, in fact, really data streams in which computer texts, fax messages, and ordinary voice conversations are mixed into a cascade of digitized information that doesn't distinguish between your phone call home and a computer check of your credit card balance.

Exponential Growth

As a result of the convergence of these three innovations, all aspects of communication are expanding at an exponential rate that doubles at every time increment: 1, 2, 4, 8, 16, 32, 64, and so on. In some cases, that time increment is only five or ten years and declining. Included in this exponential growth are (1) the *speed* with which information is transmitted, (2) the *capacity* of global systems, and (3) the *amount* of information available for transmission.

If you plot any of these aspects of communication over the last half of the twentieth century—speed of getting a news dispatch from one point to another, number of international telephone circuits, capacity of personal computers—they all follow an exponential curve that, in most cases, is approaching a vertical rise. Our interest in this book is not the technical aspects of this change, although we will return to the notion of the convergence of computers, satellites, and digitization as the basis for this communication revolution. Instead, our interest is in how the revolution is influencing global communication, particularly mass media and intercultural communication in different parts of the world, and in how it is laying the groundwork for a truly global culture.

If we step back from the dizzying changes that result from this communication revolution, four general trends in global communication at the end of the twentieth century can be detected. These trends will influence global communication well into the twenty-first century as well and form the underlying themes of this book. You will see them in one way or another in every chapter. Think of them now as a tourist guide to global communication, as an outline of the rest of the book, and as a context for understanding global communication at the beginning of the information age.

ANGLO-AMERICAN DOMINANCE

The dominance of the English-speaking world in all aspects of global communication would be cause for amazement if we didn't take it for granted. Think for a moment how extraordinary it is that Americans can travel just about any place in the world and reasonably expect to (1) get along speaking only English, (2) buy a Big Mac and a Coke, and (3) find a copy of *Time* or *The Wall Street Journal.* Even in the 1990s, it can be startling—but is no longer unusual—to walk into a hotel room in Papua New Guinea or Guinea-Bissau and see Cable News Network (CNN) on the TV or to get into a conversation in a remote city of China or Nigeria with someone who knows more about the latest rock and sports stars than you do.

The Anglo-American dominance of global communication can be categorized in various ways, but it may be useful here to separate this late twentieth-century phenomenon into four distinct areas: English as a world language, popular culture, communication technology, and news. Later chapters examine each area in some detail. At this point, a few quotes, examples, or vignettes can highlight what you may have taken for granted on an overseas vacation.

The Global Language

As tongue-tied Americans know, English is truly the world language, with a penetration around the world without parallel in history. A few statistics reinforce the experience of any international traveler. One person in seven in the world now claims to know the language; some estimates put the figure at one in four. Probably more people in China and the former Soviet Union alone are studying English today than speak it as natives. More than 80 percent of the world's research is first published in English; much of it is never translated because it doesn't need to be. In some areas of new knowledge—air traffic, for example—English is universal. Half of the world's 10,000 daily newspapers are published in English; probably a majority of the world's TV sets speak English.[2]

Pop Culture[3]

The influence of the West—mainly Anglo-America—in global popular culture is often the most visible and frequently the most contentious area of dominance. To some, this is "cultural imperialism," which, it is argued, is a deliberate policy of the culturally dominant nations to hold the rest of the world in a state of economic and political dependency while obliterating traditional cultures. Others contend that this indisputable dominance is a product of the economy of scale and market structure of the Anglo-American communication system rather than the result of any deliberate government or business policy, but the cultural imperialism argument is important enough that we will consider it in detail later.

It is not necessarily bad that you can travel just about anywhere in the world in the familiar environment of U.S. fast food, the Sony Walkman, and Levis, but you should at least be sensitive to the anomaly of this unique and all-pervasive influence. And to the advantage it gives Anglo-Americans in functioning in a world that sometimes seems a carbon copy of our own culture.

Consider a few data from recent headlines. The Academy Award TV extravaganza is shown in more than 100 countries. In many, the telecast is live. The Tournament of Roses Parade in Pasadena, California, is telecast to about the same number of countries. U.S. football is gaining popularity in Europe, where the National Football League established the World League of American Football. During the league's first year, teams in Barcelona, London, and Frankfurt did better in attendance and on the field than the U.S. teams.

Baseball is next. In Belize, thanks to a private cable system that brings in the Chicago super station WGN, the Cubs are everyone's favorite baseball team, and the kids begin their own games by humming "The Star-Spangled Banner." If you

---

[2] These examples are from *The Story of English, The Mother Tongue: English and How It Got That Way*, and several of the sources in them. See "For More Information" at the end of the chapter for citations.

[3] A similar idea is expressed in "Global Lifestyles and Cultural Nationalism." John Naisbitt and Patricia Aburdene, *Megatrends 2000* (New York: Morrow, 1990), pp. 118–153.

have traveled outside the United States at all, you may have noticed the ubiquity of U.S. college and pro sports shirts and caps and familiar faces on TV screens and in movie ads. Sometimes it's easy to forget that you've even left the United States.

Pico Iyer is an Anglo-Indian journalist for *Time,* educated in Britain and the United States. In 1985, he traveled around Asia documenting the influence of Western pop culture. The title of his book, *Video Night in Kathmandu,* gives a hint of the theme. Because he captures so well the pervasiveness of Anglo-American influence, his work deserves to be quoted at some length. Here he describes his arrival on a legendary Pacific island:

> I had come into town the previous afternoon watching video reruns of *Dance Fever* on the local bus. As I wandered around, looking for a place to stay, I had noted down the names of a few of the stores: the Hey Shop, The Hello Shop, Easy Rider Travel Service, T.G.I.Friday restaurant. After checking into a modest guesthouse where Vivaldi was pumping out of an enormous ghetto blaster, I had gone out in search of a meal. I ran across a pizzeria, a sushi bar, a steak house, a Swiss restaurant and a slew of stylish Mexican cafes. Eventually, however, I wound up at T.J.'s, a hyper-chic fern bar, where long-legged blondes in tropical T-shirts were sitting on wicker chairs and sipping tall cocktails. Reggae music floated around the place as a pretty waitress brought me my corn chips and salsa.
>
> After dinner, I had made my way to a nearby cafe for a cappuccino. Next to the cash register were enough stacks of old copies of *Cosmo, Newsweek* and the Sunday London *Times* to fill six doctors' waiting rooms. Behind the counter was a backgammon set for customers and a homemade library of faded paperbacks—Erica Jong, Ken Follett, Alexandra Penney. From Casablanca, the showy, two-story singles bar across the street, Bruce Springsteen was belting out "Dancing in the Dark." . . .
>
> I was, of course, in Bali, the Elysian isle famous for its other-worldly exoticism, its cultural integrity, its natural grace.[4]

Many travelers probably had similar experiences but were probably oblivious to the pervasiveness of Anglo-American pop culture. We shouldn't be. Even here, though, first appearances can be deceptive. Note the references to sushi and Mexican and Swiss restaurants. U.S. culture is an amalgam of the world's cultures, and the emerging global culture looks thoroughly "American" but is really a product of global influence, just as U.S. culture is.

Technology

The new communication technology ranges from satellites and supercomputers, where U.S. leadership is still strong if precarious, to the dazzling array of miniaturized consumer products that now come mostly from Asia but still are developed with the Western market in mind. As Iyer notes, it is the technology—from live

---

[4] Pico Iyer, *Video Night in Kathmandu* (New York: Knopf, 1988), pp. 29–30.

news via satellite to the ubiquitous Walkman—that jars the cultural senses in even the most isolated corners of the world. Could one visit even North Korea or Bhutan and not see the artifacts of Anglo-American pop culture? Probably not. I've seen a department store display window in Vienna full of University of North Carolina sweatshirts and a "Milwaukee University" T-shirt in Dakar, Senegal. Probably more people around the world know who Michael Jackson, Michael Jordan, and Rambo are than know who is president of the United States.

Electronic media saturate the United States as they do nowhere else. We lead the world in radio (more than two per person) and television set (almost one per person) ownership, although other industrialized countries are not far behind. Our per capita purchase of CDs, records, and tapes is actually slightly behind several other countries', and we lagged northern Europe in embracing the home VCR, but the sheer size of the U.S. market towers over every other. Because of size of the market—and, of course, our infatuation with entertainment gadgets— any consumer product must be successful in the United States if it is to succeed globally, and most are produced specifically with this market in mind.

News

Even more than pop culture, it was Western dominance of the global news flow that spawned the New World Information Order (NWIO) debate in the 1970s, a bitter global argument that sought to reduce Anglo-American influence.

The Big Four western news agencies, which supply about half of the global news according to most studies, are fairly well known. They are the Associated Press (AP) and United Press International (UPI) from the United States, British Reuters, and Agence France-Presse (AFP) from France. They are the heart of the world's news system and pump basic information to the smaller agencies and national media around the world as well as their own domestic media. First word of earthquakes and civil wars but also peace treaties and routine stock market prices is likely to flow from these giants to newspapers and broadcasters around the world.

Less well known but at least as important are the television news film organizations. Reuters Television, formerly Visnews, is the largest. It acquired its present name in 1992 when Reuters bought shares owned by the National Broadcasting Corporation (NBC) and the British Broadcasting Company (BBC). Worldwide Television News (WTN) was originally set up by UPI and Independent Television News (ITN), the news company of Britain's commercial TV network; now WTN is owned by the American Broadcasting Corporation (ABC). The U.S. commercial networks also market their news abroad, and Cable News Network (CNN) truly has become "the world's most important network." It is sold in more than 140 countries, and its signal is available to anyone with a satellite dish in most others. It is a regular feature in international-class hotels in countries from China to Switzerland and runs as background in newsrooms and government ministries around the world.

CNN is not alone, of course. The BBC's World Service Television (WST), which began operation in 1991, is billed as a competitive alternative and is expanding rapidly. It is likely to be successful in Africa and Asia, where the British accent and news formats are more familiar than the U.S. voice and style of CNN. New global and regional networks are springing up all over, inspired and financed by a new generation of internationally minded media moguls who, for the most part, are unknown to the people who watch their programs. In Britain and parts of the European continent, Rupert Murdoch's satellite Sky News channel broadcasts the ABC evening news and *Nightline,* and CBS's evening news is shown every day on domestic channels in France and Japan.

Even in the insular United States, an energetic priest from Creighton University in Omaha, Nebraska, pieced together a 24-hour TV service of nothing but TV news programs from around the world. Some, such as the Russian prime-time news show and newscasts from Mexico and Italy, are distributed live; others come on tape a few days to a week or two late. The service, called SCOLA (for Satellite Communications for Learning), is distributed by satellite around the clock to a growing number of university campuses and community cable systems, which are always looking for something new to fill their 30, 50, or 500 channels. Click through your cable system and you may find several non-English services offering programs from around the world. In 1992–93, for example, C-SPAN regularly broadcast Russian television news and the British Parliamentary question time.

Similar trends are taking place in other media. The three truly global newspapers—the *International Herald Tribune, The Wall Street Journal,* and *USA Today*—are all American, of course, but two British competitors are moving up. The *Financial Times* is printed in Germany and New York, and an international edition of the *Guardian* is printed in Germany and France for same-day European distribution. With the modern communication technology of the information age, distance is irrelevant. They could just as easily print in Singapore, New Delhi, or Lagos and may well have plans to do just that.

For the record, it should be noted that every news organization mentioned here is Western and that all but AFP are Anglo-American. However, it should also be noted that the phenomenon of globalization is not exclusively Anglo-American or even Western. China prints its *People's Daily* and an English-language newspaper, *China Daily,* in locations around the world. An international edition of *Al Ahram,* the influential Egyptian daily, is printed in London and New York. The *Yomiuri Shimbun,* one of Japan's "Big Three," publishes a combined English-Japanese edition in the United States. Other examples could also be cited. But, of course, it is the Anglo-American media that dominate the global flow of information, and they command the attention of the world's leaders and protesters.

·

RESURGENCE OF CULTURAL CONFLICT

In one sense, the search for cultural identity that is so much a part of the last decade of the twentieth century is nothing new. In the nineteenth century, it was called nationalism and was the cause of most of the wars that fill the books of European history. It is also a theme of third-world experience in the past 20 or 30 years, as new nations tried to create a sense of national identity to unite the disparate and often hostile peoples tied together by an arbitrary colonial boundary. What is new are (1) the degree to which these old conflicts create today's headlines and (2) the places where the conflicts are occurring.

Consider a brief but tragic list of current or recent battle zones: Sri Lanka, India, Lebanon, Sudan, the former Yugoslavia, Northern Ireland, and the former Soviet Union. Even the peaceful Pacific islands of Fiji and New Caledonia could be included. In all cases—and the list probably could be expanded by checking today's newspaper—the underlying cause is culture. It is language, religion, tribe, the things that traditionally separate "us" from "them." Such conflict is brutal, intractable, and often rooted in centuries of antagonism. In the absence of ideological conflict, the cultural forces that tie people together are threatened by those that rip them apart.

Language in Conflict

In some parts of the world, this cultural resurgence is taking a different form. Dramatic political changes in the old Soviet bloc have reduced the tensions between the superpowers but, curiously enough, may have made Europe safer for "traditional" war, based more on nationalism and cultural conflict than on ideology. To no one's surprise, the Serbs and Croats in what used to be Yugoslavia still don't like each other; nor do the Lithuanians and Russians, or even the Flemish- and French-speaking Belgians.

Two points in this renewed assertion of cultural identity in the Old World deserve notice. One is that the renewal often focuses on language rather than religion or ethnicity as the defining element of culture. It is significant that one of the first acts of "independence" in several of the non-Russian Soviet republics was to restore the national language to preeminence. This led to the spectacle of *Russians* in the Baltic states and Moldavia (now Moldova) claiming to be the victims of discrimination. When the wreckage of communism was cleared away after the collapse of the Soviet Union and the communist regimes of Central Europe, the traditional sources of cultural conflict remained, and language quickly rose to the surface.

The second point is the speed and intensity with which these conflicts—in many cases, centuries old—flared up. Even in Western Europe, which is moving, albeit sometimes reluctantly, toward a supranational "United States" of Europe, the power of nationalism is surprising. The 12 nations of the European Community (EC) insist on all 9 of their languages. The Belgian government fell twice in the 1980s when it removed a local mayor who had refused to take a language test after his city was switched to a Dutch-speaking province. In France, Spain, and the Italian Tyrol, demands for cultural autonomy center on language. There were even complaints about the new EC passport that put the words "European Community" above the national identity.

Language Conflict at Home

In our own part of the world, Loi 101, which was designed to protect the language and culture of French Quebec in an Anglo continent, is well known. It produced some surprising results, such as the platoons of language police rooting out violators of the French-only signage laws. With the wisdom of Solomon, the Canadian courts decided that a kosher delicatessen in Montreal could display a sign in Hebrew but an English-language bookstore could not use a small English sign to clarify its Latin name. After a period of intense conflict over Quebec's linguistic and cultural status, Canadian tempers cooled, but the issue of Quebec's linguistic and cultural status is unresolved. And the disintegration of Canada as a nation in the coming century remains a distinct possibility.

Within the past five years, about 20 states in the United States considered laws making English their official language, putting them in step with a parallel but low-profile and so far unsuccessful national campaign. The movement is partly a backlash against the bilingualism movement of the 1970s and the rapid influx of non-English-speaking (mostly Hispanic) immigrants, but the concern is legitimate and goes deeper. Alistair Cooke, the elegant British-born host of the Public Broadcasting Service's *Masterpiece Theater,* joined S. I. Hayakawa, well-known semanticist and short-term U.S. senator, to warn that "the day that the immigrant's tongue becomes the first language of any community or—God forbid—a State, the American experiment will be on its way to breaking up into a collection of feuding German republics, with several Quebecs in our future."[5] If Puerto Rico becomes a state—a distinct possibility in the 1990s—we will have one state that is officially and overwhelmingly Spanish-speaking. How that will affect the country, for good or bad, is anybody's guess.

Of course, it is a surprise to most Americans to learn that they have no official national language, and no one is quite sure what it would mean if we did have one. Language problems in North America and Western Europe seem simple—almost trivial—compared to the hopeless mire of Lebanon or the centuries-old hatreds in the former Yugoslavia and Northern Ireland. They are cut from the same cloth, however, and are likely to get worse, not better, as ideological competition between the superpowers recedes.

GLOBAL CULTURE

It is a curious counterpoint to the resurgence of cultural conflicts in the world that simultaneously the outline of a truly global culture is emerging. This trend includes, as comedians say, good news and bad news. The good news is that a global culture may offer a solution to some of the intractable conflicts noted above. If the Serbs and Croats, Sri Lankans, and Northern Irish could forget their ancient grievances, we'd all be better off. They certainly would be. A fragmented Central

---

[5] Quoted in a mass mailing by U.S. English, one of the national lobby groups, distributed in 1989.

Europe, free to rekindle the old animosities that exploded into World War I, is not much of a dividend from the dismantling of the Soviet empire. A global culture, even one heavy on Rambo films and Euro-Disneyland, might be an appealing alternative.

Universal Culture?

A controversial assessment of world events in the late 1980s, which we'll consider more later, argued that the crucial question of history has been answered (Western liberal democracy won) and that future leaders will spend their time putting out local brush wars and deciding who gets the VCRs and stereos. This is a tempting vision of a world with neither superpower confrontation nor ethnic strife. It even reinforces the point about the emergence of the first global culture. Is the continuing Anglo-American dominance of world communication a first step in that direction? And should we take it as the ''victory'' of the global purveyors of mass culture over the rough mosaic of traditional cultures, nasty as some of them may be?

Possibly, but there are drawbacks. The obvious one is the loss of the planet's cultural diversity. Although the kind of Americanization of the world that Iyer describes so well in Asia makes it easier for everyone—not just Americans—to travel around the world with something familiar to grab on to, the blandness, superficiality, and artificiality of a global culture are always disappointing. If you're going to eat Big Macs and plug your Walkman into rock's current hot group, what's the point of leaving home?

Although we would all welcome an outbreak of peace and goodwill in the world's hot spots, a global culture consisting mostly of Japanese hardware and U.S. software would be a big net loss for the planet. *Time* magazine compared the rapid loss of the world's remaining 15,000 cultures to the burning of the library of Alexandria: ''Today, with little notice, more vast archives of knowledge and expertise are spilling into oblivion, leaving humanity in danger of losing its past and perhaps jeopardizing its future as well.''[6]

Another debit is that so much of the emerging global culture is a product of multinational corporate enterprise. The new media moguls, who do exist in large part as individuals rather than anonymous corporate boards, are virtually unknown, sometimes even in their own countries. They seem to form almost a global interlocking directorate with vertical and horizontal integration of the means of production and distribution. Consider that great American, Australian-born Rupert Murdoch. His empire stretches from the South Pacific across Britain and Europe to North America—the entire Anglo-American axis of cultural influence. He owns a Hollywood film studio, a struggling TV network, and the largest TV magazine in the United States, along with assorted newspapers and magazines. In Britain and Europe, he operates the most advanced direct broadcast satellite system packages and the largest (and sleaziest) national paper in London.

---

[6] Eugene Linden, ''Lost Tribes, Lost Knowledge,'' *Time,* September 21, 1991, pp. 46–56.

His holdings also include the no-longer-so-illustrious *Times* of London, small dailies in Fiji and Papua New Guinea, a major daily in Hong Kong, and even a magazine in Hungary.

Murdoch is unusual, not because he operates globally, but because he is relatively well known. Many of the other modern moguls are not. Silvio Berlusconi in Italy, the late Robert Maxwell in Britain, the Japanese Sony Corporation, the Hachette organization in France, and Bertelsmann in Germany are all multimedia and multinational. All are taking advantage of new technology, global management strategies, and a tide of hands-off government policies to extend their operations and influence beyond national and regional borders. Until Maxwell's death in 1991, he was little known in the United States even though he had begun to follow Murdoch in establishing a strong foothold there. Many of the other individual and corporate moguls of the global communication system are sinking roots into the United States as well.

Foreign Ownership in the United States

From the U.S. perspective, a growing concern is not the old complaint of excessive cultural influence around the world—the cultural imperialism argument—but the astonishing speed with which the United States is selling off its popular culture industries to foreign buyers. The 1989 sale of Columbia Pictures to Sony, which already owned CBS Records, raised the specter of a single multinational corporation controlling a complete global package of Japanese Walkmen and Watchmen and the records, tapes, CDs, and movies to go with them.

In almost every one of the popular media—books, magazines, music, movies, even newspapers—foreign buyers are snapping up U.S. properties with speed and enthusiasm never seen before. One of the largest chains of daily newspapers in the United States is the Canadian Thomson group, which owns 120 dailies, most of them, to be sure, very small. Among the French Hachette properties is the *Encyclopedia Americana,* although it also should be noted that the prestigious *Encyclopaedia Britannica* is owned by a U.S.-based multinational. In the United States, only television is protected by law from foreign ownership (which presumably is why Murdoch cashed in his permanent resident green card to become a U.S. citizen). The prohibition is not really important, however, because the global system of production and distribution provides access to the U.S. market through joint productions, direct sales, and indirect ownership. Behind the foreign interest in Hollywood is exponential growth of broadcasting internationally that promises to double—and perhaps to double again—the numbers of receivers, channels, and program hours by the end of the twentieth century.

Is global communication in the 1990s the ''global village'' Marshall McLuhan envisioned a generation ago? Perhaps it is, in the limited sense that few events, good or evil, escape notice for long or that a few of the icons of U.S. pop culture do achieve worldwide recognition. The countervailing forces, however, seem to be growing, and even in the democratic countries of Western Europe and Canada, people are mounting the barricades to slow the advance of the global invasion.

TRIUMPH OF INDEPENDENT JOURNALISM

In recent years, followers of the global debates about the role of mass media in third-world development have heard harsh criticism, even denunciation, of the Western tradition of independent journalism as a facade for cultural imperialism. The more moderate critics argued that the fragile economic and political structures of most third-world countries need the support of mass media to assist the process of nation-building. Independent, critical media are a luxury that might be possible later.

The more radical critics, in contrast, disdained the claims of an independent press as a fig leaf covering neocolonialism—communication as a late twentieth-century surrogate for the imperial armies of earlier invasions—and argued that the developing nations could achieve real independence and "authentic" (i.e., non-Western) development only by disengaging from the Western-dominated global communication system. They also invented a new style of journalism, heavy on flattery of public officials and the "good news" of development accomplishments. "Development journalism," as it was called, was based on mobilizing news media in support of national development. Part of the idea came from Vladimir Lenin's dictum about the press as a legitimate instrument of government control. But the idea also came, in part, from the United States, where mass media had been used (and still are) by various educational systems and the federal Agricultural Extension Service to promote all sorts of social change.

After the collapse of communism in Central and Eastern Europe at the end of the 1980s, the term *third world* was used less frequently. The "second world" of communism disappeared except for China, Cuba, and North Korea, which seemed to be anachronisms from an earlier age rather than alternatives to market-based liberal democracy. However, economic and political problems, if anything, seemed to get worse, and the idea remained that mass media had some power and some special responsibility to help countries still struggling to catch up with the West. In the "emerging democracies" of the old second and third worlds, the role of journalism is still a topic for debate.

Development Journalism

In the 1970s, the goals of third-world "national development" often changed from economic and social growth along Western lines to the vagaries of cultural sovereignty and political identity. In practice, the nation often came to mean the regime in power—hardly a new idea—and development news consisted of endless puffery of government leaders and the nation's progress, even where there wasn't much.

Development journalism—very much a part of the New World Information Order debate at the United Nations Educational, Scientific and Cultural Organization (UNESCO) in the 1970s—now has a record, and it is not impressive. Several of the alternative news organizations created both to implement the NWIO and to fill legitimate gaps in the global news system have operated for 10 or 15 years, most with little evidence of success. The most ambitious was the Non-Aligned

News Agencies (NANA) pool, which transmitted stories contributed by member news agencies, almost all government controlled. In 15 years of operation, it achieved virtually no visibility, even in the media of its strongest supporters. The Pan-African News Agency (PANA), modeled on NANA, limped along as an unloved and largely ignored stepchild of its parent Organization of African Unity.[7] In 1993, it announced a shift from reliance on government-controlled national agencies to independent reporting, hoping that the "Western" style might save it financially.

In contrast to NANA and PANA, a number of regional and specialized agencies achieved modest success in filling the gaps left by the global agencies. Most operated with the very Western notion that news media ought to be independent of government, critical when necessary, and always a watchdog on the institutions of power. Two good examples are the Caribbean News Agency (CANA) and Pacnews, which serves the scattered islands of the South Pacific. Both are pragmatic news organizations, are filling a real need, and are run by professionals.

Several independent newspapers also demonstrated surprising vitality, some in unexpected places. In Zimbabwe, an independent newspaper in the provincial city of Bulawayo quickly sold out its 100,000 press run in Harare, while the government-run papers gathered dust.[8] In China, the independent *World Economic Herald* in Shanghai was increasing circulation dramatically and, not surprisingly, was one of the first voices silenced by the government in its crackdown on the democracy movement in 1989. In Russia and Central Europe, professional, independent media replaced the partisan papers that emerged from the rubble of communism.[9]

Death of Communism

Perhaps the most dramatic changes in journalism took place in the Soviet Union and Central and Eastern Europe. Under the banner of *glasnost,* journalism underwent an extraordinary metamorphosis in just a few years in that part of the world. A small Soviet weekly paper, *Ogonek,* went from 230,000 copies to more than 3 million and was limited to that by a lack of newsprint. *Moscow News,* formerly a pallid weekly distributed to tourists and as overseas propaganda, became virtually impossible to find at Soviet kiosks and was banned from distribution in anti-*glasnost* Cuba. Both of these publications were at the edge of *glasnost,* testing with each issue the limits of journalistic independence. *Izvestia,* the dull government daily, fell from 10 million copies a day to 4.5 million. *Pravda,* the party daily that also remained timid and traditional, lost 80 percent of its 10-million circulation, while the bold *Komsomolskaya Pravda* grew to 17 million copies a day. The failed coup against President Mikhail Gorbachev in August 1991 produced, among other effects, an end to the lingering

---

[7] James Brooke, "Africans Find Freeing News Isn't So Easy," *New York Times,* December 8, 1988, p. A3.

[8] Jane Perlez, "Zimbabwe Reads of Officials' Secrets," *New York Times,* January 29, 1989, p. A3.

[9] Jamey Gambrell, "Moscow: The Front Page," *New York Review of Books,* October 8, 1992, pp. 56–62.

faith in a party press.[10] The role of journalists in the momentous events that brought an end to communism in Europe and dictatorships in other parts of the world is a topic for Chapter 11 and debate well into the future.

Media in Revolution

The collapse of communist governments in Poland, Czechoslovakia, East Germany, and Romania in 1989 cannot be attributed to independent, critical journalism, but independent journalism played a role once the old regimes began to falter. In Czechoslovakia, students spread news of Prague protests with handbills and amateur newspapers until government-controlled broadcasting was "liberated" and began honest reporting. In Romania, the central broadcasting headquarters became the command center for the insurgent government. It must have been the first time in history that the inner workings of a revolution were telecast live. In both countries, videotapes of the extraordinary events that routed vicious governments were rebroadcast again and again as if needed to convince people of what they had accomplished. The full story of the influence of mass media on the social upheavals of 1989 has not been told yet, and it is still too early to determine finally whether communication played some critical role or merely was an eyewitness that gave the rest of us a ringside seat and possibly a magnified, distorted view of its own importance.

The End of History?

These changes represent the triumph of independent journalism over competing press ideologies we consider at length in later chapters. These changes also may be part of a larger trend that is also connected to the communication revolution of our time. An article in the summer of 1989 in *The National Interest,* a conservative political journal, created a considerable flutter of interest in Washington, D.C.[11] The author, Francis Fukayama, took as his text the argument by the German philosopher Georg F. Hegel that when the essential question of how to organize human society is answered, history will end.

Hegel believed that point was reached in 1806 when Napoleon, representing the ideals of the French Revolution, defeated the Prussians. Fukayama accepted the argument, contending that liberal democracy built on a system of market capitalism had outlasted its two twentieth-century competitors, fascism and communism, for the hearts and minds of men and women. He envisioned a future in which ideological struggles would be replaced by a concern with regional ethnic struggles and technical questions of the distribution of wealth. The result would be a banal culture in which the distribution of VCRs and stereos—his words—would be a major concern.

---

[10] The paperback edition of Hedrick Smith's *The New Russians* (New York: Avon, 1991), published in late 1991, carries his analysis of *glasnost* to the postcoup, postcommunist, post–Soviet Union.

[11] Francis Fukayama, "The End of History?" *The National Interest,* Summer 1989, pp. 3–18.

Is this the global culture we described earlier? Or is it simply the gloating of conservatives over the failure of communism? Possibly both, and Fukayama, who became the deputy director of strategic planning for the State Department in a conservative Republican administration, was not without his critics. A *Time* magazine headline writer called the article the beginning of nonsense, and any number of writers noted the depressing list of wars around the world and the equally depressing list of inequities and conflicts still unresolved in Western liberal democracies. If history has ended, there is still lots to do, cleaning up the wreckage of past struggles and coping with the resurgent cultural conflicts.

The criticisms, however, miss an important point, perhaps the key point in Fukayama's argument: The legitimacy of communism is gone. It can no longer claim to be the vanguard of historical change. It is not the rallying cry of the young idealists but the burden of tired, old men who tried and failed. Imagine being in charge of the ritual anniversary celebrations of the revolutions in China or Cuba. What could you say to defend the record of those regimes in the past four decades? How could you hope to mobilize the citizenry to fight for some increasingly improbable future, especially with the images of Tiananmen Square, Bucharest, and Moscow still so vivid in people's minds and part of the permanent videotape archive for future generations?

Journalism is part of the great upheaval of the end of the century. It would be foolish to predict an end to government control of communication in the third world or of government's efforts to influence the media in the West, but it is increasingly difficult to justify that control. The theories of the role of mass media in society that legitimize government monopoly (communism) or mobilization (development) were never very popular among journalists and are now on the defensive everywhere. You will seldom meet journalists from the third world or the socialist countries who, despite criticism of Western coverage of their countries, defend government control or accept the argument that professional, independent journalism is a luxury developing countries cannot afford.

The nineteenth-century British prime minister Benjamin Disraeli argued that the only preparation for liberty is liberty. Countries that are coping most success-fully with the turmoil and upheaval of our age—Costa Rica, India, Botswana, and keep your fingers crossed for Central Europe and the former Soviet republics—are doing it in the glare of honest journalism. Of course, they really have no choice because in the age of high-tech global culture, government monopoly of infor-mation, never really successful even in the old days, is now impossible.

Consider the use of fax machines and computer bulletin boards in China, audiocassettes in Iran, underground newspapers in Poland, satellite dishes and short-wave receivers everywhere. To rephrase Abraham Lincoln, you can fool some of the people some of the time, but even that's getting tough. An immediate victim of the suppression of the democracy movement in China was the credibility—if it had any to begin with—of Chinese government news media. A difference between the 1950s, when Mao Zedong adapted Lenin's principles of media control to the creation of the first third-world communist state, and the 1990s was that it was possible in the 1950s to imagine a nearly soundproof border and government monopoly of information. Now, with Sony pocket short-wave receivers, photocopiers and fax machines, and half-meter satellite dishes, it is not.

A Chinese demonstrator in Tiananmen Square invites fellow protesters to address the global media. The picture illustrates the importance of English as the language of global communication and the influence of Anglo-American news media.

SOURCE: Andy Hernandez, SIPA Press.

Accelerating Change

Global communication in the 1990s is changing so fast that anything written today can be outdated tomorrow. Who could have imagined the collapse of communism in Eastern and Central Europe or the violent end to the democracy movement in China? Who could have predicted portable phones and fax machines, compact disks and digital audiotapes, direct broadcast satellites, and portable receiving dishes? What inventions in the future will make today's technology seem as primitive as a wind-up record player or a hand-crank telephone? An understanding of global communication today will help you make sense of tomorrow's headlines. That's the purpose of this book.

MAIN POINTS

1. Global communication at the end of the twentieth century is in the midst of a revolution that is a product of the convergence of three technological innovations: communication satellites, computers, and digitization. Digitization converts any form of information—text, sound,

and pictures—into a simple binary code that can be transmitted instantly through a global network of computers linked by satellite. As a result, virtually all elements of communication are accelerating at an exponential rate. This produces rapid change in all cultures and often disruption in traditional cultures.

2. The English-speaking world dominates global communication and is still at the forefront of the information revolution even though its economic and political power are diminished. The Anglo-American dominance of language, pop culture, communication technology, and news is, according to some, a new form of domination of the developing world that seeks to maintain nineteenth-century imperial dominance. Others see it as a product of the global scale of the English-speaking world and the strongly competitive commercial structure of Anglo-American media. Despite a global debate and call for a more equitable redistribution of communication resources as part of a New World Information Order, Anglo-American dominance seems to grow stronger.

3. As ideological competition between the superpowers recedes, the assertion of cultural identity has become the basis of more and more conflict. In many countries, particularly in the industrialized nations, this cultural identity focuses on language.

4. Despite the resurgence of culture as the basis of conflict, the first outlines of a global culture are emerging. This culture is promoted by a new generation of broad-based, communication-oriented corporations. Although the content of the emerging global culture still looks Anglo-American, more and more of it is produced and distributed by European and Japanese conglomerates that aim for global markets.

5. The New World Information Order debate included calls for a new kind of journalism more supportive of third-world development than the traditional independent, critical media of the West. After a decade of practice, development journalism has failed, and the benefits of independent journalism are increasingly acknowledged. The dismantling of communist regimes in Eastern Europe also contributed to the triumph of independent journalism.

FOR MORE INFORMATION

Robert McCrum, William Cran, and Robert MacNeil, *The Story of English* (New York: Viking Penguin, 1986), based on a BBC/PBS series, covers both the evolution of English as a global language and its current varieties. The videotapes on which the book is based are probably available in your campus library. Take a look at the first segment, "An English-Speaking World."

Bill Bryson, *The Mother Tongue: English and How It Got That Way* (New York: William Morrow, 1990), covers a lot of the same ground, with more emphasis on the evolution of the language.

Pico Iyer, *Video Night in Kathmandu* (New York: Knopf, 1988). The extensive quote in this chapter gives you a flavor of the book. It is now available in paperback and recommended especially for armchair tourists who are not able to see global Anglo-American cultural dominance firsthand.

William A. Hachten, *The World News Prism: Changing Media, Clashing Ideologies,* 3rd ed. (Ames: Iowa State University Press, 1992), is an excellent, tightly written introduction to the issues that underlie much of this book. His "five concepts of the press" are the basis for my discussion of world media systems.

Robert L. Stevenson, *Communication, Development, and the Third World: The Global Politics of Information* (New York: Longman, 1988; pbk. University Press of America), emphasizes a summary of the NWIO debate and the role of communication in third-world development. Not surprisingly, the perspective is similar to the one in this book.

Cees Hamelink, *Cultural Autonomy in Global Communications* (New York: Longman, 1983), and Anthony Smith, *The Geopolitics of Information* (New York: Oxford University Press, 1980), cover some of the same ground as my 1988 book but from a different political perspective. Read them all and make up your own mind.

Francis Fukayama, "The End of History?" *The National Interest,* Summer 1989, pp. 3–18. A provocative article, especially relevant to the collapse of communist regimes in Eastern Europe and to the assertion of the triumph of independent journalism. A follow-up issue contained extensive reaction. His book, *The End of History and the Last Man* (New York: Free Press, 1992) expands the theme. Use these works as the basis of a debate over his main premise.

FOR DISCUSSION

1. Interview international students for examples of U.S. cultural influence in their countries. Ask them to account for this influence and to assess its positive and negative effects.

2. Examine media from other countries—newspapers and magazines in the library, SCOLA, C-SPAN, and other satellite TV channels—for similarities to and differences from U.S. media. International students can help you identify familiar TV programs and Hollywood films.

3. Collect data from local officials and Census Bureau documents about the ethnic origins of your community or state. Assess to what extent the data reflect "a nation of nations" and how immigrant cultures influence the dominant culture.

DATA BASE

I. The ten top entertainment companies in 1988 as measured by income were:

1. Time Warner (U.S.), sales $8 + billion ($12 billion in 1991). Substantial involvement in music, TV and film production, cable TV, books, newspapers, and magazines. Holdings include *Time, Fortune, Sports Illustrated, People, Money;* Home Box Office, Cinemax; Time-Life Books, Little, Brown & Co., Scott, Foresman & Co.; Warner Brothers movies, television (*Night Court, Murphy Brown*), Lorimar; Warner Brothers Records, Atlantic Records.

2. Bertelsmann (German), sales $6 + billion ($9 billion in 1991). U.S. holdings include 30 publishing houses (Bantam, Doubleday, Dell), RCA Records, Literary Guild, Doubleday Book Club, Mystery Guild, magazines

(*Parents, Young Miss, Expecting*); in Germany, Gruner + Jahr (*Stern, Brigette, Geo, Capitol, Schöner Wohnen, Eltern, Nicole, Impulse, Yps, art, Frau im Spiegel* magazines), 25 percent of *Spiegel, Hamburger Morgenpost* (daily newspaper), Bertelsmann Music Group (RCA, Ariola, Arista records), Ufa group, Sonopress; RTL plus (38 percent).

3. News Corp. (Australian), sales $6 billion ($9 billion in 1991). Rupert Murdoch's empire includes 20th Century Fox studios, Fox TV network, Harper & Row publishers, daily papers in Boston and San Antonio, Texas, *TV Guide, New York* magazine, and *Seventeen* in the United States; in Britain, daily papers (London daily and *Sunday Times,* the *Sun, News of the World*) accounting for one-third of total national circulation, William Collins books, 7 percent of Reuters, 20 percent of Pearson (*Financial Times, The Economist,* Viking Penguin books, Longman), Sky direct broadcast TV system; two-thirds of daily newspaper circulation in Australia; half of daily newspaper circulation in New Zealand; papers in Hong Kong, Fiji, Papua New Guinea; magazines in Hungary; STAR TV, a regional satellite service based in Hong Kong.

4. Fininvest (Italian), sales about $5 billion ($9 billion in 1991). Silvio Berlusconi controls three commercial TV networks (with a majority of total audience) and *Il Giornale* (a major daily paper) in Italy; was a partner in France's fifth channel, La Cinq, which went bankrupt; and owns 45 percent of Tele-5 in Germany and extensive TV operations in Spain, Tunisia, and the former Yugoslavia. In the United States, he collaborates with several Hollywood studios on production and distribution.

5. Fujisankei (Japanese), sales about $5 billion ($6 + billion in 1991). Privately held company that publishes *Sankei Shimbun* daily newspaper (circulation 2 million plus) and operates Japan's most successful radio and TV networks; both emphasize mass-appeal entertainment. Bought one-quarter of Britain's Virgin Music Group and arranged $10 million deal with independent Hollywood producers but so far has not bought U.S. properties. Paid President Ronald Reagan a reported $2 million for brief and controversial visit to Japan in 1989.

6. Capital Cities (U.S.), sales about $5 billion ($5.3 billion in 1991). Owns ABC network, ESPN, Arts & Entertainment network (38%), Lifeline (33%).

7. Hachette (France), sales about $4 billion ($5.7 billion in 1991). The largest magazine publisher in the world owns Curtis Circulation Company, Diamandis Communications (*Woman's Day*), *Elle* magazine, and Grolier Publications (*Encyclopedia Americana,* Dr. Seuss's Beginning Readers Program, Disney's Wonderful World of Reading) in the United States; the weekly *Paris-Match* and Europe 1 (France's number two radio station) in France.

8. General Electric (U.S.), sales about $4 billion ($3.1 billion in 1991). Owns NBC network.

9. Walt Disney (U.S.), sales over $3 billion ($6.1 billion in 1991). In addition to U.S. activities, runs Disneylands in Japan and France. Includes Touchstone Pictures, which offers racier fare than the traditional family-oriented Disney movies.

10. Sony (Japan), sales from CBS Records and Columbia Pictures over $3 billion ($3.5–4.5 billion in 1991, from entertainment activities). Owns 2,770

feature films; 23,000 episodes of 260 TV series; Columbia Television's 11 prime-time series, including *Who's the Boss?* and *Designing Women;* Merv Griffin Enterprises, including "Wheel of Fortune" and "Jeopardy"; 820 Loews movie screens in 220 locations; Columbia Pictures and Tri-Star film studios; and RCA/Columbia Home Video.

SOURCE: Data from various sources, especially "The Entertainment Industry: Survey," in *The Economist,* December 23, 1989, pp. 3–17.

II. In 1989, four popular U.S. television programs were sold to the following European countries:

	Cheers	*Golden Girls*	*L.A. Law*	*Roseanne*
Belgium		X		X
Britain	X	X	X	X
Denmark	X	X	X	X
Finland	X	X	X	X
France			X	X
Greece	X	X	X	
Iceland	X	X	X	
Ireland	X	X		X
Italy	X	X	X	X
Holland	X	X	X	X
Norway		X	X	
Portugal	X	X		
Spain		X	X	
Sweden	X	X	X	X
Switzerland		X		X
West Germany			X	
Yugoslavia		X	X	

SOURCE: Steven Greenhouse, "For Europe, U.S. May Spell TV," *New York Times,* July 31, 1989. Copyright © 1989 by the New York Times Company. Reprinted by permission.

III. Five global news agencies and four news film agencies supply most of the world's news.

1. Reuters is the world's largest and oldest news agency. It obtains information from 137 exchanges, from 3,100 subscribers in 79 countries and a network of over 1,100 journalists, photographers, and camerapeople. Distributes information via 145,000 terminals and teleprinters and directly to clients' computers. Produces services in English, French, German, Spanish, Arabic, Japanese, Danish, Norwegian, Dutch, Portuguese, Swedish, and Italian. Processes up to 5 million words a day through editing centers in London and Hong Kong. New York edits material from Western Hemisphere.

2. Associated Press serves 84 percent of U.S. daily newspapers (96% of daily newspaper circulation). Has world's largest photo service, now converting to digital format. Has total work force of 2,920, including 1,580 journalists and photographers around the world. Supplies news to 112 countries in 6 languages: English, French, German, Spanish, Dutch, Swedish. Customers include 1,500 daily papers and broadcasters in United States and about 8,500 media around the world. Each of AP's services puts out 2 million words a day in English and 50,000 in other languages.

3. United Press International (UPI) is a privately held company. Employs 2,000 full-time journalists worldwide. Produces news in English, Spanish, and Portuguese. Services include an international sports dispatch service, international science and technology service, remote-access data service for media and nonmedia customers, international news service on video circuit for hotels and airports, and international audio service. Produces total of 14 million words a day for 7,000 recipients in 100 countries. After declaring bankruptcy in 1991, was sold the following year to Saudi-owned, London-based Middle East Broadcasting Center, Ltd., which broadcasts TV programs in Arabic to the Middle East. Selling price: $3.95 million.

4. Agence France-Presse (AFP) employs 870 journalists in France and 850 journalists abroad in 180 countries. Departments include: AFP News, AFP Economy, AFP Sport, AFP Magazine, AFP Audio, AFP Video, AFP Agora Data Bank, and AFP Publications. Puts out a million words a day in French, English, Spanish, Arabic, Portuguese, and German. Has about 10,000 media customers and 2,000 nonmedia customers in 144 countries. These include 500 newspapers, 350 broadcast companies, 200 TV companies, and 99 national press agencies. Indirect customers include about 7,000 papers, 2,500 radio broadcasters, and 400 TV broadcasters.

5. Telegraph Agency of the Soviet Union (TASS) (former Soviet Union) employed 1,500 journalists in Soviet Union and in 100 foreign offices. Supplied news to 4,000 Soviet media. More than 1,000 news agencies, media, and other subscribers in 115 countries received service. Produced 4 million words a day in Russian, English, French, German, Spanish, Arabic, and Portuguese. After the collapse of the Soviet Union, it became ITAR-TASS and struggled to survive as an independent agency. ITAR stands for Information Telegraph Agency of Russia.

6. Reuters Television, originally called Visnews, is world's largest supplier of news film for TV. Bought out shares owned by NBC and BBC and changed name in 1992. Distributes stories to 409 customers in 83 countries via satellite and videocassette; material appears on approximately 650 million TV sets. Maintains one of world's largest libraries of news film and videotape. Staffs 38 bureaus and works with contract crews in about 70 countries.

7. Worldwide Television News (WTN) is 80 percent owned by ABC. Was formed in 1952 by United Press, 20th Century Fox Movietone News, and Britain's Independent Television News. Original name was UPITN. Maintains 15 overseas bureaus and contracts with film crews in about 70 countries.

8. CBS is world's second-largest supplier of news coverage from its domestic and 15 overseas bureaus.

9. CNN is shown officially in more than 140 countries and has viewers in more than 200. It operates two 24-hour-a-day news channels in the United States, a Spanish-language service (two 30-minute newscasts a day), and CNN International, the global channel pieced together from the two domestic services and some additional programming. In 1992, signed an agreement to become part of a German-language TV news service. Maintains 9 domestic and 19 overseas bureaus. Service includes innovative "CNN World Report," which consists of stories submitted by TV newscast organizations around the world.

SOURCE: *World Communication Report* (Paris: UNESCO, 1989), pp. 136–139, updated from various sources. Note that specific figures vary, even within this book. Differences result from different ways of counting, different times, and different definitions.

IV. Top money-making movies in selected countries at the end of 1992. In each country, movies are ranked according to gross earnings in the last week of the year.

France: *Home Alone 2; Death Becomes Her; The Bodyguard; Beauty and the Beast; Sister Act; La Crise; A Few Good Men; Tom and Jerry: The Film; Damage; Blade Runner.*

Germany: *Home Alone 2; Beauty and the Beast; Sister Act; Death Becomes Her; Fried Green Tomatoes; Raising Cain; Howard's End; Pet Semetary 2; Flodder Does Manhattan; Mo' Money.*

Italy: *Beauty and the Beast; The Bodyguard; Wolf! Wolf!; Dreaming about California; Puerto Escondido; Home Alone 2; The Last of the Mohicans; Death Becomes Her; A Few Good Men; Ricky and Barabbas.*

Australia: *Home Alone 2; A Few Good Men; Sister Act; Under Siege; The Muppet Christmas Carol; That Night; Death Becomes Her; Mo' Money; Strictly Ballroom; Pet Semetary 2.*

Japan: *Home Alone 2; The Bodyguard; Bram Stoker's Dracula; Death Becomes Her; Godzilla vs. Mothra; The Police Story; Byoin-e Iko; Beethoven; Ruby Cairo; Unlawful Entry.*

Canada: *Aladdin; A Few Good Men; Home Alone 2; The Bodyguard; Forever Young; Toys; The Distinguished Gentleman; Hoffa; The Muppet Christmas Carol; Leap of Faith.*

Brazil: *Sister Act; Unforgiven; Single White Female; Sneakers; Raising Cain; Boomerang; Mediterraneo; Rapid Fire; Far and Away; Mission of Justice.*

SOURCE: *Variety*, January 4, 1993, p. 52. Copyright © 1993. Reprinted by permission.

CHAPTER 2

Coping with Culture

ABOUT THIS CHAPTER

We begin our study of global communication where communication begins: culture. In this chapter, we consider what cultures are, how they evolve, and why there are so many. Then we move to culture as the basis of misunderstanding and conflict. After considering the varieties of cultural values, we move to dominant U.S. cultural values: what they are; why they are so appealing; and, as the core of the emerging global culture of the 1990s, whether they threaten the survival of other cultures.

INTRODUCTION

Charles Darwin is supposed to have asked in his early days as a naturalist, "Why are there 10,000 different kinds of beetles? Couldn't God be satisfied with 1,000?" Darwin eventually answered the first question with his theory of the evolution of species. The second remains unanswered.

Cultures are like species. They both evolve in bewildering and wonderful numbers and variety as their environments change. Some, like dinosaurs, cannot adapt and vanish. Others, like the passenger pigeon, alas, are destroyed by the intrusion of other species, usually *homo Sapiens.* Cultures are always at risk, too. A visit to the ruins of Upper Egypt, where Roman soldiers 2,000 years ago carved their initials on pillars erected 2,000 years earlier by a long-dead culture, is a good antidote to the conceit that our own culture is permanent.

We know when we encounter a different culture, but deciding exactly where we crossed the border can be difficult. The cultural difference is apparent immediately when we cross from Germany to France or from the United States to Mexico. It is not so easy to decide when we cross from the South to the Midwest or the

West in the United States or from one region of Italy to another. Cultures are sometimes hard to detect because they are hard to define. Here we do not mean "high
culture" (classical music, opera, ballet) or "popular culture" (rock and country-
western music, movies, TV) but the set of characteristics that distinguish "us" from
"them." Formal definitions of culture are tricky. One popular text puts it this way:

> Culture is the deposit of knowledge, experience, beliefs, values, attitudes,
> meanings, hierarchies, religion, timing, roles, spatial relations, concepts
> of the universe, and material objects and possessions acquired by a large
> group of people in the course of generations through individual and
> group striving. Culture manifests itself in patterns of language and in
> forms of activity and behavior that act as models for both the common
> adaptive acts and the styles of communication that enable us to live in
> a society within a given geographic environment at a given state of
> technical development at a particular moment in time . . . . [C]ulture
> is persistent, enduring, and omnipresent.[1]

That definition doesn't leave much outside of culture, and, in a sense, culture
is everything. It is everything that identifies one people and separates them from
all others. It is what they share among themselves and what holds them together
as a unique community, region, or nation. In too many cases, it's what makes
them hate others with different cultural elements. We will consider *language,
values,* and *behavior* as the key elements of culture and focus on how they are
powerful forces in global communication. Our discussion includes the dominance
of English as the global language of the twenty-first century and the unique appeal
of U.S. cultural values, especially U.S. popular culture. The behavioral component
of culture is represented by a discussion of nonverbal communication and
especially the data base in Chapter 3, which includes guidelines to understanding
nonverbal cues around the world. To repeat a point made in Chapter 1, two trends
of global communication in the 1990s are a resurgence of demands for cultural
identity and at the same time the emergence of the foundations of a global culture.
Both have their roots in the thousands of distinct cultures that flourish around
the world. The key to understanding any of them is language.

LANGUAGE: THE KEY TO HUMAN CULTURE

Roots of Culture

Culture has its roots in biology. Much of our social behavior—our culture—
is a product of some physical need or adaptation. This point is argued by both
Edward T. Hall, a noted anthropologist who specializes in communication

---

[1] Larry A. Samovar, Richard E. Porter, and Nemi C. Jain, *Understanding Intercultural
Communication* (Belmont, CA: Wadsworth, 1981), pp. 24–25.

and culture, and Edward O. Wilson, a leader in the new and sometimes controversial field of sociobiology. Wilson argues that the influence of biology is underrated:

> Evolution has not made culture all-powerful. It is a misconception among many of the more traditional Marxists, some learning theorists, and a still surprising proportion of anthropologists and sociologists that social behavior can be shaped into virtually any form . . . . Each person is molded by an interaction of his environment, especially his cultural environment, with the genes that affect social behavior. Although the hundreds of the world's cultures seem enormously variable to those of us who stand in their midst, all versions of human social behavior together form only a tiny fraction of the realized organizations of social species on this planet and a still smaller fraction of those that can be readily imagined with the aid of sociobiological theory.[2]

An intriguing thought: Even though the variety of existing cultures is dazzling, many more are biologically possible. The world that is contains a fraction of the cultural diversity of the world that could be. Still, some aspects of culture seem universal. These include the structure of the family, rearing of young, and elements of nonverbal expression such as smiles, frowns, and sounds of pain and fear. Some of these are common to social animals as well. Wilson even argues that altruism has a genetic base and claims it can be observed in animals as well as human societies. What separates humans from animals is language and the unique ability it gives us to pass on to the next generation the sum of our own experience. The legacy is transmitted partly in genes but mostly in languages.

Culture became possible when our very ancient ancestors discovered speech, probably simultaneously with the development of self-awareness. With words, they could separate ideas from the physical objects they represented. They could reconsider what happened yesterday and anticipate what would happen tomorrow. They could deal with abstractions. They could even think about who they were, why they were there, and what would happen at the moment of death. The cleverest animals can do none of these. As collective experience accumulated, it was passed on to new generations in the form of stories, legends, and rules for survival.

The human species was now different from other species and from its own ancestors. People were aware of themselves and their environment. With language, they could describe experiences and remember them. They could create and invent and influence their environment as well as respond to it. The collected experience, stored in language, was a culture. Each was a unique history of experience, adaptation, and invention. In most cases, the language was unique as well. Its vocabulary reflected the specific history and needs of its speakers; its grammar somehow facilitated the expression of the culture.

---

[2] Edward O. Wilson, *On Human Nature* (Cambridge, MA: Harvard University Press, 1978), pp. 18–19.

The First Communication Revolution

Language makes culture possible, but a written language revolutionizes culture. Surprisingly enough, there aren't that many. Most of the 3,000 to 4,000 languages thought to exist in the world today have no written form. They—and the cultures they contain—exist only in the minds of people who speak them. Most are small and weak and probably doomed to extinction, like the dodo bird and passenger pigeon.

In Chapter 13, we talk about the third revolution in the history of human communication, the convergence of electronic technologies of our own time. It follows the development of written language and the invention of printing with moveable type, two revolutions that changed the definition and distribution of power. But first things first.

Why was the invention of a written language a revolution in human evolution? Three reasons can be cited: Written language made communication across time and space possible; it allowed the body of knowledge to expand infinitely; and it challenged the authority of those who held power, the key element of any true revolution.

Imagine for a moment that English had no written form and consider how your life would change. The library, campus bookstore, and newsstand would disappear. This book would, too, along with virtually every source of information you encounter every day. Theoretically radio and television could exist, but the technical information they require is found only in books, so they would be gone, too. "Education" would consist of sitting with an elder and memorizing a few sagas, legends, and stories. Most of your knowledge would come from the experiences of hunting, fishing, cooking, raising children. Your parents could pass on a few tips they had learned from their parents. Accumulated knowledge could not exceed the collective capacity of the few people in the village or tribe to remember it.

Culture changed dramatically when words were written down. Not everyone thought a written language represented progress. In Plato's dialogue, *Phaedrus,* an Egyptian god-king, Thamus, rebukes the god Thoth, who invented writing:

> This discovery of yours will create forgetfulness in the learners' souls, because they will not use their memories; they will trust to the external written characters and not remember of themselves. The specific which you have discovered is an aid not to memory, but to reminiscence, and you give your disciples not truth, but only the semblance of truth; they will be hearers of many things and will have learned nothing; they will appear to be omniscient and will generally know nothing; they will be tiresome company, having the show of wisdom without its reality.[3]

Remember this complaint when we discuss later communication revolutions and look for parallels in the arguments for and against each new development.

---

[3] Quoted in Carl Sagan, *The Dragons of Eden: Speculations on the Evolution of Human Intelligence* (New York: Random House, 1977), pp. 222–223.

The Second Communication Revolution

Now imagine a culture based on a written language in the days before books were commonplace, such as in medieval Europe. Communication was independent of time and place. You could read a document written by someone living in a distant place or at a different time. Knowledge was no longer limited to the number of stanzas a single person could memorize. Great libraries like those in ancient Alexandria or the medieval European monasteries could aspire to collect a complete record of human knowledge. Authorities—priests, kings, chiefs—no longer could aspire to a monopoly on information or a monopoly of power.

A novel by Umberto Eco, *The Name of the Rose,* brilliantly captures the spirit of the late Middle Ages, when the Catholic church's long monopoly on authority came under increasing pressure from skeptics. One of them was the main character in the book, Brother William of Baskerville, an early-day Sherlock Holmes, who combined the logic of Aristotle and the empiricism of Roger Bacon to solve a series of ungodly murders. Unlike the leaders of the bleak northern Italian monastery where monks died mysteriously, Brother William did not believe that some knowledge was so dangerous that it must be destroyed. Two centuries later, Galileo Galilei encountered the same problem when his endorsement of Copernicus's *On the Revolution of the Celestial Spheres* contradicted church teaching on the solar system and was banned. He was forced to recant, but his view survived, and his book reinforced the modern political meaning of *revolution.* The Vatican finally admitted its mistake in 1992. The book was truly revolutionary. Many books are, in the sense that they challenge the authority of those in power.

A written language gives a culture great strength and adaptability. The whole is greater than the sum of its parts because it doesn't depend on individuals for memory. Even a small town library contains more knowledge than people of a large nation can hold in their heads. CD-ROMs promise to reduce the holdings of the greatest libraries to a size that will fit into a backpack. Against the bulldozer force of vibrant modern languages, especially global English, nonwritten languages have little power of resistance and little chance of survival. The death of language signals the death of culture. In an era of invigorated demands for cultural autonomy, it is not surprising that people from Wales to Lithuania to North American Indian reservations are insisting on the restoration of their languages, their unique experience, their culture.

CULTURAL VARIETY

Like all species of plants and animals, cultures evolve, but in most cases, it is impossible to explain why they acquired specific characteristics. Some elements are nearly universal, such as religion or at least a belief system and, of course, language. Most elements of a culture are unique. To the outsider, they are sometimes amusing, sometimes irritating, always at least a little confusing.

Explaining Cultural Differences

In a few cases, unique cultural characteristics can be explained historically. An extended hand—as in a handshake—showed that you were not armed. Avoiding the use of the left hand for everything except toilet functions was a practical health requirement in traditional Arab lands. Americans' attachment to—even obsession with—individual liberty and suspicion of government reflect the values of immigrant ancestors and perhaps the experience of settling a frontier where survival depended on self-reliance. Most elements of culture, however, are puzzles. Why is black a color of mourning in the West, whereas white is used in parts of Asia? Why do Latin Americans stand closer together than North Americans, and why are they more casual about time? Why does Russia have such byzantine verbs of motion?

Students of culture—anthropologists, of course, but also scholars in other disciplines, including communication—can document these differences and compare cultures on a long list of attributes, such as those noted earlier in the formal definition of culture. However, they lack a widely accepted theory of culture, which is a concise set of statements that explain the diversity of cultures in the world and permit scholars to predict how these cultures might evolve in the future. Schema for cross-cultural comparisons, weak in theory, are important for people who have to function in other cultures and for the rest of us who simply want to appreciate the richness of different cultures and perhaps to gain insight into our own.

Cross-cultural comparisons can be dangerous because of a tendency to declare one culture better or worse than another. At one level, all cultures and all languages do what needs to be done. They represent successful adaptations to the environment in which they developed, and they promise a future to succeeding generations. They provide a social structure for individuals to live out their lives with a sense of security, value, and purpose. Some cultures are more successful than others, and some incorporate values that are (or should be) universally repugnant. To shrug off cannibalism, slavery, human sacrifice, or present-day abominations of tribal slaughter and ethnic cleansing with a we-can't-judge-others attitude is cultural relativism at its worst. Still, an assertion that one culture is better than another puts us on the path toward racism and ends in the grotesque distortions of racial (or cultural) superiority that led Germany and Japan to assert a right—even a responsibility—to purge the world of its "inferior" peoples.

How can we compare cultures or predict whether a culture is likely to thrive, merely survive, or disappear entirely? In pioneering studies a generation ago, Daniel Lerner focused on national development in the third world—a new term at the time for poor countries in Latin America, Asia, and Africa, many of them emerging from colonial rule. How these "underdeveloped" countries of the world can become "developed" is the subject of Chapter 10; in this sentence, the use of quotation marks indicates that the definition of *development* is now a matter for debate.

Lerner defined *development* as Western political democracy. He argued that traditional cultures were becoming more like the West and concluded that the painful transition from traditional to modern culture was inevitable and positive. His justification, however—and this is an important point—was not that democracy was morally superior to the authoritarianism of most traditional cultures but that it was flexible and allowed cultures to adapt to external pressures that resulted from the end of long cultural isolation. In short, he argued that in the modern world, traditional cultures could learn to accommodate change, or they could die.

Cultural Survival

Survival ability is one criterion for measuring cultures. Another is to begin with a set of basic cultural values and see how various cultures compare. For example, traditional cultures—a term that applies to small towns and some big-city neighborhoods in Western countries as well as to the third world—usually do a better job of providing a sense of time and place. People feel secure because they are born into a stable structure of family and community that provides for them, but at a price. The price is usually rigidity, resistance to change, and intolerance of nonconformity. Respondents in Lerner's surveys in the eastern Mediterranean in the 1950s could not answer his questions about what they would do if they became the village chief or could change village life because they knew they were not the chief and knew village life had not changed in hundreds of years. In a traditional culture, you are born into a specific position and expected to do pretty much what your parents and grandparents and great-grandparents before them did. Even in Garrison Keillor's mythical Lake Wobegon, the motto is, "We Are What We Are." There, as in small towns all over the world, people who want to be something very different from everyone else have to leave town.

Twentieth-century Western cultures, in contrast to traditional cultures, do a better job of allowing people to develop unique interests and talents and are more tolerant of eccentricity and difference. There is greater emphasis on freedom and individual rights but at the price of the loss of sense of belonging. Early German sociologists compared the traditional values of *Gemeinschaft* (community) and the modern values of *Gesellschaft* (society) and found the latter responsible for the sense of alienation and other ills of industrial society. More recently, a team of U.S. sociologists updated Alexis de Tocqueville's classic nineteenth-century study of U.S. society and concluded that obsession with individual freedom in the United States threatens survival of the society itself.[4] They urged a return to the traditional values of community—more generous sharing of resources, active participation in public life, re-creation of a coherent sense of social purpose—and warned that the "cancer" of individualism may be destroying the social glue that has held the country together for more than two centuries.

We meet the same conflict between cultural forces holding a society together and the forces of individual liberty driving it apart later when we discuss press

---

[4] Robert N. Bellah et al., *Habits of the Heart: Individualism and Commitment in American Life* (New York: Harper & Row, 1986.)

freedom in other kinds of media systems in Chapters 5 through 11. If freedom means freedom from government control, then most countries with which the United States shares many cultural values do not have a truly free press. On the other hand, if the British "culturally ingrained toleration of eccentricity and iconoclasm," as Michael Kinsley of *The New Republic* put it, is more important than a written constitutional guarantee, then Americans may have to reconsider their assumptions about British media, which have to live with an Official Secrets Act and virtually unlimited power of courts to prohibit publication of material related to matters under their jurisdiction.[5] Sorting out differences among cultures is difficult, and deciding which are better or worse is even harder. Cultural conflict and the emergence of the first global culture are such an important part of global communication in the 1990s, however, that we need to take a closer look.

CULTURE IN THE AGE OF GLOBAL COMMUNICATION

Culture is historically linked to the concept of nationalism, which means in simple definition that each culture (or nation) should also be a sovereign political entity (a state). The roots of nationalism go back to the American and French revolutions, but nationalism itself became an important political force in the nineteenth century, when most of Europe was still ruled by the great empires.

Fitting Nation and State

World War I, which started when a Serbian nationalist assassinated the crown prince of the Austro-Hungarian Empire, precipitated the "fall of the eagles," the collapse of the three continental empires whose symbols were all eagles. In their place rose a dozen new states—Finland, Latvia, Albania, and Poland among them—that contained, more or less, distinct cultures. President Woodrow Wilson included the idea of political independence and territorial integrity for all states (cultures) in his Fourteen Points for a permanent postwar peace.

Even then, the job of identifying distinct cultures was impossible. Where does one end and another begin? How do you solve the problem of two cultures geographically mixed to the point that you can't draw borders or, worse, two cultures claiming the same territory? Wilson's notion of nationalism was tried in the Balkan Peninsula and produced the verb *balkanize*. According to Webster, *balkanize* means "to break up (as a region) into smaller and often hostile units." The peace settlement after World War I produced a cluster of new nation-states but did not end conflicts among them or within them. Unfortunately, it helped to set the stage for a second, more terrible world war and the resurgence of ancient conflicts in our own time.

---

[5] Michael Kinsley, "A Model of Ex-Greatness," *The Economist*, December 23, 1989, pp. 33–35.

For one thing, the new boundaries did not—could not—differentiate cultures adequately. The cultural map of Europe did not match the political map and still doesn't. Many areas inevitably were cross-hatched to show that two nations shared the same territory—two cultures with competing deeds to the same real estate. In many cases, the claims went back centuries and were hardened with long histories of conflict. When Adolf Hitler came to power in Germany, one of his first goals was to produce a Greater Germany of all the German-speaking areas in Central Europe. The World War I peace conference had produced boundaries that left significant numbers of Germans as minorities in states dominated by other cultures. Some thought Hitler would be satisfied with a Third German Reich (empire) that embraced the Sudetenland, parts of Poland, and Austria. As we know, he was not. With the collapse of Soviet influence in Central and Eastern Europe in 1989, many of the problems left unsolved at the end of World War II were resolved, but the older conflicts resurfaced. The task for the 1990s and beyond will be to solve the problems of nationalism left by the fall of eagles in 1918.

The example of nationalism "gone mad" in Germany could be applied to the Asian theater of World War II as well, where Japan also engaged in many of the practices that made the Nazi regime synonymous with the worst kind of racism: genocide. Globally, World War II was the bloodiest war in history and brought the world closer to self-annihilation than anything else ever had. When the shooting stopped, finally, in the shadow of the mushroom clouds of two atomic bombs, the survivors were sober. Culture seemed to be a deadly dangerous force, not the legitimate expression of a people's self-identity.

The recognition of the dangers of nationalism—the assertion of cultural independence—was one of the reasons that the United Nations succeeded after World War II, whereas the League of Nations, an organization similar in structure and purpose formed at the end of World War I, failed. It was also an impetus behind efforts to create a supranational Europe, which—50 years later—may become a true European Community (EC).

The tenacity of culture, however, is evident even there. EC commissioners maintain the right to speak in their nine separate languages and insist documents be translated into each language. There was some public protest against a common passport that put the words "European Community" above the nation and more serious concern about rules allowing free movement of people and goods among the 12 nations. Even now, the French, Germans, Danes, and Spaniards want to remain French, German, Danish, and Spanish, and not become mere "Europeans." The British are not even sure they want to be part of Europe.

Third-World Cultural Identity

After World War II, the focus of cultural conflict shifted to the emerging third world. The problem was especially difficult in Africa, where the colonial division of the continent was a product of accident, occasional wars, and a Berlin conference in 1985 that drew a final map of colonial Africa. The political map, of course, had little in common with a physical map and nothing in common with a map of Africa's extraordinarily numerous and diverse cultures. The problem was worse in Africa than in Asia and the Middle East, where European colonies were also becoming independent but where cultural boundaries were more clearly defined and matched political boundaries better. It was also less of a problem in Latin America, which had been politically independent for more than 100 years and whose indigenous cultures had been virtually annihilated in the Iberian conquest, still the single most successful example of cultural genocide in history.

The Organization of African Unity, a group put together in 1963 in preparation for the dismantling of the European African empires, decided early to maintain the colonial boundaries, whatever the cost to cultural integrity. The first decades of independence were not kind to most of Africa, but the agreement held, a significant accomplishment in an era of rising cultural conflict everywhere. Most—not all, but most—African post-independence wars grew from demands for independence, autonomy, or equitable access to power by one culture that felt, usually correctly, repressed by another. Consider the civil war in Nigeria in the 1960s and current conflicts in Sudan, Ethiopia, and Liberia, among others. Even conflict in South Africa can be considered war among the "tribes" of Dutch Afrikaner settlers, English colonists, and a host of indigenous peoples. The battle over apartheid is the first layer of cultural conflict that goes much deeper and is not likely to end with apartheid's inevitable abolition.

The recognition of Eritrea as an independent nation in 1993 after decades of war with the central government of Ethiopia could be the start of the unraveling of postcolonial Africa. To the continent's terrible problems of AIDS, drought, and tribal (cultural) war, add the impossible task of redrawing political boundaries to match, more or less, cultural boundaries. The task, likely to loom large in the early years of the twenty-first century, could make the job of dividing tiny Bosnia seem simple by comparison.

Many of the first generation of third-world leaders recognized the problem of creating new "nations"—political cultures, really—out of the disparate populations history had bequeathed them. Mahatma Gandhi, a Hindu, fasted to try to prevent the partition of British India and the bloodbath that followed independence. He was assassinated by a fanatic Hindu who objected to Gandhi's goal of Hindi-Muslim equality. At independence, Jomo Kenyatta, a Kikuyu who became the first president of Kenya, adopted part of the clothing of a rival tribe to demonstrate that they were now all part of one nation. Other examples could be cited as well to show how independence from colonial rule introduced new, and often more intractable, problems.

Even now, many third-world leaders argue that the goal of building a single nation from the fragile coalition of traditionally hostile cultures is so important and the social structure so delicate that they must mobilize mass media to support the goal of nation-building. An independent press—aloof, critical, focusing on the weaknesses and failures of the government—is seen as a luxury of stable, developed nations. Perhaps at some time in the future, when these new nations have developed the cultural institutions that can better adapt to change, they argue, then independent journalism may be appropriate. Perhaps never. Others argue that third-world countries need to develop independently from Western influence, just as their languages and cultures did. If so, Western notions of press freedom and responsibility may be as dysfunctional to third-world needs as elements of our pop culture seem to be. This argument, that mass media need to be mobilized to support national development—with Western perspectives of freedom postponed or dismissed—is the basis of the concept of development journalism. Chapter 10 discusses development journalism in detail.

CULTURAL CONFLICT IN THE 1990s

By now, the world collectively should know the dangers of nationalism, but a curious phenomenon of the 1990s—and one of the four trends cited in Chapter 1—is the resurgence of conflict based on culture. Cultural conflict knows no geographic boundaries and seems to prosper in the absence of ideological conflict. You can see it on the newspaper's front page in news from a dozen parts of the world: demands for linguistic and cultural autonomy in Western Europe and North America; religious and ethnic conflict in the Middle East and South Asia; ancient animosities in Central Europe resurfacing as communist control collapses. Some conflicts are a product of colonialism; others were held in check by colonial control and are now reemerging. And still others are a product of the most extraordinary event of our time, the dismantling of the Soviet Union's 40-year dominance of Central and Eastern Europe and the collapse of the Soviet Union itself, the last classical European empire.

Resurgence of Nationalism

The end of Soviet hegemony in Central and Eastern Europe brought political freedom to millions and a flowering of ancient cultures in the heart of Western civilization—but at a price. Along with the traditional cultures, old cultural conflicts have reasserted themselves. Under the communist regime in Bulgaria, the large Turkish population was denied its language, religion, and even use of Turkish names. That policy was reversed early in 1990 and immediately precipitated protests by the Bulgarian majority. Romania has a significant Hungarian minority, and conflict between Romanian Hungarians and Romanians developed within months of the collapse of the Ceauçescu regime in December 1989. Romania itself began to discuss union with the dominantly Romanian republic of Moldova.

In Yugoslavia, itself an artificial construct of diverse languages, religions, and ethnic groups, the existence of the country was threatened by all sorts of conflicts: ethnic, religious, and linguistic. Even the main language, Serbo-Croatian, is written in two alphabets; Serbian in Cyrillic and Croatian in Latin. The fragmentation of the country into several independent republics failed to stop the conflict. Television pictures daily show attempts to deal with competing claims for territory and dominance.

In the former Soviet Union, an unwieldy superstate of 15 culturally distinct (and often hostile) republics with subrepublics and autonomous regions mixed

The Golden Arches in Moscow is a global symbol of Anglo-American pop culture. Is it "cultural imperialism" or the first sign of an emerging global culture? In 1993, the Russian government required all signs to be in the Cyrillic alphabet.

SOURCE: Wide World Photos.

in, revolution seemed possible in several areas. The three Baltic states responded to Gorbachev's twin policies of *glasnost* (openness) and *perestroika* (restructuring) by quickly restoring their own languages to preeminence—and generating claims of discrimination from the Russians who lived there. This act of nationalism was followed by the republics' gaining full independence from the Soviet Union.

In Ukraine, a first demand was the restoration of the Ukrainian church, which is affiliated with the Roman Catholic church, not the Russian Orthodox church. In the two republics of Armenia and Azerbaijan, people fought both each other and the Russians, and the Soviet Army had to be brought in to maintain order. A complicating factor in that cultural conflict was that history had denied both peoples a single homeland. Significant numbers of Armenians lived in Turkey, and many Azeris were in areas belonging to Iran. The conflict there—and in so many other hot spots—seemed to involve so many cross-pressures, so many complications, so much history that even a Solomon could not find a solution.

A Global Culture?

This is a discouraging assessment of the cultures humankind has created by the end of the twentieth century—perhaps too dismal. We should remember that most people get along with each other most of the time. News, at least in the Western definition, is the exceptional event, the conflict rather than the absence of conflict. The headlines don't read: ''Most Armenians Did Not Fight Azeris Today''; ''Most Catholics in Northern Ireland Did Not Ambush British Soldiers''; ''Most New Yorkers Avoided Racial Confrontation.''

A few years ago in the midst of the ideological cold war between the two superpowers, cultural conflict seemed unimportant. It certainly did not pose the possibility of the annihilation of life on the planet in an all-out nuclear war. Now, as superpower confrontation recedes and its ability to influence world events diminishes, our TV screens are filled with pictures of conflicts in places we have never heard of. The complaints often seem insignificant to outsiders and usually derive from ancient animosities outsiders know nothing about. To outsiders, cultural conflict usually appears irrational. To insiders, it is often at the core of the culture's existence.

Is a global culture the answer to the problem of cultural conflict? The outline of a global culture is emerging in the 1990s, but it is limited. It is built on English as a common language and consists of a common definition of news, a uniform but superficial popular culture, and a set of universally recognizable icons such as the Sony Walkman, the Coke bottle, and Michael Jackson's glove. Traditional cultures—the real cultures that evolved over centuries—continue to demonstrate an amazing resilience. They can absorb elements of the global culture just as they have always adopted some external influences. England is still England with U.S. fast food (and probably better because of it), and China remains thoroughly Chinese even with TV commercials for Boeing airplanes and BBC English language lessons. ''New'' nations such as the United States, Australia, and Canada have benefited from the unprecedented influx of non-Anglo immigrants and the energy and culture they bring with them. In these countries today, it can be easy to forget that nachos, egg rolls, and tandoori cooking are not native. The 1990s are a decade of global communication and a global culture and the simultaneous flowering of hundreds of unique and enchanting traditional cultures as well. Global communication gives us a better chance to get acquainted with such cultures.

CULTURAL VALUES

Culture is a slippery concept to define. Measuring cultural values is even more difficult. For one thing, there is no agreement on what cultural values are important and how they should be described. As with many other aspects of global communication, we can look at what others have done and adapt their insights to our own purposes.

Mapping Cultural Values

Edward T. Hall, the noted anthropologist who specializes in the study of communication and culture, defines a list of ten "primary message systems" that he uses to derive a matrix of basic elements of culture. The ten are interaction, association, subsistence, bisexuality, territoriality, temporality, learning, play, defense, and exploitation. The list of ten is crossed with adjectival forms of the same list to produce categories such as "interactional association" and "organizational defense." At the intersection of (economic) subsistence and learning, for example, is the subject of rewards for teaching and learning; the intersection of defense and territoriality produces both personal privacy and collective organization of territory for defense. In all, Hall's approach produces a "cultural map" of 100 specific aspects of culture, each of which can be further subdivided. It doesn't tell us how important privacy is in a specific country or how highly education is valued in a particular culture, but it does emphasize that a study of cultural values should include these items.[6]

Other scholars have adopted a similar approach in starting with a set of basic human values (what we think is important) or beliefs (what we think is true) and deriving a kind of periodic table of cultural values. Condon and Yousef, for example, begin with three basic values: self, society, and nature. When sketched as overlapping circles, the three produce three additional values: family (an overlap of self and society), human nature (self and society), and the supernatural (nature and self). Within this set of six values, Condon and Yousef list 25 "value orientations," each of which has three categories (although they acknowledge that the division of each value orientation into the three categories is arbitrary). Here's how it works. Under the value of "self," for example, they list four value orientations and the three divisions within each.

Self

Individualism-interdependence

1. Individualism   **2.** Individuality   **3.** Interdependence

Age

1. Youth   **2.** Middle years   **3.** Old age

Sex

1. Equality of sexes   **2.** Female superior   **3.** Male superior

Activity

1. Doing   **2.** Being-in-becoming   **3.** Being

The chart is arbitrarily drawn so that U.S. cultural values are represented in the first column. The order seems reasonable. On the whole, these are the things that most Americans seem to value. We certainly have a culture that stresses

---

[6] Edward T. Hall, *The Silent Language* (New York: Anchor, 1973), pp. 193–199.

individualism, youth, sex equality, and activity. Other value orientations from the rest of the chart—democracy, high mobility, informality, happiness, and so on—also fit in.[7]

What about the other extreme? Is there a culture that values interdependence, old age, male superiority, and being (acceptance of life as it is; Zorba the Greek is cited as an example). Japan or China might qualify. Both cultures certainly are different from the United States. Many traditional cultures also fit the pattern. The mixed cultures are more of a problem to identify. Can you think of a culture that values individuality (milder than individualism), middle age, female superiority, and being-in-becoming ("the outlook of the artist")? Perhaps the middle path fits European cultures, although we could quarrel with a characterization of them as female dominant. In general, the more a set of cultural values falls into the left end of the table, the closer the culture resembles that of the United States; the more it falls to the right, the greater the cultural gap from the United States.

In fact, of course, Condon and Yousef assume that any single culture will zigzag through their list of value orientations. The effect is that their periodic table of cultures can produce almost limitless permutations. An authoritarian, low-mobility culture that emphasizes youth and equality of sexes is unlikely but possible. You may be able to think of one or two that combine opposite ends of the various value orientations. They certainly would be interesting to visit.

This way of looking at cultural values makes clear that any two cultures will share some values and disagree on others. We are all more or less like others, or more precisely, we will have some values in common with every other culture, but the degree and nature of overlap will vary from culture to culture. In multicultural societies—every country is multicultural, but nations such as the United States and Canada were founded on cultural diversity—we could describe the subcultures in the same way. One text in intercultural communication argues that the overall similarity between the dominant U.S. and British culture is greater than between mainstream U.S. and U.S. ethnic minority cultures.[8]

Of course, there are big differences within cultures as well as among different cultures. Individual differences are important to every culture but vary in degree and kind from one culture to another. Presumably there is more individual cultural variance within the U.S. culture than within, say, the more homogeneous Japanese or Korean cultures. Even the official U.S. motto of *E Pluribus Unum* ("Out of Many, One") recognizes the cultural diversity of the nation. Current trends on campuses put the emphasis on the *Pluribus,* rather than the *Unum,* a practice likely to define academic battle lines into the next century.[9]

---

[7] John C. Condon and Fathi Yousef, *An Introduction to Intercultural Communication* (Indianapolis, IN: Bobbs-Merrill, 1975).

[8] Larry A. Samover, Richard E. Porter, and Nemi C. Jain, *Understanding Intercultural Communication* (Belmont, CA: Wadsworth, 1981), p. 31.

[9] Arthur M. Schlesinger, Jr., *The Disuniting of America: Reflections on a Multicultural Society* (New York: Norton, 1992).

North American Cultural Values

Plotting how you see yourself as a member of several overlapping and/or concentric subcultures is another way of coping with the messiness and imprecision of cultural values research. President Lyndon Johnson used to say that he was—in order—an American, a Democrat, and a Texan. Or was it American, Texan, and then Democrat? That litany seems to translate into a hierarchy of subcultures, not surprisingly defined mostly by politics. Each one is part of a larger subculture. Others might see their subcultures as overlapping rather than concentric. You could be part of a religious culture and an ethnic culture, such as both Catholic and Korean. As a member of this small subculture, you could hold values of both cultures. It is quite likely that some values would conflict. This is a particular problem for immigrant groups in any culture and the basis of more and more conflict, both within the immigrant culture and between it and the dominant culture.

In the United States, an immigrant Chinese couple's marriage broke up when the husband found the wife with another man. He killed her, and the defense at his trial was that in traditional Chinese culture his action was an acceptable response to her crime of infidelity. The jury was unimpressed with the argument, and he was convicted.

In Germany, the immigration of Turkish "guest workers" has produced a generation of young people caught between two very different cultures and not at home in either. In Turkey, they're called "Deutschlanders" because they're really no longer Turks; in Germany, they find it hard to find acceptance as dark-skinned "Germans" who avoid pork and alcohol in deference to their Muslim religion. Linguistically they're caught between German in school and Turkish at home. Some speak both languages poorly. Ironically, the creation of a borderless European Community in 1992 was accompanied by imposition of stricter immigration controls and rising cultural tensions.

Globally, the conflict between trying to assimilate immigrants into a dominant culture versus expanding opportunities to maintain distinct minority culture is growing. The number of political refugees and economic migrants is at an all-time high, and they travel farther to seek asylum and opportunity.

The United States has always thought of itself as a melting pot of cultures to which any newcomer has access. It is true that it is easier for an immigrant to become an American than, say, for a Turk to become a German, but there are difficulties and prices to be paid. Usually the price of assimilation is giving up most of the old cultural values. In recent years, we have found out that the stew in the U.S. melting pot is lumpier than we thought and that some immigrant groups have melted more than others. Now the maintenance of cultural identification is seen as an individual right in a multicultural nation and the diversity of cultures as a strength of the larger multicultural society. Each generation of immigrants brings new energy and talents and adds a new spice to the melting pot. In California, where everything seems to happen first, non-Anglo whites already are a majority in schools and will be a majority of the state's population early in the next century. In New York City, white, Anglo-Saxon, Protestant males—the traditional WASPs who are supposed to control the country—are down to less than 12 percent.

In contrast to the United States, Canada has always considered itself more of a patchwork quilt than a melting pot, and immigrant cultures are stronger. Efforts to preserve cultural pluralism have produced vibrant ethnic neighborhoods within cities, even the wonder of a Vancouver restaurant offering a "Chinese smorgasbord." A unique aspect of Canadian culture is the presence of a French-speaking province in a country dominated by a culture closely tied to Britain (and, of course, the Anglo cultural giant to the south). The tensions between French and English Canada often overshadow the conflicts within Anglo Canada, especially those that accompany the rise in non-European immigration. In 1989, a Sikh applied to join the Royal Canadian Mounted Police but insisted he be allowed to wear the traditional turban. A "Mountie" with a turban instead of the famous "Smokey the bear" hat? Well, Canadians may even get used to that.

Cultural Diversity and Enduring Values

In both countries, multiculturalism is a source of great strength and energy and also the source of conflict, of course. One problem of multicultural societies is that different cultural values lead to discrepancies in the distribution of wealth, power, and other social benefits. Patchwork quilts and zesty soups are always lumpy. In Anglo North America, the immigration of large numbers of Asians has led to startling success by Asian students in academics and to claims that some California universities have adopted informal quotas to prevent them from dominating student bodies. Jews are also overrepresented (compared to their numbers in the population) in academics and the professions. Unless one is prepared to argue that admission policies and standardized exams are biased in their favor, the only argument to explain this lump in the melting pot is that these two cultures attach unusually high value to education, and perhaps to a strong family structure as well, which supports high achievement. Studies of cultural values support this.

Other discrepancies abound. Blacks are vastly overrepresented in sports and pop music; Irish and Italians still exert unusual influence in politics; WASPs dominate banking and finance, although this is changing rapidly. Institutional barriers and prejudice still play a role in North American society, but the varied cultural values of major subcultures play a larger and growing role. Cultural values seem to persist even after surface integration into the dominant culture has occurred and even when people of one culture emigrate to very different cultures. Thomas Sowell is a conservative scholar who studied Chinese, Europeans, and Africans in various "New World" immigrant cultures. He found that in most cases, cultural values persisted in the new environments, sometimes even for two or three centuries, and that these values have implications for social disparities today:

> Cultural differences have been enduring over the generations, as well as prominent at a given time. The British in South Africa still have

substantial economic advantages over the Afrikaners, though the latter have been in the country more than three centuries and the British nearly two centuries. The Chinese continue to dominate the economies of many southeast Asian nations, as they have for centuries. The descendants of ante-bellum "free persons of color" in the United States still remain greatly over-represented among American Negro leaders and high achievers more than a century after all blacks were freed, and northern blacks still score higher on I.Q. tests than southern blacks.[10]

Similar patterns can be found within countries. In 1985, a study of inner London showed that about 10 percent of "native British" schoolchildren had passed five O-level exams, roughly the equivalent of high school graduation, which qualified them for higher academic education. In contrast, about 25 percent of Indian and African-Asian (mostly Indians who had left Africa) and between 15 percent and 20 percent of Pakistanis qualified. Among Caribbean natives and Bangladeshis, however, the rate was about 5 percent.

The figures reflected more or less the proportions of well-educated parents in each group. But another factor, according to the report, was the effect of culture and religion, which put Muslims at a disadvantage more than Hindus and Sikhs. Demands of a Muslim religious education outside the regular classroom and cultural conflict between traditional Muslim values and those of modern British society distracted Muslim children and made it difficult for them to learn. In contrast, Hindu and Sikh students were usually highly motivated by a culture that emphasized entrepreneurship and hard work and took discrimination more in stride because it is built into the traditional caste system. There were also differences in academic success between West Indians from Barbados and Trinidad, where there is a stronger tradition of grammar schools, and Jamaica, where there is not.

Asian immigrants in Britain, even after several generations, tend to maintain their separate identity more than West Indians, just as they do in the United States and Canada. Each succeeding generation becomes a little more like the dominant culture—smaller families, more single parents, a wider range of occupations—but assimilation is slow. Values that are a product of generations of cultural evolution are hard to discard, yet the frequent conflict between the old and new is a problem every immigrant faces.

It's tough to retain old values in a new culture, especially when they require you to be different. Wearing a turban, abstaining from meat on Friday, even saying grace before meals all can be clear expressions that you're not really part of the mainstream. Children, for whom the pressure to conform is especially strong, often find themselves caught between the two cultures, one at home and the other on the playground. Usually the new culture wins the struggle eventually, but, as Sowell argued, the old values can persist for generations. All countries in the 1990s are multicultural, and all have to find some way to accommodate minorities

[10] Thomas Sowell, *The Economics and Politics of Race: An International Perspective* (New York: William Morrow, 1983), p. 142.

whose language, values, and behavior are different. Some countries are more diverse than others and some more successful in creating multicultural accommodation if not always harmony.

A Multicultural World

This focus on Anglo-American cultures and their values is not intended as a cover-up of the serious problems that exist in these culturally diverse nations or as claim to any innate superiority of their cultural values. But Western cultural values in general and particularly Anglo-American values have both unusual strength and appeal that help account for their dominance in the world. Lerner, you will remember, argued that it was their ability to adapt to change that gave them strength. The list of cultural values we saw in the left-hand column above is also part of the reason: independence, mobility, openness, rationality. These are popular around the world, especially to people denied cultural expression at home. Although the West has no monopoly claim on these virtues, cultures that are rigid and intolerant are incapable of creating or surviving in a global culture. Carl Sagan, without referring to any specific culture, gives the future to this kind of culture:

> Unless we destroy ourselves utterly, the future belongs to those societies that, while not ignoring the reptilian and mammalian parts of our being, enable the characteristically human components of our nature to flourish; to those societies that encourage diversity rather than conformity; to those societies willing to invest resources in a variety of social, political, economic and cultural experiments, and prepared to sacrifice short-term advantage for long-term benefit; those societies that treat new ideas as delicate, fragile and immensely valuable pathways to the future.[11]

Does this describe Western society in the past, the booming Asian cultures now rolling across the globe, or a multinational global culture of the future? Start with your own set of cultural values and predict your own future. Remember from the last chapter Wilson's comment that the world has produced only a few of the possible cultures. The future may give us an explosion of variety, or it may give us a bland, uniform culture throughout the world. Unlike other species, we have the power to choose.

U.S. CULTURAL VALUES

A separate section on U.S. cultural values is included for two reasons. One is the assumption that most students reading this book are Americans (or at least studying in U.S. schools where textbooks like this one are a strong tradition). The other

---

[11] Carl Sagan, *The Dragons of Eden: Speculations on the Evolution of Human Intelligence* (New York: Random House, 1977), p. 193.

is that the most powerful forces in global communication are generally Western, more specifically Anglo-American, and in many areas, American. Later chapters consider the complaint that this constitutes "cultural imperialism," which threatens the independence and integrity of other cultures. To understand that concern, we need to know something about the values that the largely U.S. communication system is bringing to (or inflicting on) the rest of the world.

U.S. Political Culture

U.S. culture is unusual—and perhaps unique—in that it is essentially political. We don't have the common experience of living together in one plot of land for centuries, evolving a language, religion, set of beliefs, and values together that transcend even violent political upheaval. All we have are the ideals of the founding fathers and the documents they left behind. Canada, Australia, and New Zealand are also "new," but their cultural identities evolved slowly and did not begin in revolution. The National Archives in Washington, D.C., displays the Declaration of Independence and the Constitution in what is virtually a secular cathedral, and we approach them as we would the relics of an ancient national saint. That's also why the great monuments in a sometimes pompous national capital are so moving to us. They're all we've got to tie us together as a single people. The coin in your pocket reminds you of that with the phrase, *E Pluribus Unum*—"Out of Many, One."

A TV miniseries titled "Amerika" a few years ago—before *glasnost* and all that—was built on the storyline of a Soviet conquest of the United States. One of the most effective scenes was a high school band marching in a parade accompanied by giant red banners with the faces of Marx, Lenin, and—Abraham Lincoln. The scene, which was actually filmed in Canada, emphasized the incongruity of juxtaposing the icons of the two great twentieth-century secular cultures. Of course, communism also tried to create a culture based on words and images of its founding fathers, but as events in 1989 showed us so dramatically, it failed. Why?

One reason is that communism was superimposed over traditional cultures, which showed remarkable tenacity despite brutal efforts to produce a new culture derived from Marxism. After decades of indoctrination, Russians, Poles, and Chinese were still Russian, Polish, and Chinese, and they all wanted to stay that way. As Johann Goethe put it, the United States had it better because we didn't have the burden of an ancient culture to overcome. The big blemish in the evolution of U.S. culture, of course, was that it pushed aside the real Native Americans and excluded those Americans who had been brought here on slave ships and their descendants, who were legally barred from participation. The genius of Martin Luther King, Jr., was that he preached an inclusive social revolution and identified the aspirations of blacks with the famous cultural values of life, liberty, and pursuit of happiness. Despite later demands for black separatism and pressures for maintenance of other distinct American cultures, the dominant U.S. culture is one of inclusion. Anyone can become an American. Most of us keep the "hyphenated" link to our cultural roots a generation or two, and then disappear into the melting pot.

U.S. Values

People from other countries are often surprised to hear the phrase, ''She's a good American.'' They rarely describe someone as a ''good Swede'' or a ''good Nigerian.'' With tongue in cheek, a visiting Hungarian novelist describes how he'll become an American:

> As an American I'll have a credit card. Or two. I'll use and misuse them and have to pay the fees. . . . And I'll buy the best dishwasher, microwave, dryer and hi-fi in the world—that is, the U.S.A. I'll have warranty for all—or my money back. I'll use automatic toothbrushes, egg boilers and garage doors. I'll call every single phone number starting 1-800. . . . I'll buy a new TV every time a larger screen appears on the market. . . . My life won't differ from the lives you can see in the soaps: nobody will complain. I won't complain either. I'll always smile.[12]

A accurate portrait of U.S. culture, or a gentle caricature? A little of both probably, but we need to remember that a stereotype is the linking of individual characteristics with membership in a culture: ''Americans are . . . [fill in the blank]''. The only thing all Americans are is American. The same goes for subcultures such as African Americans, Italian Americans, and Chinese Americans. The only characteristic they all share is ethnic origin, and the larger commonality of U.S. citizenship. Any sentence beginning with the words, ''Americans are . . .'' is false and dangerous. It is false because the only thing all Americans share is citizenship, the basis of our common political culture. It is dangerous because it inevitably contains a stereotype. Still, values and characteristics vary from culture to culture, and, let's face it, most Americans do rely on credit cards, buy lots of gadgets, and smile a lot. They are common attributes of our culture and reflect our cultural values. Many—if not all—of us are like that much—if not all—of the time. Is U.S. culture built only on materialism and superficial pleasantries?

The Good and Bad of Individualism

Some would argue that it is, but there is more. The one cultural value that stands out is individualism. As you will remember, Condon and Yousef contrasted it with individuality, suggesting an almost pejorative definition of the word, an excess of a good thing. Americans' concern with individual liberty goes back to the founding of the republic. It is not surprising that it is a powerful cultural value, as most of us had ancestors who came here precisely to get away from oppressive governments and stifling cultures. They asked for little except a chance to make their own lives free from outside interference. Our current mistrust of government is a product of that cultural tradition. Traditional Anglo culture, of which modern U.S. culture is a product, also stresses individualism or individuality, but in the United States it has become almost an obsession. Canadian law promises peace,

---

[12] Milos Vamos, ''How I'll Become an American,'' *New York Times,* April 17, 1989, p. A19.

order, and good government as common goals, but the American Declaration of Independence called for life, liberty, and the pursuit of happiness. There is a significant difference between the two sets of values.

Alexis de Tocqueville was an early nineteenth-century philosopher/social scientist from France who traveled widely in the United States to see how the first field experiment in the philosophy of the Enlightenment was faring. The French Revolution, which occurred the same year the U.S. Constitution was put into effect, foundered, whereas the American Revolution produced a stable government and a culture that seemed to preserve the cultural values that had inspired both revolutions. Tocqueville's long account of his exploration of U.S. democracy is still a classic and still offers fresh insight into the secular culture of the United States.

In it, he contrasted ''egoism'' with ''individualism''—a new word then. The former, he said, was characteristic of European aristocracies, the latter a feature of the young U.S. republic. Tocqueville was ambivalent about the value of individualism and worried about its long-term effect:

> As social equality spreads there are more and more people who, though neither rich nor powerful enough to have much hold over others, have gained or kept enough wealth and enough understanding to look after their own needs. Such folk owe no man anything and hardly expect anything from anybody. They form the habit of thinking of themselves in isolation and imagine that their whole destiny is in their own hands.
>
> Thus not only does democracy make men forget their ancestors, but also clouds their view of their descendants and isolates them from their contemporaries. Each man is forever thrown back on himself alone, and there is a danger that he may be shut up in the solitude of his own heart.[13]

If anything, the emphasis on individualism has increased since Tocqueville's visit. In 1924, a public opinion poll found that 29 percent of U.S. mothers thought it was important to instill independence in their children, whereas 50 percent emphasized loyalty to church and 45 percent said strict obedience was important. In 1988, the poll was repeated. In our own time, 76 percent of mothers said independence was important to their children, whereas only 22 percent cited loyalty to church, and 17 percent mentioned strict obedience as important values. The proportion of mothers counseling tolerance in their kids went from 6 percent to 47 percent, so the selfish cultural values of the yuppies and NIMBY (''not in my back yard'') didn't completely dominate the 1980s.[14] Still, too many Americans in the 1990s are shut up in the solitude of their own hearts, a condition that can lead to selfishness as well as to self-reliance.

---

[13] Alexis de Tocqueville, *Democracy in America,* trans. George Lawrence (New York: Doubleday Anchor, 1969), vol. 2, p. 508. The quote is reprinted in Robert N. Bellah et al., eds., *Individualism and Commitment in American Life: Readings on the Themes of Habits of the Heart* (New York: Harper & Row, 1987).

[14] University of Michigan ISR surveys cited in *USA Today,* January 20–22, 1989.

The American Dream as Cultural Value

The conflict between the cultural values of individualism (modern and very American) and commitment to community (very traditional and seemingly out of place in the 1990s), which was a theme throughout Tocqueville's work, was also the theme of an unusual study of U.S. society in the 1980s. The book was written by a small group of sociologists who rejected random samples and sophisticated data analysis in favor of long interviews with a small number of more or less typical Americans. They quote poets and philosophers more than statisticians, which is unusual enough, and conclude that somewhere in our relentless search for individual freedom we have lost our sense of community:

> For over a hundred years, a large part of the American people, the middle class, has imagined that the virtual meaning of life lies in the acquisition of ever-increasing status, income, and authority, from which genuine freedom is supposed to come. Our achievements have been enormous. They permit us the aspiration to become a genuinely humane society in a genuinely decent world, and provide many of the means to attain that aspiration. Yet we seem to be hovering on the very brink of disaster, not only from international conflict but from the internal incoherence of our own society. What has gone wrong?

A page later, they provide part of the answer:

> The American dream is often a very private dream of being the star, the uniquely successful and admirable one, the one who stands out from the crowd of ordinary folk who don't know how. And since we have believed in that dream for a long time and worked very hard to make it come true, it is hard for us to give it up, even though it contradicts another dream that we have—that of living in a society that would really be worth living in.[15]

In a later book, the same authors argued that the American dream could be attained by strengthening the traditional social institutions that many Americans had tried to escape. Their solution: less individualism, more community.[16] The phrase "the American dream" is known around the world. It usually means unlimited opportunities for personal achievement. Even though it has lost a lot of its glitter in the past several decades, it is still identified with personal freedom and unlimited opportunities. The lines around the visa section of U.S. embassies around the world are testament to its strength today. Are the cultural values of the nation of nations, the American dream, a proper basis for the global culture of the 1990s? This is a question to consider after we look more closely at language and particularly at English, the language of global communications.

---

[15] Robert H. Bellah et al., *Habits of the Heart: Individualism and Commitment in American Life* (New York: Harper & Row, 1986), pp. 286, 287.
[16] Robert H. Bellah et al., *The Good Society* (New York: Knopf, 1991).

MAIN POINTS

1. Cultures evolve, like species of plants and animals, from a genetic base. Cultures are the sum of language, values, and behavior that make one people distinctive from all others.
2. Human culture became possible when our ancient ancestors first acquired language. The development of written language was the first communication revolution.
3. Cultures can be judged on the basis of the values they contain as well as their ability to adapt to a changing environment.
4. The notion that each culture should be a sovereign political state grew out of the nationalism movement of the nineteeth century and was strengthened in the dismantling of European empires of the twentieth century. This, in turn, has led to a resurgence in the assertion of cultural independence in the 1990s.
5. Anglo-American or U.S. cultural values, which emphasize individual liberty and opportunity, remain popular throughout the world and are reflected in the emerging global culture.

FOR MORE INFORMATION

Two books cited frequently in this chapter are useful as introductory texts to the topic of intercultural communication. They are Larry A. Samovar, Richard E. Porter, and Nemi C. Jain, *Understanding Intercultural Communication* (Belmont, CA: Wadsworth, 1981), and John C. Condon and Fathi Yousef, *An Introduction to Intercultural Communication* (Indianapolis, IN: Bobbs-Merrill, 1975). Three books by Edward T. Hall are *The Hidden Dimension* (1969); *The Silent Language* (1969); and *Beyond Culture* (1977). All are published in paperback by Doubleday Anchor Books in New York. They are applicable to both the study of communication and culture and nonverbal communication, which is discussed in Chapter 3.

The Tocqueville classic, *Democracy in America,* still offers insight into U.S. political culture and is easy to read. A paperback edition translated by George Lawrence and edited by J. P. Mayer was published by Anchor Books in 1969. *Habits of the Heart,* by Robert N. Bellah, Richard Madsen, William M. Sullivan, Ann Swidler, and Steven M. Tipton, is the 1980s update based on Tocqueville and free from jargon, statistics, and mathematical models. It was published in paperback by Harper & Row in 1986. A follow-up volume, *Individualism and Commitment in American Life* (edited by Robert N. Bellah et al., published by Harper & Row, 1987), contains comments on U.S. cultural values from Thomas Jefferson to Ronald Reagan. Their prescription for strengthening U.S. society is contained in *The Good Society* (New York: Knopf, 1991).

A massive study of changing cultural values in 26 countries in the 1970s and 1980s is reported in *Culture Shift in Advanced Industrial Society,* by Ronald Inglehart. The book was published by Princeton University Press in 1990. You can also find regular international studies of public opinion in a variety of sources. Start with *Public Opinion Quarterly* (a research journal) and *Public Opinion,* a policy journal that became *The American*

Enterprise in 1990. Many surveys are carried out by the Gallup Organization and reported in most newspapers.

Critical studies of contemporary U.S. culture, particularly disparities of subcultures, are Sowell's *The Economics and Politics of Race: An International Perspective* (New York: Morrow, 1983); Lawrence E. Harrison, *Who Prospers? How Cultural Values Shape Economic and Political Success* (New York: Basic, 1992); Charles J. Sykes, *A Nation of Victims: The Decay of the American Character* (New York: St. Martin's, 1992); Arthur M. Schlesinger, Jr., *The Disuniting of America: Reflections on a Multicultural Society* (New York: Norton, 1992).

Upbeat interpretations are Ben J. Wattenberg, *The First Universal Nation: Leading Indicators and Ideas about the Surge of America in the 1990s* (New York: Free Press, 1991); Joseph S. Nye, Jr., *Bound to Lead: The Changing Nature of American Power* (New York: Basic, 1990).

FOR DISCUSSION

1. Debate the following proposition from Schlesinger, cited above: "The American population has unquestionably grown more heterogeneous than ever in recent times. But this very heterogeneity makes the quest for unifying ideals and a common culture all the more urgent."

2. Compile a list of social conflicts around the world and try to identify causes. What aspects of culture are most at issue? How would you propose to solve these conflicts?

3. Survey students in the class to see what cultures and subcultures they see themselves as part of. Sketch the various concentric and overlapping cultures to see how differently people of similar backgrounds define themselves. Determine what and how much members of the class have in common, and on what and how much they differ.

DATA BASE

I. Global cultural values: At the end of 1989, affiliates of the Gallup Poll in 36 countries asked people, "Do you think 1990 will be a peaceful year, more or less free of international disputes, a troubled year with much international discord, or remain the same?"

	Peaceful (%)	*Remain Same (%)*	*Troubled (%)*	*No Opinion (%)*
United States	37	32	26	5
Soviet Union (Moscow)	64	16	11	9
Belgium	16	48	33	3
Denmark	31	29	31	10

	Peaceful (%)	Remain Same (%)	Troubled (%)	No Opinion (%)
France	10	42	39	9
West Germany	30	32	25	1
Great Britain	29	38	26	7
Greece	19	33	20	28
Ireland	31	40	18	11
Italy	36	36	20	8
Luxembourg	28	32	37	4
Netherlands	25	41	30	3
Portugal	24	30	17	30
Spain	26	27	28	19
Austria	23	37	31	9
Finland	25	50	20	5
Hungary	22	29	31	17
Iceland	48	39	6	6
Sweden	35	41	16	8
Switzerland	29	34	27	10
Turkey	33	14	23	30
Argentina	43	23	23	11
Brazil	35	18	37	9
Canada	24	46	27	4
Chile	46	22	26	6
Costa Rica	24	26	35	15
Mexico	28	31	42	4
Uruguay	36	22	30	12
Australia	20	44	28	7
Hong Kong	28	31	34	7
Israel	36	20	23	21
Japan	12	36	22	30
South Korea	34	18	28	21
New Zealand	30	45	22	3
Philippines	24	45	29	2
South Africa	25	36	28	11

SOURCE: The Gallup Poll News Service, vol. 54, no. 32c, December 31, 1989. From *The Gallup Poll Monthly,* no. 29110, December 1989, p. 12. Copyright © 1989 The Gallup Poll. Reprinted by permission.

II. The Euro-Barometer asked Europeans in 1985, "Would you say you are very proud, quite proud, not very proud, or not at all proud to be (nationality)?"

Country	Percentage saying "very proud"
United States	*76
Greece	72
Australia	*70
Hungary	*67
Mexico	*65
Spain	64
Canada	*62
Luxembourg	62
Iceland	*58
Britain	54
Ireland	53
Argentina	*49
Italy	45
Norway	*41
France	42
Denmark	40
Sweden	*30
Netherlands	34
Portugal	33
Belgium	26
Japan	*30
West Germany	20

NOTE: *Data from comparable national survey in 1981.
SOURCE: Ronald Inglehart, *Culture Shift in Advanced Industrial Society* (Princeton, NJ: Princeton University Press, 1990), p. 411. Copyright © 1990 by Princeton University Press. Reprinted by permission of Princeton University Press.

III. Perspectives on the United States: *Newsweek* magazine in 1983 gave people in six countries a list of 14 characteristics and asked them which ones they associated with Americans.

	Most often associated with Americans	Least often associated with Americans
By the French	Industrious	Lazy
	Energetic	Rude
	Inventive	Honest
	Decisive	Sophisticated
	Friendly	

	Most often associated with Americans	Least often associated with Americans
By the Japanese	Nationalistic Friendly Decisive Rude Self-indulgent	Industrious Lazy Honest Sexy
By the West Germans	Energetic Inventive Friendly Sophisticated Intelligent	Lazy Sexy Greedy Rude
By the English, Scottish, and Welsh	Friendly Self-indulgent Energetic Industrious Nationalistic	Lazy Sophisticated Sexy Decisive
By the Brazilians	Intelligent Inventive Energetic Industrious Greedy	Lazy Self-indulgent Sexy Sophisticated
By the Mexicans	Industrious Intelligent Inventive Decisive Greedy	Lazy Honest Rude Sexy

SOURCE: "What the World Thinks of America," *Newsweek,* July 11, 1983, p. 50. From *Newsweek,* July 11, 1983. Copyright © 1983 Newsweek, Inc. All rights reserved. Reprinted by permission.

IV. Are U.S. cultural and social values unique? Responses by people in nine countries suggest differences between the United States and other countries.

U.S.	Austral.	Switz.	G.B.	Neth.	W. Ger.	Aust.	It.	Hung.

Agree strongly/agree that government should provide everyone with a guaranteed basic income.

U.S.	Austral.	Switz.	G.B.	Neth.	W. Ger.	Aust.	It.	Hung.
21%	38%	43%	61%	50%	56%	57%	67%	79%

U.S.	*Austral.*	*Switz.*	*G.B.*	*Neth.*	*W. Ger.*	*Aust.*	*It.*	*Hung.*

Agree strongly/agree it is the responsibility of the government to reduce the differences in income between people with high incomes and those with low incomes.

| 29% | 44% | 43% | 64% | 65% | 61% | 81% | 82% | 80% |

Agree strongly/agree differences in income in (name of country) are too large.

| 58% | 61% | 68% | 76% | 66% | 76% | 90% | 87% | 76% |

Those with high incomes should pay a much larger/larger proportion of their earnings in taxes.

| 58% | 65% | NA | 76% | NA | 90% | NA | 86% | NA |

Agree strongly/agree the government should provide a job for everyone who wants one.

| 45% | 40% | 50% | 59% | 75% | 77% | 80% | 82% | 92% |

Agree strongly/agree the government should provide a decent standard of living for the unemployed.

| 37% | 36% | 46% | 65% | 61% | 66% | 43% | 68% | NA |

For those with low incomes, taxes are much too high/too high.

| 70% | 75% | 69% | 87% | 80% | 85% | 78% | 85% | 60% |

For those with middle incomes, taxes are much too high/too high.

| 70% | 64% | 51% | 41% | 60% | 52% | 47% | 62% | 39% |

Agree strongly/agree that the wearing of seatbelts should be required by law.

| 49% | 92% | NA | 80% | NA | 82% | 81% | 81% | NA |

Agree strongly/agree that smoking in public places should be prohibited.

| 46% | 56% | NA | 51% | NA | 49% | 58% | 89% | NA |

Definitely/probably should be the government's responsibility to provide health care for the sick.

| 89% | 93% | NA | 99% | NA | 98% | 98% | 100% | NA |

Definitely/probably should be the government's responsibility to provide industry with the help it needs to grow.

| 63% | 87% | NA | 95% | NA | 54% | 75% | 84% | NA |

Ambition essential/very important for getting ahead in life.

| 89% | 86% | 65% | 80% | 68% | 68% | 79% | 49% | 73% |

Knowing the right people essential/very important for getting ahead in life.

| 40% | 33% | 45% | 39% | 44% | 60% | 68% | 76% | 41% |

A person's political beliefs essential/very important for getting ahead in life.

| 9% | 5% | 14% | 5% | 3% | 19% | 21% | 22% | 25% |

U.S.	Austral.	Switz.	G.B.	Neth.	W. Ger.	Aust.	It.	Hung.

Strongly agree/agree the way things are in (name of country) people like me and my family have a good chance of improving our standard of living.

U.S.	Austral.	Switz.	G.B.	Neth.	W. Ger.	Aust.	It.	Hung.
72%	61%	59%	37%	26%	40%	47%	45%	33%

SOURCE: *The American Enterprise,* March/April 1990, pp. 113–116.

CHAPTER 3

Communicating Across Cultures

ABOUT THIS CHAPTER

Language, more than anything else, is the heart of culture. The history of a culture is recorded in its books and oral expressions. Its values are embedded in vocabulary and even, it seems, in grammar. Languages evolve with cultures and are as varied and puzzling as the cultures they contain. In this chapter, we examine the linkages between language and culture—psycholinguistics, expression of cultural values, sociolinguistics—and then consider why language is so often at issue in the 1990s when cultures and subcultures from the U.S. Southwest to the Baltic assert a right to independence and self-determination.

INTRODUCTION

The Hitchhiker's Guide to the Galaxy, the first book in a hilarious four-part science fiction "trilogy," describes one of the most improbable products of evolution: the Babel fish. When you stick the tiny Babel fish in your ear, you instantly understand everything said to you in any language. The end to all problems of cultural misunderstanding? Unfortunately, as *The Hitchhiker's Guide* notes, "the poor Babel fish, by effectively removing all barriers to communication between different races and cultures, has caused more and bloodier wars than anything else in the history of creation."[1]

---

[1] Douglas Adams, *The Hitchhiker's Guide to the Galaxy* (New York: Simon & Schuster, 1979), pp. 60–61.

Of course, the Babel fish is the product of a zany imagination, but the story highlights two issues at the heart of any discussion of communication and culture. One is whether instant and complete communication would eliminate the cultural conflict that is so prevalent in the last decade of the twentieth century. The answer is probably not. The other is why languages are so different and how languages influence the way we communicate from culture to culture. This question requires a complex answer.

PSYCHOLINGUISTICS

Charles V, emperor of the Holy Roman Empire in the sixteenth century, is supposed to have said, "I speak Spanish to God, Italian to women, French to men, and German to my horse."[2] Charles had to know several languages because he was also king of Spain and archduke of Austria. He didn't mention English because in the 1500s, English was a minor language, virtually unknown outside of Britain and not universally used even there.

Language and Thinking

Language is at the heart of any culture, and in the 1990s, it is increasingly the basis of assertions of cultural independence. Especially in Western countries, language has replaced religion as the demarcation line between cultures and has become the battlefield for cultures demanding recognition and autonomy. Consider Welsh insistence that a regional fourth TV channel be programmed in Welsh or the use of Irish in Ireland's radio and television, even though in both countries only a tiny minority of the population speaks the ancient tongues.

In Belgium the central government fell twice in the 1980s when the mayor of a small town, which had been transferred from French to Dutch administration, refused to take a test to demonstrate his knowledge of Dutch. Closer to home is the French-only movement in Quebec, which at one time threatened Canada with civil war and continues to divide the country. In the United States, more than 20 states have considered laws making English their official language, and a similar national movement is endorsed by Alistair Cooke of *Masterpiece Theater.*

Why is language, of all things, drawing people to the barricades, and why now? Part of the answer is the dominance of Anglo-American culture throughout the world and with it, the emergence of English as the first truly global language. (We consider this more in depth in Chapter 4.) Part of it is the assertion of cultural independence, with language—often the most visible aspect of culture—leading the charge. Language protects a culture. It keeps outsiders out and insiders in. What better way for a Welshman to remind an Englishman of his outsider status than to speak Welsh and to insist that as much of Wales as possible do the same? The French

---

[2] Thomas G. Aylesworth and Virginia L. Aylesworth, *If You Don't Invade My Intimate Zone or Clean Up My Water Hole, I'll Breathe in Your Face, Blow on Your Neck, and Be Late for Your Party* (New York: Condor Publishing, 1978), p. 85.

Canadian and English-speaking American accomplish something similar. They remind the Anglo Canadian and non-Anglo-American that they must pass the cultural initiation rite of learning the language. Only then can they become part of the culture.

Languages protect cultures and, as we have already noted, they also seem to contain the culture. Can you really understand the French, the Chinese, or the Mexicans without knowing their language? Most people would say no. Part of the differences among languages, and therefore cultures, have to do with the idiosyncrasies of grammar and structure that make direct translation impossible. Beyond that, however, there is a vague sense that some languages just work better—certainly differently—in certain circumstances. Maybe Charles V was right: Spanish is better for talking to God and German better when you talk to a horse.

The Whorf–Sapir Hypothesis

The argument that language directly influences cognitive processes—perception and thinking—is the basis of psycholinguistics, a field of research and study that is still associated with two pioneering scholars, Benjamin L. Whorf and Edward Sapir. They studied Native American languages of the U.S. Southwest, which had evolved in cultures very different from and independent of those of Europe. The languages operated very differently from Indo-European languages. In Hopi, they noted, verbs refer to anything of short duration—lightning, flame, a puff of smoke—whereas anything of long duration—man, mountain, house—is a noun. One word is used for birds, another for anything else that flies. Sapir argued that this and other unique qualities of every language have important implications for the way we perceive the world:

> Human beings . . . are very much at the mercy of the particular language which has become the medium of expression for their society. It is quite an illusion to imagine that one adjusts to reality essentially without the use of language and that language is merely an incidental means of solving specific problems of communication or reflection. The fact of the matter is that the ''real world'' is to a large extent built up on the language habits of the group. . . . We see and hear and otherwise experience very largely as we do because the language habits of our community pre-dispose certain choices of interpretation.[3]

Even languages closer to English than Hopi and Navajo seem to ''do'' things differently. Consider a German who looks at a masculine moon (*der Mond*). To a Frenchman across the Rhine River, that same moon is feminine (*la lune*). The sun is the opposite for both: feminine in German (*die Sonne*) but masculine in French (*le soleil*). To the Englishman across the English Channel, of course, the sun and moon are neither masculine nor feminine; they are simply *the sun* and *the moon*. Common sense tells us that these differences must have some influence on the way

---

[3] Quoted in Wilbur Schramm and William E. Porter, *Men, Women, Messages, and Media*, 2nd ed. (New York: Harper & Row, 1982), pp. 77–78.

the French, the Germans, and the English perceive the heavenly bodies, some impact on the way these two common objects fit into the three distinct cultures. When you move from the comparatively close relatives of the Indo-European language family to Hopi, Chinese, or any of the several thousand unwritten languages still found in isolated areas, the differences get bigger. In many cases, the Indo-European notion of a language made up of nouns, verbs, and adjectives no longer fits. Surely the process of thinking, the way we perceive our environment, must be affected by the language we use. Perhaps even the brain functions differently.

But wait a minute. Most of the problems we seem to encounter are vocabulary. The common example is Arabic with 10 (or is it 100?) words for camel but none for snow, whereas Eskimo languages have a dozen (or 100) words for snow and presumably none for camel.[4] Do Arabs *perceive* snow and rain to be the same because they have only one word for both? Are Eskimos unable to distinguish among cows, horses, and camels because their language contains only one word for "big animals that don't live here"? Probably not. We create or adapt the words we need. If you're from Miami or Los Angeles, snow is snow (and not much different from ice or sleet, all of which you know only from the weather report on TV). If you're from the "snow belt" or you're a skier, then you know the differences between powder and crust, dry snow and wet snow, sleet and hail. All languages develop the vocabulary they need. A lack of a specific word doesn't mean speakers of that language cannot perceive differences among objects. All languages borrow or invent new words to accommodate new experiences. English does it with unusual speed and enthusiasm, but all languages do it.

There are more complex problems of psycholinguistics, of course. Once you get away from the Indo-European language family, structural differences among languages get larger and more complex. Direct translation from one to the other may be impossible. However, most people who are truly fluent in two languages will tell you that it is possible to express the same thought in either language. This suggests that the differences are in the cultures, not in the languages, and that all languages function more or less the same way: They all do the job of communicating that the culture requires of them.

The Chomsky Argument

The counterargument to traditional psycholinguistics is represented by Noam Chomsky, who asserts that everyone is born with predisposition to language but not to a specific language. We know that up to about age six a child can learn any language with equal ease. After that age, any other language is never quite the same as our "native" language. But how do we learn? By imitating what we hear from mommy and daddy and *Sesame Street?*

Chomsky contends that we don't learn a language merely by imitation, as the rare "talking" animal does, because even small children can invent grammatical structures—sentences—that could not possibly have come from listening to their

---

[4] Eskimo languages really have only two words for snow. See Geoffrey K. Pullum, *The Great Eskimo Vocabulary Hoax and Other Irreverent Essays on the Study of Language* (Chicago: University of Chicago Press, 1991).

parents. They also seem to learn the formal rules of grammar at a remarkably early age. We often hear the amusing result when small children follow the rule instead of the exception: "I goed to the park today," "We singed in school." Chomsky argues in favor of an innate ability, acquired through centuries of evolution, that allows a small child to learn a language—any language—early in life. He suggests that each of us arrives at birth with a kind of physical template, a flexible computer program wired into our brain, that incorporates a "deep grammar," or set of rules that apply equally to all human languages. The idiosyncrasies we struggle with in coping with a foreign language, in this view, are really superficial and unrelated to the real biological grammar of all human languages.

Chomsky's work puts him on the side of heredity in the debate on the relative influence of heredity versus social environment on human behavior. On the same side are Wilson's sociobiology and Carl Sagan's fascinating speculation on the evolution of human intelligence in *The Dragons of Eden*. Cognitive science is a rapidly expanding field and includes both empirical research and speculation about language and the mind.

On the whole, the arguments of the traditional psycholinguists are in decline in the 1990s and the arguments of the Chomsky school are ascendant. Of course, certain differences in cultural aspects of language cause us problems even after we get past the unique hurdles of any foreign language we try to learn. Sociolinguistics deals with the whole range of linkages between language and society, but an important part of the field involves the different meanings that different cultures give to words. This is probably a greater obstacle to cross-cultural understanding than a lack of comparable vocabulary or any of the other unique aspects of languages.

CULTURAL ASPECTS OF LANGUAGE

At the biological level, as far as anyone knows, all languages operate the same. We haven't found any differences in brain wave activity between thinking in English and thinking in Chinese. Nor have we discovered any difference in the genetic structure or brain capacity of different races or language groups. As a result, contrary to both popular belief and common sense, we don't think differently in different languages. Any thought you come up with in English can be expressed in any other language, provided you can find or invent the right vocabulary.

Language teachers are right: Stick with it, and at some point, you'll discover that you can function just about as easily in Spanish, German, or Japanese as you can in your native English. Or if you're struggling with English as a foreign language and find this book difficult, don't despair. Improvement comes quietly but steadily with practice. And remember that English, with its great subtlety and huge vocabulary, to say nothing of its cultural varieties, remains a challenge even to native speakers.

Double Meanings

The real problem of cross-cultural communication (or miscommunication) is not one of language per se. Dictionaries can tell us that German *Haus*, French *maison*, and Spanish *casa* are all equivalent to English *house*. They can't tell us what those words mean to the people who use them, the individual and collective cultural experience they embody. In this sense, *Haus* and *house* are never the same word.

All words have two parts to their "meaning." One part is the *denotative* meaning, the one you find in the dictionary. This is the easy part to translate. It tells us that *maison* is equivalent to *casa,* but it tells us nothing about what *maison* means culturally to the French or how that differs from the cultural meaning of *casa* to the Spanish. The second part of a word's meaning is its *connotative* meaning, which is its subjective or cultural meaning. This meaning is never in a dictionary and cannot be translated from one language to another, or even from one culture to another in the same language. Words contain both meanings, but dictionaries contain only the denotative one.

Connotative meanings are a product of both individual and collective experience. Differences in the connotative or cultural meanings of words, which are a product of our personal experiences with them, exist among people of the same culture and are even bigger among different cultures. Ask a Russian child to draw a picture of his or her *dom* (house) and you probably would get a big apartment complex with an extended family and perhaps even neighbors sharing facilities. Space would be cramped, and few amenities would be available. However, family ties probably would be stronger than in the United States. The cultural experience of "home" would include grandparents, unlike the United States where grandma and grandpa are likely to be in a Florida condo or in a nursing home.

In many other cultures, "home" is the place where your family has lived for generations, maybe even centuries, pretty much as it does now. Home is stability, security, tradition. Change, even if it promises a better life, is threatening. A German TV series called *Heimat* ("home" or "homeland") covered the history of a German community from pre–World War I monarchy to the turbulent 1960s. It struck a particular chord among Germans, who had endured significant disruptions of their sense of *Heimat.* In the United States, we pride ourselves on looking forward, not backward, but it still is disconcerting to return to the place where we grew up and find that our childhood home—our *Heimat*—is now a shopping center parking lot. Our lack of interest in the past may be linked to individualism as a cultural value. Other cultures, which have roots that go deep into the soil of a specific piece of real estate, have a different meaning of *Heimat.*

Measuring Cultural Meaning

Obviously cultural differences in the meaning of words can be a problem. One problem is that you can't go to a dictionary to find out what these meanings are. Think back to any recent discussion that involved abstract concepts such as justice, peace, freedom, or love. If you disagreed with a point made by someone else, consider how much (or how little) you know about that person's personal experience with the concepts those words represent. Your cultural meaning of the word could well have been very different from the other person's. If the other person came from a part of the world you know little about, the possibility of shared understanding is remote. Without a reasonable overlap of connotative meaning as well as denotative meaning, it's difficult to share meaning, which is a good working definition of communication. It's easy to say, "I know where you're coming from," but actual understanding is hard.

Cultural meanings overlap but are never exactly the same for any two people even in the same culture. Between two cultures, the differences are larger, sometimes to the point that common understanding is extremely difficult. Even with the Babel fish to eliminate the simple problem of denotative translation, things didn't go well, and the earth was destroyed to make way for an intergalactic bypass. In the global culture of the 1990s, we're already in trouble despite a nearly universal language and global communication technologies.

Studying cultural differences of meanings is different from studying how and whether language influences cognitive processes of perception and thinking. The physiologist wants to understand how the brain works, and the psychologist tries to understand the mind. The sociolinguist wants to understand cultures and especially the linguistic glue that holds them together.

A notable effort in that direction began in the 1950s when Charles E. Osgood and colleagues at the University of Illinois developed a technique to measure subjective meaning.[5] They gave people lists of words—everything from simple words such as *boy* to abstract words such as *love.* Adjectives and verbs were included as well. Research participants rated each word on 7-point bipolar scales, such as pleasant-unpleasant, hot-cold, angular-rounded, and so on. When the researchers ran the results through a computer with a statistical routine called factor analysis, they found that the scales tended to fall into three distinct groups, regardless of the word being rated or the variety of scales used in the evaluation. Even people who evaluated a word very differently tended to use the same underlying dimensions.

Osgood and his colleagues concluded that subjective meanings of words— what we have been calling the cultural or connotative meaning—could be broken into three distinct and independent dimensions: evaluation (good or bad), potency (strong or weak), and activity (active or passive). Thus, when you think about two people such as President Bill Clinton and President Boris Yeltsin, your cultural meaning of the two people is a combination of the three dimensions. A student in Russia, with very different feelings toward the two leaders, would still use the same three dimensions. You can plot your "meaning" of a word on a three-dimensional Cartesian graph and compare it with, for example, the "meaning" of the same word to the student sitting next to you. Try it with this example. To keep things in two dimensions, we'll use only the first two dimensions and one adjective-pair for each word. Copy the following and mark how you see Presidents Clinton and Yeltsin with an X in the appropriate category.

---

[5] Charles E. Osgood, George J. Suci, and Percy H. Tannenbaum, *The Measurement of Meaning* (Urbana: University of Illinois Press, 1957).

Bill Clinton

| Good | ___ | ___ | ___ | ___ | ___ | ___ | ___ | Bad |
| Strong | ___ | ___ | ___ | ___ | ___ | ___ | ___ | Weak |

Boris Yeltsin

| Good | ___ | ___ | ___ | ___ | ___ | ___ | ___ | Bad |
| Strong | ___ | ___ | ___ | ___ | ___ | ___ | ___ | Weak |

Now convert the ratings to numbers (good, strong = $+3$; bad, weak = -3; other ratings in between) and plot them as shown in Figure 3.1.

Finally, plot the ratings of one or two other people near you, and you have a simple, graphic representation of how the two or three of you feel about these national leaders. The graph shows, in a limited way, the differences in cultural values. You can expand the technique by adding an active-passive dimension and plotting it on a three-dimensional graph, but this simplified exercise in subjective meaning should be enough to demonstrate how differently similar people from the same culture can evaluate fairly straightforward concepts. Try it with someone from a very different culture or with highly abstract, emotional words to see how much of the meanings of words are outside the dictionary definition.

Cross-Cultural Meaning

Osgood and his associates took the *semantic differential* (as the technique was called) to more than 30 cultures and languages and evaluated a list of 620 basic words. The project, which took more than 15 years, produced the first cross-cultural dictionary and began, in a very primitive way, to chip away at the age-old problem of finding ways to compare linguistic equivalents with very different cultural meanings.

A few of the findings about colors are indicative of how social science can add to—and occasionally contradict—subjective impressions. Osgood described differences across cultures in terms of the three basic dimensions, evaluation

FIGURE 3.1   Measuring the cultural meaning of two presidents.

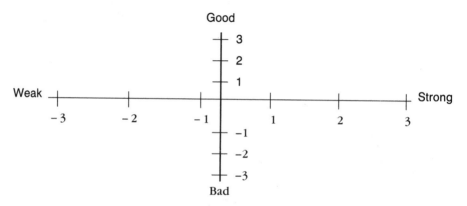

(good-bad), potency (strong-weak), and activity (active-passive). A few cultural evaluations were universal. The concept *color* itself and the color blue were positive in evaluation (good). Black and gray were negative in evaluation (bad) in all or virtually all cultures. Red and black were high in potency (strong); gray, yellow, and white were low in potency (weak). Color itself and red were high in activity (active); blue and gray were low in activity (passive).

Now for a few differences. American English-speaking subjects (school boys in central Illinois) rated black as low potency but high activity, possibly a function of racial interpretation. Western Europeans rated green as low potency (weak); two Scandinavian languages rated yellow high in evaluation (good). When colors were linked to days of the week, Monday was universally linked with gray, suggesting that our familiar "blue Monday" is really more gray. Only in Japan was Monday linked to blue. Sunday, in contrast, was uniquely linked to green for Americans, whereas most language cultures associated Sunday with white. The weekdays tended to be linked to different colors in different cultures. On the whole, American English and Japanese were the most isolated, meaning they tended to form linkages different from those in most other languages.

Osgood found that in general colors in the red end of the spectrum were strong and active and colors in the blue-green tones were more weak and passive. He speculated that this reflected the universal phenomenon that most food, such as meat and ripe fruit, is brightly colored, whereas our background environment is made up of earth tones.[6] Is this a reflection of the universal elements of all human cultures, behind the mosaic of cultural differences? It's possible.

Cross-Cultural Misunderstanding

This kind of research doesn't tell us why black is associated with mourning in most Western cultures whereas white has the same connotative meaning in many Asian cultures, but it does begin to lay out some of the differences that make cross-cultural communication both exhilarating and occasionally treacherous. Of course, it invites us to speculate how different cultures evolved with distinct subjective meanings for denotatively equivalent words. At a practical level, it warns us to be sensitive to unanticipated meanings. Imagine receiving a Christmas present wrapped in black paper or a sympathy card in neon pink. You could make a comparable mistake by offering red roses to a German or Polish acquaintance, yellow or white chrysanthemums to most Europeans, any purple flowers to a Brazilian, or white lilies to a Canadian. All of these are associated with funerals or death in the respective cultures.[7]

Even if you try to be sensitive to the cultural component of words and objects (such as the color of flowers), you still face obstacles to reaching the goal

---

[6] Charles E. Osgood, William H. May, and Murray S. Miron, *Cross-Cultural Universals of Affective Meaning* (Urbana: University of Illinois Press, 1975).

[7] These interpretations are included in Roger E. Axtell, *Do's and Taboos around the World,* 2nd ed. (New York: Wiley, 1990). Additional tips are reproduced in the Data Base at the end of this chapter.

of shared meaning that we have defined as communication. One of the hurdles is that the type of language you use is also a clue to your position in the culture. As an outsider, you can't avoid dealing with linkages of language and society, or with sociolinguistics.

SOCIOLINGUISTICS

In the previous section, we referred to sociolinguistics in the discussion of the connotative or subjective meaning of words. That's an area that really touches both psycholinguistics and sociolinguistics. The latter is more typically concerned with aspects of language such as dialect and pronunciation and how these and other aspects of language relate to social structure.

The Importance of Accents

Professor Henry Higgins, of *Pygmalion* and *My Fair Lady* fame, was a socio-linguist. He underscored the importance of sociolinguistics when he sang that the moment an Englishman speaks, he makes some other Englishman despise him. The New England Yankee and Deep South sharecropper have a similar problem. In *Pygmalion,* George Bernard Shaw was referring to the wide variety of dialects in British English and their importance in a then highly stratified British society. Accents remain stronger and more important in Britain than in North America, New Zealand, and Australia. But we're not exempt from making judgments or decisions based on someone's accent.

Despite a continual stirring of the melting pot and the leveling influence of pop culture, regional, class, and ethnic accents in the United States are getting stronger and more widely acceptable. A large part of this can be credited to recent social movements that have demanded acceptance of subcultures into the main-stream culture. Institutions are also less willing to insist on adherence to a tradi-tional standard or to provide instruction in it. Few schoolchildren today are taught elocution (as it was called a century ago) or drilled in pronunciation. Regional and cultural variations appear more frequently in radio, television, and movies as well. One of the artificial elements in 30- or 40-year-old movies is that the characters almost always speak in complete, grammatically correct sentences. Now movie characters speak like many people really do, grammatical errors, sentence fragments, careless pronunciation and all.

Many cultures consider maintenance of the language important enough that they sponsor official institutions to arbitrate language use. The French Academy is the most famous, mostly because of its efforts to hold back the tide of "Franglais." It also tries to set standards for pronunciation and grammar. For decades, the British Broadcasting Corporation (BBC) has set the standard for British English, although the BBC standard varies slightly from "received pronunciation," or "RP English," which is transmitted through the British private schools to the elites of each generation.

American English, for better or worse, has no single standard, although the accent used by TV announcers and newscasters is close to a standard. It is about the same as the pronunciation in general use in the upper Midwest and on the West Coast. Except for those on stations broadcasting to distinct audience segments such as blacks or country-western fans, most U.S. broadcasters tend toward the flat, slightly nasal accent native to South Dakota-born Tom Brokaw. Texas native Dan Rather and Canadian-born Peter Jennings had to smooth the edges of their ''native'' speech as they moved up the ladder of network television news. Even on local radio and television stations, the sound is clearly American, though it may not match the local accent.

Regional accents in both Britain and the United States retain amazing strength despite the bulldozer effect of national and global media. Schoolchildren in North Carolina may learn to read and count on *Sesame Street,* but when they go off to school, they speak with the distinct sounds of their parents, not those of Big Bird or Kermit the Frog, who use the network standard. Usually we retain the accent we learn as children, unless we move to a different part of the country. Even then, we slip back into our accents easily when we visit or move back where we came from. In Britain, too, the influx of U.S. movies and TV programs seems to have made little dent in the distinctive British language and accents. Kids have picked up American words and slang since World War II, but the accents remain distinctly British. In all cases, the accent seems to embody the specific subculture we identify with, and we give it up as reluctantly as we give up the culture.

Language and Social Standings

Sociolinguists are also concerned with other aspects of language use, such as vocabulary and grammar, when they are linked to social position. Most of us, in fact, move between at least two subcultures easily and adjust our use of language accordingly. Consider how your speech changes when you move from an informal gathering of students to an important job interview. ''Yeah'' and ''nah'' become a carefully articulated ''yes'' and ''no''; ''hey, watch it, man'' becomes a grammatically correct ''excuse me, sir.'' Unlike most languages, which distinguish two or more degrees of formality in the second person, English has only a single egalitarian ''you,'' reserving the archaic, informal ''thou'' for occasional hymns and prayers. Still, we manage to build all manner of hierarchies and social distinctions into our speech, probably as much as languages that continue to make use of ancient cultural distinctions.

English may be one of the few languages that recognizes degrees of formality in usage. Language usage guides and even some dictionaries distinguish among degrees of formality. What is right for informal speech is inappropriate for formal settings, and what we say is often different from what we write. For example, most of us would say ''It's me'' but probably not write it. ''He don't know it,'' or ''she ain't here,'' although not recognized as acceptable by very many authorities, are often heard in informal speech. Some well-educated people were drilled with the grammatical error of ''it is me'' (the correct form is ''it is I'') and overcompensate by saying things such as ''on behalf of my wife and I'' or ''she gave it to myself.''

The words we use tell others a lot about us and allow us to communicate across cultures. But they can also create problems. This chapter has discussed how words acquire unique cultural meanings that are difficult to translate and how language itself can be a barrier. Now it turns out that a large part of communication—some claim a majority—doesn't even involve words. Maybe we don't need the Babel fish!

NONVERBAL COMMUNICATION

The hardest part of cross-cultural communication doesn't even involve words. Nonverbal communication, according to one scholar who specializes in the field, contains two-thirds of the total "meaning" that is exchanged between two people in an ordinary conversation.[8] He stipulates that this is true for people from the same culture speaking the same language. Edward Sapir, the psycholinguist, calls nonverbal communication "an elaborate code that is written nowhere, known by none, and understood by all."[9] This is an optimistic assessment because cultural differences in nonverbal communication add a layer of potential misunderstanding that is difficult to avoid. Within a single culture or subculture, everyone may understand the nonverbal code, but outside of that culture nonverbal communication can be a disaster waiting to happen.

Communicating without Words

You can see the importance of nonverbal communication with one or two simple experiments. Go to a place where couples are engaged in ordinary conversation. Discreetly watch a couple out of voice range and write down what seems to be going on. You can certainly tell whether they're discussing their studies or something more personal, whether the relationship is formal or informal, whether it's going well or not. For another experiment, watch a TV program with the sound turned off—a soap opera or drama is best—and make the same kind of observations. To add a cross-cultural element, look for a subtitled foreign film on TV or rent one and cover up the subtitles with a piece of masking tape. Can you interpret the nonverbal behavior with the same degree of confidence you achieved among your peers?

In most cases, the cross-cultural element adds a significant barrier to understanding. Some gestures and facial expressions are universal, but many are not. Sometimes you can figure out something about the conversation from the nonverbal cues that accompany it, but not always. Nonverbal behavior that is widely understood in one culture can be misunderstood in another. Almost anyone who has traveled abroad can tell of experiences in which he or she misinterpreted a simple nonverbal cue. The best any cross-cultural traveler can hope for is

---

[8] Ray Birdwhistell, quoted in Wilbur Schramm, *Men, Messages, and Media: A Look at Human Communication* (New York: Harper & Row, 1973), p. 67.

[9] Quoted in Wilbur Schramm, *Men, Messages, and Media: A Look at Human Communication* (New York: Harper & Row, 1973), p. 68.

sensitivity to the problem and enough flexibility and candor not to let misunderstanding destroy the pleasure of exploring other cultures.

Elements of Nonverbal Communication

One problem is that we lack any theory of nonverbal communication, which is a concise explanation for the extraordinary differences among cultures or, for that matter, for the universal elements of nonverbal behavior. We're not even sure what the term includes. One text lists 24 nonverbal communication topics including hand gestures, facial gestures, posture and stance, clothing and hair styles, time symbolism, timing and pauses within verbal behavior, and silence. Another text defines nonverbal communication as "all those stimuli within a communication setting, both humanly generated and environmentally generated, with the exception of verbal stimuli, that have potential message value for the sender or receiver."[10] This doesn't leave anything—except words—that isn't potentially nonverbal communication. Note, too, that nonverbal communication continues even when the words stop. In nonverbal language, you cannot *not* send messages.

Another text adopts a set of fancy phrases to describe the kinds of nonverbal behaviors researchers have looked at: kinesics (gestures, facial expressions, body positions, body movement), oculesics (eye movement and contact), proxemics (spatial relations), chronemics (use of time), sensorics (smell, taste), haptics (touching), and paralinguistics (qualities of speech).[11] All of these deal with different aspects of the nonverbal communication that goes on continuously, even among people who cannot understand each other's language.

In practice, most studies have focused on body actions, space, and aspects of language other than words and their meanings. Obviously you can communicate a great deal through kinesics, proxemics, and paralinguistics (or metalanguage), as these nonverbal behaviors are often called. Albert Mehrabian, one of the best known scholars of nonverbal communication, claimed that in ordinary conversation, words accounted for only 7 percent of the transferred meaning, whereas paralanguage accounted for 38 percent and facial expressions for 55 percent.[12]

Behavior as Communication

The basis for this precise claim isn't clear, and the numbers probably wouldn't hold up across cultures. Still, when you carry out any of the simple experiments suggested above, it is surprising to see how much you can learn about what others may be "saying," even without their words—or how much you can misunderstand. Researchers do not agree on how much of nonverbal communication is

---

[10] Larry A. Samovar, Richard E. Porter, and Nemi C. Jain, *Understanding Intercultural Communication* (Belmont, CA: Wadsworth, 1981), p. 156.

[11] Carley H. Dodd, *Dynamics of Intercultural Communication,* 2nd ed. (Dubuque, IA: William C. Brown), ch. 9.

[12] Albert Mehrabian, *Silent Messages,* 2nd ed. (Belmont, CA: Wadsworth, 1981), p. 77.

universal—perhaps genetically based—and how much is culture-specific. Facial expressions seem to be close to universal. Smiles and frowns are about the same in every language and often have a counterpart in animals. The rule breaks down quickly, though. In Western cultures, a big, toothy smile is an expression of friendship, openness, and welcome, but in some Asian cultures, showing your teeth is considered rude and in poor taste. A comparable cultural difference is found in giggling, which is an expression of silliness and lack of seriousness in the West but is associated with embarrassment in many Asian cultures.

When you move from simple behavior that may have its origin in biology, both cultural differences and the opportunities for misunderstanding become greater. Even the venerable "V for victory" sign is considered an obscene insult in some parts of Europe, especially when it is presented with the palm toward the person making it. Nor do the first two fingers mean "two" in most parts of Europe, as they do in North America. To indicate to a European that you want two Cokes, two beers, or two seats, you gesture with your thumb and index finger.[13]

Popular books apply the findings of scholarly research on nonverbal communication, usually focusing on careful use of nonverbal cues to get ahead. Wear a red or yellow "power tie," men were advised a few years ago; get an office at the corner of the building with extra windows and floorspace; drive a Volvo (or is it a BMW this year?). Women are given comparable tips, especially regarding how to break into the traditionally male domains of corporate and political power.

At the international level, the importance of understanding nonverbal communication is obvious. The difficulty is greater, too, because so much of nonverbal communication is culturally acquired and culturally specific. Although plenty of guides for dealing with specific cultures exist—the Data Base of this chapter contains excerpts from one—nonverbal communication is usually not controllable and not repeatable. If presented with some token of honor—such as a sheep's eyes at a Middle East feast or a cooked dog in Asia—you probably can't hide your real response even with the most lavish words of praise for your hosts. Nor can you repeat the nonverbal reaction, which, in this case, is probably just as well.

The only guidelines for reducing the problems of communication failure are to try to learn as much as you can before you enter a different culture and to be flexible and honest when you do. If you know that promptness is expected in northern Europe and you're unavoidably late, a sincere apology is appropriate and probably adequate. If you're in Latin America and know that meeting times are flexible, you can avoid frustration by anticipating that others will show up 15 minutes to an hour after the appointed time. Although guide books don't always mention it, an honest approach can bring the murky areas of nonverbal communication into the open. Admit you're new to the country or culture and ask for an explanation, or apologize when the nonverbal response to your actions is not what you expected. For example, if you receive a special invitation to dinner

---

[13] Desmond Morris et al., *Gestures* (New York: Stein and Day, 1979), ch. 20. This interesting book is based on a study of 20 key gestures in 40 localities in 25 European countries. North Americans may be surprised to learn the variety of differences and how they have immigrated to the United States and Canada.

in a foreign friend's home: "I know the invitation says 7:00 p.m., but could you tell me the best time to arrive? And what kind of gift may I bring?" If there is a shocked nonverbal response and a mumbled "thank you" to a gift you've just presented: "I'm afraid my gift surprised you. I'll explain why I chose it if you can help me understand why you responded as you did."

There is no nonverbal Babel fish, so we're probably condemned to continue stumbling over our nonverbal mistakes as much as over our verbal miscues. However, the delight of discovering new cultures is enough reward that we shouldn't be deterred from cross-cultural adventures. One of the advantages of increased contact among cultures—and certainly a product of the emerging global culture—is that we all know more about other cultures and their unique nonverbal cues. Perhaps a global nonverbal language is emerging alongside English, the verbal language of global communications.

LANGUAGE AND SOCIAL CONFLICT

One of the four trends in global communication we encounter throughout this book is a resurgence of demands for cultural autonomy in all parts of the world. In many cases, this is defined by language rather than religion, which in the past, was probably the most frequent basis of cultural conflict. Why language? In the Western world, religion is less important now than in the past, and most of the dominant religions there accept the principle of religious pluralism. Language, in contrast, remains the repository of an active culture, often one that has been suppressed. It is a cultural symbol that you encounter every day. Unlike religion, you can't avoid it. Language makes a statement about a culture and the people who use it. When French and Anglo Canadians choose one language to the exclusion of the other for an ordinary conversation, their decision says something about the two cultures. One is primary, the other subordinate. When the European Free Trade Association agreed to use English exclusively, a language native to no nation in the organization, it guaranteed that none of its member nations would get an advantage over the others. The same principle is at work in India, which was supposed to replace colonial English with native Hindi but never has because the non-Hindi states don't want to be at a disadvantage.

Three current examples of language conflict, all of which have been mentioned in passing, deserve a closer look. All are close to home, and all are likely to be in tomorrow's headlines. They demonstrate that cultural conflict in the 1990s is not limited to warring factions in Beirut or the newly liberated tribes of Central Europe. They also show that ancient feuds and injuries that seem so irrational to outsiders are not the only source of conflict. Linguistic conflict is very much part of the powerful Anglo-American world in the 1990s as well.

Wales and Welsh

In Wales, English became the official language when the principality was annexed in 1536 and the exclusive language of instruction in 1870. From the time of annexation, the Welsh culture, including its language, was suppressed. Elderly people can remember when students early in this century were made to wear signboards around their necks if they were caught speaking Welsh in school. As a result, the proportion of Welsh people who could speak the language dropped from 50 percent in 1901 to a mere 19 percent in 1981, about 500,000 in all. Only in parts of northern Wales is the language used for ordinary discourse.

Like Irish Gaelic across the Irish Sea, Welsh got a big boost when government policy in the 1970s reversed itself. Bilingual education was introduced in the schools, and a regional fourth TV channel was awarded to a group that promised to broadcast most of its primetime programs in Welsh. Is it worth it to devote a TV channel to a maximum audience of 500,000, only one-fifth of the people living in Wales, 1 percent of Britain's total population? A lot of Welshmen would argue that it is, even if they can't understand the programs themselves or prefer the English channels most of the time.

Some progress can be measured in restoring the culture. The proportion of bilingual young people has increased—modestly—for the first time in decades, if not centuries. Welsh-language television has boosted literature and theater, both of which are thriving, and Cardiff is Britain's (and possibly Europe's) second most active film center. It is particularly strong in production of cartoons, which can be adapted easily to various language soundtracks. Most argue that the Welsh-language TV channel was a good investment.

Unfortunately, revival of the Welsh language and culture has not eliminated the ancient animosities between the Welsh and their still dominant English neighbors. Economic disparities persist and are probably made greater by a policy of separate and inevitably unequal cultures. Most Welsh seem to be prepared to pay that price for some measure of cultural identity. In this regard, they are like the French Canadians, who are also a minority within a large nation (and near-continent) of English.

Canada and French

The 5 million French Canadians represent about one-fifth of all Canadians and are concentrated in the province of Quebec, which was added to British Canada in the 1700s. Although bilingualism and biculturalism were long recognized, the future of francophone Canada was threatened by the overpowering strength of anglophone Canada and the United States as well as one of the lowest birth rates in the world. When the Parti Québécois (PQ) won control of the provincial government in 1976, it was committed to a policy of French-first, not merely bilingual equality.

The PQ's program to bolster the French language and culture included two controversial provisions. One required immigrants to the province—especially important because native Quebecers were declining in numbers—to attend French-language schools unless they could prove that their parents were English-speaking. Because most immigrants wanted to be part of the dominant English-speaking culture, many moved on to other provinces where their kids could become part of the dominant North American culture

The other controversy involved establishing French as *the* official language of Quebec, not French and English equally. Businesses were instructed to function

The universal (but English) "STOP" in a Quebec traffic sign is defaced to become "101," a reference to the law—later declared unconstitutional—that mandated exclusive use of French in the province. In many countries, language is used to assert cultural independence and is the basis of cultural conflict.

SOURCE: James Seeley.

in French. Only French was permitted on signs, and platoons of "language police" were dispatched to root out violators. For a while, the fight to cleanse the province of English made good news copy: a business was fined for using an English date stamp to mark incoming mail; hundreds of shops were cited for posting both English and French signs; a few shopkeepers became famous for refusing to obey the law, despite repeated citations. The French-only signage provision of Loi 101 was declared unconstitutional and replaced with another law that tried to accomplish the same thing but gave more flexibility to signs inside a store and allowed some English provided the French was more prominent. The serious side of the controversy was a migration of English-speaking residents and businesses to other provinces and a decline in immigration that raised the specter of a defiant Quebec holding on to its French-ness while most of its businesses and people simply moved away.

While the PQ was in power, some Québécois refused to speak English to other Canadians, prompting some monoglot tourists from the United States to wear lapel flags so they could get service in restaurants and gas stations. The PQ even championed succession from Canada, which led Prime Minister Pierre Trudeau—a French Canadian—to counter with the threat of armed force to maintain the nation. All very nasty in a country known for its civility and tolerance.

The PQ stayed in power until 1985, by which time much of the passion over Loi 101, which established the French-only policy, had subsided. The incoming Liberal party negotiated an agreement that renewed Quebec's commitment to the Canadian confederation but also recognized Quebec as a distinct society. It also promised a more relaxed interpretation of the more divisive elements of the law. From the English side, the controversy generated a greater awareness of the French minority and a new commitment, mostly through innovative bilingual schools, to the official bilingualism that had been Canadian policy in principle but seldom in practice.

Although not as spectacular (or violent) as conflicts in other parts of the world, the issue of bilingualism will not go away. In 1990, a delicately crafted agreement recognizing Quebec's special linguistic and cultural status was rejected by two English-speaking provinces. Among other factors was a newly recognized autonomy for Canada's indigenous peoples that gave their small numbers disproportionate clout in provincial legislatures.

After more negotiation, a second agreement—named after Charlottetown in Prince Edward Island, where it was written—was rejected in a popular referendum in October 1992. The Charlottetown non-accord gave something to everyone—special status to Quebec, more autonomy to the other provinces, recognition for native peoples—but ended up as a symbol for the long list of grievances Canadians felt about other regions and subcultures. Only the three poor and isolated Atlantic maritime provinces voted yes.

The failure of Charlottetown left Canada with its 1982 constitution that Quebec had never ratified and a big question mark about its future: independence for Quebec, disappearance of the whole country into the U.S.-dominated North American free trade area, or perhaps the birth of a multicultural, continent-wide renaissance?

As in Wales, the assertion of cultural identity seemed to spark creativity. The number of publishing houses in Quebec increased from three 30 years earlier to 150. More than 30 cultural magazines are published in Quebec, and the province is home to over 200 cultural festivals annually. Internationally, the province is a key member of *la Francophonie,* the French-language equivalent of the Commonwealth, and a major producer of textbooks and computer software for the still-significant French-speaking world. Movies and TV are less successful as exports but growing. The future of French Canada remains part of a broader search for Canadian cultural identity that includes the free trade agreement with the United States (approved with exceptions for cultural industries) and its extension to Mexico (very much in doubt).

The United States and English

In the United States, the conflict over language is different from that in Wales or Quebec. The last two involve minority cultures trying to preserve their language against a much larger and more powerful English language and culture. In the United States, the issue is to what degree (or whether) minority languages should be recognized and encouraged. Although other languages are also involved, the debate focuses mostly on Spanish and the fast-growing Hispanic enclaves in Miami and along the border between the United States and Mexico.

It may come as a surprise that English is not the official language of the United States. The country doesn't have an official language because it never seemed necessary. Most immigrant groups maintained their own cultural enclaves for a while and then disappeared into the melting pot. Only where the new Americans maintained a critical mass in numbers and chose to avoid slipping into the melting pot did something like separate subcultures exist. Even now there are pockets in the United States where English is a foreign language—mostly the "ethnic" neighborhoods in big cities that contain a concentration of people still tied to the old culture and replenished by a steady stream of immigrants. In contrast to earlier times, most cities now are trying to preserve their "Chinatown" and "Little Italy" neighborhoods. Cities such as Milwaukee, Baltimore, and Seattle have tried to renovate decaying city cores by emphasizing their ethnic diversity, past and present. The present cultural diversity of the United States is greater than at any time in its past and becoming more so. Even though the country is one of the most monolingual in the world, not everyone speaks the unofficial national language.

Monoglot Multiculturalism

According to the 1980 census, 11 percent of Americans—23 million—spoke a language other than English at home, a number that has grown steadily since then. Of these, 43 percent, or about 10 million, spoke Spanish.[14] The figures don't mean

---

[14] Edith McArthur, "What Language Do You Speak?" *American Demographics,* October 1984, pp. 32–33.

that these 23 million people knew no English. In fact, more than 80 percent said they could speak English "very well" or "well."

So what's the problem? Most of us had ancestors who arrived with no knowledge of the language. They—or their children—struggled with a new language and new culture. Eventually most succeeded in becoming simply Americans. For most of today's immigrants, the situation is no different. Classes in English as a second language are oversubscribed. No one knows the value of English more than new arrivals who cannot speak it. Are today's Hispanic and Asian immigrants any different from the Italians and Russians of the past century?

At one level, the answer is no. Most have the same dreams and the same energies as earlier generations. But two things are different. One is that the attitude toward immigrant cultures changed in the 1960s and 1970s and then did a fast 180-degree switch in the 1980s. The second is the rapid increase in Hispanic immigration and the creation of a kind of third nation along the United States–Mexico border, which in 50 or 100 years could create within the United States a new Wales or new Quebec, separate and definitely unequal.

The attitude change in the 1970s was a spin-off of the civil rights movement and argued that Americans shouldn't have to speak English and that they certainly were entitled to education in their first language. As a result, California became officially trilingual, requiring that government services be available in Chinese and Spanish as well as English. Miami became bilingual; new employees had to be able to speak Spanish as well as English. The biggest push came from the federal government, which decided that local schools had to provide education in any language spoken by a student in the school.

Most schools already had various kinds of special programs to help non-English-speaking students, but was it reasonable to try to provide full bilingual education in any language? Most districts had students with a dozen or more linguistic backgrounds. In big districts, the number of languages reached several dozen. Charlotte, North Carolina—hardly a mega–melting pot like New York or Los Angeles—in the mid-1980s had 800 students from 50 countries with 42 languages enrolled in a model bilingual program. There, as in most other school districts, the goal was to get the students up to speed in English, not to offer instruction in the 42 native tongues.

Special programs to help kids who didn't know English were never a political issue, but the rise in all-Spanish barrios and occasional all-Vietnamese or all-Korean neighborhoods coupled with demands that government promote separatism rather than integration were. Advocates of multilingualism argued that opposition was racist and based on fears of the rapid rise of non-Anglo immigration. Proponents of all-English argued that government's role was to promote integration into the mainstream culture and pointed to places such as Sri Lanka, Lebanon, and India where cultural conflict had led to full-scale war.

Official English

The backlash was a movement in the 1980s to declare English the official language of the United States, whatever that meant. A national campaign called U.S. English was founded by S. I. Hayakawa, a noted semanticist and one-term senator from

California. Supporters included *Masterpiece Theater's* Alistair Cooke, novelist Saul Bellow, child psychologist Bruno Bettelheim, and Nobel Prize physicist Rosalyn Yalow. The national effort was directed toward a constitutional amendment or at least federal legislation declaring English the official language. The national effort was not successful, but by 1990, 16 states had passed some kind of laws recognizing English, and several others had legislation under consideration. In early 1991, the Arizona law was struck down by a federal court, so the question was guaranteed to keep lawyers busy well into the new decade and probably into the twenty-first century.

One problem was that no one was quite sure what it meant to have English as the official language. It did not mean that schools, emergency services, and government bureaucracy in general would stop offering services in other languages, although non-English outreach efforts to encourage voting or participation in social programs might be curtailed. Some local ordinances outlawed signs in languages other than English, but they seemed vulnerable to First Amendment challenges. A United States in the twenty-first century with English as the official language probably would not be much different from one without an official language, but no one can be sure. The issue is likely to be part of the debate over multiculturalism in the next century.

In the United States as in Canada, the debate involved two issues. The first was achieving a balance between integration of subcultures into a broader national culture and accommodation of the diverse cultural mix that gives both countries a unique strength. The second was recognition of the special circumstances of the French in Canada and the Spanish in the United States but withholding the same kind of special status from smaller subcultures. If Quebec is French, why shouldn't the Chinese in Vancouver or the Balts in Ontario have the same kind of special recognition and protection? Why should Vietnamese immigrants in Texas not have the same opportunities as Mexican Americans for education in their own language? In New York City, the issue of who got special recognition reached the point that immigrant Russians did not qualify for special programs but fifth-generation, native African Americans did. Italian Americans were included among cultural subgroups entitled to special consideration as were new immigrants from the Caribbean who qualified for programs intended to help long-resident blacks.

For the 1990s, the problem of non-English-speaking immigrants pretty much solved itself. Second-generation Cubans not only spoke English easily, but also many lost their Spanish. Sons and daughters of immigrants remained "hyphenated Americans" but with the emphasis on *American*. In all parts of the country—and especially among the Hispanics—adult courses in English as a second language were oversubscribed. All cities and school districts faced the problem, not of encouraging immigrants to study the national language, but of accommodating all those who wanted to participate. No one seems to appreciate more the importance of knowing English in the United States than those who don't.

The long-range future is more uncertain, especially as the "third nation" between the United States and Mexico grows. The possibility of Puerto Rico's entry as the fifty-first state raises the additional problem of an American Quebec, a completely Spanish-speaking state. Would Congress have to become bilingual, as the Canadian Parliament has done? History may be a good guide to the future. As each wave of immigration washed ashore in the United States—Italians, Russians, Jews, Chinese railway workers—the same complaints about the threats to the culture were heard. Eventually, the mainstream culture accommodated them and in the process became a little less Anglo and a little closer to the nation of nations many of us want our country to be.

Assimilation versus Multiculturalism

There is always a price to be paid when you assimilate into a different culture. You leave part of your past and some of yourself behind. For some people, the price is too high, and they never become part of the new culture. Children carry less of their old cultural baggage and usually assimilate easily. That's why the second generation of hyphenated Americans usually produces a generation that drops the hyphenation and becomes, like the millions who preceded them, simply American. Will the United States become bilingual in fact with distinctly Anglo and Hispanic cultures under the flag of one nation? Or will the power of the mainstream culture continue to absorb, more or less, everyone who enters it? We'll know the answer sometime in the middle of the twenty-first century.

Meanwhile, the final word can go to someone who went through the experience that made most of us—or our parents, grandparents, or great-grandparents—Americans. Ricardo Rodriguez was born in Sacramento to parents who spoke little English. On his first day in school, the nuns insisted that he become *Rich-heard Road-ree-guess.* He did and entered the American mainstream to become a distinguished writer and lecturer. His autobiography recounts the pain of that journey and the price he paid in estrangement from his parents' culture. He concluded, however, that it was worth it:

> Only when I was able to think of myself as an American, no longer alien in *gringo* society, could I see the rights and opportunities necessary for full public individuality. The social and political advantages I enjoy as a man result from the day that I came to believe that my name, indeed, is *Rich-heard Road-ree-guess*. . . . I celebrate the day I acquired my new name. Those middle-class ethnics who scorn assimilation seem to be filled with decadent self-pity, obsessed by the burden of public life. Dangerously, they romanticize public separateness and they trivialize the dilemma of the socially disadvantaged.[15]

It would be nice if people of good will could get together and redraw political boundaries in such a way that each language/culture had its homeland, but for all the reasons we mentioned in the previous chapter, they can't. A United Nations

---

[15] Richard Rodriguez, *Hunger of Memory: The Education of Richard Rodriguez* (New York: Bantam, 1983), p. 27.

recognizing all of the several thousand languages still alive in the world today would become a new Tower of Babel. There's something to be said for a global language. In Chapter 4, we'll see what has become the *de facto* language of global communication in the 1990s. Later chapters consider the argument that it's also the medium of a new global hegemony.

MAIN POINTS

1. Psycholinguistics considers whether a specific language influences how we think and how we perceive the social environment. Although intuitively appealing, psycholinguistics is in disfavor, with most scholars of the opinion that all languages are surface manifestations of a general language ability we are all born with and that any language can communicate as well as any other.

2. The biggest linguistic barrier to understanding is not psycholinguistic but cultural-linguistic, meaning the differences in connotative or cultural meanings of words. Connotative meanings derive from personal and collective cultural experience and are never the same for two people or two cultures.

3. Sociolinguistics emphasizes social factors related to the use of language—accent, pronunciation, vocabulary—that carry messages about the speaker's social standing. Although English no longer recognizes a difference between formal and informal "you" as most Indo-European languages do, the language we use still varies from subculture to subculture and from one social setting to another.

4. Nonverbal communication transmits more information than the words used in ordinary interpersonal communication. Cross-cultural nonverbal communication presents special problems because so much of nonverbal meaning is culture specific, unwritten, and not subject to repetition or control.

5. Conflict over language is common in many cultures, replacing religion or ethnic identity as the basis of conflict. Important examples of this new source of social conflict can be found in Britain (over Welsh), Canada (over the status of French in Quebec), and the United States (over English-Spanish bilingualism).

FOR MORE INFORMATION

Lots of "pop" literature is available, especially about nonverbal communication (and how to use it to your advantage) and tips for getting along in different cultures. A few recent books: Robert A. Kapp, *Communicating with China* (Chicago: Intercultural Press, 1983); John C. Condon, *Good Neighbors: Communicating with Mexicans* (Chicago: Intercultural Press, 1985); Edward C. Stewart, *American Cultural Patterns: A Cross-Cultural Perspective* (Yarmouth, ME: Intercultural Press, 1972). Similar books focusing on other countries are available from the same publisher.

More scholarly works include George A. Borden, *Cultural Orientation: An Approach to Understanding Intercultural Communication* (Englewood Cliffs, NJ: Prentice Hall, 1991); Carley H. Dodd, *Dynamics of Intercultural Communication,* 2nd ed. (Dubuque, IA: William C. Brown, 1987); Mark L. Knapp, *Nonverbal Communication in Human Interaction* (New York: Holt, Rinehart & Winston, 1972); Desmond Morris et al., *Gestures* (New York: Stein and Day, 1980). Morris is also well known for *The Naked Ape, Manwatching,* and *The Human Zoo,* all basic anthropological studies of human cultures. S. I. Hayakawa's *Language in Thought and Action,* 3rd ed. (New York: Harcourt Brace Jovanovich, 1972) is a classic on semantics.

Most of the books recommended in Chapter 2 apply to material covered in this chapter as well.

FOR DISCUSSION

1. Use the semantic differential described in this chapter to test cultural differences in the meaning of words. Include international students to see if differences between them and American students are greater than among American students.

2. Survey people from other countries or those who have traveled or lived abroad to compile a list of cross-cultural differences in nonverbal communication. Compile a list of humorous, embarrassing, and serious misunderstandings that arose.

3. Debate the following proposition: The assertion of cultural independence around the world is likely to (increase) (decrease) conflict in the twenty-first century.

DATA BASE

More than 80 percent of the Parker Pen Company's sales are outside of the United States, so they obviously know something about functioning successfully in other cultures. After 22 years living and traveling abroad for the company, Roger E. Axtell, vice-president for worldwide marketing, edited a light-hearted guide to navigating the murky waters of cross-cultural communication. Following are excerpts from the chapter "A Quick Guide to the Ways of the World," in his book *Do's and Taboos around the World.* Most apply to business encounters, which tend to be more formal than casual contact, but a good rule is to err on the side of tradition and formality. It's easy to ask someone to call you by your first name; it's impossible to tell someone you find their uninvited use of your first name insulting.

> In Belgium and Luxembourg, privacy is a jealously guarded right and is carefully respected. Avoid sending a gift of chrysanthemums. They are a reminder of death.
>
> In Britain, avoid the word "English." Scotch is what you drink. The people are called Scots or Scotsmen. Avoid striped ties in case they are copies of British regimentals.
>
> In Italy, handshaking and gesturing are national pastimes. All university graduates have a title and usually expect you to use it. Punctuality is not an Italian virtue—at least for social events.

In Spain, men who are close friends often give each other an *abrazo* (hug). Women friends greet and part with a slight embrace and a kiss on each cheek. An oddity in Spain is the lateness at which people eat dinner. Restaurants do not generally open until after nine and do not get into full swing until about eleven.

In Germany, respect titles ("Doktor") and never jump to a first-name basis until invited. Answer the phone by immediately saying your last name.

In Egypt, the workweek runs from Saturday to Thursday. Friday is the Muslim day of rest. Remember to remove your shoes before entering a mosque.

In Côte d'Ivoire (the official name of the Ivory Coast since 1986), handshaking is customary. Make appointments well in advance and be punctual, but do not be surprised if the host is not so particular.

In Tanzania, gifts are often given by hosts at the time of departure from the country. At the same time, visitors may reciprocate by presenting their hosts with a gift. Topics for discussion include the Tanzanian National Parks, African culture, and international politics. Subjects to be avoided in conversation include the prevailing political climate.

In the Middle East, local Islamic religious custom demands everything stop five times a day for prayers. While you are not expected to kneel or face Mecca, you must not interrupt or display impatience when your host does. It is an insult to sit in such a way as to face your host with the soles of your shoes showing.[16] Even if an Arab invites you home, his wife (or wives) will probably not be seen (although she may well be in the kitchen supervising dinner). It is not polite to inquire about her (them), and if you do meet, be warm but undemonstrative. Do not even shake hands unless she takes the initiative, which she no doubt will not.

In China, a slight bow is appropriate when meeting someone. A handshake is also acceptable. The Chinese are quite formal and will use the full title of their guests during introductions.

In India, men may shake hands with other men when meeting or leaving. If introduced to a woman, a man should not shake hands but should place his palms together and bow slightly. Men should avoid touching a woman and should not talk to a lone woman in public.

In Japan, the usual form of greeting is a bow and not a handshake. Never address a Japanese by his first name. Only his family and very close friends use the first name. To say "Mister (last name)," simply say the last name and add the word *san*. The Japanese enjoy receiving gifts, which should be wrapped in pastel-colored paper, no bows.

---

[16] A special predicament for those who arrive at the University of North Carolina and find themselves "Tarheels."

In Thailand, avoid stepping on doorsills, where Thai tradition says a spirit resides. Never touch a person's head—even a child's—as the head is considered the seat of the soul.

Canadians are somewhat more conservative than U.S. citizens. Canadians are proud of their country and take exception to exaggerated comparisons with the U.S.

In Mexico, flowers are not expected by host or hostess. If you do send flowers, remember that for some classes of Mexicans yellow flowers connote death, red flowers cast spells, and white ones lift the spells. The two- or three-hour midday siesta is the most common time for business appointments.

In Brazil, remember that Portuguese is the language. Never start right into business discussions unless your host does so first.

SOURCE: Roger E. Axtell, *Do's and Taboos Around the World,* 2nd ed. (New York: Wiley, 1990). Reprinted by permission.

CHAPTER 4

English: The Global Language

ABOUT THIS CHAPTER

Language is the heart of culture and the center of the wave of cultural resurgence that touches all parts of the world in the 1990s. Despite efforts to establish indigenous languages in places as disparate as Wales and Pakistan, English is the global language. English represents both a common tongue for the emerging global culture and a source of conflict. Some claim that it gives unfair advantage to Anglo-American culture and even that it is the opening wedge of a deliberate effort to dominate world culture and, through it, world commerce and politics. In this chapter, we consider how English became the language of global communication, whether it is a good choice, and whether alternatives exist. Later we return to the question of whether global English is a form of "cultural imperialism."

INTRODUCTION

The crew of an Italian airliner in Italian airspace talking to an Italian control tower speaks only one language—English.[1] In fact, English is the only language used in international air traffic control and is virtually the only language of a whole range of other activities from scientific research to pop music. Two-thirds to three-quarters of all computer data bases are in English, and more than 80 percent of all scientific research is published first in English. Watch television news, and you'll note English-language protest signs and sound-bites from around the world, from Beijing to Bucharest. English is, as no language in history has ever been, the language of global communication.

---

[1] This is the opening sequence of the BBC/PBS series, *The Story of English*.

English-language newspapers are published in most countries of the world, and several Anglo-American dailies are distributed globally. *Time* and *Newsweek* publish several distinct international regional editions. Here are the same week's U.S. domestic and Asian editions of the two influential weeklies.

The emergence of English as *the* world language is dramatic and improbable. At the peak of the Roman Empire, English did not exist. A few years before the founding of the first English colony in the New World, a British scholar called the English language "of no account, stretching no further than this island of ours, nay not there over all."[2] Today one person in four on the planet claims

---

[2] "English: Out to Conquer the World," *U.S. News & World Report*, February 18, 1985, p. 49.

some knowledge of it, and the number is increasing faster than the population. Where does English come from? How did it become the dominant language of the twentieth century? Are there alternatives? These are questions we need to address to understand why English is a critical element of the mosaic of global communication.

DEVELOPMENT OF ENGLISH

To trace the growth of English, we have to start somewhere in north-central Europe sometime between 4000 and 6000 B.C. In that cold, inhospitable climate—perhaps in the Russian steppes, perhaps in the Danube Valley—lived primitive tribes that developed a simple language now called "Indo-European prototype." But don't look in the library for any books in this language or expect to find any bilingual Indo-European–English dictionaries in the bookstore. What little we know about the language and the people who spoke it comes indirectly from the linguistic evidence contained in a vast extended family of languages that survive today from India to the Atlantic edge of Europe.

Common Roots

The evidence is found mostly in a short vocabulary list of common words— *mother, father, sister, brother*—that are similar in all of the Indo-European languages. Linguistic historians can start with present-day words, trace them back through their known history, and use them to point toward a common ancestry. After all, German *Bruder,* Russian *brat,* Sanskrit *bhratar,* and English *brother* have some obvious common root. The root is the shadowy Indo-European language. Some elements of Indo-European culture can also be inferred from the vocabulary. The first Indo-Europeans had several words appropriate for winter but none for the ocean, which they had never seen, and obviously none of the words we need to function in an advanced industrialized democracy.

The people who spoke this language—there was no written form—migrated over the centuries from their original home to all parts of Europe, the Middle East, and the Indian subcontinent, carrying their simple language with them and passing it on to other peoples along the way. Colonial conquest carried Indo-European languages to the Americas, Africa, and parts of Asia and the Pacific. About one-third of the people on the earth today speak languages that belong to this huge extended family.

We don't speak Indo-European today because all languages constantly drift, evolve, and adapt to new circumstances. Like animals and plants that cannot adapt, some languages die out. Others emerge in response to changes in their environment. In the millennia that followed the birth of the Indo-European prototype, its branches changed to the point where they became unintelligible to one another. The common heritage was discovered only by eighteenth- and nineteenth-century linguists and remains shadowy and imprecise.

The Origins of English

Now fast-forward to the first century A.D. The Celtic tribes (pronounced KEL-tic; only in Boston basketball is it SEL-tics) of what are now Great Britain, Ireland, and the Brittany coast of France spoke languages that are much like today's Welsh, Gaelic, and Breton. They were a part of the Indo-European family but far removed from the Latin of the Roman Empire and early Germanic that dominated the heart of the European continent. The Roman invasion of Britain in 55 A.D. established the northern rim of the great Roman Empire that united a large part of Western Europe for several centuries. In Britain, Caesar's legions subdued what is now more or less England and held the Celtic tribes at bay in Scotland and Wales. The Romans brought their language with them, of course, but it had little influence on the native Celtic tongues. When the Romans withdrew in 410 A.D. or there-abouts, the Celtic languages and cultures remained largely intact, but the heartland of Roman England was made vulnerable to a new generation of invaders. Except for some place names, the Roman invaders left little linguistic imprint.

The new invaders came from the east. Over the next several centuries, a variety of tribes conquered pieces of England. The Jutes and Angles came from Denmark and the Schleswig-Holstein region of Germany, and the Saxons invaded from the German coast. The sketchy historical record that survives suggests a grim life of invasions, wars, frightful religious practices, and hardships. The Angles, one of several invading tribes, eventually gave their name to the country, but the Saxons gave their language. By the year 1000, the name *England*—or some variant of it—was well established, and the dominant language was Saxon or what scholars today call Old English.

Our Germanic Cousins

We can now answer one of the questions with which we began the chapter—the pedigree of present-day English. Old English was a form of Low German, one of several strands of a Germanic root that also produced High German (modern German). Saxon Low German produced modern Dutch as well, so the closest relative of English is Dutch, a first cousin, and modern German is still kissin' kin but a more of a second or third cousin. If you have ever tried to read a Dutch or German newspaper, you may be skeptical of any claim of kinship between English and these two modern tongues. Modern German often strings small words together to form seemingly unpronounceable long words, but beneath the forbidding surface, German grammar and vocabulary are a lot like those of English.

You may also wonder why, as the Romans left so little apparent linguistic influence, modern English has so many Latin-based words. The answer lies in one final invasion of Britain and a remarkable change that made English very different from its linguistic relatives.

The French Connection

The Norman invasion of 1066 was the last time Britain was successfully attacked by outsiders. The Normans were French-speaking Vikings from the northern French coast who established the modern British monarchy and a French-speaking regime that lasted nearly 300 years. William the Conqueror, crowned in Westminster Abbey on Christmas Day in 1066, tried without much success to learn the language of his new kingdom. His court apparently didn't do much better. Norman French became the language of government, and Saxon English—well established as the spoken language of the people but with limited use as a written language—became almost an underground tongue.

These two languages, one for the royal court and the other for the people, competed with a third tongue, Latin, which was as close to a world language as any until our own time. Latin was the language that bound together the Catholic Church, the most influential multinational conglomerate of its day, and European universities, which maintained a modest exchange of ideas and scholarship. If you were literate in Norman Britain, you probably could read French and Latin, but not Old English, which had little written literature to offer and little use in circumstances that required written documentation. The speakers of Old English carried their culture, even then a remarkably vigorous body of legends, songs, and stories, in their heads.

French-speaking Norman Britain lasted about 300 years. By the mid-1300s, English had resurfaced in all areas of British life. The authors of *The Story of English* attribute the decline of French to the French-English Hundred Years' War (1337–1454), which isolated the adversaries from each other; the black plague, which depleted the educated elites of the monasteries and universities; and the integration of the Norman English people with the much more numerous Saxon English. By the end of the fourteenth century, English was in use at all levels of government and education. Norman French, except for an occasional symbol such as the monarch's assent to legislation passed by Parliament, became a historical curiosity.

Middle English Emerges

The English that emerged after a couple of centuries underground, however, was very different from the Saxon Old English. The difference is seen between *Beowulf* and *The Canterbury Tales. Beowulf,* a long, gloomy poem about the grisly days when various Scandinavian and Germanic invaders were at war with the Celtic natives and each other, is written in Old English. It is a foreign language we cannot read except in translation. Some versions even include a few letters unfamiliar to us. *The Canterbury Tales,* in contrast, looks familiar. With a little help in vocabulary and word endings, we can tackle it in its original form.

Middle English, usually identified with the years 1150 to 1500, took advantage of the language's earlier contact with Latin and French and has a large and diverse vocabulary that is, for the most part, familiar to us. The language itself changed during its years underground and now functions in a way that is fundamentally different from Old English and most of English's linguistic relatives. Among other changes, English dropped the distinction between the formal "you" and familiar "thou" that survives in other languages and the noun genders that make the sun feminine in German but masculine in French.

More important is that most Indo-European languages retain inflections that show the function of words in sentences with distinctive endings. Middle

English, in contrast, emerged as a *distributive* language that relies on position to show how words are linked. In the next section, we consider this unique change in detail and how it serves as both an advantage and disadvantage for English as today's global language. At this point, we can just note that the grammatical rules of English are extraordinarily simple. The big problems for all of us—native speaker as well as foreigner—are spelling, pronunciation, and bewildering multiple meanings. Despite these drawbacks, Middle English represented the rebirth of a flexible, vigorous language that continues to serve its users well.

Modern English and the Printing Press

Modern English, which is essentially the language we know today, is usually dated from 1500 and is a product of the second revolution in human communication: Johannes Gutenberg's invention of printing with moveable type in the mid-1400s. Modern English is characterized by more or less uniform spelling, pronunciation, and word definition. It is anchored by dictionaries, grammar books, and experts who tell us what is good or bad writing as well as what is right or wrong grammar. This could not happen until books, newssheets, and handbills were widely available.

William Caxton introduced modern printing to Britain about 1476 and opened the English culture to a relatively wide public for the first time. The sudden availability of printed material stimulated unprecedented scholarship and invention and, as happens in all revolutions, challenged the monopoly on authority, which in this case belonged to the crown and the church. It also gave the early printers unusual power, because Caxton and his colleagues often decided how words would be spelled and what rules of grammar would apply. At the time, no single version of Middle English existed. Variations in vocabulary, word meaning, spelling, and grammar could be found from county to county, almost from town to town. Even today, British English enjoys (or suffers) much more regional variety than the language of the "younger" English-speaking countries.

Because Caxton worked in London, the modern English that grew out of the early printed volumes reflected the language of that part of the country. For several reasons—the numerous variants in use at the time, the lack of a central authority to establish standards, a large foreign vocabulary already in place—Caxton's English suffered from one problem that still plagues it: a frustrating lack of regularity in spelling and pronunciation. Although the language is rich in vocabulary and subtle in meaning, English spelling and pronunciation are a nightmare for people who try to learn it as a foreign language and can be a plague even for those who claim it as a native tongue. None of the reforms proposed since Caxton's time has been adopted, and none is likely to be approved by the dozens of countries that recognize the language and the hundreds of millions of people around the world who depend on it for global communication.

ENGLISH TODAY

The dominance of English in global communications today is a product of three factors: the influence of the British Empire during the eighteenth to mid-twentieth centuries, the emergence of the United States as an economic and political super-power after World War II, and, finally, at the end of the twentieth century, a global economic and political structure that needs a common tongue and has appropriated English as the obvious choice.

British Beginnings

The first two, of course, are linked to the power of two specific countries at specific periods in history. If the Roman Empire had survived or if the Spanish Armada had defeated the English, we might be speaking a variant of Latin or Spanish. History, including the history of global communication, is filled with "if." To large extent, we speak English because the Roman Empire did fall, the British fleet did defeat the Spanish, and a long sequence of other historical events turned out the way they did. Britain was a true (and very successful) European colonial power whose permanent imprints included language and culture. The United States, uniquely powerful at the end of World War II, spread its influence through a mixture of necessity, default, and design. If English triumphed over French, Spanish, or Arabic, it could be argued that its advocates were simply bigger and more clever than the competition and happened to appear at a propitious moment in history.

The third factor, however, is new to the world: Never before has the planet been so tightly linked that a "global" language is necessary. A few jet-setting executives from Japan or Germany may be in Africa one day, Latin America the next, and back home the third. Music stars and many journalists follow similar frenetic schedules. Protesters appeal to a global TV audience. All of them require not one or even two or three foreign languages, but a single language that will get the job done; English serves them all.

At its height, as generations of British schoolboys learned, the sun never set on the British Empire. One-quarter of the world's population lived under the rule of the Union Jack, a feat of diplomacy and military skill no other nation has ever matched. The British Empire was unusual because of its size and because the British knew when to fold the flag and leave. British colonies existed on every continent. There was British Honduras—now Belize—in Central America and Guyana in South America in addition to Gibraltar, Cyprus, and Malta in Europe itself. This gave Britain and its institutions, language among them, footholds all over the planet. When the continuation of the empire became politically and economically unacceptable around World War II, the British converted it into the Commonwealth, a collection of 47 nations plus the remaining remnants of the empire, presided over by the British monarch. The common bond is the colonial experience, a smattering of surviving British institutions—and English.

The U.S. Contribution

Winston Churchill understood that the sunset of the British Empire was inevitable as the World War II grand alliance moved toward victory. His vision of the postwar world included a condominium of Anglo-American leadership, perhaps using U.S. clout to maintain British global leadership. He got something less: an Anglo-American "special relationship" that was more emotional than practical and an inevitable dissolution of the unique wartime bond between him and President Franklin Roosevelt. After the war, global influence and responsibility shifted across the Atlantic, and with it came a new accent for global English.

When the United States inherited global political influence and responsibility at the end of World War II, the driving force of English shifted as well, but with a difference. In those years—and even more so now—American English traveled on waves of popular culture and consumer-oriented commerce rather than politics. Early on, the French, who still try to promote French as an alternative to an English-saturated world, called English *la langue du Coca-Cola,* and others began to refer to "Coca-Colonialism," meaning a domination of the world by popular ("pop") culture rather than armies. A large part of the appeal of American English as separate from the British version was precisely the cultural component. This included a lifestyle that promised freedom from traditional cultural fetters, as well as life, liberty, and the pursuit of happiness as inalienable rights. The language of Shakespeare was transformed into the language of pop music, advertising, and music videos.

Everyone's Second Language

In the global environment at the end of the twentieth century, a new force propels English. Even in the twilight of the "American century" (*Time* magazine founder's jingoistic phrase for the twentieth century), the influence of English grows. The language has developed its own momentum, independent of British or U.S. influence and beyond their control. English is the language of a global economy, a global culture, a global information society. A Scandinavian businessman organizing a deal to build a factory in Argentina with Swiss financing and Italian management to export Japanese-designed products to Africa needs English. A French movie producer working in Hungary with an international cast and crew needs English. A Russian biologist collaborating with scientists in Germany and India needs English.

English today is a "native language" in 12 nations with a total population of about 350 million, according to *U.S. News & World Report.*[3] These include the countries that come immediately to mind—the United States, Britain, Canada (except for Quebec, of course), Australia, New Zealand, and Ireland—and also several former colonies without a true native language—Guyana, the Bahamas,

---

[3] "English Spoken Here . . . and Here . . . and Here." *U.S. News & World Report,* February 18, 1985, pp. 50–51. *The Universal Almanac 1991* says English is an official language in 87 nations and territories and is spoken by one-third of the world's people. John W. Wright, ed., *The Universal Almanac 1991* (Kansas City, MO: Andrews and McMeel, 1990), p. 306.

Barbados, Grenada, Jamaica, and Trinidad and Tobago. In 33 others with about the same number of people, English is an official or semiofficial language. Most of these are former British colonies, but the list includes the Philippines and Israel as well. In many of these countries, English is a second language, used widely in government, business, and education, but not in the home. It is often called a link language because it is the common link in a nation of disparate peoples.

In most countries, English is studied widely. Countries such as the Netherlands, Denmark, and Sweden maintain a thriving culture in their own tongues but recognize that participation in global affairs requires English. As a result, knowledge of English (and usually one or two other languages) is expected as a part of ordinary education. The Dutch minister of culture even proposed adoption of English in Dutch universities. The suggestion was rejected, but the European Community's emphasis on educational exchange will inevitably strengthen English in European higher education in the twenty-first century. Over French protests, English is the dominant language of the European Community and, with French running a distant second, the language of the UN, OPEC, NATO, ASEAN, and other international organizations.

The number of people who know English as a foreign language may well approach 1 *billion*. If the definition is the ability to use a few English words, the figure could be twice as high. No one knows for sure how many of these people there are or how to measure knowledge of English, but a few figures are helpful.

In France and Germany, where a foreign language is required in secondary school, 80 percent to 90 percent of students choose English (rather than the neighboring country's tongue). More than half of Soviet high school students studied English, a number that certainly has increased since the collapse of communism. Some estimates have put the number of English students in China alone at one-quarter of the population, including an audience of millions for the BBC TV series *Follow Me,* which turned its host into a major national Chinese celebrity. This estimate would put the figure of Chinese English students, most of whom study informally, at more than 250 million, exceeding the entire population of the United States. It is significant that President Bush's first promise of aid to Hungary and Poland was to send Peace Corps volunteers—to teach English.

LINGUISTIC COLONIALISM?

To many, English is a passport to a better life, a boarding card to the global culture. That's why commercial English instruction is a thriving industry around the world as well as a popular subject in schools everywhere. But not everyone is happy with the invasion of "Coca-Colonialism." Language, they contend, cannot be imported without the baggage of culture. With American English particularly, that means a set of cultural values that in some countries clash with the indigenous values that evolved over centuries, and it may even threaten the survival of the indigenous culture(s). In some cases, even languages seem to be at risk.

The most visible critics of English are the French (in both France and Quebec), who have complained for years about "Franglais," a hybrid that includes words such as *le weekend* and *le fast-food.* In 1984, French President François Mitterand established the Commissariat Général Française, which was supposed to guard against Franglais and provide alternatives acceptable to French sensibilities. Five editions of the *Dictionary of Official Neologisms* have appeared, the latest with 2,400 English words or expressions that should be avoided in official French. Acceptable alternatives are provided: *le gros-porteur* for jumbo jet; *une exclusivité* for scoop; *prêt-à-manger* for fast food. Technical jargon is more of a problem, but French offers alternatives, which, for the most part, are ignored.[4]

Other languages are subject to (or victims of) the same infiltration. A Russian will put on his *dzhinzi* (jeans) and go to a *dzhazz-saission* and order a *dzhin-in-tonik.* Germans are at ease with *der Bestseller, die Software,* and *das Tee-shirt.* They also appropriate verbs such as *feuern* (to fire) and *eincheken* (check in). "Japlish" includes "mongrel" words such as *man-shon* (mansion), *mai-homu* (my home, i.e., apartment), and *aisu-karimu* (ice cream), as well as more than 20,000 English words that are in common use in more or less their original form. In Japan more than in other countries, whole phrases get adopted, almost as icons of the pop culture they embody. As *The Economist* notes, "Beyond the medium, there is no need for a message." A few examples it offers: "I feel Coke & Sound Special" (from a street vending machine); "OD on Bourgeoisie Milk Boy Milk" (a tee-shirt); "With the biggest dream in your heart moving towards your biggest wish, try to brighten up your lifestyle. For your life" (a package of instant noodles).[5]

In most parts of the world, the quality of English is high—certainly higher than anything most English-speakers could produce with their high school Spanish or French. Still, the European Community's translation service collected these examples from hotels around the world:

1. Paris: Please leave your values at the front desk.
2. Acapulco: The manager has personally passed all the water served here.
3. Moscow: You are welcome to visit the cemetery [across the street] where famous Russian and Soviet composers, artists, and writers are buried daily except Thursday.
4. Bucharest: The lift [elevator] is being fixed for the next day. During that time we regret that you will be unbearable.[6]

THE LANGUAGE OF GLOBAL COMMUNICATION

For better or worse as we approach the twenty-first century, English is the global language with a steamroller force no nation can block or direct. It is no longer the language of British imperialism or U.S. economic hegemony. It

---

[4] James M. Markham, "Pardon My English, but Did Someone Say 1992?" *New York Times,* May 12, 1989, p. A4.

[5] "Japperish," *The Economist,* October 31, 1987, p. 64.

[6] Charles Goldsmith, "Look See! Anyone Do Read This and It Will Make You Laughable." *Wall Street Journal,* November 19, 1992, p. B1.

is the language of the world, with a life of its own. But how good a choice is it for a world language?

Let us stipulate that a world language is needed but that the term has a limited definition. If trade and tourism around the world are going to operate and a global economy function and a global culture flourish, a widely shared, reasonably accessible language is requisite. If Alitalia pilots need a single language to navigate the world, it's probably just as simple to use it when they talk to air traffic control in Milan as in Tokyo or New York. Unless someone finds the Babel fish, we're going to need a single language, and English is the obvious candidate. However, establishing a global language does not necessarily mean that other languages will disappear. Denmark, the Netherlands, India, and Nigeria are examples where English and other languages do coexist. And it certainly does not mean native speakers can sit back smugly and assume there is no reason to study other languages because everyone else speaks ours. If the world collectively could sit down and rationally choose a common language, it might not select English. Alternatives, which we will consider below, do exist. On its merits, English might be the best choice, or it might not.

Technical Arguments for English

1. English has strong links to the entire Indo-European family of languages, which, you will remember, are native to one-third of the people in the world. That doesn't help the Chinese or Fijian studying English as a true foreign language, but a Russian, Iranian, or Brazilian comes to English with a basic understanding of part of the grammatical structure and vocabulary.

2. English has dropped a lot of the "baggage" that makes other Indo-European languages less "user-friendly": formal and informal address, noun genders, most inflections. As *The Economist* put it, "English, in short, is easy to speak badly—and that is all that is required of a world language."[7] With a surprisingly short list of words and a few simple rules for stringing them together, anyone can enter the global culture. You don't have to spend a semester or two memorizing rules of verb conjugation and adjective declension to get some practical use out of English. On the other hand, no one, not even a native speaker, really masters the language. There is always room to expand vocabulary and polish syntax, to get a step closer to the power of Shakespeare or a perfect advertising slogan.

3. English has the largest vocabulary of any language in the world and invents, adopts, and modifies words with ease. Although most ordinary English prose gets by with only 1,000 to 2,000 words, English has, by common reckoning, at least 500,000 words and at least as many additional distinct technical terms. German, by contrast, has about 185,000, French fewer than 100,000. If a word

---

[7] "The New English Empire," *The Economist,* December 20, 1986, p. 128.

doesn't exist in English, you can borrow one from another language or make up your own. About 80 percent of English words are imported or expropriated, which means they did not exist in English's Saxon roots. Ordinary use includes a virtually complete duplicate vocabulary of Latin and Germanic stems. Although the basic vocabulary is overwhelmingly Romance-Germanic—a big help to Europeans and Latin Americans—English also borrows from all other language families. No other language comes close to the diversity, flexibility, and adaptability of English.

Cultural Arguments for English

1. English is a native or official language on every continent. This gives it a strong anchor around the world. The core of English-speaking countries, though clearly diminished from the dominance they exerted earlier in the twentieth century, are still major political, economic, and cultural forces regionally and globally. The rising nations, particularly Japan and Germany, lack the ability and will to project their languages internationally. Regional organizations, such as the EC and ASEAN, have already adopted English as the dominant language.

2. English is already, for practical purposes, the global language. This is a circular argument, of course: It should be the world language because it already is. But the alternatives, to be considered below, are impractical. Even if a wonderful alternative appeared unexpectedly (a pocket supercomputer? the Babel fish?), it would be futile to try to dismantle a language that has evolved so successfully.

3. Much of the global culture already exists in English, and it is impossible to translate it into any other "world language." Imagine trying to re-invent computers or even typewriters in Chinese. Could anyone reconstruct the body of modern scientific knowledge in classical Arabic or Amharic? Although language does not seem to be a filter that directly influences cognitive processes, as the early psycholinguists believed, languages do differ in their ability to adapt to changing circumstances, and English is probably the most subtle, flexible, and adaptable.

Technical Arguments against English

1. Spelling and pronunciation are English's Achilles heel and the despair of millions of students around the world. Beyond a few simple rules of pronunciation, the best way to learn is simply to memorize—without asking why—the meaning of an English word along with whatever oddities of pronunciation and spelling go with it. An old rhyme offers this advice:

> Beware of *heard*, a dreadful word
> That looks like *beard* and sounds like *bird*,
> And *dead*: it's said like *bed*, not *bead*—
> For goodness sake, don't call it *deed!*

The differences in pronunciation among *tough, through, though,* and *thought* alone defy all logic and probably are enough to discourage most people. Can you imagine tackling a language with comparable irregularities? Of course, spelling and pronunciation are not the only problems. The lack of inflected endings to specify precisely how a word fits into the meaning of a sentence makes for simple grammar, but at a price. Consider the hotel workers writing out the notices cited in the previous section. Many of the examples were logical and consistent. The problem is that English is neither.

So far, language reform efforts have failed. These include a campaign after World War II to develop a simplified English vocabulary and grammar that could serve as a kind of starter-language and occasional campaigns to eliminate the British and American variants in spelling and pronunciation. A recent light-hearted effort to promote "Canadean" is also doomed.[8]

2. The distributive nature of English changes meaning in ways speakers may not intend or understand. First, consider these simple sentences:

> He overlooked the table.
> He looked the table over.
> He looked over the table.

It is possible to come up with a set of rules to explain the differences (*overlook* is a compound verb; *look over* is a simple verb with separable prefix; *looked over* (the table) is a simple verb, with *over* a preposition introducing a phrase used as an adverb). But it's easier to say simply, "Because that's the way it is," and offer a "translation" of other words as required.

Beyond the subtle grammatical differences, English changes when words are shifted around in a sentence. In an essay on English as a world language, a student recently wrote, "English is spoken roughly by 750 million people." I assume the student meant, "English is spoken by roughly 750 million people." A clearly different meaning results from the reversal of only two words. Even native-speaking wordsmiths make mistakes, some of which appear each month on

---

8 "Canadean" would eliminate "q" and all silent and extra letters and add the verb "to must." The main difference would be phonetic spelling: "We urj all owr reeders tu abandon the obsolete, anoying english langwaje, and tu adopt the emerjing, rasional canadean langwaje," an editorial calling for linguistic change said. "It iz so eezy." "Language Activist Wants to Make 'Reeding Eezier,'" AP dispatch in the Chapel Hill (NC) *Newspaper,* January 24, 1990, p. A3.

the inside back cover of *Columbia Journalism Review*: "Unemployed/Attack Dogs/in Barracks"; "N.J. Jails for Women/in Need of a Face Lift"; "FBI Called/in Bomb Threats/to Adams." Maybe it's just too hard for nonnative speakers to pick up such subtleties. When nonnative speakers and native speakers use the language, the native speaker always has an advantage. When nonnative speakers use it as a link language, no one can be sure what gets lost in the "non"-translation.

Cultural Arguments against English

1. Most of the complaints against English center on two factors. One is simply that it gives native speakers an unfair advantage. It is hard to appreciate this until you've studied abroad or tried to engage in a serious conversation in a foreign language. You run into all sorts of problems, among them the fact that everything you know about the topic is stored in memory in English. It's hard to think in one language when the data base is in another. The secretary-general of the European Free Trade Association, a six-nation group of non-EC members, none of which has English as a native language, notes that even though English is the official language of the group, "using English means we don't talk too much since none of us knows the nuances."[9] The question is whether this would be an unfair advantage in negotiations involving native speakers.

2. The cultural argument against English is part of the broader argument about the dominance of Anglo-American popular culture in global communication. Although purists object to Franglais and the infiltration of English into other languages, it is really the culture that is at issue—the realities of punk rock and fast food—not the words. English, it is argued, is a Trojan horse hiding a whole set of cultural values that disrupt and threaten other cultures. Even languages themselves are on the endangered species list. Languages without a written form, which includes most of the estimated 3,000 to 6,000 languages in use today, are most vulnerable.

3. English also gives the native speaker a unique cultural advantage. It is possible to travel to most parts of the world and get by easily using only English. Can you imagine someone speaking only French or Swedish, to say nothing of Swahili, Mandarin, or Arabic, surviving as a tourist in the United States or Britain? In most European countries, in contrast, university students are expected to know English, and readings are assigned and guest lecturers introduced in English without apology or warning. English, of course, is the first language of the tourist information center.

---

9 "The New English Empire," *The Economist*, December 20, 1986, p. 129.

Not only can we expect to find English-speaking flight attendants, desk clerks, and waiters everywhere, but also English-language publications and other pieces of Anglo-American culture. In the novel *The Accidental Tourist,* a major character writes guide books for business travelers who hate unfamiliarity. His books tell where to find Chef Boyardee spaghetti in Rome and Burger King Whoppers in Paris. In contrast, the visitor to Anglo-America from Angola or even Austria virtually draws a curtain across his or her homeland.

Mixed Arguments

1. We could repeat some of the technical arguments because they contain implications for culture as well: size and distribution of the family of English speakers, vast resources of knowledge already in English, flexibility and adaptability of the language. Beyond that, of course, English already is the global language. Almost all of the global culture is now produced and stored in English.

2. A second cultural reason favoring English as the global language is precisely the same as a reason against it: the culture that goes with the language. The Anglo-American cultural values of individualism, opportunity, and a better future attract students of English to the language. It is really condescending to say to people of the third world, yes, it's fine for us to have Walkmen and a "California lifestyle," but you should be happy with your generations-old culture of rigid authoritarianism and poverty. If you learn English, you'll just want to give it all up.

   Some "good liberals" were aghast to find that East Berliners, when the wall was opened at Christmas 1989, went first to the overloaded shops along the Ku'damm in West Berlin to marvel at— and occasionally to buy—bananas, Whoppers, sex magazines, and rock tapes. If others want to learn English as their entry into the mass culture of Anglo-America, who are we to discourage them?

ALTERNATIVES

If English, for technical or cultural reasons, is unsuitable as a language for global communication, what would be a better choice? There are alternatives, but no clear favorite.

Alternatives from History

Latin was as close to a global language as the world had for the first millennium A.D. and still has influence. Even though it is no longer used in liturgy, Catholic churches around the world usually have some remnants of Latin inscription, a tribute to the days when you could participate in an identical mass in any country (but probably not understand much of it in any, even your own). Latin survives in medicine and law, a tribute to its influence in scholarship and authority, but it is, well, a dead language and lacks a living culture. The occasional modern book translated into Latin—*Winnie the Pooh* is a favorite—seems artificial to the few who can read it. Except for modern Hebrew, no language has been brought back from extinction and restored to life.

Occasionally Hebrew or Aramaic (the language of Jesus) is proposed as a world language, but the suggestion is impractical. Modern Hebrew is the language of one small country, and Aramaic is on the verge of extinction in Syria, the victim of the more powerful Arabic. When the topic moves to science or other "modern" subjects, Israelis shift into English. It is hard to imagine that an ancient, isolated tongue such as Aramaic could be modernized to accommodate all that global communication requires.

Living Alternatives

Let's scrap dead languages and those with unique cultural value to part of the world. How about one of the several modern-day languages that meet two reasonable criteria: (1) number of native speakers and (2) diverse use. Chinese, of course, has more native speakers than any other—well more than a billion in China alone plus 20 million in Taiwan and several million more in Chinese communities in other countries. But there are problems. The spoken language includes various mutually unintelligible dialects, and the tonal aspects are more difficult for foreigners than the "th" sound in English or the inflections of other Indo-European languages. The language as a whole is not widely used outside of China and is difficult to adapt to electronic hardware. Realistically Chinese is not a strong candidate.

Several other languages are not as difficult as Chinese and offer the advantage of size and diversity of use. They are Hindi-Urdu (with 330 million speakers, the third largest language), Russian (280 million speakers), Spanish (200 million), or Arabic (150 million speakers). Portuguese (140 million speakers) and French (120 million) have the advantage of use in countries around the globe.[10] Arabic and Hindi-Urdu have alphabets that are difficult to adapt to keyboards and are more regional than global in use. Both are closely linked to cultures that are peripheral to the twentieth century. Some other languages have some claims of global reach. In fact, we sometimes forget that Portuguese is the language of the single largest Latin American country as well as five countries of Africa and Macau in Asia. Spanish can claim the former African colony of the Spanish Sahara and some lingering influence in the Philippines.

---

[10] These conservative estimates include both native speakers and those who use a language as a second tongue. Other languages with more than 100 million total speakers are Indonesian-Malay (140 million), Bengali (125 million), Japanese (110 million), and German (100 million). Michael Malherbe, *Les Langues de L'Humanité* (Paris: Editions Seghers, 1983), p. 25. Slightly different numbers are given in John W. Wright, ed., *The Universal Almanac 1993* (Kansas City, MO: Andrews and McMeel, 1992), p. 324.

French, of course, was a rival to English until about World War I and can claim a distinguished history as an international language of diplomacy and literature as well as outposts in all continents. French influence includes French Guiana in South America; several Caribbean islands; French Polynesia in the South Pacific; and widespread use in Indochina, Maghreb, and the eastern Mediterranean. However, if you add together all the speakers of English as a native language, second language, and foreign language, only Chinese approaches it in size, and no other language comes close in influence. Is English the global language by default?

Esperanto

One other choice remains to be considered: Esperanto. As you will read in the Data Base at the end of this chapter, Esperanto, now a little more than 100 years old, was invented as a rational, simple tongue incorporating elements of the Indo-European language family. Esperantists don't like to hear it called an artificial language; they think of it as a planned language with only 16 simple rules of grammar and no exceptions. The language is overwhelmingly Eurocentric. It looks and sounds a little like Italian with a strong overlay of English/Germanic vocabulary. It is virtually without irregularities or nonliteral meanings. Starting from a knowledge of English, you can learn it reasonably well in less than 100 hours.

Estimates of the number of Esperanto speakers (who wear green star-shaped pins so other speakers will recognize them) vary from less than 1 million up to 8 million. More than 10,000 works have been published in Esperanto, including some modern fiction and poetry. It is most popular in countries whose languages do not travel well, such as Iran, the Scandinavian countries, and Japan. In some countries such as China, Esperanto has been promoted as a domestic link language.

Esperanto reached its peak after World War I, when it was proposed as a universal language to overcome the cultural misunderstandings and conflicts that precipitated the war. However, no international organizations ever adopted Esperanto, and none is likely to. Groups such as the UN, EC, and the OECD have enough trouble with the languages they already use and are happy to rely more and more on English. Since the mid-twentieth century, the use of Esperanto has declined, and it is not a serious contender to replace English.

No language, certainly not a planned one such as Esperanto, is likely to displace English because it is precisely the culture that comes with English that has such powerful appeal. As *The Economist* notes:

> [A]t least a few novice students of EFL [English as a foreign language] look forward to the treasures of Shakespeare, Mark Twain and Yeats. And those language students who have less exalted ambitions—refining their appreciation of Bob Dylan's lyrics, following ''Dynasty'' without the subtitles, securing the local McDonald's franchise, emigrating to America—have even less reason to be diverted from their English studies.[11]

---

[11] ''Estas neniu alternativo,'' *The Economist,* December 20, 1986, p. 130.

The Force of Culture

Of course, it is the appeal of the culture that also is usually the impetus for English speakers to study a second language and is the great value of the junior year in college abroad. English speakers can function as tourists in any country in English, but it is only when we achieve some reasonable command of a foreign language that we can step inside the culture and, even if only for a semester, become part of it.

For better or worse, we cannot separate a global language from a global culture. In both cases, English is so far ahead of the competition that no change is likely—except one. Language drift is constant, and at some point a dialect or regional variety becomes a separate language. Compared to the evolution of physical species, the process is remarkably fast. It took French, Spanish, Italian, and the other Romance languages only a few centuries to become separate from Latin, and Afrikaans a shorter time to break from Dutch. Even in the twentieth century, Shaw's Professor Henry Higgins (from *My Fair Lady*) claimed that English had completely disappeared in the United States. He was, if not entirely wrong, perhaps only premature.

If a London friend tells you to take the lift to his first-floor flat and knock him up at 7 o'clock, you'll probably know to take the elevator to his second-story apartment and to come by at 7:00 P.M. But differences between British and U.S. language exist now and may be getting bigger. The editor of the *Oxford English Dictionary* predicts a drift that will eventually produce two distinct languages. Other reputable sources disagree, but the news agencies already have lists of words that must be translated from one to the other, and you can buy a serious British-American dictionary in bookstores.

In other English-speaking countries, the divergence is already greater. Consider this sentence from an English-language paper in India: "Condemning the police zulum, Mr. X said the management created a hungama by unleashing its goondas on workers protesting against talabanki by observing peaceful hartal."[12] A good case could be made that the queen's English has already disappeared from that part of the world. A common language for global communication seems likely to stay in place for the next several centuries. In other parts of the world, however, the drift is fast enough that your grandchildren may well have to study in a Department of Englishes or English Languages and read the scholarly journal *World Englishes,* which already exists.

The likeliest candidates for separation from the Anglo-American standard are countries or regions that have a rich base of native languages to serve as a source for new words and grammatical constructions or those where English has become a creole, a distinct language with full vocabulary that evolved from simple pidgin languages of explorers, soldiers, and traders. These regions include the Indian subcontinent, Nigeria in West Africa, and the Caribbean. Even in the United States, regional differences seem to be gaining strength, and it is not too difficult to

---

[12] From the *Tribune* of Chandigarh, quoted in *World Press Review,* February 1988, p. 44. See also Anthony Spaeth, "If You Are Queasy, Avoid India's Papers—And This Article," *Wall Street Journal,* February 8, 1989, p. 1.

distinguish a standard Canadian pronunciation from its U.S. equivalent. *Oot* and *aboot* instead of *out* and *about* and the final *eh?* often give the Canadian away.

In a century or two, we may have a root English that is used internationally and by educated speakers in traditional English-speaking countries. Even in these countries and certainly in those where the language is now a second language, separate languages will have evolved to the point where they are as distinct from each other as Italian is from Spanish. They are likely to form a spectrum of overlap, with greater differences between the international standard and African and Indian variants than between the ''Spanglish'' of the southern United States and the ''Franglais'' of New England and Canada. In all cases, the driving force will be the global culture, not the influence of any single country.

MAIN POINTS

1. English has achieved dominance in global communication to a degree unknown in history. Its influence is a product of British and U.S. political and economic power in the past and also of its current use as the language of the emerging global economy and culture.

2. English evolved from Germanic roots but contains an unusually large vocabulary from Latin and other languages as well as German. Modern English emerged as a distributive language with simple rules of grammar. Despite terrible irregularities of spelling, pronunciation, and meaning, English can be put to use with a minimum of formal study yet retains the sophistication and flexibility that challenge even the well-educated native speaker.

3. Alternatives to English as the global language are impractical, and the language is likely to increase in importance as the language of science, commerce, and popular culture. However, drift is inevitable, and the future can be expected to produce a family of languages that are similar but not mutually intelligible.

FOR MORE INFORMATION

Robert McCrum, William Cran, and Robert MacNeil, *The Story of English* (New York: Viking Penguin, 1986). This companion to the BBC/PBS series was recommended in Chapter 1. If you didn't check out the videotapes then, do so now.

A. C. Baugh and Thomas Cable, *A History of the English Language* (London: Routledge & Kegan Paul, 1978), is the standard history.

Bill Bryson, *The Mother Tongue: English and How It Got That Way* (New York: Morrow, 1990), is a popular treatment.

Three international news magazines published major stories on the global influence of English. They are good for relatively recent information and examples and discuss related topics. They are: ''English, English Everywhere,'' *Newsweek,* November 15, 1982, pp. 98–105; ''The English Language: Out to Conquer the World,'' *U.S. News & World Report,* February 18, 1985, pp. 49–59; ''The New English Empire,'' *The Economist,* December 20, 1986, pp. 127–131.

FOR DISCUSSION

1. Use the arguments in this chapter to debate the following proposition: ''English: a (insert an adjective of your choice) world language.''

2. Interview a few people about their experiences studying English as a foreign language. Survey some friends for embarrassing mistakes they have made in speaking languages other than their native language.

3. Interview an Esperantist to find out why he or she studied the language and what hopes he or she has for its future. Look for Esperanto books in a library or bookstore and see how much you can read.

DATA BASE

Esperanto is one global language that is easy to learn and offers a wide range of literature. Most countries have information centers that offer instruction. The Esperanto Information Center, 410 Darrell Road, Hillsborough, CA 94010, offers a free course by mail. Here is part of the first lesson.

Language is all about things (nouns) and actions (verbs) of energetic things:

One Thing . . .	*Acts On . . .*	*Another Thing*
Birdo . . .	*kaptas . . .*	*insekton.*
A bird	catches	an insect.

Esperanto is ''grammar-coded''—you can tell what part each word plays in a sentence from the word endings:

_____*o*   _____*on*
SINGLE SUBJECT NOUN   SINGLE OBJECT NOUN

If there is more than one of the same thing (PLURAL NOUN):

_____*oj* (as in boy)   _____*ojn*
PLURAL SUBJECT NOUN   PLURAL OBJECT NOUN

To show when the action takes place, the verb TENSE (time) is changed by putting these endings on the verb roots:

PRESENT TENSE	_____*as*	
PAST TENSE	_____*is*	
FUTURE TENSE	_____*os*	
Birdoj	*kaptis*	*insektojn.*
Birds	caught	insects.
Birdoj	*kaptos*	*insektojn.*
Birds	will capture	insects.

EVERY NOUN AND EVERY VERB FOLLOW THE ABOVE RULES WITHOUT EXCEPTION.

In Esperanto, things have no gender. There is only one word for "the," no matter if the noun is singular or plural, subject or object. Therefore:

La birdoj kaptas la insektojn.

La birdo kaptis la insekton.

Here are some words in Esperanto (hyphens separate root words and their noun endings):

NOUNS	*VERBS*	*MORE NOUNS*
AMIK-O (friend)	FAR' (do, make)	KAF-O (coffee)
FIL-O (son)	FORGES' (forget)	KUK-O (cake)
FRAT-O (brother)	HAV' (have)	LAKT-O (milk)
INSTUIST-O (teacher)	TRINK' (drink)	PAN-O (bread)
KNAB-O (boy)	VEND' (sell)	SUKER-O (sugar)
PATR-O (father)	VID' (see)	TE-O (tea)

Each Esperanto letter has only one sound. Here is a guide to some of the sounds. The stress is always on the next-to-last syllable of a word:

A	*E*	*I*	*O*	*U*
palm	there	three	glory	too

C = ts (in lots); OJ = oy (in boy); G = g (in go)
KN is always pronounced separately: K-Nabo.

Translate the following sentences into Esperanto. Example: THE MEN SOLD CAKES.

La viroj vendis kukojn.

Note the word "a" does not exist in Esperanto; the simple noun is enough. Also, a dash indicates that two English words are translated into one Esperanto word.

1. FATHER MAKES A CAKE.
2. THE BOY WILL-HAVE THE MILK.
3. THE SON FORGOT THE MILK.
4. THE BOYS DRINK TEA.
5. THE FRIEND SOLD THE BREAD.

For more information, contact the Esperanto League for North America, P. O. Box 1129, El Cerrito, CA 94530 U.S.A., or the Canadian Esperanto Association, C. P. 126, Succursale Beaubien, Montreal, Quebec, H2G 3C8.

A more sophisticated example is from this *Time* magazine essay (August 3, 1987):

La Espero de Esperanto

En 1887 Ludoviko Zamenhof, multlingva pola okulisto, publikigis libron prezentantan novan lingvon sub la kaŝnomo Doktoro Esperanto. Zamenhof arde deziris ke lia inventita lingvo fariĝu la dua lingvo de la mondo. Kvankam tiu espero estas ankoraŭ nerealigita, preskaŭ sesmil fervoraj esperantistoj—historia le plej granda renkontiĝo—tiel foraj lokoj kiel Japanio kaj Brazilo estas ĉi-semajne en Varsovio por honori Zamenhofje la okazo de la centa datreveno de lia lingvo. Ili celebras per diversaj arranĝoj, ĉiuj en Esperanto, plus vizito al la hejmurbo de Zamenhof, Bjalistoko.

Multaj homoj supozas, ke Esperanto estas unu mortanta lingvo, vorta eksperimento kiu simple no elsukcesis. Fakte, exparantistoj estat troveblaj tra la tuta mondo. Taksoj pri ilia tuta nombre multe varias, inter 1 milionoj kaj 8 milionoj aŭ pli. Marjorie Duncan, 65-jara, emerita instruistino el Sidneo, Aŭstralio, kredas, ke la movado bezonas pli da gejunuloj. Sed, ŝi diras, ili preferus ''veturigi autojn aŭ iri surfumi.''

The Hope of Esperanto

In 1887 Ludovic Zamenhof, a multilingual Polish oculist, published a book introducing a new language under the pseudonym Dr. Esperanto, meaning ''one who hopes.'' Zamenhof fervently wished that his invented tongue would become the world's second language. Although that hope is still unrealized, nearly 6,000 zealous Esperantists—the largest gathering ever—from as far away as Japan and Brazil are in Warsaw this week to honor Zamenhof on the occasion of the 100th anniversary of his language. They are doing so with a variety of events, all in Esperanto, plus a visit to Zamenhof's hometown of Bialystok.

Many people assume that Esperanto is a dying language, a verbal experiment that has simply not worked out. In fact, Esperantists can be found all around the world. Estimates of their total number vary widely, from 1 million to 8 million or more. Marjorie Duncan, 65, a retired Sydney, Australia, schoolteacher, believes the movement needs more young people. But, she says, they would ''rather drive cars or go surfing.''

SOURCE: ''The Hope of Esperanto,'' from *Time*, August 3, 1987. Copyright © 1987 Time Warner, Inc. Reprinted by permission.

CHAPTER 5

The Armchair Tour
of Global Media

ABOUT THIS CHAPTER

In this chapter, as the first step in a whirlwind tour of the world's mass media, we consider several theories of mass media. These are efforts to describe key aspects of mass media in different countries and to sort them into a few categories that permit us to see the essential similarities and differences. After looking at several theoretical frameworks other scholars have devised, we consider our own set of criteria for comparing and contrasting media systems and anticipate some of the differences we can expect in various countries. Then it's all aboard for a fast visit to the world's media in the 1990s.

INTRODUCTION

Cultures form the context for global communication, but it is modern mass media—newspapers, magazines, radio, television, and telephones—that link the world. It does not take more than a few minutes with a foreign newspaper or newscast, even if you don't understand the language, to realize that national media systems are as varied as the cultures in which they're found. Despite the dominance of Anglo-America in all aspects of global communication, mass media reflect a variety of social, political, and economic systems. In some countries, they are almost opposite images of the media Americans are familiar with.

In 1977, a charter flight from Germany to San Francisco stopped briefly in Bangor, Maine, for refueling and customs clearance. One tourist, a German brewery worker who knew almost no English, went through customs and on into the city, believing he had arrived in California. He managed to get a hotel room and spent the next three days sightseeing in Bangor, a quiet New England town of 30,000. He assumed he was in the San Francisco suburbs. Then, with his few words of English, he asked a taxi driver to take him to San Francisco, which, of course, is about 5,000 kilometers from Bangor. The cab driver took him instead to a local German restaurant, whose owners explained to the poor man where he was and why he hadn't been able to find the Golden Gate Bridge.

Different cultures can be confusing, of course, as we have seen in previous chapters. Even a common language is no protection against misunderstanding. For the next several chapters, we are going to be armchair tourists. We will examine the wonderful and bewildering variety of mass media around the world and consider key aspects of global communication at the end of the twentieth century. We will use mass media to try to understand something about cultures and use cultures to try to understand mass media. To do that—and to avoid the problems of the German tourist in Bangor—we need a guide book.

Role of Theories

In science, theories serve as guide books, because they tell us what to look for and help us understand what we have seen. Good theories are succinct, precise, and broadly applicable. Like good guide books, they point us in the right direction but are not so rigid that they inhibit the unexpected pleasure of serendipitous discovery. You can travel without a guide book, of course, and often the most memorable moments result from chance encounters and unplanned experiences. It's disconcerting, though, to return home and find that you came within a block or two of a famous landmark and didn't see it. Or maybe you let your snapshots stay in a mess in a drawer because you can't remember where they were taken or what they represent. Organizing principles are always useful for these reasons. Good theories are very practical.

We don't have a single theory to help us understand the bewildering variety of mass media in the 170 or so countries in the world, and we don't have time to explore more than a small fraction of them. As tourists, we're in a hurry, so we need to be selective and hit the high points.

Scholars who made the trip before us have supplied different criteria for comparing mass media systems and different ways of organizing them into general categories. In the absence of a single unified theory, these various semi-theories, concepts, and perspectives can serve as our guide book. We won't see everything, and some of our snapshots won't fit neatly into the categories, but we can cover a lot of ground in a short time and probably avoid getting completely lost.

The Value of Getting Lost

By the way, the German brewery worker's vacation wasn't lost after all. He spent two weeks in Maine, where he was given an acre of land and made an honorary member of the Penobscot Indian tribe. Then he flew on to San Francisco, courtesy of a newspaper there, where he was briefly a hero and a celebrity, before returning to the relative obscurity of his hometown near Augsburg. The moral of the story is not to despair if the museum closes at 2:00 P.M., and you arrive at 2:15. Find a small café, relax, and enjoy the pleasure of serendipity.

THEORIES, CONCEPTS, PERSPECTIVES

The first attempt to provide a framework for studying the world's media systems was the product of a large and influential study of the role of mass media in the United States. A national Commission on Freedom of the Press, chaired by Robert Hutchins of the University of Chicago, was organized in 1946 by Henry Luce of *Time* magazine.[1] The commission's report and several separate studies by commission members tried to define the social responsibilities of mass media in an age of sudden and unexpected U.S. superpower status and media influence. The commission's interest was domestic, but its report had international implications, both because of the U.S. media's growing international influence and because of the new awareness that U.S. concepts of media freedom and responsibility were not always exportable. A follow-up study of media social responsibility, commissioned by the National Council of Churches, was headed by Wilbur Schramm, one of the most influential and prolific scholars of mass communication throughout a long career that continued until the late 1980s. The Council of Churches study included a comparative look at different media systems, which became the first of several theories of the press. The study is still widely cited.[2]

FOUR THEORIES

Fred S. Siebert, Theodore Peterson, and Wilbur Schramm, who collaborated on *Four Theories of the Press,* divided the world's diverse media into four distinct groups or theories: authoritarian, libertarian, social responsibility, and Soviet communist. In defining the four, they considered these criteria: historical development of the system; philosophical basis; social, political, and economic purpose; right to use media; control; what is forbidden (censorship); and ownership. At the heart of any media system, they said, is the relationship between media and government.

The media-government axis is still crucial to any examination of global media. In a short introduction to the book, Schramm argued that the four theories derived from the simple dichotomy of media controlled by government (authoritarian and communist) and media independent of government (libertarian and social responsibility). That essential difference continues today.

Authoritarian Theory

The authoritarian concept developed in England in the sixteenth and seventeenth centuries. It was a product of the communication revolution that followed Gutenberg's invention of printing with moveable type. That revolution ended the church and state monopoly on knowledge and allowed the owners of the first *mass* medium—the simple press that could quickly produce large quantities

---

[1] Hutchins Commission [or Zachariah H. Chafee, Jr.], *A Free and Responsible Press* (Chicago: University of Chicago Press, 1947).

[2] Fred S. Siebert, Theodore Peterson, and Wilbur Schramm, *Four Theories of the Press* (Urbana: University of Illinois Press, 1963).

of books, pamphlets, or newspapers—to challenge authority to a degree that none had done before. Governments, which still claimed absolute authority, responded by allowing printing but subjected it to severe restrictions.

In general, printers were allowed to operate, even to the point of publishing newspapers, as long as they did so with government's permission and did not challenge government's authority. In some cases, the new medium was used openly by governments to maintain their power, a pattern of media-government relations that is not obsolete. In a majority of countries in the world today, the government has the power (1) to prevent publication of information it does not want available or (2) to force publication of information it does want disseminated.

Libertarian Theory

According to *Four Theories,* the libertarian press theory evolved over several centuries in Britain and the United States as a reaction to the authoritarian press theory. A dividing line between the two could be drawn in 1689, the year the English Bill of Rights was approved by Parliament. The bill contained no explicit mention of press freedom, but Siebert argued that the basic principle of press independence was established. Libertarianism had two core ideas. One was that no one—certainly not a hereditary king or queen—had a monopoly on truth and should have a monopoly on information. Instead, the libertarians argued that truth—if a single truth even existed—was discovered only through a clash of competing claims. The second idea was that citizens of a democracy, not the inner circle of aristocrats who had ruled in Europe's traditional royal courts, had the right to participate in political debate and ultimately to decide which version of truth should be accepted. Libertarian press theory goes hand-in-hand with multiparty political democracy and, in most cases, free-market capitalism.

You will recognize the close links between the theory of libertarianism and the dominant U.S. social values discussed in Chapter 2. It is no accident that many of the founding fathers of libertarianism were among the founding fathers of the U.S. republic. We know the arguments of libertarianism from the writings of John Milton, John Stuart Mill, Thomas Paine, Thomas Jefferson, and others who inspired the American Revolution and expanded the Anglo-American principles of individual rights and freedoms.

At this point, we can see the clear dichotomy between a political system built on a unity of media and government, on the one hand, and a political system built on separation of press and government, on the other. The first, almost by definition, requires a permanent one-party state, whereas the second, also by definition, assumes a multiparty system with government temporarily in power by popular mandate. To the authoritarian government, the media are either a tool to maintain power or at a minimum annoyances that must be denied any ability to threaten or challenge power. To the libertarian government, the media are part of the competition for power and usually function as watchdogs on those in political positions of power. Media can be advocates of specific parties or segments of society, as they often are in Europe, or they can be common carriers of information from different parties and groups, as they try to be in the United States.

Despite the rhetoric of the New World Information Order, an independent press is ascendant in the 1990s. One of the key demands in the wave of social revolutions that swept through Central and Eastern Europe in 1989 was to end government's control of the media. Even though government control is more often the rule than the exception in the third world, the trend is toward press independence there as well.

Communist Theory

The remaining two theories are twentieth-century variants of the first two. The communist theory flows from Lenin, the architect of the first communist revolution, more than from Karl Marx, who was a theorist of revolution but not a practitioner. Lenin's communist theory of the press recognized an active role for media in creating a revolution, and then the media were to be used to produce the kind of ultimate socialist state Marx's theory envisioned. In Lenin's writing, which we consider in detail in Chapter 8, some statements on the role of the press may sound strange to Anglo-American ears. Lenin talks about the press—remember that he was writing around the turn of the nineteenth century, before the press became the media—as a collective propagandist, agitator, and organizer. In another pamphlet, he describes the press as a scaffold that holds up a single-party political system. These ideas are very different from those of, for example, Thomas Jefferson.

Social Responsibility Theory

Libertarianism underwent a revival of sorts in the 1980s, a product of broadcast deregulation and new desktop publishing technology that allowed people to produce newsletters and other materials in their basements. In the 1940s and 1950s, however, the concern was not with getting government off our backs and letting the marketplace take advantage of the explosive growth of communication capacity. Instead, media scholars and practitioners were interested in improving a system that seemed to work reasonably well but not perfectly—or maybe it didn't even work that well. Peterson put it this way:

> Freedom carries concomitant obligations; and the press, which enjoys a privileged position under our government, is obliged to be responsible to society for carrying out certain essential functions of mass communication in contemporary society. To the extent that the press recognizes its responsibilities and makes them the basis for operational policies, the libertarian system will satisfy the needs of society. To the extent that the press does not assume its responsibilities, some other agency must see that the essential functions of mass communication are carried out.

Peterson was also explicit on what those responsibilities were:

(1) servicing the political system by providing information, discussion, and debate on public affairs; (2) enlightening the public so as to make

it capable of self-government; (3) safeguarding the rights of the individual by serving as a watchdog against government; (4) servicing the economic system, primarily by bringing together the buyers and sellers of goods and services through the medium of advertising; (5) providing entertainment; (6) maintaining its own financial self-sufficiency so as to be free from the pressures of special interests.[3]

In the cynical 1990s, these noble-sounding "responsibilities" may sound a little hollow, even to a staunch defender of U.S. media. Radical critics argue that the whole notion of socially responsible, privately owned mass media is an oxymoron. Many of these critics are almost as contemptuous of "public" media, which at least have the redeeming quality of being nonprofit. In Western Europe, the traditional noncommercial public broadcast systems, always subject to varying degrees of political control, are losing ground to U.S.-style radio and television: entertainment oriented, heavy on advertising, programming selected to maximize audiences. In the United States, even minimal public service programming is harder to find as light-handed government oversight is relaxed and station and network owners acknowledge their prime interest in the "bottom line" rather than the public interest.

Despite their cheerful optimism about socially responsible Anglo-American media and their cold-warrish description of "totalitarian" communist media theory, the Four Theories, as they are universally referred to, remain an indispensable system for classifying global media systems. There are important differences between, say, U.S. and Russian media, even in the 1990s when just about everything that was thought essential to a communist system has been discarded. Closer to home, there are also very basic differences between broadcasting in Western Europe and broadcasting in the United States and surprisingly big differences between media-government relations in the United States and the same relations in Britain. The Four Theories remain a useful template for categorizing and studying the national media systems in the 1990s, but perhaps they could use a little sprucing up.

FIVE CONCEPTS

The most useful updating of the basic Four Theories was done by William A. Hachten in his readable, insightful book on global communication in the 1980s.[4] His "five concepts" change the Four Theories three ways.

---

[3] Fred S. Siebert, Theodore Peterson, and Wilbur Schramm, *Four Theories of the Press* (Urbana: University of Illinois Press, 1963), p. 74.

[4] William A. Hachten, *The World News Prism,* 3rd ed. (Ames: Iowa State University Press, 1992), ch. 2.

Western Concept

First, he combined the libertarian and social responsibilities theories into a single "Western" concept. This acknowledges the high level of public (as opposed to government) involvement in broadcasting in most Western democracies, the significant communication-related activities of government even in the United States, and the blurring of the line between government and private sectors in all facets of communication. If anything, new technology has made many of the justifications for socially responsible media—limited broadcast spectrum, lack of media outlets, and need to promote culture and education among them—obsolete. Western media are becoming more alike in the 1990s and, on the whole, the Western concept is more libertarian and less socially responsible.

Development Concept

Second, Hachten defines a distinct "development concept" that is particularly pertinent to the global debate over the role of mass media in the third world. The development concept takes some of its ideas from the authoritarian theory (media cannot be too critical of government), some from the communist theory (media should be mobilized to support the political system), and, curiously enough, some from the North American experience of the Agricultural Extension Service, which still uses communication to try to improve life in rural areas of the United States and Canada.

In its benign manifestation, development journalism is not too far from social responsibility and is compatible with public broadcasting and the boosterism that some small newspapers still practice. In some forms, however, it smacks more of authoritarianism or the cult of personality that traditionally filled communist media with page after page and picture after picture of the noble leader guiding the nation toward a Marxist utopia. The role of mass media in national development is still a major concern to that vast expanse of geography and humanity referred to as the third world. The development concept will figure prominently in our armchair media tour of these areas.

Revolutionary Concept

Third, Hachten specifies a separate "revolutionary concept" of mass media. From Tom Paine's pamphlets to Lenin's polemics, journalism has been a part of every revolution, of course, but in the age of global communication, media have taken on new power and new importance. Pictures of tanks rolling across Tiananmen Square, of Germans chipping away at both sides of the Berlin Wall, and of a sober Daniel Ortega conceding electoral defeat are vivid reminders of the extraordinary events that modern mass media have allowed us to witness. But are the media themselves part of these revolutions or merely bystanders able to record dramatic events that would have taken place anyway? Chapter 11 considers this question in detail and explores recent revolutions in which media may have played a significant role. Hachten underlines the role of journalism in past revolutions and notes the additional power that new technology gives revolutionaries. In an age of revolution—and the 1990s are certainly that—revolutionary media deserve special attention.

Authoritarianism and Communism

Hachten's last two concepts are the traditional authoritarianism, now found frequently in Latin America and in some Asian countries, and communism, which is mostly an artifact except for a few outposts such as Cuba and North Korea.

THREE PERSPECTIVES

At this point, can we conclude that there are four theories or five concepts of the press, or maybe some other number that will allow us to sort the world's media into a comprehensible set of categories? A third approach recognizes that the three political "worlds" political scientists use frequently can also be the basis of classifying media systems.[5]

In this admittedly simplified way of looking at the diverse nations of the planet, the "first world" includes the industrialized democracies of Western Europe, North America, and Japan. Sometimes South Africa and Israel are also included. The "second world" comprises the industrialized socialist countries of Eastern and Central Europe, which are now trying to move into the first-world category. Occasionally China, Cuba, and the few other communist countries in the developing world are also included. The "third world" is most problematic because it is the most diverse. Usually the term is based on level of economic development (or lack of it), but listings of third-world countries often include the highly industrialized and rapidly growing "tigers" of Asia (Hong Kong, which isn't even a separate country, Taiwan, Singapore, and South Korea) as well as several oil-exporting countries in the Persian Gulf whose per capita gross national products are among the highest in the world.

If "third world" is conceived in political terms, it means nonaligned in the sense of independence of the two superpowers. However, the Non-Aligned Movement, which is sometimes considered synonymous with the third world, includes Cuba, which is about as nonaligned as Canada, and several of the U.S. "client states" in Latin America and Asia. So the third world is neither totally underdeveloped nor totally nonaligned. It is big and diverse.[6] With the collapse of the second world of communism in the 1980s, terms such as "third world" and

[5] L. John Martin and Anju Grover Chaudhary, eds., *Comparative Mass Media Systems* (New York: Longman, 1983).

[6] Sometimes the "fourth world" is used to separate those countries that have little potential for development because of population or lack of resources. The group frequently includes Bangladesh and the African nations of the Sahel. The term "fifth world" is occasionally used for the small group of very rich oil-exporting countries, which are usually treated separately in economic reports by organizations such as the World Bank and the United Nations.

"nonaligned" lost much of their meaning, but they remain useful in sorting out the countries of the world.

Martin and Chaudhary accept the imprecision of carving the sections into three worlds but find the classifications useful, nevertheless, because media in each of the three regions tend to be similar and different from those in the other two regions. They organize the three world perspectives around six functions that mass media fill in all countries: (1) the concept of news; (2) the social, political, and economic role of the media; (3) the educational, persuasive, and opinion-making function; (4) the entertainment function; (5) press freedom; and (6) the economic basis of the media. Obviously, as they note, news is different in Moscow, Idaho, and Moscow, Russia. The educational, persuasive, and opinion-making function varies from Santiago, Chile, to Santiago, Spain. Their authors address these various functions from the different perspectives of first-, second-, and third-world media systems, recognizing that generalization inevitably requires both simplification and the occasional linking of countries that really share very little.

THE THREE-PART SYMPHONY

Another classification system recognizing that each of the three "worlds" has evolved, more or less, its own media philosophy is J. Herbert Altschull's thoughtful analysis of the role of news media in human affairs.[7] Altschull, a journalist and scholar, dismisses the notion of social responsibility as "absurd," arguing that every media system pursues the interests of those who control it. He defines three distinct systems that are similar to Hachten's Western, communist, and development concepts. Altschull calls them "market," "Marxist," and "advancing" and argues that they produce a global symphony with a variety of themes and melodies. Here, in outline, are the distinctive characteristics of each.

Purpose of Journalism
Market: To seek truth; to be socially responsible; to inform (or educate) in a nonpolitical way; to serve the people impartially; to support capitalist doctrine; to serve as a watchdog of government.

Marxist: To search for truth; to be socially responsible; to educate people and enlist allies (in a political way); to serve the people by demanding support for socialist doctrine; to mold views and change behavior.

Advancing: To serve truth; to be socially responsible; to educate (in a political way); to serve the people, by seeking, in partnership with government, change for beneficial purposes; to serve as an instrument for peace.

---

[7] J. Herbert Altschull, *Agents of Power: The Role of News Media in Human Affairs* (New York: Longman, 1984), ch. 11.

Articles of Faith

Market: The press is free of outside interference; the press serves the public's right to know; the press seeks to learn and present the truth; the press reports fairly and objectively.

Marxist: The press transforms false consciousness and educates workers into class consciousness; the press provides for the objective needs of the people; the press facilitates effective change; the press reports objectively about the realities of experience.

Advancing: The press is a unifying and not a divisive force; the press is a device for beneficial social change; the press is meant to be used for two-way exchanges between journalists and readers.

Views on Press Freedom

Market: A free press means journalists are free of all outside control; a free press is one in which the press is not servile to power and is not manipulated by power; no national press policy is needed to ensure a free press.

Marxist: A free press means the opinions of all people are published, not only those of the rich; a free press is required to counter oppression; a national press policy is required to guarantee that a free press takes the correct form.

Advancing: A free press means freedom of conscience for journalists; press freedom is less important than the viability of the nation; a national press policy is needed to provide legal safeguards for freedom.

It is obvious that the guide books will not always agree on what aspects of media systems around the world we should look at or how we should interpret what we discover. This is an advantage, however, because it gives us the opportunity to develop our own guide book, our own theories, concepts, and perspectives, and perhaps even a new symphonic variation. The scholars who preceded us in touring the world's media systems blazed a trail and left us with a good supply of brochures and travel tips. With all these materials spread out before us, we need to piece together our own itinerary.

A GUIDE FOR ARMCHAIR TOURISTS

Hachten's five concepts of the press are the most current and useful way of dividing up global media systems. We will devote a chapter to each, after a special consideration of media in the dominant English-speaking world. All of the authors noted above included some aspects of mass media—relationship between media and the government or social and political functions, for example—but they did not agree on others. Although making no claim that the list is all-inclusive, we consider these aspects of media systems in various countries around the world: the links to culture, availability, ownership and control, legal guarantees and restrictions, social and economic purposes, and audiences. A sampling of what we'll see later can help explain why these aspects are important and perhaps sensitize us to differences we might otherwise overlook.

Links to Culture

Think for a moment how U.S. mass media reflect our culture. We noted earlier that individualism is a powerful trait in U.S. culture along with a concomitant suspicion of government. It should come as no surprise, then, that the U.S. media system is among the most decentralized in the world and the most independent of government control. It might come as a surprise that even many countries that share the Western media concept have a different view of the media system.

For these other countries, all media, but especially broadcasting, have an obligation both to maintain and to promote the national culture, and government's role is to make sure they do. Thus, even in democratic countries such as Canada and Britain, there is concern that lowbrow but admittedly popular U.S. imports represent a threat to their cultural integrity. In a move that looked decidedly undemocratic from our side of the Atlantic, the European Community in 1989 called for limits to imported U.S. television programming and increased government-supported efforts to expand and improve European production. From their perspective, this was a logical extension of the well-established principle that broadcasting should not be privately owned or overly commercial—better to have the occasionally heavy hand of government supporting national (cultural) identity than the steamroller power of the multinational entertainment conglomerates obliterating it.

Another cultural difference: When forced to choose between the power of government and the power of big business, Americans typically opt for the latter. Most Europeans would go for the former. They tend to see government as a legitimate expression of the nation; Americans are likely to quote Jefferson's famous remark that the government is best that governs least. Americans are not too concerned about massive media conglomerates with headquarters in distant cities, even other countries. Europeans—and people in many other parts of the world as well—often see the power of private, commercial mass media as a greater threat to their liberties than government and are unimpressed by Jeffersonian fears of big government.

The EC action on TV imports is an example of the use of government as a counterweight to the power of global media. As we examine other nations' media, we need to be sensitive to this close link between media and efforts to maintain cultural identity.

Availability

It may not be surprising to find that the United States is the most broadcast-saturated country in the world or that radio and television are still rarities in some parts of the planet. In the United States, we now have more than two radio receivers per person and almost one TV set per person. We also have the most stations to choose from. More than half of all households have cable or a satellite dish in the backyard. Cable systems offering 35–40 channels are standard; those with up to 100 channels are not unusual. Even over the airwaves, most of us can receive at least 5 or 6 channels of television and 30 to 50 radio stations. With the Walkman and Watchman, we can take radio and television with us to the shopping mall, the beach, or even to a dull lecture.

The rest of the world is catching up. In Europe, traditionally limited public broadcasting is feeling the pressure of a rapid expansion of the number of channels and stations, most of them privately owned and commercial. In all parts of the world—and especially in the third world—the number of radio and TV sets is growing geometrically, doubling every three to five years. Growth is fastest in the poorest countries. By the end of the century, very few people will be "media poor" in the sense that they have no access to radio or television, but few will be "media rich" in the U.S. sense of having personal, portable radio and TV.

The situation is very different when we look at newspapers. Here you may find some surprises, such as the fact that the United States is not the world leader in newspaper readership—not even close. Between 1967 and 1988, the proportion of adults in the United States who read a newspaper "every day" dropped from 73 percent to 51 percent. Total daily newspaper circulation dropped from about

Newspapers from home and abroad dominate public life in Europe in a way that has disappeared from the United States. This kiosk in Paris offers dozens of dailies and hundreds of magazines.

SOURCE: Edwin Martin.

350 copies per 1,000 people at the end of World War II to about 250 copies per 1,000 in 1990. The United States ranked 19th in the world in per capita circulation in the mid-1980s, ahead of Kuwait and Hungary but behind Singapore and Czechoslovakia.[8]

Newspapers Down

Elsewhere in the world, the newspaper picture is mixed. In parts of Western Europe, newspapers are booming, mostly thanks to the belated arrival of new technology. In several countries—Britain, Austria, Spain, and Italy, for example—the most influential papers are less than a generation old. In the late 1980s, London saw the birth of two dailies and two Sunday papers. Figures from Eastern Europe are a muddle in the aftermath of the social revolutions, but new and newly independent newspapers are thriving while those still associated with the old regimes and parties are dead or dying.

In many parts of the third world, newspapers are not thriving. In Africa, perhaps a dozen countries have no daily paper at all. In others, the only paper is a scrawny sheet, poorly printed and subsidized or owned outright by the government. In Latin America and most of Asia, newspapers are healthy and crisply printed by the newest technology but fail to keep up with population growth. As a result, circulation is declining on a per capita basis. Several factors are at work.

One is the rapid growth of population, which governments can't keep up with. As a result, literacy is declining, and illiterates are not newspaper readers. Another is the high cost of everything used in the newspaper business—newsprint and ink included—which must be imported with scarce hard currency. In the poorer countries, advertising revenues are limited or nonexistent. In all countries, of course, broadcasting is a powerful competitor for people's time, attention, and money. It would be unwarranted pessimism to forecast the death of newspapers in the poorest countries of the world in the twenty-first century, but in some countries in Africa and in a few in Asia, the question is not whether they will thrive but whether they will survive.

Telecommunication Up

Telecommunication, too, is changing rapidly in all parts of the world. We used to think of it as POTS, plain old telephone service. The telephone still provides that, of course, but more and more telephone circuits now connect computers and fax machines. In New York City, the area code 212 ran out of numbers, and another area code had to be added. Other cities in the country are now facing the same problem.

In most countries, telecommunication is expanding at an explosive rate and undergoing a revolution of availability and capability. In 1989, a ceremony in Honiara, the capital of the Solomon Islands, inaugurated a satellite-based telecommunication system that, for the first time, linked the capital and outlying

---

[8] Marion Lewenstein, "Global Readership," *Presstime* (published by the American Newspaper Publishers Association), September 1987, pp. 10–12. See this chapter's Data Base for an update.

islands with telecommunication services. After each regional governor greeted the prime minister by phone, the governor sent a fax message that appeared instantly on a machine next to the prime minister. It was a clever symbol of how telecommunication now embraces a variety of technologies and, of course, how important it is to the third world.

Telecommunication is especially important to global communication in the 1990s for two reasons. One, preliminary evidence indicates that it seems to be a significant factor in promoting third-world economic growth. This question was a major part of the decade-long debate over the role of communication in the third-world that was known as the New World Information Order (or New World Information and Communication Order, NWICO) debate. Chapter 10 deals with the NWIO/NWICO debate and communication and development in detail.

Second, telecommunication is intimately entangled with news flow. The news gets to your radio, TV, and newspaper through a complex web of telecommunications that includes satellites, probably optical fiber cable, and maybe even old-fashioned wires looped from pole to pole. This is exactly the same system that allows people in Moscow, Russia, to pick up the phone and direct-dial someone in Moscow, Idaho. The satellites that link computers, fax machines, and people also have more complex circuits that send the TV news pictures from Berlin, Germany, to Berlin, Wisconsin. It is impossible to talk about news media in the 1990s without talking about global telecommunication. As messages bounce from earth station to satellite and down to another earth station on the other side of the planet, it is equally impossible to distinguish a reporter's voice report or news copy from any other voice or text. Often the two are merged into a single digitized data stream that one day will include television pictures as well.

Information as Power

If knowledge is power and information the basis of wealth in the information age of the 1990s, then availability of mass media becomes an important factor in the distribution of wealth and power within a country or among countries. Countries that cannot afford to develop their media systems will be left behind. Information poverty is probably as significant in the 1990s as economic disparity among nations has been in the past.

Disparities exist within countries as well, of course. Governments that claim a monopoly on information, which is a common characteristic of communist and authoritarian regimes, may be able to prevent the development of revolutionary media systems for a while, but in the long run, they can't. In the information-rich West, it is easy to overlook the information poverty that exists in much of the world. To avoid that, we need to ask at each stop on our tour who has access to mass media and who controls access and availability.

Ownership and Control

When discussing the role of mass media with foreign colleagues, U.S. journalists, particularly owners of newspapers and broadcast stations, often divide the world into a simple dichotomy: "government" media versus "free" media. In this very simple view of global media, ownership and control are the same thing. "Government" media can never be free, and "free" media can never be subject to "government" influence—end of debate.

There are two errors in this argument. First, ownership and control are not the same thing. Most newspapers and broadcast stations in the United States are owned by giant corporations, some of them foreign companies. However, these owners rarely try to control the media in any direct sense. They look at the bottom line on the financial statements more than at editorial page policy. If anything, U.S. media are controlled by its customers. TV officials are right when they say they'd be happy to give us the highest quality cultural and current affairs programming hour after hour. All we have to do is watch it, which we don't. The same principle applies to newspapers. U.S. media may not give us what we *should* get, but they certainly give us what we want. In a lot of other countries, many of them firmly in the tradition of Western democracy, this approach is looked upon as foolish and dangerous.

The other error is that the argument omits the possibility of public ownership and control, which can free the media from undue influence from either government or private ownership. Our own puny public radio and TV are good examples. A majority of the world's broadcast systems are publicly rather than privately owned. Political control varies widely.

In most authoritarian media systems today, the media are privately owned but subject to significant government influence. This combination of private ownership and government control is particularly strong in Latin America but can be found in some Asian countries as well, such as Singapore and South Korea. In some cases, government control is overt, as it was historically in Britain and is now in most countries in Africa. In others, it is subtle and covert. In Mexico, for example, newsprint was traditionally imported by a government-owned corporation. Newspapers that got too critical of government could find their supply reduced or even eliminated. In many countries, critical journalists are subjected to anonymous threats, arrested on vague charges, and sometimes they simply disappear.

Government-Media Embrace

Even in the United States, the wall between government and media is not as impenetrable as professional organizations sometimes claim. Newspapers can be exempted from antitrust laws and allowed to establish more efficient joint printing arrangements with government approval. Broadcasters must still satisfy minimal requirements of public service and responsibility before their licenses are renewed, but nonrenewal is rare. Special postage rates can be viewed as an indirect subsidy to newspapers and magazines. In all countries—especially democracies—a symbiotic relationship exists between government and media. They need each other, and they influence each other in different ways, in different degrees, and with different results.

Journalists and their media are subject to ordinary laws in every country, but many democratic countries provide special considerations for media. In Sweden, reporters cannot be forced to reveal sources in court proceedings. At the same time, an advertising tax is redistributed in reverse proportion to news-papers' market penetration. The point of the plan, which has helped Sweden maintain healthy newspaper competition and avoid the one-newspaper cities of the United States, is to redistribute a little of the wealth from the biggest papers to the smallest. Do these government interventions reflect the social responsibility theory in practice, or are they part of a traditional Swedish paternalism that calms the media watchdog?

Swedish journalists themselves would not agree on the answer. On one hand, Swedish newspaper circulation is about twice that of the United States, and no Swedish daily has died since the subsidy plan was started in 1971. On the other hand, Swedish journalism is tame and reluctant to use its special protections. The media collectively did not investigate the murder of Prime Minister Olaf Palme or scandals in arms sales to the third world with the vigor one might expect from the *Washington Post* or *60 Minutes*.

The ability of the White House to influence what the *New York Times* prints is much less than the power of the British government to influence what the BBC or London *Independent* reports. Certainly the influence of both governments differs in kind and degree from that of the Mexican government. The point is that ownership and control are both important aspects of media systems, but they are not the same thing.

Public Service Media

Nor are the only choices government-owned and -controlled media, on one hand, and privately owned, "free" media, on the other. A third choice is public media, which can be free of both government and private influence but aren't auto-matically. The U.S. public media system is weak financially, but it presents some of the best and most critical coverage of U.S. government and society. Advocates of the free/government dichotomy often forget that. In fact, around the world, public broadcasting is more common than privately owned, commercial broad-casting. Public radio and television, dedicated to something more lofty than maximizing audiences for advertisers, was the standard in Western Europe, and to a large extent it still is, although its future is in doubt. It was also the model for most of Africa, Asia, and the Middle East, although direct and massive govern-ment control is now the rule in these regions, not the exception.

On paper, broadcasting systems in Britain, France, and Germany a generation ago looked similar. The BBC was a noncommercial monopoly financed by license fees owners paid on receivers. The French ORTF, dismembered in 1974, was similar in that it was a monopoly that programmed multiple national and regional services that supposedly complemented one another. The German ARD was a consortium of regional broadcasters that provided a commercial-free, national television service financed by government and user licenses.

Even though ownership was vested in a public body in each country, control varied widely. The BBC developed a reputation for honesty and accuracy in news coverage that no other broadcaster in the world can match today. Despite severe legal limitations we consider below, the BBC has always been a model of independence and excellence. The ORTF, on the other hand, was a creature of direct political control. Top officials were appointed by the government and answered to the government, right down to clearing the rundown of TV news stories. President Charles de Gaulle once dismissed criticism of his heavy and obvious control of TV news by saying the papers were all against him, so why shouldn't he control TV?

ARD policy was—and is—determined to some degree by a supervisory board representing "socially significant" groups in Germany. These include the churches, the labor unions, business, and the political parties. In theory, ARD answered to the supervisory board, and the people who actually produced the programs were nonpartisan civil servants. Many public broadcasting outlets and a few cable systems in the United States maintain similar advisory boards whose members are supposed to reflect and protect the interests of subcultures as well as the general public.

Throughout the world, the public service model is under attack. Outside of Latin America, very few third-world countries maintain even a pretense of public or private commercial control, claiming instead that development-oriented media, mobilized by the government to support national goals, are a necessary part of national development. Deregulation and commercialization of broadcasting threaten the tradition of public media as well. Although this trend is most notice-able in Europe, it is a force pressing against the concept of development media as well.

The great political upheavals of the late 1980s moved the world away from government control and toward the America notion of "free" media, financed by advertising and intent on maximizing audiences by offering mass-appeal entertainment. The global entertainment conglomerates, abetted by deregulation-minded governments, are one force behind the decline of public media, but global audience attraction to "frothy" entertainment is another. Game shows and soap operas, raucous music videos, and even sex and violence appear to be popular around the world.

Given Americans' hostility toward government in general, it is not surprising that the United States developed a media system that is rooted in private owner-ship and largely divorced from government influence. Whether the global media system evolving in the 1990s in the image of the Anglo-American model will continue to grow in that direction is something we cannot predict, but the forces behind new global media suggest that it will.

Legal Guarantees and Restrictions

Because mass media are locked in a symbiotic embrace with governments and often are a creature of governments as well, it is reasonable to expect big differ-ences among media systems in the kinds of legal protections they enjoy, the restrictions they must endure, and the responsibilities they are expected to fulfill. An obvious starting place is a nation's constitution or basic law, but, in fact, no constitution denies press freedom. To the contrary, all of them guarantee it. Very few go beyond a general statement establishing the right to a free press, although some cite specific guarantees or exceptions. Consider this excerpt from a national constitution:

> [Citizens are guaranteed] freedom of speech, of the press, and of assembly, meetings, street processions, and demonstrations. Exercise of these political freedoms is ensured by putting public buildings, streets, and squares at the disposal of the working people and their organizations, by broad dissemination of information, and by the opportunity to use the press, television, and radio.

The phrase "working people" is a clue to its socialist origin, but the first sentence sounds remarkably like the First Amendment to the U.S. Constitution. The quote comes from the constitution of the Soviet Union, a country that, until recently, was notable for its lack of press freedom.

The Chinese constitution declares that "citizens enjoy freedom of speech, correspondence, the press, assembly, association, procession, demonstration, and the freedom to strike, and have the right to speak out freely, air their views fully, hold great debates, and write big-character posters.[9] To an outsider, that is exactly what the protesters in Tiananmen Square were doing in June 1989, when the government sent in the tanks to crush them. Written constitutions are a poor guide to the real measure of press freedom in different countries.

Defining Press Freedom

The U.S. First Amendment is notable for its brevity and, if anything, is less explicit than either the Soviet or Chinese statements. The general principle of all three seems to be similar, but you would get an argument from most people if you suggested on that basis that there really is no difference among the three world giants. Also, it is not too inaccurate to argue simply that the First Amendment means at any given time what a majority of Supreme Court justices say it means. More generally, press freedom in any country is defined collectively by constitutional guarantees, laws, and the daily activities of judges, lawyers, and government officials who give these laws meaning.

To start with the familiar, we can define press freedom in the United States as the right to speak, print, or broadcast what you want to without prior restraint but with limited liability afterward. The grounds for bringing a post-publication action traditionally include sedition, obscenity, and libel. Lawyers and legislators argue at great length about where the fine line between protected speech and unconstitutional behavior lies, but the Supreme Court has never accepted the claim of Justice William O. Douglas and some civil liberties lawyers that the First Amendment means exactly what it says: no law restricting free speech or press,

---

[9] Both quotes are from Manny Paraschos, *Constitutional Provisions on the Press: A World View.* Paper presented to the Association for Education in Journalism and Mass Communication, meeting in Washington, D.C., July 1989.

period. Not even in the "land of the free and the home of the brave" is press freedom absolute.

In practice, even the classic formulation of press freedom in the First Amendment is hard to interpret. Laws to guarantee access to information, such as freedom of information laws and open meeting statutes, recognize the importance of government openness and accountability and suggest that freedom of access to information is important if freedom to publish is to have any meaning. On the other hand, cases charging bureaucrats who leak information with theft of government property or holding officials to nondisclosure contracts demonstrate how determined governments can protect information they don't want to see in the papers.

In most Western countries, governments exert a greater influence on mass media than in the United States. In Britain, which lacks both a written constitution and an independent judiciary with the power to overturn parliamentary action, the government has almost a free hand to determine what information will be made public and how violators will be dealt with. If press freedom is defined as the ability to publish or broadcast without government interference, either before or afterward, then the United States has the freest press in the world, and Britain has at best a severely restricted press. Some listings of press freedom do not put Britain into a "most-free" category.

Beyond Government Control

Of course, other considerations may be important, too, such as the right of access to the media and a right of reply if you're maligned. It's one thing to be able to stand on the street corner and pass out political handbills, but freedom of the press means something very different to private citizens than to the big companies that own newspapers and broadcast stations. You benefit from socially responsible, aggressive news reporters acting on your behalf in the corridors of power, but you probably have very little opportunity to use the common constitutional rights yourself in any meaningful way.

In a few countries, some kind of access and right of reply are built into the legal system so ordinary people can use the media. Consistent with the European view of government, many there would argue that it is government's responsibility to restrict the power of the media on behalf of the citizens, not the other way around. The public broadcast systems, of course, rest on the assumption that the public good is better served by insulating the media from market pressures and putting the public more or less directly in charge.

Our checklist of things to look for in each national media system must include the constitutional guarantees, but they are only the first step. We also need to look at the full range of legal restrictions and protections as well as the working definition of press freedom. We also should consider media responsibilities and how they are enforced. The acceptance of press freedom as freedom from government control puts us clearly on one side of the original dichotomy of media systems. Advocates of the other position, that media are a legitimate part of government, are fewer and quieter in the 1990s than even a few years earlier, but they are still around. In practice, government influence on mass media covers the full range from a little to almost total.

Social and Economic Purpose

A compromise declaration on the role of mass media was approved by the United Nations Educational, Scientific, and Cultural Organization (UNESCO) in 1978 after a long and bitter debate on the dominance of the West in all aspects of global communication. The declaration took 128 words to list the "contributions" of mass media to solving many of the world's ills. The word "contributions" replaced "responsibilities" in earlier drafts because the Western delegates argued that media really had no "responsibilities" to deal with these issues. Governments were responsible for war, racism, apartheid, and so on; journalists weren't.

It was an argument that many delegates to the conference couldn't understand. Nor would they have understood the statement attributed to William Peter Hamilton of *The Wall Street Journal,* quoted in the "Social Responsibility" chapter of *Four Theories:*

> A newspaper is a private enterprise owing nothing whatever to the public, which grants it no franchise. It is therefore affected with no public interest. It is emphatically the property of the owner, who is selling a manufactured product at his own risk.[10]

Social Purpose or Freedom

If our first dichotomy of national media systems was made on the basis of their relationship to government, a second could be over social purpose. On one side are Mr. Hamilton and most U.S. media owners, who stand with John Stuart Mill: The common good or national interest is the sum of all the private goods or interests pursued selfishly by individuals. On the other side are advocates of the social responsibility theory, development theory, and communist theory, who contend that media should do something besides giving us constantly what we want to watch or read—and making money.

Although the argument that media ought to be independent of government is accepted in many parts of the world, the notion that media ought to be privately owned, commercially based, and dedicated to earning as much money as possible for their owners is far less popular. In most countries, as we have already noted, broadcast media more than newspapers and magazines are expected to serve some higher purpose. Even in the United States, broadcasters were traditionally granted temporary licenses to serve the public interest, convenience, and necessity. In theory, but seldom in practice, a broadcaster that failed to do so would lose its license.

---

[10] Fred S. Siebert, Theodore Peterson, and Wilbur Schramm, *Four Theories of the Press* (Urbana: University of Illinois Press, 1963) p. 73.

Most European broadcasters and those modeled on European systems would argue that broadcasting is a limited resource that should serve to advance education, culture, and maybe the government in power. These goals can be achieved by vesting control over broadcasting in a single public system not subject to pressures from advertisers, private owners, and viewers.

The contrasting position, which curiously enough is being advocated in Britain more than in the United States, argues in favor of auctioning off broadcast licenses. Let licenses go to the highest bidders to operate as the owners want. If you can make money with highbrow culture and public affairs, fine. If the audience prefers hour after hour of *Dallas* and *The Texas Chainsaw Massacre*, that's fine, too. Every night almost 99 percent of U.S. households choose not to watch some of the finest programming in the world on public television. It's democracy in action.

Britain was the first country to test its faith in the marketplace in 1991 when it auctioned off franchises for regional commercial TV broadcasting that had previously been administered by the Independent Broadcast Authority. Although other considerations were taken into account, most franchises went to the applicants bidding the most money. Not even the "antigovernment" Reagan administration tried that.

Opposing Pressures

Globally, two trends in social and economic purpose are evident. Sometimes they pull media in the same direction. In other places, they tend to pull in opposite directions. One is the trend of rapid expansion of media, particularly broadcasting, which is spearheaded by profit-minded private industry. This pulls the media toward popular entertainment, commercial sponsorship, and audience preference as the basis of content. At greatest risk are the high-quality, sometimes politically controlled, radio and TV stations of Western Europe, which are losing their monopoly status and their guaranteed revenues.

The other trend is away from the social function of support for the government as defined in the communist theory and the new development concept. The decade of the 1990s promises to witness the ascendancy of "free" media as we define the term in the West. Authoritarian control over media is still prevalent but harder to defend (observe Singapore, China, and the Middle East, among others) and still harder to maintain (see Chapter 11, "Revolutionary Media"). The classical communist theory is now a historical artifact except for a few outposts such as Beijing, Havana, and Pyongyang. Even in these places, cadres with surreptitious audio and videotapes may be slowly undermining the political regime.

Audiences

We have already noted the possibly surprising statistic that the United States is well down the list in newspaper circulation but solidly in first place in radio and TV ownership. About half of the adult population reads a newspaper more or less daily, about the same proportion as watches the evening network news on TV. Does that mean that half the population, by choice or due to lack of a quarter or two to buy a paper, is cut off from the flood of information that distinguishes this age of global communication?

Possibly, but almost everyone in the United States encounters news on a daily basis somewhere, whether scanning the headlines over a first cup of coffee, jogging while listening to a Walkman, or pausing to catch the news breaks sandwiched in a favorite TV program. We just don't pay very much attention or take it seriously. In other countries, the situation is different.

For one thing, TV news in "prime time" rather than at the periphery of the TV schedule is common in most countries. In countries with limited channels, no other choice may be available. News also is treated more seriously than in the United States, sometimes to the point that it almost assumes the character of a state religion, with repeated pictures of national leaders and the symbols associated with them.

Access as Elitism

In many parts of the world, access to mass media is still limited. Despite the proliferation of cheap radio and TV sets, they are too expensive for most people in the world. A few spots—but not many—are still outside the range of broadcast signals. A bigger problem is illiteracy, which is increasing. You don't need to be literate to watch TV or listen to the radio, but you do need to be literate to read a newspaper.

Newspapers and to a lesser extent television are elite media in most of the third world. They often are available only in the capital city. They require knowledge of the national language rather than the local tribal or ethnic language and, relatively speaking, they cost a lot of money. In rich countries with a diversity of newspapers, something that has disappeared in the United States, readership divides along class and income lines. The "quality" papers represent a tiny part of the total national circulation. The average British reader sees either a tabloid with more bare breasts than serious news or a weak local paper that ignores everything outside the city limits. At each stop of our media tour, we will want to ask who pays attention to the media; what constraints limit access; and how fragmented the audience is, by economics, class, or geography.

In most countries, the term *mass media* is already or about to become obsolete, because it implies that a single audience exists for each medium and that the country's media collectively reach people uniformly. This is seldom the case, even in countries, such as the pre-1989 Soviet Union or China, that use the media as massive propaganda weapons. At the low end of economic development, media are limited to the elite. Most people are excluded by illiteracy, poverty, and lack of access to outside sources. At the high end of development, particularly where media are commercial and privately owned, audiences become fragmented. In the media-saturated West, people can select a varied diet from a menu groaning with choices segmented by intellectual level, content, and ideology.

Rules of TV Programming

Two flexible rules of thumb seem to influence who pays attention to what. The first concerns news: News produced independently of government is favored over news controlled by government. In the long run, news produced by professionally competent, ideologically neutral journalists is preferred over partisan journalism. Witness the credibility and popularity of Western media in communist and third-world countries as evidence of the first statement and the recent growth of nonpartisan journalism in Europe as evidence of the second.

The second rule is less optimistic: In every country, audiences prefer entertainment to public affairs and culture if given a choice. The global success of Hollywood TV and films is less evidence of cultural imperialism than of the universal appeal of entertainment that emerges triumphant from the brutal competition of the very commercial U.S. entertainment industry.

A corollary to the second rule of thumb is that audiences tend to prefer local entertainment to Hollywood imports if the quality is roughly comparable. British television has long recognized that Shakespeare will never win in the ratings over *Benny Hill* or *The Eastenders,* but Britain is one European country that traditionally provided both. *Dallas* and *Dynasty* were at the top of the ratings in Germany until *Black Forest Clinic* and *Linden Street,* both potboilers of the same genre as the U.S. shows, dethroned them. In Latin America, locally produced soap operas have pushed U.S. imports to the periphery of prime time and also are finding audiences around the world.

Despite a continuing Anglo-American dominance in media around the world, more channels and simpler technology are making it possible for more local production and greater diversity. Now it's time for a firsthand look, so return your tray table and seat back to their original, upright position for takeoff. The armchair tour is underway.

MAIN POINTS

1. The relationship between media and government is crucial. Although the basic dichotomy is between government-controlled media and independent media, the line blurs quickly. In all countries, a symbiotic relationship between the two exists.

2. Authoritarian press systems are usually privately owned and independent of government but subject to various overt and covert government pressures. The function of mass media in an authoritarian state can be entertainment or information, but challenges to government authority are not permitted. The authoritarian concept is found in most Latin American countries and some nations in Asia.

3. In the Western concept of the press, the media are mostly independent of government and function as advocates of political views, common carriers of information, and watchdogs on government. They are usually privately or publicly owned, although governments maintain

various levels of influence. The Western concept is gaining strength worldwide in the 1990s.

4. The communist concept is built on Lenin's assertion that the media are part of the state's apparatus of political indoctrination and control. Information is a monopoly of the state or party. The communist concept of journalism was discarded in Central and Eastern Europe along with other elements of communism, but in the few remaining communist countries, the traditional Marxist-Leninist theory of the media is still in place.

5. The revolutionary concept of media acknowledges the importance of mass media in undermining existing governments. The phenomenon is as old as Thomas Paine's pamphlets and as new as networks of fax machines and computer bulletin boards in China. Can mass media really overthrow a government by themselves, or are they only eyewitnesses to revolution? Events of the late 1980s can be used to support either side of the argument.

6. Development media are mobilized by government to assist in promoting national development objectives (and usually the regime in power). In many parts of the third world, development journalism is justified as a temporary expedient to help poor countries catch up to the West. In other areas, advocates argue that development media should serve as a barrier to protect indigenous cultures against the destructive influence of the Western global culture. Although it has been largely discredited, elements of development journalism remain in force in most developing countries.

FOR MORE INFORMATION

The original formulation of the four theories of the press is still a good starting point: Fred S. Siebert, Theodore Peterson, and Wilbur Schramm, *Four Theories of the Press* (Urbana: University of Illinois Press, 1963). William A. Hachten's restructuring of the four theories into five concepts is in his short and insightful *The World News Prism: Changing Media, Clashing Ideologies,* 3rd ed. (Ames: Iowa State University Press, 1992).

The three perspectives of first, second, and third world are represented in essays from a wide range of authors in L. John Martin and Anju Grover Chaudhary (eds.), *Comparative Mass Media Systems* (New York: Longman, 1983). A very useful interpretation of global media along the same lines is J. Herbert Altschull, *Agents of Power: The Role of the News Media in Human Affairs* (New York: Longman, 1984). Altschull employs a similar trichotomy to describe the world's media systems and some of the political issues of the 1980s. The book contains a good critique of the social responsibility concept.

A data-packed survey of broadcasting is *World Broadcasting in the Age of the Satellite,* by W. J. Howell, Jr. (Norwood, NJ: Ablex, 1986). A chapter on broadcasting in culturally diverse countries is especially pertinent to our consideration of the role of culture and cultural conflict in the 1990s. Three other useful surveys of global broadcasting are George H. Quester, *The International Politics of Television* (Lexington, MA: D. C. Heath, 1990); Donald R. Browne, *Comparing Broadcast Systems: The Experience of Six Industrialized*

Nations (Ames: Iowa State University Press, 1989); and Eli Noam, *Television in Europe* (New York: Oxford University Press, 1991).

Global Journalism: A Survey of the World's Mass Media, 2nd ed., edited by John C. Merrill (New York: Longman, 1991), is the standard tour guide of global media systems. It is organized geographically rather than by type of media system.

Current Issues in International Communication, edited by L. John Martin and Ray Eldon Hiebert (New York: Longman, 1990), contains a wide range of current materials related to global media systems. Many of them are quantitative studies addressing the political questions raised in this and previous chapters in this book.

FOR DISCUSSION

1. Debate the following proposition: Social responsibility in journalism is (needed now more than ever) (obsolete) (impossible).

2. Compare and contrast a sample of major U.S. newspapers with newspapers from Britain, Canada, Australia, and New Zealand, using the criteria presented in this chapter. Include radio and TV if samples can be collected.

3. Select a major world event and compare coverage of it in as many countries as possible. Look for differences consistent (or inconsistent) with the prevailing concept of media in each region.

DATA BASE

I. Each year, Freedom House in New York City evaluates the level of political rights and civil liberties in each country of the world. Political rights "enable people to participate freely in the political process." Civil liberties "are the freedoms to develop views, institutions and personal autonomy apart from the state." To score high (1) on the political rights and civil liberties indexes, a country must have a media system that is independent of government control, among other criteria. A score of 1 indicates most free; 7 indicates least free. Freedom House also assigns an overall "freedom rating" to each country: free (F), partly free (PF), or not free (NF). Data for 1992 are shown below.

The Human Development Index, compiled by the United Nations Development Program, combines life expectancy, literacy, educational attainment, and adequacy of income (buying power) into one measure. The scale is ranged from 0 to 1. Ratings for 1992 are shown below.

Country	Political Rights Index	Civil Liberties Index	Freedom Rating	Human Development Index
Afghanistan	7	7	NF	.074
Albania	4	4	PF	.791
Algeria	4	4	PF	.533
Angola	6	4	PF	.169
Argentina	1	3	F	.833
Australia	1	1	F	.971

Country	Political Rights Index	Civil Liberties Index	Freedom Rating	Human Development Index
Austria	1	1	F	.950
Bahamas	2	3	F	.875
Bahrain	6	5	PF	.790
Bangladesh	2	3	F	.185
Barbados	1	1	F	.927
Belgium	1	1	F	.950
Belize	1	1	F	.665
Benin	2	3	F	.111
Bhutan	6	5	PF	.146
Bolivia	2	3	F	.394
Botswana	1	2	F	.534
Brazil	2	3	F	.739
Brunei Darussalam	6	5	NF	.848
Bulgaria	2	3	F	.865
Burkina Faso	6	5	NF	.074
Burundi	7	6	NF	.165
Cambodia	6	6	NF	.178
Cameroon	6	6	NF	.313
Canada	1	1	F	.982
Cape Verde Islands	2	3	F	.437
Central African Rep.	6	5	PF	.159
Chad	6	6	NF	.088
Chile	2	2	F	.863
China	7	7	NF	.612
Colombia	2	4	PF	.758
Comoros	4	3	PF	.269
Congo	6	4	PF	.372
Costa Rica	1	1	F	.842
Côte d'Ivoire	6	4	PF	.289
Cuba	7	7	NF	.732
Cyprus	1	1	F	.912
Czechoslovakia	2	2	F	.897
Denmark	1	1	F	.953
Djibouti	6	5	NF	.084
Dominican Republic	2	3	F	.595
Ecuador	2	3	F	.641
Egypt	5	5	PF	.385

Country	Political Rights Index	Civil Liberties Index	Freedom Rating	Human Development Index
El Salvador	3	4	PF	.498
Equatorial Guinea	7	7	NF	.163
Ethiopia	6	5	PF	.173
Fiji	6	4	PF	.713
Finland	1	1	F	.953
France	1	2	F	.969
Gabon	4	3	PF	.545
Gambia	2	2	F	.083
Germany	1	2	F	.955
Ghana	6	6	NF	.310
Greece	1	2	F	.901
Guatemala	3	5	PF	.485
Guinea	6	5	NF	.052
Guinea-Bissau	6	5	PF	.088
Guyana	5	4	PF	.539
Haiti	7	7	NF	.276
Honduras	2	3	F	.473
Hong Kong	4	3	PF	.913
Hungary	2	2	F	.893
Iceland	1	1	F	.958
India	3	4	PF	.297
Indonesia	6	5	PF	.491
Iran	6	5	NF	.547
Iraq	7	7	NF	.589
Ireland	1	1	F	.921
Israel	2	2	F	.939
Italy	1	1	F	.922
Jamaica	2	2	F	.722
Japan	1	2	F	.981
Jordan	4	4	PF	.586
Kenya	6	6	NF	.366
Kuwait	6	5	NF	.815
Laos	6	7	NF	.240
Lebanon	6	4	PF	.561
Lesotho	6	4	PF	.423
Liberia	7	6	NF	.227
Libya	7	7	NF	.659

Country	Political Rights Index	Civil Liberties Index	Freedom Rating	Human Development Index
Luxembourg	1	1	F	.929
Madagascar	4	4	PF	.325
Malawi	7	6	NF	.166
Malaysia	5	4	PF	.789
Maldives	6	5	NF	.490
Mali	6	4	PF	.081
Malta	1	1	F	.854
Mauritania	7	6	NF	.141
Mauritius	1	2	F	.793
Mexico	4	4	PF	.804
Mongolia	2	3	F	.574
Morocco	6	5	PF	.429
Mozambique	6	4	PF	.153
Myanmar	7	7	NF	.385
Namibia	2	3	F	.295
Nepal	2	3	F	.168
Netherlands	1	1	F	.968
New Zealand	1	1	F	.947
Nicaragua	3	3	PF	.496
Niger	6	5	PF	.078
Nigeria	6	4	PF	.241
North Korea	7	7	NF	.654
Norway	1	1	F	.978
Oman	6	6	NF	.598
Pakistan	4	5	PF	.305
Panama	4	2	PF	.731
Papua New Guinea	2	3	F	.321
Paraguay	3	3	PF	.637
Peru	3	5	PF	.600
Philippines	3	3	PF	.600
Poland	2	2	F	.874
Portugal	1	1	F	.850
Qatar	7	5	NF	.802
Romania	5	5	PF	.733
Rwanda	6	6	NF	.186
São Tomé/Principe	2	3	F	.186
Saudi Arabia	7	6	NF	.687

Country	Political Rights Index	Civil Liberties Index	Freedom Rating	Human Development Index
Senegal	4	3	PF	.178
Sierra Leone	6	5	PF	.062
Singapore	4	4	PF	.848
Solomon Islands	1	1	F	.434
Somalia	7	7	NF	.088
South Africa	5	4	PF	.674
South Korea	2	3	F	.871
Soviet Union	3	3	PF	.873
Spain	1	1	F	.916
Sri Lanka	4	5	PF	.651
St. Lucia	1	2	F	.712
St. Vincent	1	2	F	.693
Sudan	7	7	NF	.157
Suriname	4	4	PF	.749
Swaziland	6	5	PF	.458
Sweden	1	1	F	.976
Switzerland	1	1	F	.977
Syria	7	7	NF	.665
Taiwan	3	3	PF	N/A
Tanzania	6	5	NF	.268
Thailand	6	4	PF	.685
Togo	6	5	NF	.218
Tonga	3	3	PF	N/A
Trinidad/Tobago	1	1	F	.876
Tunisia	5	5	PF	.582
Turkey	2	4	PF	.671
Uganda	6	6	NF	.192
United Arab Emirates	6	5	NF	.740
United Kingdom	1	2	F	.962
United States	1	1	F	.976
Uruguay	1	2	F	.880
Vanuatu	2	3	F	.536
Venezuela	1	3	F	.824
Vietnam	7	7	NF	.464
Western Samoa	2	2	F	.591
Yemen	6	5	PF	.232

Country	Political Rights Index	Civil Liberties Index	Freedom Rating	Human Development Index
Yugoslavia	6	5	NF	.857
Zaire	6	5	NF	.262
Zambia	2	3	F	.315
Zimbabwe	5	4	PF	.397

SOURCE: from *Freedom in the World, '92–'93*. Copyright © 1993, Freedom House. Reprinted by permission.

II. Daily newspapers sold per 1,000 inhabitants, 1991–1992.

Norway	619
Japan	584
Sweden	522
Finland	521
Germany	335
Switzerland	415
Austria	409
Czech Republic	396
United Kingdom	362
Singapore	348
Denmark	340
Luxembourg	333
Netherlands	317
New Zealand	364
United States	244
Russia	222
Canada	214
Australia	199
Estonia	195
Slovakia	179
Ireland	177
Belgium	173
Israel	158
France	157
Poland	126
Italy	115
Malaysia	112
Cyprus	91

Greece	83
Spain	81
Argentina	79
Turkey	56
South Africa	44
Philippines	43
Portugal	39
Uruguay	35
Tunisia	30
India	24
Brazil	15

SOURCE: Walt Potter, "News of the World," *Presstime,* July 1993, p. 66. Copyright ©
1993 Newspaper Association of America. Reprinted by permission of *Presstime,* the
magazine of the Newspaper Association of America.

III. Videocassette recorders in 1988 as percent of television households and
increase from 1987.

	Percent of TV Households with VCR	Percent Increase 1987 to 1988
Argentina	3	38
Australia	63	11
Austria	39	30
Bahrain	64	5
Barbados	4	35
Belgium	26	20
Bermuda	55	18
Brazil	15	28
Brunei	49	50
Bulgaria	4	39
Canada	58	14
Chile	5	22
China	2	7
Colombia	39	17
Costa Rica	10	32
Cyprus	52	10
Denmark	38	15
Ecuador	17	18
Egypt	14	23
El Salvador	9	28

	Percent of TV Households with VCR	Percent Increase 1987 to 1988
Finland	39	20
France	38	27
West Germany	51	15
Ghana	9	5
Greece	38	30
Guatemala	10	17
Hong Kong	64	15
Hungary	9	33
Iceland	60	16
India	49	11
Indonesia	22	9
Iran	25	8
Iraq	32	7
Ireland	50	11
Israel	57	9
Italy	17	40
Japan	70	6
Jordan	18	5
Kenya	28	19
South Korea	23	8
Kuwait	78	2
Lebanon	65	3
Luxembourg	46	17
Malaysia	44	10
Mexico	19	22
Netherlands	49	15
New Zealand	52	15
Nigeria	17	3
Norway	41	15
Oman	36	− 4
Panama	43	11
Peru	38	13
Philippines	36	− 15
Poland	7	15
Portugal	40	11
Qatar	69	4
Saudi Arabia	52	10
Singapore	39	11

	Percent of TV Households with VCR	Percent Increase 1987 to 1988
Spain	35	21
Sri Lanka	34	5
Sweden	38	13
Switzerland	36	15
Thailand	12	4
Turkey	34	5
United Arab Emirates	76	4
United Kingdom	60	8
United States	59	14
Uruguay	6	5
Soviet Union	1	29
Venezuela	39	8
Zimbabwe	31	42

SOURCE: *World Communication Report* (Paris: UNESCO, 1989), pp. 159–160. Original data from *Screen Digest,* November 1988.

IV. Number of hours per week spent watching television in various countries.

United States	29 hours 05 minutes
Japan	28 hours 28 minutes
United Kingdom	25 hours 35 minutes
France	20 hours 54 minutes
Belgium	20 hours 08 minutes
Austria	19 hours 24 minutes
Germany	19 hours 15 minutes
Denmark	17 hours 33 minutes
Ireland	16 hours 55 minutes
Netherlands	16 hours 48 minutes
Switzerland	15 hours 25 minutes
Sweden	15 hours 01 minutes
Norway	14 hours 22 minutes
Finland	12 hours 28 minutes

SOURCE: Figures from A. C. Nielsen Co., quoted in Andrew L. Shapiro, *We're Number One: Where America Stands—and Falls—in the New World Order* (New York: Vintage, 1992), p. 166. Copyright © 1991 by Andrew Shapiro. Reprinted by permission of Vintage Books, a Division of Random House, Inc.

V. The Committee to Protect Journalists documented 1,264 cases of attacks against journalists in 1991, the highest number since the annual survey began in 1981.

Total Cases by Region

Latin America and the Caribbean	299
Middle East and North Africa	269
Europe and the former Soviet Union	268
Africa	267
Asia and the Pacific	159

Documented Abuses (Partial List)

Journalists

Killed	61
Missing, feared dead	5
Detained	324
Threatened	164
Attacked physically	156
Attacked through the courts	151
Expelled	42

News media

Publications confiscated	96
Publications/stations banned	66
Editorial offices/broadcast centers raided	27

Journalists Killed or Missing by Country

Azerbaijan	3
Brazil	1
Colombia	10
Ethiopia	1
Guatemala	1
Haiti	3
India	5
Iraq	4
Israel and Occupied Territories	1
Latvia	2
Mexico	2
Pakistan	1
Paraguay	1

Peru	6
Philippines	1
Russia	1
Thailand	1
United States	1
Yugoslavia	21

Journalists in Detention as of February 1992, Including Journalists Missing but Believed to Be Alive

Burundi	1
China	29
Cuba	1
Ghana	1
Haiti	1
India	2
Indonesia	1
Iran	2
Iraq	1
Israel and Occupied Territories	5
Ivory Coast	3
Kuwait	11
Lebanon	2
Libya	1
Maldives	4
Mauritania	1
Myanmar (Burma)	6
Peru	1
Rwanda	1
Sri Lanka	1
Sudan	3
Syria	9
Tunisia	5
Uganda	1
Vietnam	10
Western Sahara	1
Yugoslavia	3

SOURCE: *Attacks on the Press 1991* (New York: Committee to Protect Journalists, 1992). Copyright © 1992 Committee to Protect Journalists. Reprinted by permission.

CHAPTER 6

English-Speaking Media

ABOUT THIS CHAPTER

We begin our global tour of world media in familiar territory: the English-speaking world. There are several reasons for this. One is that exposure to different cultures can be discomfiting as well as exciting. It is easier if we cushion ourselves against too much culture shock at the beginning. We can also understand other media concepts better if we begin with a review of our own. Perhaps the most important reason is that the English-speaking media have unique influence in the world at the end of the twentieth century. We will see them and their influence on other media systems in all parts of the world.

In this chapter, we consider some of the reasons for Anglo-American dominance and then look at the interplay of culture in media in the larger English-speaking countries of the world: the United States, Canada, Britain, and Australia. The Data Base includes comparative statistics from these countries, which will help us put comparable figures from other parts of the world into perspective.

INTRODUCTION

If your travel itinerary includes Cuba or North Korea, you might not find Anglo-American news media easily, but just about everywhere else in the world the newsstands will have *Time, Newsweek, The Economist,* the *International Herald Tribune,* and probably the London *Times* and the *Wall Street Journal.* Even the aggressively domestic *USA Today* publishes international editions. The copies you find may be outdated and ragged, but just about every downtown news-stand and street vendor will have a few. Even in Havana, Cuba, and Pyongyang, North Korea, a small short-wave radio—a valuable asset on any international trip—will keep you in touch with the BBC World Service or Voice of America. In short, mass media from the English-speaking nations have a unique reach and influence around the world. It is just about impossible to travel anywhere in the world outside their range and influence.

One argument is that media dominance is part of the larger pattern of cultural imperialism, a deliberate effort by Anglo-American governments, their military forces, and multinational corporations to use media as a replacement for the British and occasionally U.S. armies that conquered one-quarter of the world's peoples in the previous two centuries. The dominance is obvious as soon as you check the airport newsstand or turn on the TV in your hotel. The explanation for it, however, is not simple, and certainly not as simple as advocates of the cultural imperialism argument suggest.

EXPLAINING DOMINANCE

Cultural Imperialism

To understand the argument that Anglo-American global influence in all areas of communication is a product of deliberate government policy, we need to go back a century. During the nineteenth century, a large part of the world was controlled from a few centers of power. The key cities were London and Paris, supported by a number of "minor league" centers such as Brussels, Berlin, the Hague, and Washington, D.C. Then, according to some modern theorists, the world functioned as a single economic and political system, with the European colonial powers at the center and their colonies at the periphery, purposefully maintained as poor, powerless, and dependent on the centers.

Two examples offer a glimpse of how this system worked. In India, British laws required raw cotton to be exported to England, where industrialists grew rich spinning and weaving the raw cotton into finished goods that were sold back to Indian consumers. In the later years of colonialism, phone calls from Ghana to the neighboring Ivory Coast had to be routed through London and Paris because the only phone lines went from the colony to the colonizer, from the periphery to the center, not laterally from periphery to periphery. Without question, the colonial system of the eighteenth and nineteenth centuries was designed to the advantage of the colonial powers and had the effect—whether intentional or not—of establishing a system of global communication whose benefits continue to accrue to a handful of Western nations. The global flow of information, which is likely to constitute the wealth and power of the twenty-first century, looks a lot like the flow of goods, services, and colonial armies of the nineteenth century.

Look at the flow of news, movies, or TV programs around the globe. Plot international airline routes, phone calls, and mail. The centers are London, Paris, and New York City (and, in some ways, Tokyo). The flow of information and influence is still from these centers to the rest of the world. The now politically independent nations of Africa, Latin America, and Asia are still at the periphery of the system, still the endpoints of vectors that originate in the centers. The system looks a lot like the previous one except for a diminished role for France and the other continental powers and a greatly increased prominence for the United States. But is it really a deliberate policy of using information to maintain a global system of dominance and exploitation: cultural dominance as imperialism?

Herbert Schiller, who linked the older world system and dependency theories to communication, thought so:

> Unavailable to expansionists of earlier times, modern mass communications perform a double service for their present-day controllers. . . . Abroad, the antagonism to a renewed though perhaps less apparent colonial servitude, has been quite successfully (to date) deflected and confused by the images and messages which originate in the United States but which flow continuously over and through local informational media. . . .
>
> Expanding across all continents, the sphere [of U.S. investment and trade] grows significantly larger year by year. A powerful communications system exists to secure, not grudging submission by an open-armed allegiance to the penetrated areas, but by identifying the American presence with freedom—freedom of trade, freedom of speech and freedom of enterprise.[1]

A decade later, when U.S. global economic and military influence clearly had begun to shrunk while cultural influence continued to expand, Schiller concluded that the cultural values associated with the First Amendment were being used as a fig leaf to mask an open conspiracy between government and the multinational corporations that controlled global communication:

> Any attempts by foreign countries to regulate the flow of information across their borders are regarded as interference with the "free flow of information.". . . By conferring on billion-dollar private combines the [First Amendment] right of individual free speech, the government is weakening legitimate concern for genuine individual liberties. And its attempt to impose American laws and institutions on other countries encourages chauvinism abroad and at home.[2]

These strong words represent one position in a debate that dominated global communications in the 1970s. The fallout continues to color most topics we encounter in a global tour in the 1990s. But is cultural imperialism the only explanation of the unique Anglo-American influence in world communication?

---

[1] Herbert I. Schiller, *Mass Communications and American Empire* (Boston: Beacon, 1971), pp. 2–3.

[2] Herbert I. Schiller, "Information: America's Global Empire," *Channels,* September–October 1981, p. 33.

Market and Cultural Factors

Although the U.S. government has actively promoted the export of U.S. ideas of free expression since World War II, neither U.S. foreign policy nor British colonialism explains why British and U.S. media are growing in influence at the end of the twentieth century and are the model for media in most other countries. Several other factors need to be considered.

1. Anglo-American cultural values, which encourage initiative and creativity and tolerate eccentricity. Of course, those qualities are combined with the lure of financial and popular success in the global market. Aspiring actors still head for Hollywood and New York City; rock bands certain that they are the Beatles of the 1990s still head for London. Those three cities form the axis of the emerging global culture.

2. Economy of scale in the global English-language market. A publication in English has, in theory, a potential audience of up to one-quarter of the world's population. A similar advantage accrues to broadcast and film, which can be shipped around the world without dubbing or subtitling.

3. The competitive, market-oriented structure of most Anglo-American media. Regardless of its artistic and cultural merits, a TV series that emerges from the fire of U.S. commercial network competition with the magic 15 percent rating and 30 percent audience share has proved its popular appeal. With a few exceptions, these Anglo-American hits become hits in other countries as well.

4. Anglo-American dominance in other areas of global communication, which creates a synergy or mutually supporting embrace of all aspects of global communication. Dominance in news supports dominance in popular culture, which supports dominance in technology, which supports dominance in journalistic style, which supports dominance in the English language, and so on.

Keep these unique factors in mind as embellishments to the several media theories we considered in Chapter 5. From whatever perspective you adopt, the global influence of Anglo-American media is unique.

UNITED STATES

Press Freedom

We have already used the United States as the basis of comparison in Chapter 5, so now our discussion can focus on aspects of its mass media system that are similar to (and occasionally different from) those in the other English-speaking countries. Given the U.S. cultural values of individualism and suspicion of government, it is no surprise to find a media system that is even more decentralized, more independent of government, and more commercial than in other English-speaking countries. When third-world governments talk about the responsibilities of media to support development programs and Marxists talk about media as instruments of agitation, propaganda, and social control, most Americans get uncomfortable. Some of them—the Reagan and Bush administrations, for example—don't even like the idea of tax-supported "public" radio and television.

If press freedom is defined as freedom from government influence before and after publication, then the U.S. media are the freest in the world. Remember Mr. Hamilton of the *Wall Street Journal,* who claimed that a newspaper's only responsibility is to its owner. It is a commercial product offered to the public, who decides whether to buy it or not. A similar marketplace rule applies to broadcasting. Despite a few references to public responsibility in a license, which were never enforced vigorously, a radio or TV station exists to make money for its owners. That presumably is why U.S. broadcasting is so heavy on mass-appeal entertainment and so low on cultural, educational, and public affairs programming. The station owners are absolutely correct when they say they'd give us the highest quality programming in the world—all we have to do is watch it.

In the U.S. context, press freedom is essentially the right to speak or print with no prior restraint and minimum legal accountability afterward. The definition could be extended to include certain elements of public access, such as freedom of information laws, open public meetings, and records accessibility statutes, but many of the restrictions other democratic countries take for granted are anathema in the United States. Is freedom from government control the only true definition of press freedom, or is it an inadequate definition or a false definition that gives freedom only to the handful of moguls who own the media? Journalists from the English-speaking countries like to debate these questions—and you can, too.

Media Characteristics

U.S. media are also among the most decentralized in the world. This was almost a necessity in a continent-size country until satellite communication developed, but it also reflects the lack of a single political-commercial-cultural capital such as London and a federal system that was designed to keep political power away from Washington. Unlike media in most nations, U.S. newspapers are local or, at most, regional, with three exceptions: the *Wall Street Journal,* a specialized paper that pioneered printing at dispersed sites; the national edition of the *New York Times;* and *USA Today,* which tried to redefine news in the name of all of us. The short life of the first national sports daily, the *National,* is evidence of the difficulty of creating truly national newspapers in the United States, even in the age of satellite-based remote printing and efficient distribution.

The national dailies, except for the *Wall Street Journal* with its specialized audience, have not established themselves as successes. They are relatively small in circulation: London alone publishes a half dozen national dailies with more than a million circulation whereas *USA Today* reaches under 2 million in a country four times as large after pumping hundreds of millions of dollars into the effort. The *New York Times,* even with its national edition, has a circulation of 1.1 million.

The "average" U.S. daily is probably a regional or big-city daily with 50,000 to 100,000 circulation. It gives lots of attention to sports, comics, and recipes and not very much to world affairs or local controversies. Unlike the British dailies, which openly appeal to distinct segments of the public, U.S. dailies balance their generally bland editorial pages with "op-ed" pages devoted to different views and readers' letters. However, the "marketplace of ideas" in the average U.S. daily ranges from A to about C.

Compare the tame editorial and op-ed pages of most U.S. papers with the vigorous and open partisanship of most London dailies to see how invigorating partisanship can be. Of course, farther from our Anglo-American home, the differences are even greater. In Paris, a dozen papers compete for readers' attention with partisanship as sharp as the right-wing ideology of Robert Hersant and the left-wing perspective of the French Communist party. They don't even try to separate news from opinion and, curiously enough, print no letters from readers.

Media Fragmentation

U.S. newspapers, which are read daily by about half the adult population and by an additional third on an occasional basis, are the last remaining *mass* medium in a system that is increasingly fragmented. Mass appeal magazines such as the old *Life, Look,* and *Saturday Evening Post* are dead, replaced by hundreds of small-circulation, specialized publications that appeal more to specific readers and advertisers. Radio, too, has gone from a national network service to local stations competing for tiny, carefully defined audience segments. Even some of the syndicated radio news services are fragmented to the point that different newscasts are matched to specific radio formats.

Television is in the process of fragmenting. Twenty years ago, the three commercial networks dominated the audience. They geared their programming to maximize viewership, which meant in practice aiming at the lowest common denominator. There wasn't much competition except maybe a weak public station and a UHF commercial station running old situation comedies (sitcoms) and movies. Network programming hasn't changed in philosophy, but the arrival of cable has reduced the networks' prime-time audience share to less than 70 percent. Many of the cable channels are geared toward small but clearly defined audiences—sports, arts, news, religion—that nibble away at mass appeal network programming. If the new technologies of high-definition television (HDTV) and direct broadcast satellites (DBSs) arrive as promised in the twenty-first century, the proliferation of choice and fragmentation of audiences will continue.

Elite versus Mass Media

With more radio and TV receivers per person than in any other country, Americans are surrounded by electronic media. Not so with print. Not only is the United States below many industrialized democracies in newspaper circulation and readership, but it is weak in magazine circulation as well. Magazine readership by definition makes one a member of the elite. The largest general-circulation magazines are *TV Guide* and *Reader's Digest,* with 16 million copies each. The major news magazines, which we seldom think of as elite, really are because they reach less than one-quarter of the population. *Time*'s U.S. circulation is 4.4 million; *Newsweek* sells 3.3 million copies, *U.S. News & World Report* 2.3 million. Opinion journals such as *New Republic* and *National Review* reach even fewer people. Compared with most third-world nations and European countries such as Italy, Spain, and France, the United States is still rich in print media, but it is well behind Japan, most of the northern European countries, and even some developing countries. Comparisons with the media systems of other major English-speaking countries produce similarities and several surprising differences.

CANADA

Both geographically and psychologically, Canada lies between Britain and the United States, not always certain where to look for inspiration and comparison. Its emergence from colonialism was slow and peaceful, and ties with Britain are still strong. However, in geography, demography, and economy, it is so much like the United States that outsiders sometimes forget the two countries are separate and distinct.

Geography alone made it inevitable that ties between Canada and the United States would be strong. Although Canada is the world's second largest country geographically, it can be viewed as a narrow nation of 26 million people huddled along the U.S. border. A majority of the Canadian population lives within 100 kilometers of the United States, and the flow of people, goods, and information has always been more north and south than east and west. The province of British Columbia and the state of Washington have more in common with each other than either does with its national capital several thousand kilometers to the east. The free trade agreement between Canada and the United States in 1988 strengthened the world's largest trading relationship and further reduced obstacles to movement across the world's longest unguarded international border. In a world of rising nationalism and ethnic hostility, the cooperation between the United States and Canada remains an exemplary exception.

Yet we should not think of Canada's 10 provinces and territories as merely second-class states without congressional representation in Washington. Two separate cultural conflicts play a central role in Canadian life now and are likely to continue well into the twenty-first century.

Cultural Factors

One, which we have already mentioned in Chapter 3, involves the status of French-speaking Quebec. After decades of relative quiet and slow decline, the Québécois began in the 1960s to demand special status for their language and culture. At one point, the debate reached the level of serious calls for the province's secession from Canada. A series of compromises giving French special status in Quebec and committing the whole country to very limited bilingualism eliminated the possibility of a civil war but did not defuse the issue.

The question of Quebec resurfaced in the 1980s when Canada repatriated its constitution from Britain and rewrote it. Quebec decided it would not sign the constitution unless it included special recognition of Quebec's linguistic and cultural uniqueness. The delicately crafted Meech Lake agreement, intended to relieve Quebec's reservations, was then rejected by two English-speaking provinces precisely because of the special status it accorded the French language and culture. A second effort at balancing French and English demands, with indigenous peoples emerging as a small but powerful third force, failed in 1992. As a result, Canada faced the rest of the 1990s with a constitution Quebec had not ratified and the renewed possibility of national disintegration. Ironically, the Canada–United States free trade zone made Quebec secession easier and perhaps more likely. A gloomy Canadian pastime was to develop scenarios for the disintegration of the country: The maritime provinces would petition Washington, D.C., to become states, Quebec would become a separate nation, and so on.[3]

The second issue was the cultural identity of Canada in a continent dominated by the United States. In the 1970s, Canada had passed several laws designed to protect its own media. The most effective—and most strongly opposed by U.S. media—denied Canadian companies a tax deduction on advertising in foreign media. The effect was narrow but significant. *Time* and *Reader's Digest* dropped special Canadian editions but lost very little overall circulation in Canada, and several U.S. commercial broadcasters near the Canadian border lost most of their Canadian advertising accounts.

The effect in Canada was not readily apparent, although the change did help *Maclean's* become a successful and influential weekly news magazine. Laws limiting foreign TV programming were less successful because most Canadians still could watch U.S. channels, and they continue to do so in large numbers. Except for news, Canadian television remains a weak also-ran in a market dominated by U.S. spillover and cable channels, capturing a minority of the audience with a diet still heavy on U.S. and British imports and homemade imitations. In some cases, the U.S. commercial networks sell episodes to Canadian television for airing before they appear in the United States. This serves financial interests on both sides of the border by increasing the domestic ratings of Canadian TV and increasing the selling price of the Hollywood productions.

It is noteworthy that the U.S.-Canadian free trade agreement exempted culture industries. No one expects the modest Canadian film and TV industry to challenge Hollywood or the southward flow of Canadian talent to stop, but the agreement underscores the resentment of U.S. dominance even in countries that share the Anglo-American traditions and values of free expression.

---

[3] One less than serious response to Quebec's demand for recognition as a "distinct society" was to declare ROC (the Rest of Canada) indistinct instead. Mordecai Richler, *Oh Canada! Oh Quebec! Requiem for a Divided Country* (Toronto: Penguin, 1992), p. 150.

Print Media

Canadian newspapers look a lot like their counterparts south of the border. Newspaper circulation per capita is similar, competition is rare, and chains dominate. Fat, advertising-heavy papers carry a similar bland diet of news and entertainment. Except for the internationally minded *Globe and Mail* in Toronto, which circulates across Canada, the papers tend to be regional in outlook and muted in their coverage of government.

Although obviously in the environment of "free media," Canadian journalists face legal obstacles their colleagues south of the border would find intolerable. Libel laws are stricter, access to public records is more limited, and reporting of legal proceedings is circumscribed, all similar to the situation in Britain. This is a product of the long British legal influence and a society built on the principles of "peace, order, and good government" rather than "life, liberty, and the pursuit of happiness."

BRITAIN

Cultural Factors

Great Britain can serve both as a model for Western European media systems and as a key element of the English-language media empire. Like most other European countries, it is *relatively* small and *relatively* homogeneous and is dominated by a single political, economic, and cultural capital. The emphasis on *relative* is a reminder that culture and geography are, well, relative. You can't take the train from London to Edinburgh for an afternoon movie and return in time for dinner, but compared to Canada and the United States, Britain is small and homogeneous, and London dominates it as no Canadian or U.S. city dominates its nation. A map of roads, rail lines, or air routes shows how all radiate out from London.

National Media

Media, too, are concentrated in the capital. British newspapers can be separated into three groups. The first cut is between the national press—the 12 general-circulation dailies published in London but readily available throughout the country—and the local or regional papers published elsewhere. With a few exceptions, the provincial papers are small and undistinguished.

The London dailies, in contrast, are woven into the fabric of national life to a degree that disappeared in North America a half century ago. Buying one or more papers at a street-corner kiosk or train station (home delivery is uncommon) is still part of the daily routine for millions of Britons. A survey of major print stories is a routine part of broadcast news, and a preview of tomorrow's front pages is a regular feature of late-night TV news.

The London papers can be split into two groups, the five "quality" papers that are frequently quoted abroad and the seven "popular" tabloid dailies that

A dozen dailies are published in London and distributed throughout Britain. The splashy tabloids outsell the influential quality papers by a wide margin.

range from the feisty *Daily Mirror* to the truly awful *Sun*. Most of the spectacular circulation figures derive from the popular dailies. The *Sun,* with its daily feature of a naked woman on page 3, alone sells 4 million copies. In contrast, only one of the quality dailies, the conservative *Daily Telegraph,* circulates more than a million. The *Guardian;* the young *Independent,* now often considered the best and most influential of the qualities; and the venerable *Times* are stuck at about

400,000. Whether the North American reader with his or her bland but professionally crafted regional daily is better served than a British cousin depends on the papers you pick for comparison as well as the criteria for deciding what's good and bad.

At the top, the London quality dailies define news more broadly than their U.S. counterparts, offering superb coverage of arts and ideas as well as informed and thoughtful reporting of world affairs. The writing style is often personal, and the use of language is masterful, although accuracy occasionally suffers. A morning spent with two or three of the quality dailies and a cup of bad English coffee is one of the great pleasures offered by London.

Recent Technical Change

British papers together maintain circulation of about one copy for every three people, whereas in North America the figure is one copy for every four people and dropping. Several factors seem to be operating. One is that British papers have yet to face the competition from a deluge of commercial television. A second is the distinctive class and political appeal that permeates the British papers, encouraging a routine second or third buy. A third is the combination of supply-side economic growth in the 1980s and the dramatic defeat of powerful labor unions over the issue of reduced staffing of new electronic editing equipment.

This produced a spurt of innovation and profitability that proprietors across the Atlantic could envy but not emulate. While circulation stagnated in North America, two new dailies and two Sunday papers (one short-lived) were successfully introduced in London. *Today,* which was clearly patterned on *USA Today,* faltered in a competitive market already glutted with midscale tabloids, but the *Independent* soon joined the elite dailies that represent the best of English-language journalism. A pub discussion among journalists or thoughtful readers frequently ranks the *Independent* as the best of the best, while the daily *Times,* under Rupert Murdoch's tutelage, is dismissed with a nostalgic reference to its glorious past and the assertion of a steady decline since Murdoch took over.

Ironically not a single daily is now published on Fleet Street, the most famous "newspaper row" in the world. Most have moved to the renovated Docklands on the Thames River and are edited and printed in postmodern buildings that seem more appropriate to the space age than to the newspaper age of the nineteenth century. A law outlawing secondary strikes was what finally allowed the newspaper owners—first Eddie Shah with his tabloid *Today,* then Murdoch, and then the rest—to end the stranglehold the byzantine newspaper unions had maintained for decades. With the speed of the collapse of the Berlin Wall, the Victorian system of manufacturing newspapers from lead plates, with separate unions controlling each tiny piece of the process, gave way to electronic technology that eliminated most of the traditional backshop work force. British proprietors finally fought the battle North American publishers had won a quarter century earlier.

Broadcasting Tradition

British broadcasting began with premises quite different from those that guided the development of radio and television in the United States. Whereas U.S. electronic media from the start were privately owned, local, and left to find their audience in a commercial marketplace with a minimum of government oversight, the British decided early to make their radio and then television a centralized, noncommercial monopoly charged with social responsibilities and subject to public scrutiny. Unlike many other countries where the "public service model" (as opposed to the U.S. "market model") of broadcasting became a pretext for direct government control, Britain evolved a system admired worldwide for its independence, quality, and innovation.

British broadcasting is a reminder that *public* is not inevitably synonymous with *government* when applied to broadcast ownership and control and that noncommercial (or mildly commercial systems such as Britain's Independent Television) are not necessarily doomed to crank out only mind-numbing "quality" educational and cultural programming. For reasons that defy simple explanation, British broadcasting is able to produce *Monty Python's Flying Circus, Spitting Image,* and *Benny Hill* as well as the complete Shakespeare plays, the costume-drama gems that end up on PBS's *Masterpiece Theater* series, and the socially conscious sitcoms that were models for *All in the Family* and *Sanford and Son.*

Part of the explanation is the periodic review of broadcasting in preparation for the exercise of renewing broadcast charters. Although the theoretical possibility of stripping the BBC of its authority isn't taken seriously, the review permits a serious discussion of the system and the possible changes. As a result of such reviews, the Independent Broadcast Authority (IBA) was set up in 1954 as a mild competitor to the BBC. IBA's Independent Television (ITV) was created as a a privately owned, regionally based, commercially funded network more akin to the U.S. system than to the BBC's centralized, noncommercial monopoly. Similar commission reviews led to the establishment of Channel 4 in 1983 (dedicated to offering alternative programs, serving minority audiences, and supporting independent producers) and the introduction of a fifth BBC radio channel (serving children, among other "minority groups") in 1990. The established ITV regional broadcasters were shocked in 1992 when several lost their franchises in a shakeup of the system that could lead to a thorough restructuring—and possible Americanization—of the entire broadcast system.

Broadcasting Today

The same system of periodic review produced a Thatcher government proposal to promote new technologies of cable and direct broadcast satellite TV, to privatize the BBC, and to subject the entire industry to the rigors of marketplace competition in the 1990s. A big change occurred in 1991 when the government auctioned franchises of the 16 regional companies that made up ITV. In half, the winning applicants had offered the most money, whereas in the others, the Independent Television Commission decided that other factors were more important. The biggest surprise was the loss of four existing franchise holders, including Thames Television, which was responsible for the weekday London service and produced half of ITV's programming, and TV-AM, which produced ITV's breakfast program.

From your London hotel, you can probably tune in the two BBC TV channels (BBC1 and BBC2), the commercial ITV channel (whose programs will vary slightly from the equivalent channel in other parts of the country), Channel 4 (which is also regional and broadcasts substantial programming in Welsh to viewers in Wales), and possibly Murdoch's Sky TV package of direct broadcast satellite (DBS) channels. Because it is distributed via a satellite whose footprint extends beyond the British Isles, Sky TV, including a round-the-clock news channel similar to CNN, is widely available in hotels in Europe.

Your radio will bring in the five national BBC services, unimaginatively named Radio 1, Radio 2, and so on. Each is geared to a specific audience. This demonstrates that a single broadcaster operating a limited number of services under the principle of complementary rather than competitive programming can achieve greater variety than independent broadcasters competing for the same audience with virtually identical programming. Radio 1 is a grab bag of rock and other pop music. Radio 2 emphasizes classical music, much of it recorded by the BBC's diminishing stable of in-house performance groups. Radio 3 is the "light" music and entertainment service. Radio 4 supplies a diet of drama, talk, and quirky programs that are unique to the "Beeb." The new Radio 5 is seeking to establish its identity with children's programs.

In recent years, the BBC has developed regional programs so that the original concept of a centralized national service no longer applies as forcefully as it once did. The first of a patchwork quilt of local, commercial stations operating under the umbrella of the IBA are also on the air. In London you can find an all news/talk station and an all jazz station. The trend is toward a broadcast system that resembles the U.S. model more and the original BBC concept less. Still, it is hard to think of another country where quality, diversity, popular appeal, and innovativeness mingle as well as they do in Britain. On our scorecard of media systems, one factor tarnishes an otherwise superlative record: press freedom.

Press Restrictions

Britain has no written constitution, no separation of powers, and virtually no check on a determined prime minister (Margaret Thatcher, for example) except the threat of a vote of no-confidence in Parliament. A no-confidence vote can send the government into the streets for a blessedly short campaign and overnight transition of power. Until that happens, however, the government in power is able to do pretty much what it wants, including restricting critical reporting to a degree that a besieged U.S. president can only envy.

Three types of restrictions are in force. The first is the Official Secrets Act, which was strengthened in the 1980s. It allows the government to send a "D-slip" or "D-notice" to publishers, enjoining them from publishing anything about a specific incident or activity the government doesn't want publicized. The committee that discusses possible D-slips and decides when to issue them and to whom, curiously enough, includes both government and media representatives. From a U.S. perspective, this example of prior restraint—the use of the law to prohibit publication rather than to settle claims after publication—is particularly dangerous. The fact that journalists participate in the process makes it worse.

Although limited appeal is possible and newspapers occasionally violate a D-notice, the act sanctions prior censorship to a degree that would be unthinkable in the United States. Though both countries derive their understanding of liberty from the Magna Carta and the Declaration of Independence, the U.S. Freedom of Information Act, on the one hand, and the British Official Secrets Act, on the other, represent the differences in understanding of press freedom.

On a day-to-day basis, a more serious obstacle to press freedom in Britain is the routine restrictions on court reporting. In most cases, once a case comes under the jurisdiction of the courts, journalists can report only what takes place in open court and sometimes not even that. The result is that the determined probing of activities of government or private industry is just about impossible.

Could a British Woodward and Bernstein team uncover a British Watergate? The answer is probably no, although an Anglophile will point out that the strong political opposition in Parliament, where the prime minister and Cabinet must face a regular question period, serves a similar watchdog function. With the first hint of scandal, the opposition party likely would have launched a barrage of questions and inquiry that would have brought the government down in weeks.

A third area of control is the government's power to pass routine legislation without judicial review. In 1988, for example, the government used national legislation to ban broadcasters from carrying the voices of members of 11 "terrorist" organizations, most of them associated with the independence movement in Northern Ireland. Ironically, the ban included Sinn Fein, the Irish Republican Army (IRA) political party, which had run candidates for Parliament and even got one elected. An exception to the law—difficult to put into practice—was made for candidates and members of Parliament (MPs) as long as they were campaigning or dealing with constituency affairs, but in general, newscasts could cover members of the banned organizations only with a voice-over summary of their statements or even someone else repeating their actual words. The law, still in effect as the country entered the 1990s, probably did little to silence fringe groups committed to violence but did challenge the Anglo-Saxon claim of commitment to freedom of speech. Defenders of the Iranian "death sentence" on Salman Rushdie, for example, sometimes cited the British precedent as being one step removed from Ayatollah Khomeini's solution to threatening speech.

AUSTRALIA

Cultural Factors

If Britain is the mother of the English-speaking countries, then Canada, the United States, Australia, and New Zealand are first cousins. In most cases, cousins bear some family resemblance but usually develop distinct personalities. It is not too far-fetched to suggest that Canada and New Zealand share a certain British reserve while Australia and the United States have a common exuberance and openness. Perhaps these characteristics are products of geography and climate.

Australia is about the same size as the United States without Alaska, but more than half of it is inhospitable desert. Think of the Lower Forty-eight as a flat, arid land with 16 million people living around the edges, most of them in an arc along the south and east coasts. Like its English-speaking cousins, Australia's first immigrants were English settlers (many in convicts' chains) who pushed the indigenous people aside. Coping with that legacy is part of the unfinished social agenda of all English-speaking countries and a current political issue in Australia.

Until the mid-1970s, Australia's immigration policy excluded most non-Europeans. Now its doors are generally open, and Australia is becoming a zesty mix similar to that of North American culture, especially the flavors of Asian nations. Unassimilated aborigines, who constitute 1 percent of the population, remain an important exception as a separate and distinct group.

Media System

Like the United States and Canada, Australia is a federal system with broad powers left to the six states and two territories. Because of that and the distances involved, media—especially newspapers—tend to be regional rather than national. Only one general-interest daily, the *Australian,* can claim to be a national paper like *USA Today* or the *Globe and Mail.*

Broadcasting follows the Canadian and British pattern of a mixed public/private system. The Australian Broadcasting Corporation (ABC) operates a national radio and TV network. The ABC TV network competes with several commercial networks, all of which look more like U.S. commercial networks than like the BBC. They are heavy with commercials and imported U.S. series. A few major Australian series have been exported, but none has achieved recognition in the crucial U.S. market. U.S. programming in Australia includes NBC's *Today* show, which appears live at midnight.

Although Australia is fully independent of British authority, as are Canada and New Zealand, the British monarch remains the nominal head of state of the three nonrevolutionary English cousins. As in Canada and New Zealand, the British penchant for secrecy presents problems for Australian journalism. A celebrated case occurred in 1985, when a retired British intelligence officer wrote a memoir that was embarrassing to British intelligence but clearly no threat to current operations or national security. The British government brought suit in Australia and temporarily stopped publication of the memoir. The government lost the case eventually and gave up further efforts to prevent publication when the publisher brought out a U.S. edition. The British government had no legal standing in the United States and could expect that any attempt to prevent publication would fail. For several years, the absurd situation meant that copies of *Spycatcher* were available everywhere except Britain, where even media discussion of the case was prohibited.

Rupert Murdoch

Australia's most famous media mogul, the son of a native-born, minor-league media baron, took control of a local paper in Adelaide and built it into a global empire. Murdoch's News Corporation controls 60 percent of the Australian daily newspaper market (including the *Australian*) and half an airline, but his operations there are a tail that wags a global dog. From its Australian base, the corporation sweeps across the full arc of Anglo-American media. It owns papers in Fiji, Papua New Guinea, and Hong Kong and has pursued interests in the newly independent countries of Central Europe.

Of course, the empire is anchored in Britain (the *Sun,* the *Times,* and Sky Television) and the United States, where Murdoch now claims citizenship. His U.S. holdings include the 20th Century Fox studio and budding Fox TV network as well as *TV Guide,* newspapers in Boston and San Antonio, Texas, and HarperCollins book publishing (formerly Harper & Row). Even though the Japanese-owned Hollywood studios are bigger, Murdoch remains the first and most famous of the new generation of global media giants.

ENGLISH MEDIA ABROAD

Monoglot U.S. tourists often can be spotted in Rome, Paris, or Berlin with a look of confusion on their faces and a copy of the *International Herald Tribune* clutched in their hands. In a city filled with an unfamiliar language and incomprehensible headlines, the *IHT* (or *Trib* to old-timers) can be a lifeline to the familiar, as much a part of the experience of international travel as a cup of strong European morning coffee.

Global Dailies

The *Herald Tribune,* however, is more than a hometown paper for tourists. It is one of a handful of truly global newspapers—all in English, all Anglo-American—that have influence far above their modest circulation figures. They are part of a special group of elite Anglo-American media: the English-language paper in non-English-speaking countries. These newspapers, well over 100 in number, can be divided into three different groups.

The first group comprises the four dailies that are distributed globally or nearly globally. The oldest and most famous is the *International Herald Tribune,* edited in Paris and printed in 11 locations from Paris to New York City to Tokyo for distribution around the world. It was founded in 1887 by James Gordon Bennett, Jr., as a European edition of the *New York Herald* published by his father. Until the mid-twentieth century, the Paris *Herald* was mostly a community paper for expatriate Americans and tourists, famous for the quirkiness of its founder and later the antics of writers such as Art Buchwald, who worked there for 13 years.

After the high-quality parent *New York Herald Tribune* died in 1966, the Whitney family—as in Whitney Museum of American Art—sold a part interest in the Paris newspaper to the *Washington Post* and to the *New York Times,* (the latter then folded its own young and struggling Paris edition). With new management, the *IHT* evolved into a serious daily, noted for coverage of world affairs and very American but detached perspective on its homeland. Sports and comics remained a special link to the United States. The *IHT* pioneered the use of satellite technology to transmit pages, still edited in Paris, to remote printing plants in Europe, then Asia, and finally New York City, which supplies copies to Latin America and major cities of the northeastern United States. Although the paper is still popular with homesick Americans, a majority of its 180,000 copies are sold to foreigners, especially to global-minded businesspeople, bureaucrats, and government officials, who appreciate its concise, professional reporting of the world and insightful coverage of the United States. Its relatively small circulation belies the *IHT's* global influence.

IHT competition comes from the European edition of the *Wall Street Journal* and the *Asian Wall Street Journal,* edited in Hong Kong, and from the London-based *Financial Times,* which prints in Frankfurt for continental circulation and in New York City for same-day delivery and newsstand sales in the United States. *USA Today* began printing scaled-down versions of its domestic edition in Europe and Asia. However, circulation is small and its appeal is limited to Americans abroad or foreigners who somehow developed a taste for the domestic news that is the publication's trademark.

Except for *USA Today,* the global papers share several characteristics. They emphasize international business and politics and represent a style of journalism—independent and nonpartisan coverage, succinct writing—that is lacking even in many democratic countries. They benefit from the information-gathering and -distributing resources of the dominant Anglo-American global communication system. However, they are not the only English-language papers abroad.

Local Dailies

A second group of papers is the local English-language dailies that are published in almost every non-English-speaking country of Latin America, Asia, and the Middle East. Europe, of course, doesn't need local English-language dailies because of the presence of the global dailies, although small English-language papers are produced in several European countries as well.

The local papers are often owned by the companies that publish the national papers in Spanish, Arabic, or Japanese. In Japan, for example, each of the three giant newspaper houses also publishes a small English-language daily. A fourth English daily in Tokyo gives the city more English-language daily newspapers than any U.S. city outside of New York City.

These local dailies—the *Asahi Evening News* (Japan), the *Bangkok Post,* and the *Daily Journal* of Caracas, Venezuela, are good examples—serve the largely Anglo-American local community and often look like a small U.S. daily, complete with sports, comics, and cable TV listings. Local coverage is typically limited to the activities of the Anglo-American community and superficial national coverage rewritten from the national-language papers or taken from the Anglo-American news agencies.

Technical quality of writing, editing, and printing varies, although most of these papers are now professional in appearance and professionally crafted. With a few exceptions such as the *Buenos Aires Herald* and the *Jerusalem Post,* which is an important paper in its own right, very few challenge local authorities or attempt aggressive local reporting. Still, they are part of the global mix of journalism and offer young journalists a good shot at an international career.

Government Voices

It is sometimes hard to draw the line between the local English-language dailies that are private enterprises run for profit or prestige, more or less independently of government, and those that are part of governments' efforts to reach an international audience. The latter represent a third group of international English-language newspapers.

In many cases, the local media are either government owned or controlled, and English-language papers are obvious extensions. Examples include the *Moscow News* (before *glasnost*), the *China Daily* (mainland) and *China News* (Taiwan), the *Jordan Times,* and the *Indonesia Times.* The amount and visibility of government influence range from the *Pyongyang Times* and *Baghdad Observer* (shrill, heavy-handed, fawning over the national dictator to the point of embarrassment) to the slick and good-looking *Arab News* and *China Daily,* which are more professional and independent than their local-language counterparts. In most cases, these papers operate under the same rules as the local-language press and allow outsiders a glimpse of the country and its perspective on the world that is unavailable to those who walk around with the *IHT* under their arms. In many countries, English-language radio and TV newscasts serve a similar function.

The accidental tourist, of course, doesn't want to peer into different worlds, but the rest of us can travel just about anywhere with the assurance that our knowledge of the global language will keep us in touch with familiar Anglo-American media. Through these media, we can sometimes also experience the pleasure of other cultures.

MAIN POINTS

1. The media of the English-speaking nations occupy a unique influence in the world at the end of the twentieth century. This is part of a broader pattern of Anglo-American cultural dominance.
2. U.S. media are more independent of government and public control than any others and also are more commercial. Newspapers are professionally edited but local or regional in focus. They rarely provide thoughtful or extensive coverage of global affairs.
3. Canadian media resemble those in the United States. Canada faces the challenge of maintaining national (cultural) identity from two

sources: the separatist movement in French-speaking Quebec and the powerful influence of the United States.

4. British media are similar to those in many European countries. National newspapers are distinctly ''serious'' and ''popular'' in appeal; broadcasting is organized on a public service rather than commercial model. Compared to those in the United States, British journalists are subject to severe restrictions on freedom in reporting government affairs.

5. Australian media resemble their U.S. cousins more than the British. Papers tend to be local; broadcasting is a mixture of public and private services.

FOR MORE INFORMATION

An excellent source of current information about major countries in the world is books by journalists returning from overseas assignments. In each of the following chapters, you will find references to several such books. They often include a separate chapter on mass media and always include background that helps readers understand today's headlines.

Books that were useful in writing this chapter include David Hooper, *Official Secrets: The Use and Abuse of the Act* (London: Coronet, 1987); Richard Critchfield, *An American Looks at Britain* (New York: Anchor, 1990); Harold Evans, ''The Norman Conquest: Freedom of the Press in Britain and America,'' in Simon Serfaty, ed., *The Media and Foreign Policy* (New York: St. Martin's, 1991); Anthony Sampson, *The Changing Anatomy of Britain* (New York: Vintage, 1984); Ralph Negrine, *Politics and the Mass Media in Britain* (London: Routledge, 1989); *Restricted Subjects: Freedom of Expression in the United Kingdom* (New York: Human Rights Watch, 1991); Peter Desbarats, *Guide to Canadian News Media* (Toronto: Harcourt Brace Jovanovich, 1989); Mary Vipond, *The Mass Media in Canada* (Toronto: James Lorimer, 1989); Andrew H. Malcolm, *The Canadians* (New York: Times Books, 1985); and Mordecai Richler, *Oh Canada! Oh Quebec! Requiem for a Divided Country* (Toronto: Penguin, 1992).

Material on U.S. mass media is overwhelming. A good place to start is any one of several general textbooks used in introductory survey courses. Check the sources cited in these texts for more information and more specific sources.

The best-known source of professional criticism of the media is the bi-monthly *Columbia Journalism Review*. Academic research journals abound as well. They range from the general *Journalism Quarterly* to journals in each subfield (*Journal of Broadcasting, Journal of Communication, Newspaper Research Journal, Journal of Media Economics,* etc.). All include reviews of current books. Most bookstores have a section devoted to media or communication.

FOR DISCUSSION

1. Debate the origin of Anglo-American dominance of global communication, with one side advocating a cultural imperialism explanation and the other advocating some or all of the alternative explanations cited early in this chapter.

2. Assume you are a U.S. journalist in London or a British journalist in Washington, D.C. Argue that the media system in your native country is better than the one you find where you work. Begin by defining the criteria you will use to compare systems and what constitutes good and bad.

3. Compare newspapers and magazines from several English-speaking countries (and broadcast samples if you can) and look for both similarities and differences.

4. Debate the following proposition: A monopoly or near-monopoly public broadcast system serves the public interest (better) (worse) than a privately owned competitive system.

DATA BASE

I. The following list shows communication statistics from English-speaking countries (number per 100 population).

Country	Newspaper Circulation	Radio Sets	Television Sets	VCRs	Phone Lines
Australia	25	127	48	22	45
Canada	23	160	59	23	55
Ireland	21	60	31	11	26
New Zealand	33	103	37	19	43
United Kingdom	39	144	62	28	41
United States	26	224	74	26	50

SOURCE: Newspaper circulation figures are mid- to late-1980s and from UNESCO figures and other sources; phone line data are from American Telephone & Telegraph's (AT&T) *The World's Telephones,* 1991, and the International Telecommunication Union's (ITU) *Yearbook of Common Carrier Telecommunication Statistics* (18th ed.). Radio, TV, and VCR data from *World Radio and TV Receivers,* ed. by Carol L. Forrester. Copyright © 1991 IBAR-BBC World Service. Reprinted by permission.

II. Circulation figures for the leading newspapers from the main English-speaking countries:

United States

*Wall Street Journal**	1,795,000
*USA Today**	1,418,000
Los Angeles Times	1,177,000
*New York Times**	1,111,000

No other U.S. daily paper has more than 1 million daily circulation. The three marked (*) circulate nationally.

Canada

Toronto Star	509,000
Globe and Mail	323,000

Britain

Sun	3,665,000
Daily Mirror	3,641,000
Daily Mail	1,684,000
Daily Express	1,519,000
Daily Telegraph*	1,058,000
Daily Star	837,000
Evening Standard	486,000
Today	460,000
Guardian*	410,000
Times*	387,000
Independent*	372,000
Financial Times*	287,000

Those marked with an asterisk are the "quality" daily papers; all others are popular tabloids. All are published in London for national circulation.

Australia

Australian (national)	153,000
Daily Mirror (Sydney)	396,000
Daily Telegraph (Sydney)	274,000
Sydney Morning Herald	267,000
Sun-Herald (Sydney)	671,000
Age (Melbourne)	234,000
Herald-Sun (Melbourne)	623,000
West Australian (Perth)	261,000

Ireland

Irish Independent (Dublin)	150,000
Evening Herald (Dublin)	100,000

SOURCE: Robert U. Brown, ed., *Editor & Publisher International Yearbook 1992* (New York: Editor & Publisher, 1992), and Arthur S. Banks, ed., *Political Handbook of the World 1992* (Binghampton, NY: CSA Publications, 1992).

III. The following shows British TV audience shares (in percentages).

ITV	39.6
BBC1	34.7
Channel 4	10.3
BBC2	10.1
Other	5.3

SOURCE: From regular reports in *Variety;* data are from late 1992 and early 1993.

IV. Many Canadian entertainers and journalists emigrate to the United States, especially broadcast journalists and stars of *Saturday Night Live.*

Canadian-born journalists include Morley Safer (CBS), Peter Jennings (ABC), Robert MacNeil (PBS), Arthur Kent (formerly of NBC), Peter Kent (formerly of *World Monitor*), Bob McKeown (CBS), Doug James (CNN), Barrie Dunsmore (ABC), and Sheila MacVicar (ABC).

SOURCE: *USA Today,* February 26, 1991, p. D1.

V. Canadian-born entertainers include Paul Anka, Dan Aykroyd, Conrad Bain, Genevieve Bujold, Raymond Burr, John Candy, Hume Cronyn, Yvonne DeCarlo, Glenn Ford, Michael J. Fox, Phil Hartman, Melissa Hayden, Doug Henning, Margot Kidder, k. d. Lang, Art Linkletter, Rich Little, Howie Mandel, Joni Mitchell, Rick Moranis, Anne Murray, Mike Myers, Kate Nelligan, Leslie Nielsen, Christopher Plummer, Jason Priestley, Mort Sahl, Paul Shaffer, William Shatner, Martin Short, Alexis Smith, Hank Snow, Donald Sutherland, Alan Thicke, Alex Trebek, and Neil Young.

SOURCE: Mark S. Hoffman, ed., *The World Almanac and Book of Facts 1993,* (New York: Pharos, 1992), pp. 350–363.

VI. In 1991, Canadian Conrad Black took control of the bankrupt Fairfax media organization in Australia, giving him and Murdoch control of most of the country's daily and Sunday newspaper circulation.

Ownership of capital city and national daily newspapers:

Title	*Ownership*	*Circulation September 1992*	*Percent of Total Circulation*
New South Wales			
Daily Telegraph/Mirror	Murdoch	468,152	17.8
Sydney Morning Herald	Fairfax	270,447	10.3
Victoria			
Herald-Sun	Murdoch	598,009	22.7
Age	Fairfax	236,110	9.0
Queensland			
Courier Mail	Murdoch	249,119	9.4
South Australia			
Advertiser	Murdoch	205,528	7.8
Western Australia			
West Australian	W. Aust.	260,306	9.9

Title	Ownership	Circulation September 1992	Percent of Total Circulation
Tasmania			
Mercury	Murdoch	53,890	2.0
Northern Territory			
NT News	Murdoch	19,940	0.7
Australian Capital Territory			
Canberra Times	Stokes	47,570	1.8
National			
Australian	Murdoch	148,574	5.6
Financial Review	Fairfax	75,898	2.9

Murdoch owns 7 of 10 Sunday papers (73.4 percent of total circulation); Fairfax owns 2 (25.3 percent of circulation).

SOURCE: Paul Chadwick, "The Knowledge Lost in Information," *Index on Censorship,* vol. 22, no. 1, January 1993, pp. 17–23, by Paul Chadwick. Copyright © 1993 Index on Censorship. Reprinted by permission.

CHAPTER 7

Western Mass Media

ABOUT THIS CHAPTER

Much of what we discussed in Chapter 6 applies to this chapter as well. Mass media in the English-speaking countries belong to the Western tradition, of course, but there are important differences. In this chapter, we consider how mass media in the countries of Western Europe and Japan (very much "Western" in politics and economics) differ from those in Britain and North America.

Later chapters look at how the principles and practices of Western journalism have been exported to other countries. A theme of the later discussion of development journalism and the New World Information Order is that the theory of Western mass media is inappropriate—even dysfunctional—for third-world development needs. Perhaps this is so, but the values inherent in Western mass media remain appealing to other parts of the world and continue to inspire journalists.

INTRODUCTION

The ferry ride across the English Channel is short and routine and will become even simpler when the "chunnel" finally links Britain and the European continent. But Britain remains aloof from the Continent and is often a reluctant partner in the construction of the common European Community. When you step off the ferry in France, Belgium, or Holland, you immediately sense the differences between Britain and the Continent. But what are these differences? Do they go beyond language and the superficial aspects of culture?

CHARACTERISTICS OF EUROPEAN MEDIA

European Culture

Europe is closely identified with the concept of nationalism, the idea that the boundaries of a nation (culture) and state (political entity) ought to be the same. Most of European history, of course, is a succession of wars involving that end. The last war fought in the name of nationalism—World War II—nearly destroyed the Continent.

On the whole, postwar Europe from the Atlantic to the former Iron Curtain has moved from nationalism to a tentative supranationalism represented by the European Community (EC) and the still-unfamiliar Conference on Security and Cooperation in Europe (CSCE). Some countries are more enthusiastic participants than others. In recent years, when the movement toward a single economic market began in earnest, opposition was surprisingly strong. Some people objected to the new EC passports, which put the words *European Community* above the nation. The 12 member nations have insisted on using all 9 of their official languages at EC headquarters. A superculture called "Europe" might evolve in the twenty-first century, but at present, the EC is still a loose and uneasy coalition of independent nations whose common history is marked more by conflict than by cooperation.

Media Characteristics

Europe, of course, includes as much cultural diversity as other continents—probably even more—but several general patterns related to the media systems stand out.

Size and Homogeneity.   Like Britain, the countries of the Continent are relatively small and culturally homogeneous. The united Germany is a partial exception because of size and religion. Of the nations in Western Europe, only Switzerland, a loose confederation of diverse cantons speaking four separate languages, can claim to be truly multicultural. In Central Europe, the two explicitly multinational nations—Yugoslavia and the Soviet Union—disintegrated into their component and hostile ethnic parts. Even the Czechs and Slovaks, who seem to outsiders to form a common cultural identity, chose to split into two separate nations after 70 years as a single nation and only 3 years as a postcommunist democracy. Violence against Turks in Germany in 1993 and the growth of nationalistic, right-wing parties in other countries raised the difficult question of how—or even whether—the strong culture-based countries of Europe could become multicultural in the sense that the United States and Canada are.

Wars and migrations over the centuries have matched—more or less—the political and cultural boundaries, but even today there are exceptions. The Basques in Spain, the Bretons in France, and the Tyrolians in the Alps are examples of minorities who were never completely absorbed into the broader national cultures. Many of them are now demanding greater autonomy and occasionally even independence. The arrival of immigrants from colonies and the more recent influx of political asylum–seekers have added to the blurring of cultural boundaries. Still, compared to the English-speaking countries, continental Europe is a collection of cream soups more than mixed stews. One of the pleasures of traveling on a Eurail Pass is the speed with which even the landscape seems to change as you whiz across national boundaries.

Emphasis on Community.   Compared to the Anglo-American tradition of individualism, Europeans tend to put more emphasis on the larger entities of the culture, particularly institutions such as churches, political parties, and traditional organizations that mediate between individual and state. In most parliamentary systems, you vote for a party, not an individual. The idea of organizing a citizens' group to lobby for a specific entitlement would not occur to most Europeans.

One U.S. writer argues that a cause of European cultural solidarity is its long history of war. "Imagine being ten years old," he writes, "and learning that for two thousand years, the city you live in has been under attack, ten, fifty, a hundred times. Attacks come to seem like air and sunshine, not incidental occurrences in an otherwise peaceful world but essential elements of life."[1]

The compact European cities reflect a history of collective security and tight social cohesion. The above quotation reinforces the European idea that too much direct democracy is dangerous. What Americans see as the expression of true democracy—putting everything from selection of political candidates to choice of television programs to the test of the marketplace—most Europeans would consider dangerously close to mob rule. From the Data Base in Chapter 2, you can see some of the differences between North American and European cultural values. On the whole, Europeans seem to be less suspicious of government (and more suspicious of big business) than Americans and to have a sense that government and mass media are not necessarily hostile to each other. Whatever their origin, the differences are striking when you compare U.S. and European media systems.

Public Service Broadcasting.   For one thing, the wall of separation that the U.S. Bill of Rights established between government and the mass media does not exist in most European countries. Government is actively involved in broadcasting and influences the print media to a degree that U.S. journalists would find unacceptable. The European would react to the American's concern with a shrug and a puzzled look. As a quote from Georg Hegel in Chapter 8 will emphasize, the preservation and strengthening of the national culture are legitimate goals, the European might argue, and government represents the expression of culture, not a threat to the individual.

Even in the 1990s, European broadcast systems operate under a mandate of promoting education and culture. Providing mass entertainment is near the bottom of the list of purposes. Advertising is limited and controlled. With the partial exception of tiny Luxembourg, all national broadcasting institutions in Europe

---

[1] Stuart Miller, *Painted in Blood: Understanding Europeans* (New York: Atheneum, 1987), p. 6.

operate as public institutions—like the BBC or PBS—not as privately owned companies dedicated to profits. On paper, most systems look pretty much alike: a single public entity providing several complementary (rather than competing) national radio and TV services. Funding is provided by a combination of advertising, user license fees, and direct government payments.

Programming is strong on education, culture, news, and public affairs but—compared to fare in the United States—light on action, frothy entertainment, and advertising. On an extended stay in Europe, you will find most of your favorite U.S. series, but, on the whole, television tends to be, well, comparatively tame. The public interest, to which broadcasting is dedicated, is defined not by privately owned stations competing for the maximum number of viewers but by the interplay of government, political parties, and various kinds of public control authorities.

Control varies. In most countries, overall programming directions are determined by boards that are supposed to represent the public. Accountable to these boards are broadcasters who operate the services, which are technically slick and professional. Above the boards are the politicians, who exert influence in different ways but have more influence on programming than in the United States.

Television news and public affairs programming ("magazine" programs such as *60 Minutes* and documentaries, which have all but disappeared from U.S. television) occupy a big chunk of the evening schedule in Europe. In most countries, the main network news programs are in prime time and are staggered so you can watch the news on one channel, say, at 8:00 P.M., and on the other channel at 9:00. In content and technique, television news is almost universal: two or three major world events plus domestic happenings and the weather, all introduced and surrounded by universal icons of clocks, telephones, and globes or maps that put the home country at the center of the world. In a few European countries, the news is still presented with a slant reflecting the party in power, but in general, the system of government/political/public oversight produces high-quality but bland coverage. Investigative journalism is especially lacking in television news. The pleasure of a Mike Wallace "ambush" interview of a public official or CNN's disclosure of a secret government document is missing from most European TV screens.

Despite the lack of aggressive news reporting, television seems to be more homogeneous, more similar from country to country—more American—than newspapers, which still retain a unique national identity.

Partisan Newspapers.   In contrast both to television in Europe and to newspapers in the United States, European papers tend to be rich in diversity and openly partisan. In this area, Britain is a better basis for comparison than the United States or Canada. The dozen London dailies, split between the "qualities" and the "populars," circulate throughout the country with clear editorial policies and specific audiences; the pattern applies to the Continent as well.

On newsstands throughout Germany, you will see the serious but typographically dull *Frankfurter Allgemeine* alongside the chaotic *Bild Zeitung*. In France, the kiosks display the intellectual *Le Monde* and the splashy *France-Soir*. Throughout Japan—which, you recall, we're including in our "Western concept" of mass media—the newsstands offer a bewildering assortment of the national papers. They include some of the largest circulation dailies in the world. The national dailies are interspersed with local papers and specialized publications, befitting a country that prints the largest number of daily papers per capita in the world, more than twice as many as the United States and Canada. This is a far cry from the United States, where the average street-corner newsracks offer the local daily, *USA Today* and the *Wall Street Journal,* and one or two specialized weeklies.

The idea of what journalism is differs, too. Studies have shown that Anglo-American journalists tend to see their job as reporting the news rather than advocating a point of view. A lot of people don't believe it, but U.S. papers do try to keep opinion to the editorial pages (for their own) or the op-ed pages (the page opposite the editorial page where a narrow range of outside views and readers' letters are printed). Not so in Europe, where, for example, the French papers do not even have separate editorial pages and most French journalists would simply dismiss the idea that they should try to remain aloof from the events they cover.

The partisanship of European journalism—along with the distinction between mass appeal "popular" papers and intellectual "quality" press—makes for lively reading and is one reason Europe remains newspaper rich. Even the smaller capitals have a half dozen daily papers that circulate throughout the country and help to sustain a lively national political debate. If the best ones are not as aggressive as the best U.S. papers, they still are an integral part of vibrant democracies and strong cultures.

Narrow Press Freedom. If you put a group of Anglo-American and European journalists together, they will probably agree that governments and journalists, even though symbiotically entangled, function best with some daylight between them. They may not agree on whether the U.S. or European journalist operates in a freer environment, but they probably will agree that the distance between government and media is much smaller in Europe than in the United States. Does that mean the European media are less free than the U.S. media?

The American is likely to argue that freedom from government control is the *only* definition of press freedom. He or she is willing to take a chance with a privately owned media system backed by a 200-year-old legal tradition that defines press freedom as the right to publish without prior restraint and limited accountability afterward. Given the choice between a powerful government and a powerful private sector, most Americans would choose the latter, especially for their media system.

The European, on the other hand, would probably opt for government as the better protector of liberty as well as culture. Some aspects of European media law—lack of a common law tradition, government power to control information, tough libel statutes— make it difficult for the aggressive reporter. With occasional exceptions, the U.S. style of investigative journalism is rarely found in European media. In some countries, notably Scandinavia and Germany, statutes give journalists special protections their U.S. counterparts lack, even though this rarely results in exposés of scandal and corruption. These include protection of anonymous sources and guaranteed access to public records.

Governments also get involved in newspaper operations through various subsidies. In Sweden, an advertising tax is redistributed to newspapers in inverse ratio to their market strength. The result is stability in number of papers and strength for small, weak papers that probably would die without the subsidy.

The public broadcast systems, too, provide certain elements of freedom that privately owned, commercial U.S. television lacks. In some countries, these include a right to reply and in all countries a chance to influence programming through the oversight body. The U.S. station owner could argue that he or she gives viewers what they want. Every time viewers change channels, a vote is cast. What is more democratic than that? The response might be that radio and television have social obligations beyond the owner's balance sheet and that governments represent the public, whose interests should be protected. Children will always choose candy over vegetables, but few parents would condone that kind of diet in the name of democracy. As adults as well, social institutions can protect us from a diet too heavy in what we want and too light in what we need to function as responsible citizens.

Does the cozy relationship between media and government represent a lack of true press freedom? From the U.S. perspective, the answer is probably yes, but in Europe, the question does not seem so simple.

EUROPE 1992

In 1992, a historic change united the 12 nations of the European Community into a common market. All internal trade controls were abolished a year later as a first step toward what may become a ''United States'' of Europe. In the near future are probably a common currency and the skeleton of a common foreign policy. The distant future holds the promise of political union and the emergence of a supranational European culture. After 1992, traveling around Europe is becoming simpler, even though the texture of cultures is likely to remain vibrant and varied.

European Identity

In the preparations for Europe 1992, two issues emerged that influenced European media. One was the development of ''European'' rather than national media. The northern European countries were already heavily cabled and accustomed to television from neighboring countries. All countries, of course, were used to large doses of foreign programming and the occasional special program from the European Broadcasting Union. They were not used to regional programming—in English—that new technology and the idea of a common market implied. The first efforts toward a common European media system faltered.

Rupert Murdoch's Sky Television system—a handful of specialized channels delivered by direct satellite broadcast, which merged with the failed British Satellite Broadcasting to become BSkyB—generated only modest interest in Britain and even less on the Continent. The few other services directed to European satellite dishes did no better. Even multilingual Europeans, it turned out, would rather watch programs in their own languages. A joint German-French cultural channel, Arte, tried to function as an alternative to the entertainment-heavy English services, and a multilingual Euronews channel was founded as an alternative to CNN, but neither made more than a small ripple in a growing TV landscape dominated by local services heavily reliant on Hollywood programming.

The first European newspaper met a similar response. British media baron Robert Maxwell started the *European* in early 1990 as a weekly after long delays and earlier plans to make it a daily. The paper was supposed to appeal to the new generation of "Eurocrats," international businesspeople, and private citizens who thought of themselves first as Europeans. The *European* was slickly edited and printed, but circulation stagnated.

Several reasons accounted for the failure of the first generation of European media. First, all EC countries were rich in national media and already had easy access to papers from neighboring countries. The specialist who wanted to keep up with the *Financial Times* or *Le Monde* could already find them on newsstands from the North Sea to the Mediterranean. Radio and television were less important in Europe in general than in the United States, certainly to the elites who found themselves jetting from one hotel room to another.

Second, the internationally minded Euro-elites were already well served by the existing global media such as the *International Herald Tribune,* the European *Wall Street Journal,* and CNN and Sky News, which were widely available in hotels. Finally, there was the lack of pan-European identity that the new regional media needed to wean readers and viewers away from their familiar national media.

Holding Hollywood at Bay

The second Euro-issue directly involved the United States and its powerful entertainment factories. EC policy occasionally seemed designed to create a common internal economic policy but also a *Fortress Europa* against outsiders (read Japan and the United States). The EC in 1989 announced a policy—with something less than the force of law—that member countries should limit TV programming produced outside the Community (read in Hollywood) to less than 50 percent. The announced goal was to encourage European production and to protect European culture against the admittedly powerful Hollywood programming that already dominated traditional national services and was virtually all the new supranational carriers such as BSkyB Television carried.

"Foul!" cried both Hollywood and the trade negotiators in Washington, who were already fighting what they saw as unfair protectionism against U.S. products in Japan and Europe. From the U.S. perspective, the issue was free trade and the EC policy another example of U.S. trading partners trying to attack the few areas in global commerce where the United States still held the high cards. The European response, of course, emphasized the media's responsibility for maintaining national culture and the importance of creating a European identity that contained more than warmed-over Hollywood pop culture. They did not explain why the cultural identity of, say, Italians, would be threatened by watching too much Hollywood lowbrow programming but not by watching programming of exactly the same genre produced in Britain or Germany.

The issue, of course, was a case study in the different perspectives on the social role of media on opposite sides of the Atlantic. Although sharing a common cultural heritage—and most cultural values—with Europe, the United States puts greater faith in the marketplace. There is not much difference between the economic marketplace and the marketplace of ideas. Print media, broadcasters, purveyors of high culture, pop culture, and news all live or die in an economic marketplace while government stands on the sidelines, avoiding both interference and support. Not so on the other side of the Atlantic, where, despite the emergence of a global culture, national cultures remain strong and the embrace between media and government close.

WESTERN MEDIA IN THE TWENTY-FIRST CENTURY

Change in European and Japanese media is evident in the one-meter DBS TV dishes popping up on medieval roofs. They are symbols of a global communication revolution that threatens to shake the strong cultures of the West as much as the fragile cultures of the third world. In the twenty-first century, we can expect the following trends to change the Western media landscape.

Privatization and Commercialization

The public service model of broadcasting is threatened by rising costs that governments and the public are unwilling to pay, by audience dissatisfaction with limited choice and low appeal programming of traditional systems, and by new technologies and global entrepreneurs that circumvent national control bodies. Videotape rental—including most of the popular U.S. TV series—took off in Europe before it did in the United States because it offered an appealing alternative to over-the-air fare.

VCRs, the new satellite services, and occasional new commercial terrestrial services all threaten traditional public service broadcasting. The number of channels and variety of services available to European and Japanese viewers will double by the end of the twentieth century and probably double again shortly after. The existing services will have to change drastically to survive. In Britain, a goal of the Conservative government was to privatize the BBC and possibly even to turn it into a premium (pay) subscription service. On the Continent, most of the traditional broadcast bodies are either already commercial or about to become so. The future for all lies in entertainment programming with success determined in the marketplace.

Nonpartisan Journalism

A major factor in the global success of Anglo-American journalism is its nonpartisan character. It is intellectually invigorating to compare the world through the leftist intellectual perspective of *Le Monde* and the conservative *Frankfurter Allgemeine*, but for a quick summary of today's major events, sans ideological filter, you can't beat the tightly edited *International Herald Tribune*. That, of course, is the main reason the paper is so popular. The same is true for the BBC or CNN. Speed, brevity, and nonpartisanship are the hallmarks of twentieth-century Anglo-American journalism and twenty-first-century global journalism.

The trend is visible in Europe today, where several of the most successful papers are less than a generation old and dedicated to the principle of ideological independence. Examples include the *Independent* in Britain (founded in 1986) and *Der Standard* in Vienna (also founded in the late 1980s). The irony is that the emergence of what most Americans would call more professional and better journalism may be the death sentence of Europe's great newspaper diversity. As newspapers become more alike, there is less reason to buy more than one. That's why almost no North American cities have more than one daily. Watch for a consolidation of European papers—and with it, the loss of some of Europe's rich newspaper diversity.

Integration of European and Global Media

The growth of European media—rather than distinct national media within Europe—is a product of politics and the market. Although supranational media such as the *European* and Sky television may succeed eventually, the pattern for the next few decades seems more linked to cooperative reporting and joint production. Already several major newspapers routinely collaborate on regional stories that are then translated for publication in national papers. Cooperative polls routinely measure the public pulse in the 12 EC countries.

Joint TV production has a longer history. In fact, the identification of a major movie or TV series as "American" or "French" or "German" is almost impossible already because it may be a western shot in Italy in English with an international cast and German director and crew, financed and distributed by a Japanese-owned Hollywood studio with junior partnerships in a dozen countries. European TV is moving rapidly in that direction in order to spread around increasing production costs and to increase sales.

The non-European multinational entertainment corporations—mostly U.S. and Japanese—are expanding their European ties to have a foothold on the Continent when the drawbridge goes up around Fortress Europa. This will let them avoid non-EC production quotas on TV and similar national restrictions on foreign-made movies.

FRANCE

Cultural Tradition

If we had to pick one country to represent Western media—strong culture centered on the national capital, public service broadcasting subject to political influence, diverse selection of partisan newspapers—France could be the best case study. It has all of these in abundance and is about the only alternative to the

Anglo-American global communication system we have discussed in detail in earlier chapters. In the eighteenth century, the French language and culture dominated the Western world. In the nineteenth century, French was still the global language of diplomacy and educated discourse. France's success as a colonial power spread its language and culture widely in Africa, the Middle East, and Asia.

The combination of British colonialism before World War II and U.S. postwar influence was a steamroller that crushed French hopes for twentieth-century global influence. Instead, it has maintained the relatively small Francophone sphere of influence while promoting alliance with Germany in the emerging European Community. In the whole spectrum of global communication—news, pop music, movies, and TV—France is a surprisingly weak player. This seems to be a product of traditional hostility toward the Anglo world, an inward-looking culture, and a politicized media system that is not easily exportable.

Broadcasting

French broadcasting has undergone rapid and dramatic change in the past 20 years, becoming more like media in the Anglo world while retaining some of its uniquely French character. Although on paper the Office de la Radio et Télévision Française (ORTF) looked like the BBC, it was subject to open political control. President de Gaulle was reported to have dismissed criticism with the comment, "My opponents have much of the Press on their side, so I keep television."[2]

A slow evolution toward independence of French broadcasting began when de Gaulle resigned in 1969. ORTF was dissolved in 1974 and replaced with a set of quasi-independent networks that, like the BBC and ITV, were supposed to compete with each other, but not too much. The three networks—Télévision Française (TF1), Antenne 2, and France Régions (FR3)—formed the heart of French television, although ownership and control changed dramatically after the socialist regime of François Mitterand took over in 1981.

Mitterand's minister of culture, Jack (not Jacques) Lang, first adopted a policy of mobilizing television in support of the national culture while he himself became a leading critic of Anglo-American "cultural imperialism" in international circles. Then the government moved to expand TV by adding a national pay channel and two commercial networks, a curious ideological move for a socialist government. Even more astounding was the decision to sell TF1. When the bidding ended in 1987 (by which time the conservatives had regained control of the National Assembly), TF1 went to a consortium that included British publisher Robert Maxwell, and Channel 5 went to an alliance of Italian TV mogul Silvio Berlusconi and right-wing French press baron Robert Hersant. The sixth channel went to Radio-Télé-Luxembourg.

In 1992, two changes had a significant effect on what appears on French television. The first was the bankruptcy of La Cinc (Channel 5), which went off the air. The second was a reshuffling of the remaining parts of the national public

---

[2] Quoted in John Ardagh, *France Today* (London: Penguin, 1987), p. 558.

system, including a renaming of the second and third channels into France 2 and France 3. The old mission of quality (minus the Gaullist political control) was revived along with a determination to lead in the creation of an identifiable European medium not dependent on or dominated by the United States. Arte, a high culture cable channel funded by the French and German governments, also went on the air, but was met mostly with complaints from those involved and indifference from the audience.

Your hotel TV set in France now brings you all of these channels and possibly several of the regional satellite services and signals from neighboring countries. France 2 and 3 retain some of the character of public channels, whereas the others look more and more like U.S. networks, heavy on advertising, slick lowbrow entertainment, and glitzy news. Even the *CBS Evening News with Dan Rather* appears with subtitles the morning after its New York telecast.

Newspapers and Hersant

Whereas French television is characteristically European, the nation's newspapers vary from the trends outlined above. For one thing, circulation is relatively low— less on a per capita basis than in the United States or Canada—and the regional press is stronger than in most other European countries. Parisians can choose from among a dozen dailies, but press runs are small, and few of the Paris papers circulate nationally. Over all looms the figure of Robert Hersant, a press baron in the tradition of William Randolph Hearst and Joseph Pulitzer.

Hersant, stridently right-wing with a questionable record of collaboration during during World War II, owns three Paris dailies (*Le Figaro, France-Soir* and *l'Aurore*), which represent about 40 percent of national sales, and 30 titles around the country that comprise more than a quarter of regional sales. He openly defied a 1984 law designed to prevent him from expanding his media empire. With his entry into broadcasting, Hersant joined the small group of moguls who dominate European media in the 1990s. Unlike most of his brothers in this elite fraternity (for they are all men), Hersant is political (he was also elected to the European Parliament) and uses his media empire to advance his view of the world.

At the opposite end of the political spectrum is *Le Monde,* the elite newspaper that is included in any list of the world's great papers. Founded after the end of World War II (as were most of the Continent's newspapers), *Le Monde* reached a circulation of nearly 600,000 copies, the highest in Paris. In the 1980s, however, economic and political reversals humbled the great paper to the point that it had to sell shares to the public and accept the discipline of modern business techniques. *Le Monde* still looks like a tabloid edition of the *Wall Street Journal*—gray and nearly pictureless—and its survival may well depend on its ability to adapt to changing reader interests and the invasion of Anglo-American-style journalism.

To the Anglo-American, reading French papers can be either intellectually invigorating or irritating. If you like long stories, full of opinions but short on facts, then a paper like *Le Monde* will appeal to you. If you like investigative reporting in the tradition of Woodward and Bernstein, French papers will disappoint. If you like a quick summary of events in the style of *USA Today,* you're better off with a British or U.S. import. Recall that French papers have no separate editorial page and rarely distinguish between a news story and the personal columns that are put on the op-ed page in a North American paper. Accuracy counts less than a clever turn of phrase or thoughtful insight.

The difference between Anglo-American journalism, on the one hand, and French journalism, on the other, is more than a product of different professional standards. John Ardagh, a British journalist and long-time resident in France, argues that French journalism reflects a difference in the style of basic education, which teaches students to present a thesis and then marshal facts and opinions in support of it, not to lay out the facts and then see what conclusions can be induced, as Anglo-American scholarship generally does. The French approach, he notes delicately, "whatever its intellectual merits, is not the ally of objective enquiry."[3] The French style seems out of step in the global communication system of the 1990s.

GERMANY

Cultural Influences

Unlike most other countries of Europe, Germany's history as a nation is short and broken. Only in 1871 did a single state emerge from the kingdoms of Prussia, Saxony, and Bavaria, which differed then as now in both religion and cultural affinities. The German nation never included Austria or German-speaking Switzerland and evolved from a tradition of loose confederation, not the powerful centralism of France.

World War II left Germany without even a national capital. For almost 30 years, the wall cut across Berlin's main arteries, turning a grand imperial city into a bizarre place that typically startled most observers. Imagine turning onto Pennsylvania Avenue in Washington, D.C., and seeing a 12-foot concrete wall cutting across the Mall and avenue, isolating the Capitol from the White House. The Berlin Wall had a similar effect, especially at the Brandenburg Gate, which was the traditional ceremonial center of the city.

For almost a century, roads and rail lines had radiated out from Berlin as they do from Paris and London. The Iron Curtain—a singularly apt description of the postwar fortified border between the two Germanys—forced each half of the nation to grow new arteries. Note on a pre-reunification map how the train lines, *Autobahns,* and air routes in West Germany flow from the north along the Rhine to Frankfurt in the center, and then farther south toward Stuttgart or southeast toward Munich. Note also how quickly the German nation began to knit itself back together after unification in 1990. Even though Berlin is now at the edge of the country, we can expect the traditional lines of communication to reform as spokes radiating out from the national capital.

---

[3] John Ardagh, *France Today* (London: Penguin, 1987) p. 577.

Broadcasting

World War II left several influences on German media. Most apparent is that mass media are dispersed, not centralized, as they are in most other European countries. The constitution of the Federal Republic of Germany, strongly influenced by the United States after the war, made broadcasting a responsibility of the states (*Länder*). With no single cultural and political capital, the national papers were edited in several regional centers. The result, at least until Berlin again emerges as the true national capital, is the absence of a single media center to rival London or Paris.

German television in many ways resembles the British system. It is a mixture of public and private, national and regional, commercial and noncommercial services, but unlike the BBC and ITV, German TV has never developed an international reputation or influence. It is serious, high quality, and often dull. Language is one reason German television is not as widely exportable; politics and purpose are others.

Regional broadcast organizations follow, with several exceptions, the borders of the German states. Thus, Bavarian Radio serves Bavaria in southeastern Germany with both radio and TV and is an agency of the Bavarian state government. Hessian Radio does the same for the state of Hesse, and so on. After unification, the system in the former East Germany was reorganized and incorporated into the existing system in the west. The various regional organizations, plus several others representing national organizations such as Deutsche Welle, the overseas short-wave broadcast service, come together at the national level in ARD. ARD, which is identified on the air as the First Program, stands for Arbeitsgemeinschaft der öffentlich-rechtlichen Rundfunkanstalten Deutschlands and translates approximately as Public Broadcast Organization. Programs are produced by the various regional organizations and, except for a few hours before prime time, are presented as a unified national service.

The almost commercial-free ARD is controlled, in theory, by an advisory board whose members represent the range of significant social groups in the country. Included are the political parties, of course, but also the labor and employers' organizations, churches, and youth groups. The idea is that the divergent interests of the nation are better protected by such an oversight body than by market competition or an openly partisan system.

In fact, German television is a mixture of ''proportion'' and politics, the latter reflected in the partisan appointment of heads of the regional organizations by the state governments. Because broadcasting policy is in the hands of the states, a national consensus on matters such as privatization and expansion of commercial services is difficult to achieve. In states controlled by the conservative Christian Democrats, new media—cable television, DBS, and local radio—are encouraged. In states dominated by the Social Democrats, innovation generally is resisted. Partisanship of the state agencies—especially in news and public affairs programming—is always a topic of debate in Germany. Although not openly linked to the government or major parties as French broadcasting was under de Gaulle, the regional organizations do reflect the governments that support them in varying degrees. Some critics argue that a symbiotic relationship exists at the national level as well.

A second national network—unimaginatively called Zweites Deutsches Fernsehen (ZDF) for "Second German Television"—complements the First Program. It is financed by limited commercials and operates as a centralized national service. In theory, ARD and ZDF compete, but the competition is more like that between BBC and ITV, not that between CBS and NBC. A third channel is operated by the regional ARD organizations and emphasizes educational and special-interest programming.

In your German hotel room, you can watch the First and Second Programs (ARD and ZDF) and one or more of the regional third programs. Depending on the location, you may get one or more of the new private, commercial services as well, delivered by either ground transmitter or satellite. The fancier hotels may also supply CNN and Sky Television. A few even include the American Forces Network (AFN), which is broadcast on low-power UHF channels in southern Germany where U.S. armed forces are stationed. AFN uses the U.S. NTSC standard, which means a normal European TV set will not decode the picture; nor can a standard U.S. set be used to receive European channels. Germans can buy an attachment that allows them to receive AFN-TV, but few do. In contrast is the AFN radio network, which attracted a wide audience of young listeners during the years after World War II and continues to attract a significant audience of Germans who prefer the AFN mix of contemporary rock, country, jazz, and soul to the more sedate German services.

Until Berlin reemerges as the national capital of German culture, there is no single city that dominates the nation like Paris or London. Television is decentralized (except for the modern sprawl of the ZDF headquarters outside of Mainz), and national papers are published in three cities, none of them in the small political capital of Bonn.

Newspapers

The most famous German paper is the *Frankfurter Allgemeine Zeitung* (*FAZ*). (*Zeitung* means newspaper; *allgemein* means general or common; *Frankfurter* is the adjective form of the city.) Like all German papers, the *FAZ* dates only to the end of World War II and, like most, got its start with the blessing of Allied occupation forces. The *FAZ* is gray and conservative in appearance and content. Unlike those in the French papers, the *FAZ*'s editorials are clearly marked, but the overall tone of the paper is traditional and serious. Like the best of other European papers, its strength is thoughtful coverage of hard news, including more attention to the arts and ideas and international affairs than in even the best U.S. dailies.

By common agreement, the *Frankfurter Allgemeine* is placed slightly to the right of the German political center, and the *Süddeutsche Zeitung* ("South-German Newspaper") in Munich is slightly to the left. They, along with the very conservative *Die Welt* ("the world"), published in Hamburg, and the liberal *Frankfurter Rundschau* represent the main serious national dailies. This group of sober national dailies coexist with serious local papers and a few splashy tabloids. The worst of the latter is *Bild Zeitung* ("Picture Newspaper"), which is published by the Axel Springer organization in Hamburg, the same group that publishes *Die Welt*. *Bild* sells about 6 million copies daily, making it one of the largest circulation papers in the world. It is a mixture of the London *Sun* and the U.S. *National Inquirer,* put together with no apparent intervention of a layout editor but read at least occasionally by one German adult in five.

The regional papers are owned by a small number of chains. Even major cities like Wiesbaden, Mainz, and Darmstadt are served essentially by a single news-paper, with a different nameplate and local news section wrapped around a common core. Ardagh, whose reporting career included Germany as well as France, describes the German newspaper scene as "rather as if Britain had nothing but the *Sun* and *Financial Times* and then lots of superior *Yorkshire Posts* all looking like *Le Monde*."[4]

From a U.S. perspective, German journalism reflects both the strengths and weaknesses of the craft in other European countries. At its best, it is thoughtful, serious, and well informed. At its worst, it is opinion masquerading as news and subservience to authority under the guise of professional restraint. A British journalist in Bonn argues that German journalists tend to be both too opinionated and intimidated. The media, he writes,

> do not enjoy the almost instinctive self-confidence of the Anglo-American kind. Journalists in West Germany are under less professional pressure to bring out the news than in the U.S. and Britain, and are often expected to adopt some form of political cause.[5]

The result, he claims, is "more moral skirmishing than straightforward reporting."

An exception to the charge of subservience but not partisanship is the weekly newsmagazine *Der Spiegel* ("The Mirror"). Modeled after *Time* magazine even to its inventive use (or misuse) of the language, *Der Spiegel* is one of the few German media noted for investigative reporting and assaults on the establishment. Its perspective is unabashedly leftist, although it has attacked the Social Democrats as well as the conservative Christian Democrats. With a weekly circulation of nearly a million, *Der Spiegel* is a major force in German politics in its own right and often sets the agenda for other media.

Although the U.S.-inspired German constitution gives journalists more protec-tion than they have in France or Britain, hard-hitting journalism like the type that opened up Watergate or the Pentagon Papers is rare. Revelations about German industry's role in supplying Libya and Iraq with components for their poison gas factories came first in U.S. media. Marsh argues that "Criticism of the party in power is still sometimes regarded as an attack on the state."[6]

---

[4] John Ardagh, *Germany and the Germans: An Anatomy of Society Today* (New York: Harper & Row, 1987), p. 313.

[5] David Marsh, *The Germans: The Pivotal Nation* (New York: St. Martin's, 1989), p. 168.

[6] *Ibid.*

JAPAN

Cultural Factors

In some ways, Japan resembles Germany. It is a strong, homogeneous culture—probably the most homogeneous in the world—with a recent past of military aggression and U.S. occupation, now emerging from U.S. tutelage and influence as a major economic power. Like Germany, its own influence in international culture is minor. The world dances to Sony and Panasonic hardware, but the music is Anglo-American, almost never Japanese. Japanese cultural influence typically is derivative. Very few people in the world—or even in the United States—realize that much of the global pop culture product comes from conglomerates increasingly owned by the Japanese. The issue of Japanese ownership of U.S. companies—especially the culture industries—is likely to remain a contentious issue well into the twenty-first century.

Politicians and headline writers have difficulty categorizing Japan. Geographically and historically, it is not part of "the West," but politically, economically, and militarily it clearly belongs to the same loose grouping that includes Western Europe and North America. At first glance, the Japanese culture seems to set it apart from other Western nations, but a closer examination suggests similarities to continental Europe if not always Anglo-America. These include a strong sense of national identity, an emphasis on the group rather than the individual, and a suspicion of outsiders. In Japan, these characteristics can become obsessions.

You Gotta Have *Wa*[7]

The nature of Japanese culture is generally a puzzle to Westerners. It begins with *wa,* which is defined as "harmony" or "peace," and represents a constant adjustment of personal behavior toward group values and goals. From an early age, Japanese children learn that *wa* is both essential and difficult to achieve. They also learn the importance of striving for it in all they do. As adults, it takes the form of extraordinary dedication to work—often in a giant conglomerate offering lifetime employment in return—and to what outsiders sometimes call "Japan, Inc." This refers to the confluence of government, private industry, and people in striving toward common national goals, which now sometimes seem to include the seizure of the global economy.

A Dutch journalist with many years of experience in Japan notes two aspects of Japanese culture that are often misunderstood by outsiders.[8] One is that *wa* is achieved by voluntary accommodation to the group, not by authoritarian dictate, as group values are enforced in many other countries. Foreign visitors to Japanese elementary schools expect the order and purpose that prevail in the

---

[7] This is the title of a delightful book that uses baseball as a metaphor to explain the unique Japanese culture to Americans. Robert Whiting, *You Gotta Have Wa* (New York: Collier Macmillan, 1989).

[8] Karel van Wolferen, *The Enigma of Japanese Power* (New York: Vintage, 1990).

classrooms but are often surprised to learn that it emerges from even young students themselves, not from teachers. His second point is that *wa* produces a system of nearly universal agreement on just about everything but little individual responsibility or authority. As a result, government negotiators and corporate officials simply cannot promise to open markets or change manufacturing practices—or when they do, nothing happens. *Wa* always prevails.

Another unusual aspect of Japanese cultural values is the sense of uniqueness that can be traced to long periods of isolation from other countries. Many Japanese assume that outsiders can never learn their language or understand their culture. They really don't seem to understand foreigners, either, or to be willing to acknowledge that their relations with the rest of the world—both past and present—have left unhealed wounds and deep scars. The misunderstanding on both sides is especially dangerous now that Japan has emerged as the economic dynamo of the global economy and stands, inevitably, on the brink of political superpower status as well.

Japanese Media

Japanese media are what you might expect from a country with the highest level of development in the world (according to new UN definitions) but one where *wa* is still the pervasive value. Per capita newspaper circulation is the highest in the world. Television is even more pervasive than in the United States. Yet all are part of Japan, Inc., the monolithic culture.

Three publishing giants dominate the Japanese newspaper industry: the *Asahi, Mainichi,* and *Yomiuri Shimbun* (*Shimbun* means "newspaper"). Two smaller dailies, including a business paper resembling the *Wall Street Journal,* make up the "big five" that form the national press. From giant offices in Tokyo and multiple satellite printing plants come separate morning and evening papers, divided into more than a hundred localized editions. With morning and afternoon circulation combined, the three giants each produce from 6 to 14 million copies a day, the largest circulation figures in the world.

The papers operate with the most modern equipment in the world. Electronic page layout, for example, has been used for more than two decades, and high-speed presses barely blink as they move from one edition to another. Staff size, too, staggers the imagination of a U.S. journalist. The giants each employ news staffs that number several thousand, and Japanese journalists are the single largest foreign national group in Washington, D.C., and New York City and probably most other cities in the world. There are more Japanese journalists in Paris than *Newsweek* has in its entire global operation.

What does the Japanese reader, which is just about everyone in the country, learn from the one or two or three papers that arrive punctually on the doorstep? According to Edwin O. Reischauer, one of the most influential U.S. students of Japan,

> the Japanese on average are provided with fuller and more accurate newspaper coverage of both national and international news than any

Japan has the highest newspaper circulation per capita in the world, twice that of the United States. Three giants dominate the industry with daily circulations from 6 to 14 million copies. Each also publishes an English-language daily. The fourth paper is a financial newspaper, often compared to the *Wall Street Journal*.

other people in the world, and only an occasional newspaper elsewhere surpasses their great national dailies in either quantity or quality of news.[9]

However, even Reischauer complains of the Japanese media's uniformity of coverage and lack of critical reporting. Van Wolferen is more critical. He describes the "monotonous tones of a virtually fettered press" and pervasive self-censorship that derive from *wa* and promote Japan, Inc. As a result, he says, "all Japanese

---

[9] Edwin O. Reischauer, *The Japanese Today: Continuity and Change* (Cambridge, MA: Harvard University Press, 1988), p. 220.

read approximately the same things every day and have their opinions formed by what is in effect a single source.''[10]

Kisha and Dentsu

Beyond the general cultural factors, two unique elements of Japanese journalism also contribute to this situation. One is the 400 or so *kisha* (reporter) clubs attached to every major government and private institution. The 12,000 journalists who belong (virtually no foreigners) serve as the only conduit between the institutions that run the country and the public. Every day, the club members and officials of the office they cover decide what to report, how to play it, and, sometimes more important, what not to report. Club members who break the rules by reporting anything other than the agreed-on story can be thrown out. When the crown prince set out on the lengthy journey to find a suitable wife, the Japanese press agreed collectively to cooperate by publishing nothing about the search—a restraint Prince Charles and Princess Diana probably could not imagine. When the Harvard-educated bride-to-be was chosen and agreed to the marriage, the story was broken not by Japanese reporters but by the *Washington Post.*

A second factor is the giant advertising agency Dentsu, one of the largest in the world. Dentsu is responsible for a third of Japanese TV advertising (almost all of prime-time advertising), a fifth of newspaper advertising, and a third of magazine advertising. It is equal in size to the next eight largest Japanese agencies combined.

Dentsu is also a public relations agency with close ties to the government, major corporations, and media themselves. It can influence news coverage and TV programming and even decide how much major clients will spend on advertising and where. With close links to TV rating services and public opinion polling groups, the organization has influence over both media content and public policy that would be unthinkable in Europe or the United States.

High-Tech Broadcasting

Japanese broadcasting is a mixture of public and private systems like those we saw in Europe. In contrast to European systems, however, the public component is weak. NHK (Japan Broadcasting Corporation) operates one national channel devoted to education and high culture and one that competes for the mass audience with five private, advertising-financed networks. Programming on the commercial channels is largely domestic in origin but mirrors the typical U.S. commercial menu of game shows, sitcoms, and action serials more than the sedate offering of a European public channel.

It probably will not surprise you to learn that Japan introduced the first direct broadcast satellite (DBS) system and in the 1990s began operating the world's first high-definition television (HDTV) service and expected to introduce the first satellite-delivered digital audio programming, which will give a home radio receiver the perfect reproduction quality of the compact disk player. As in Europe,

---

[10] Karel Van Wolferen, *The Enigma of Japanese Power* (New York: Vintage, 1990) p. 96.

a hotel radio-TV brings in the national services, several new local radio stations, and probably CNN. An unusual aspect of Japanese broadcasting is that the occasional imported U.S. or European series or movie is frequently also broadcast with the original sound in one stereo channel and the dubbed Japanese in the other.

Even more unusual is that many of the network news programs are also simulcast in English, perhaps as an incentive for Japanese to practice the language most study but few learn to speak or understand orally. Check the instructions of the set in your hotel to see whether the newest technology allows you to use English to get inside this intriguing and important culture.

MAIN POINTS

1. Western and Japanese cultures tend to be more homogeneous than the powerful Anglo-American cultures and to put more emphasis on maintenance of the culture than on freedom of the individual.
2. Western media reflect this with broadcast systems that tend to be centralized, subject to partisan or public control, and noncommercial. Newspapers are usually openly partisan and often reflect the wide spectrum of a multiparty political system.
3. Privatization and commercialization are beginning to challenge traditional broadcast systems. The Anglo-American journalistic values of independence and criticism are influencing European newspapers. Ironically, as Anglo-American political and economic power recede, Anglo-American influence on global culture and international journalism increases.
4. The development of the European Community and the growth of regional trading blocs serve to strengthen the emerging global culture and require supranational media systems. Western and Japanese media are becoming more Anglo-American as a result.

FOR MORE INFORMATION

As noted in Chapter 6, foreign correspondents often complete an assignment and then write about the country or region in detail. Their books usually include a discussion of the media that is more current (and frequently more interesting) than those in textbooks. The following books are cited or used in this chapter.

John Ardagh, *France Today* (London: Penguin, 1988); John Ardagh, *Germany and the Germans* (New York: Harper & Row, 1987); and David Marsh, *The Germans: The Pivotal Nation* (New York: St. Martin's, 1989). Marsh is Bonn correspondent for the *Financial Times*.

Anthony Smith, ed., *Television and Political Life: Studies in Six European Countries* (London: Macmillan Press, 1979), deals with the broadcasting philosophy of six European countries.

Edwin O. Reischauer, *The Japanese Today* (Cambridge, MA: Harvard University Press, 1988), is a rewrite of a classic. Karel van Wolferen, *The Enigma of Japanese Power* (New York: Vintage, 1990), is the most critical of the works mentioned here but deals most comprehensively with the issue of Japanese culture. Robert C. Christopher, *The Japanese*

Mind (New York: Ballantine, 1983), is written by a *Newsweek* journalist whose contact with Japan goes back to the end of World War II. This book is outdated but still readable.

FOR DISCUSSION

1. Argue the strengths and weaknesses of a European system of public broadcasting and multiple partisan newspapers versus the U.S. system of commercial broadcasting and nonpartisan, common carrier, watchdog newspapers.

2. Which system would you recommend as a model for the emerging democracies of Central and Eastern Europe?

3. Is the maintenance of cultural identity sufficient reason to justify the imposition of significant (by U.S. standards) restrictions on free expression?

DATA BASE

I. Communication statistics from Western countries (number per 100 population).

Country	Newspaper Circulation	Radio Sets	Television Sets	VCRs	Phone Lines
Austria	36	72	46	16	41
Belgium	22	76	43	17	39
Denmark	37	83	49	19	56
Finland	54	73	48	19	52
France	19	108	40	18	48
West Germany	34	98	49	17	46
Greece	13	54	35	12	380
Ireland	18	56	28	11	25
Italy	10	96	61	7	370
Netherlands	31	79	43	20	45
Portugal	5	39	24	7	9
Spain	8	59	34	12	30
Sweden	53	155	67	21	67
Switzerland	50	80	46	17	56
Turkey	—	18	16	2	11
Japan	57	94	61	20	42

SOURCE: Newspaper circulation figures are mid- to late-1980s and from UNESCO figures and other sources; phone line data are from American Telephone & Telegraph's (AT&T) *The World's Telephones,* 1991, and the International Telecommunication Union's (ITU) *Yearbook of Common Carrier Telecommunication Statistics* (18th ed.). Radio, TV, and VCR data from *World Radio and TV Receivers,* ed. by Carol L. Forrester. Copyright © 1991 IBAR-BBC World Service. Reprinted by permission.

II. Circulation figures for the leading newspapers of some Western nations:

France
Le Figaro	453,000
France-Soir	405,000

Le Monde	343,000
Le Parisien	339,000
International Herald Tribune	179,000

Germany

Bild Zeitung	5,978,000
Frankfurter Allgemeine	520,000
Süddeutsche Zeitung	408,000
Die Welt	274,000

Japan

Yomiuri Shimbun	14,547,000
Asahi Shimbun	12,811,000
Mainichi Shimbun	6,275,000
Sankei Shimbun	3,150,000
Nihon Keizai Shimbun	4,364,000

The figures for Japan are total circulation—morning and evening editions—and include all regional editions.

SOURCE: Robert U. Brown, ed., *Editor & Publisher International Yearbook 1992* (New York: Editor & Publisher, 1992), and Arthur S. Banks, ed., *Political Handbook of the World 1992* (Binghampton, NY: CSA Publications, 1992).

III. Television audience shares (in percentages):

France		Japan		Germany	
TF-1	40.3	Fuji TV	23	ZDF	20.8
FR-2	24.7	NTV	19	ARD	20.4
FR-3	16.1	NHK-1	16	RTL +	18.1
M-6	10.8	TV Asahi	16	Other, SAT-1	14.0
Canal +	4.9	TBS	15	Pro-7	7.6
Other	2.1	TV Tokyo	9	Tele-5	3.7
Arte	1.1	Other	2		

Italy		Netherlands		Denmark	
RAI-1	21.0	RTL-4	28.7	TV-2	40.0
Canale-5	18.9	Nederland-2	19.0	DR/TV	34.0
RAI-2	16.1	Nederland-3	17.7	Other	14.0
RAI-3	12.5	Other	17.6	TV-3	8.0
Italia-1	12.3	Nederland-1	17.0	Kanal-2	4.0
Rete-4	11.7				
Other	7.5				

SOURCE: Data compiled from regular reports in *Variety;* figures are from late 1992 and early 1993.

CHAPTER 8

Communist Media

ABOUT THIS CHAPTER

In this chapter, we consider how mass media were used in a theory of journalism that is almost the reverse of everything in the Western concept. We look at the nineteenth-century German intellectual whose grand theory of history was the basis of communism and the twentieth-century Russian revolutionary who tried to use communism to propel a nation directly from a medieval past to a post-capitalist future. Then we explore how the communist system collapsed in most countries where it was tried and what, if anything, remains of a communist concept of the press.

INTRODUCTION

Nothing will have a greater impact on the twenty-first century than the collapse of communism at the end of the twentieth. The global media were there to record the images that marked the dramatic events: the emergence of the charismatic Mikhail Gorbachev as an international media star and the dismantling of the Berlin Wall, and then the clumsy, failed coup against Gorbachev and the ascent of Boris Yeltsin as head of a new Russia. On the other hand, television also showed the world the Goddess of Liberty in Tiananmen Square and the tanks that crushed the pro-democracy movement in China. These events served as a reminder that the triumph of democracy is not guaranteed, even at the "end of history."

But a word of warning: Things in the former communist world are changing so quickly that almost everything you read—including this chapter—can be outdated. To find out what is happening now to mass media in the former Soviet Union and the remaining outposts of traditional communism, check today's paper.

COMMUNISM AND HISTORY

For most of the twentieth century, communism stood as a challenge to the principles of democracy that had been developed and imperfectly practiced in Western Europe and North America over the past three centuries. Remember Francis Fukayama's argument in Chapter 1 that World War II left the world with two competing ideologies: multiparty, liberal democracy in a free-market economy on the one hand, and the communist ''dictatorship of the proletariat'' in a controlled, ''command'' economy on the other. For almost a half century, conflict between these two ideologies was the driving force behind global politics. The superpowers glared at each other across an Iron Curtain that split Europe and competed with each other for influence in most of the rest of the world.

When Gorbachev led the Soviet Union and countries of Central and Eastern Europe to an embrace of democracy and free markets, it was, Fukayama claimed, the ''end of history.'' No more great questions about the proper organization of society were left unanswered; the West had won.

It was, as we also noted in Chapter 1, also the triumph of Western journalism. The revolutions of 1989 certainly did not end government use of media as an instrument of social control—China demonstrated that—but it may well have killed the *legitimacy* of such a system. In the 1990s, Western-style journalism is breaking out all over, not just in the former Soviet Union and the formerly communist nations of Central Europe.

MARX AND LENIN

Marx and History

We are so accustomed to seeing the giant parade banners with Marx and Lenin side by side that it is easy to forget that the two men came from different countries, never knew each other, and lived in different epochs. Karl Marx, born in 1818, was a German intellectual and historian who created a grand theory that predicted Vladimir I. Lenin's failure as a revolutionary. Lenin, a Russian political activist born a generation later, took Marx's ideas and used them, with considerable license, to fashion a giant state that dominated most of the twentieth century.

Marx, like Fukayama, was a student of Georg Hegel and adapted the Hegelian method of inquiry to world history. Instead of using the marketplace of ideas to determine truth from among the contending claims, Hegel advocated the dialectic, a method of argument developed by the Greeks. You start off with an idea or an assertion called the *thesis*. The counter argument is the *antithesis*. After the two clash, what emerges is not triumph for one and failure for the other but a *synthesis* of the two, combining the strongest elements of both the thesis and its opposite. The synthesis becomes a new thesis, and the process continues, each step of the dialectic bringing you a little closer to the truth.

Marx took the dialectic and applied it to history, not to the study of specific events but to the broad sweep of human experience from the earliest civilizations to what he predicted would be the inevitable future of all nations. In Marx's vision, history proceeded, via the dialectic, through five stages: an idyllic primitive communism, feudalism, capitalism, socialism, and, finally, communism. In each stage, class conflict over the means of production provided the antithesis that propelled society to the next stage.

Capitalism, whose early stages Marx witnessed in Germany and Britain, would lead toward the accumulation of more and more wealth in fewer and fewer hands, Marx argued, until an inevitable workers' revolution established a socialist dictatorship of the proletariat. Then, with society freed for the first time in history from the curse of private property, class conflict would cease, the state would wither away, and true communism would emerge. The organizing principle of the final stage of history would be the famous injunction: from each according to his or her ability, to each according to his or her need.

Marx spent most of his adult life, first in Germany and then in permanent exile in Britain, dividing his time between further development of his grand theory and development of an international organization to promote workers' rights (and his political vision). His contacts with journalism were irregular. He edited a radical newspaper in Germany that was frequently harassed by the government and later, from London, wrote for the *New York Daily Tribune,* edited by the famous journalist Horace Greeley.

Marxist Press Theory

Nowhere in Marx's voluminous writings is there a statement of a "Marxist theory of the press." It has to be pieced together from the prolific writings of a long, active life and from his actions as head of an international political-action organization. The words and actions are not consistent. As a young journalist in Germany, he pleaded—sometimes eloquently—for the rights of unpopular dissenters challenged by an autocratic government. As head of the International Working Men's Association (or First Communist International), however, he was intolerant of critics and unwilling to allow his organization's newspapers to be used for free political discussion.

Early in his newspaper career in Germany, a debate in the provincial parliament over press freedom (there wasn't any in Germany at the time) inspired a series of articles. In one, Marx offered a poetic view of the role of a free press:

> The free press is the omnipresent open eye of the spirit of the people, the embodied confidence of a people in itself, the articulate bond that ties the individual to the state and the world, the incorporated culture which transfigures material struggles into intellectual struggles and idealizes its raw material shape. . . . The free press is the intellectual mirror in which a people sees itself, and self-viewing is the first condition of wisdom.[1]

---

[1] Saul K. Padover, ed., *Karl Marx on Freedom of the Press and Censorship* (New York: McGraw-Hill, 1974), p. 31.

However, actions throughout Marx's life reflected a different side of his character: a brilliant, driven mind not tolerant of lesser intellects or criticism. One of his last skirmishes was to move the First Communist International to the United States, where it died, finally, in Philadelphia in 1876, an ironic event that has escaped popular notice since then.

Lenin and Revolution

The heart of the communist concept of the press comes not from Marx but from V. I. (Vladimir Ilyich) Lenin, who oversaw the creation of the first Marxist-inspired state and pioneered the use of mass media as an instrument of government control. Ironically, Lenin seized upon a revolution and created a communist state in a country where Marx predicted neither was possible. The question of whether the Marxist progression of history was inevitable and inviolable was a source of discord among Marx's followers from the beginning. Marx said it was and believed a workers' socialist revolution was possible only in an advanced capitalist country. The success of "Marxist" revolutions first in Russia and then in China and the failure of communism as a political force in Western Europe and North America probably would have puzzled him.

Lenin, of course, believed differently and used Marxist theory of history to inspire his own practice of revolution. He came from a middle-class family and was radicalized when a brother was executed for trying to overthrow the tsar. After a period of internal exile himself, he fled to Western Europe and spent 17 years writing, organizing, and waiting for the right moment.

That moment came when the autocratic tsarist regime crumbled in the face of popular opposition to World War I, and Lenin was sent across Germany in a sealed railroad car to take control of his Radical Socialists on the promise of Russian withdrawal from the war. Later, when the coalition of revolutionaries fell apart (which often happens after successful revolutions), Lenin's Bolsheviks ("majority-ists") seized control and the world's first Marxist experiment was born.

Lenin worked prodigiously to organize, mobilize, and inspire the various groups at home and in exile that shared only an opposition to the tsarist regime. Six months after leaving Russia, he founded a newspaper, *Iskra* ("Spark"), that became a major voice for his ideas. In 1901, *Iskra* printed a long blueprint for a revolutionary structure that contains the key elements to Lenin's press principles:

> The role of a newspaper, however, is not limited solely to the dissemina-
> tion of ideas, to political education, and to the enlistment of political
> allies. A newspaper is not only a collective propagandist and a collective
> agitator, it is also a collective organiser. In this last respect it may be
> likened to the scaffolding round a building under construction, which
> marks the contours of the structure and facilitates communication
> between the builders, enabling them to distribute the work and to view
> the common results achieved by their organised labour.[2]

---

[2] *Lenin about the Press* (Prague: International Organisation of Journalists, 1972), p. 71. The statement is from "Where to Begin," published in *Iskra,* no. 4, May 1901.

Note these key words: *propagandist, agitator,* and *organizer.* Sometimes a fourth, *controller,* is inferred from the text that follows the quote. These are hardly descriptions of mass media in the West, but they represent the key political functions of journalism in the communist concept. In 1902, Lenin expanded the *Iskra* article into a short book, *What Is to Be Done?* that defined the first two terms:

> [The propagandist] must present "many ideas," so many indeed that they will be understood as an integral whole only by a (comparatively) few persons. An agitator, however, speaking on the same subject, will take as an illustration a fact that is most glaring and mostly widely known to his audience . . . [and] . . . will direct all his efforts to presenting *a single idea* to the "masses" . . . ; he will strive to *rouse* discontent and indignation among the masses against this crying injustice, and leave a more complete explanation of this contradiction to the propagandist. Consequently, the propagandist operates chiefly by means of the *printed* word; the agitator by means of the *living* word.[3]

The pejorative connotative meaning most of us attach to the words *propaganda* and *agitation* stems from their association with communist mass media. To communists, of course, they are part of everyday vocabulary. Lenin wrote before the advent of electronic media and about a largely illiterate peasant society. Today, he might replace "living word"—spoken exhortation or interpersonal communication—with "electronic media." However, from Lenin's seizure of power to the arrival of *glasnost,* the distinction between the two referred less to media than to audiences and purposes. The difference is important.

The Marxist theory of history is complex and recognizes contradictions that presumably can be understood only by elites who control a communist state. They are the audience for propaganda, which consists of complex material presented to a small audience. In contrast, the presentation of simple ideas—often only a few simple slogans—to a mass audience is agitation. Combine propaganda and agitation with collective organization and control, and the concept of mass media becomes the opposite of the image in the Western concept. It is not surprising that communist and Western journalists "talked past" one another for decades when they tried to find common ground in exploration of their very different social and political functions.

GLASNOST

Mikhail S. Gorbachev, who became head of the Communist party in the Soviet Union in 1985 and later national president as well, was an unlikely revolutionary. His career was in the party bureaucracy, his wife was a dogmatic professor of Marxism-Leninism, and he had little exposure to life outside the Soviet Union. He succeeded a generation of colorless, geriatric leaders under whose stewardship

---

[3] V. I. Lenin, *What Is to Be Done?* (Peking [Beijing]: Foreign Languages Press, 1973), pp. 82–83.

the Soviet Union remained a military superpower but sank steadily economically. By the 1980s, the country was further from the visionary model of Marx and Lenin than at any time since the revolution.

Yet within months of his accession to power, Gorbachev introduced changes to the Soviet Union that triggered the collapse of the communist superpower, his own political defeat, and the end of communism as a widely viable ideology. If Fukayama proves right, Gorbachev will be known in history as the man who recognized communism's terminal illness and arranged for its death with dignity.

The cause of death can be represented by two words that the global media added to every language of the world: *perestroika,* which means economic restructuring, and *glasnost,* whose root is the Russian word for voice but which is usually translated as "openness." The full story of Gorbachev's strategy may not be known until he writes his memoirs, but he clearly recognized the dismal state of the Soviet economy and the slow strangulation of the nation by the massive bureaucracy—immune to market, public, or political pressures—that controlled every aspect of the lives of the nearly 300 million Soviet citizens.

From the beginning, Gorbachev seemed to recognize the failure of using information as an instrument of national development and the futility of maintaining a government monopoly. Even before he took power, he told a conference on party ideology that "Broad, timely, and frank information is testimony to trust in people, respect for their intelligence and feelings, their ability to interpret events themselves."[4] This is a radically different view of the media role than his predecessors had espoused.

Gorbachev and *Glasnost*

Gorbachev apparently was less concerned with openness as a virtue by itself than with using it as a tool to implement *perestroika.* As head of the party, he could set off reforms at the top, but he needed a revolution from the bottom as well to blast loose an entrenched bureaucracy that stifled the whole system. It was a big gamble because it encouraged both the mass media and the *intelligentsia* to strike out on their own. As the old Chinese proverb puts it, "Once you climb onto the tiger, you can't climb back off."

Both interest groups, in fact, responded enthusiastically. However, the famous poet Yevgeny Yevtushenko told the Russian writers' union that more than words were needed. In the name of *glasnost,* he urged an assault on the distortions of the official version of Soviet history and on the system of privileges that had created one of the most rigid and inequitable class systems in the world. The tiger was beginning to take control of the rider.

The mass media's first response to *glasnost* seemed to be a product of individual editors' and journalists' initiatives. Two publications became known as the most daring. One was a small weekly, *Ogonek* ("Flame"); the other was *Moscow News,* another weekly published in several languages for tourist and overseas propaganda consumption. As they tested the limits of openness with

---

[4] Quoted in Hedrick Smith, *The New Russians* (New York: Random House, 1990), p. 98.

Two traditional giants of Soviet journalism—the Communist party's *Pravda* and government's *Izvestia*—now fight for readers and a role in post-communist Russia, while *Renmin Ribao* (*People's Daily*) continues its traditional functions in China.

each issue, circulation soared, but demand increased even more. Copies were rare and prized.

Pravda, the party daily that had been the most important paper in the country, remained in the hands of traditionalists, and its circulation dropped. By some accounts, it lost half its sales. In contrast, *Izvestia,* the government paper, became a leader among *glasnost*-minded journals, and its circulation increased by several million. The biggest obstacle to further expansion of the reform media was a lack of newsprint.

Broadcasting, which was controlled by the party through a state committee, equivalent to a federal executive agency in the United States, was slower to jump on the *glasnost* bandwagon. By the late 1980s, however, television viewers had become used to what was to them a new style of aggressive, critical reporting and sophisticated production that resembled *60 Minutes* more than the predictable fare of ceremonies and trumped up economic production figures that they had been familiar with.

Watching Soviet media in the late 1980s was a little like seeing someone peel an onion, layer by layer. Each new revelation exposed another layer of secrecy. Almost every week brought a new disclosure, another taboo topic reported for the first time. First it was the inefficiencies of the economic system and the failures of low-level officials. Then it was the privileges of the party elites and the performance of the Soviet Army in Afghanistan. Then the dreadful legacies of Stalin and Lenin himself were aired. Gorbachev remained serene; a nation should have no blank pages on its history, he said.

By the end of the 1980s, it was difficult to think of any topic that had not been discussed and debated thoroughly, any blank page left in Soviet history. And it was difficult to find anything left of the system Marx had envisioned and Lenin had tried to create. Amid a collapsing economy kept afloat by food shipments and management advice from the West, Soviet journalism abandoned any pretense of functioning as collective agitator and propagandist for a one-party state. It became instead an actor in the shift to a multiparty political system and a market economy.

Maybe history wasn't dead as Hegel had predicted, but a distinct communist concept of the press was. On Christmas Day, 1991, the red and gold hammer-and-sickle banner that had inspired hope and fear around the world for most of the twentieth century was lowered for the last time at the Kremlin and replaced with the former tricolor Russian flag. The Soviet Union was replaced by a vaguely defined commonwealth of most of the former Soviet republics, and Gorbachev, using a pen borrowed from the head of CNN, signed the proclamation abolishing his job and his nation.

Counterreform and Coup

The West—indeed most of the world—was infatuated with Gorbachev and his startling reforms. After decades of colorless Soviet leaders, the charismatic Gorbachev was a fresh breeze that promised to end the half century of cold war while creating the possibility of a single, united Europe. At first, encouraged by reform-minded journalists and intellectuals, *glasnost* seemed to succeed. Gorbachev remained nonplussed as the Central European nations discarded their military and economic ties with the Soviet Union, and the former East Germany, the strongest and most loyal of the client states, dissolved itself to become five new states of the powerful and very Western Federal Republic of Germany.

By 1990, however, the forces that *glasnost* set loose had outrun Gorbachev. More often than not, he was identified with the conservative wing of the party, while Boris Yeltsin, popularly elected president of the huge Russian republic, became the leader of those in the "fast lane" of change. The two managed to maintain a proper public relationship, but Yeltsin, whose domain encompassed a majority of land, people, and resources, was clearly in the driver's seat. Gorbachev seemed indecisive at best and a brake on the accelerating pressure for change at worst. When he reined in radio and television and tried to restrain independent-minded newspapers, the glow of *glasnost* began to dim.

Then came the morning of August 19, 1991, when the 250 million Soviet people—along with the rest of the world—awoke to find that an "emergency committee" of party hard-liners had imprisoned Gorbachev in his vacation *dacha* and assumed control of the country. For four days, it looked like Red Square might be a repeat of Tiananmen Square and *glasnost* might suffer the same fate as the

Chinese reform movement. After all, Marx and Lenin had described how a country would become communist, but no one had written a book explaining how a country could transform itself into a democracy. Giving up power was not part of communism's theory or practice.

After four days, responding to domestic and international outrage and perhaps suffering from a loss of nerve in the face of live television cameras, the emergency committee essentially abandoned the coup, and the reformers returned with even greater strength and commitment. The legitimacy of communism was destroyed along with the remnants of the Soviet media system. But before we consider these extraordinary events in some detail, we need to check our guide book for background about the country that figured so prominently in the last half of the twentieth century and its media system.

SOVIET UNION

Cultural Influences

The Soviet Union was, depending on your perspective, (1) a voluntary union of 15 sovereign socialist republics pursuing the Marxist vision of the inevitable march toward communism, (2) a supernation in which traditional nationalities were merged to produce a new socialist citizen, or (3) a twentieth-century extension of the old Russian Empire. In the 1990s, it would be hard to find anyone to argue in favor of either #1 or #2; #3 might be the popular choice, but with the reservation that the survival of the remnants of the Soviet Union in anything like their former form was impossible.

Following the attempted coup, most of the republics declared some form of independence from the central union. The three Baltic states, whose annexation during World War II was finally acknowledged, were allowed full political independence, while Gorbachev struggled to hold the remaining pieces of the former Soviet Union together as a loose confederation. Leningrad became St. Petersburg again, and Boris Yeltsin pushed a radical transformation of Russia away from the remaining vestiges of communism.

Statues of communist leaders were unceremoniously pulled down, and in late 1991, the Russian Communist party itself was declared illegal. Things that had been "Soviet"—embassies, rubles, nuclear weapons—became "Russian." The awkwardly named Commonwealth of Independent States that was supposed to replace some of the functions of the Soviet Union staggered from an awkward beginning into an uncertain postcommunist future.

Nevertheless, even after the collapse of communism, the countries that had formed the Soviet Union still represented (1) the largest country in the world geographically and the third largest in population and (2) the most culturally diverse country in the world, with dozens of languages and hundreds of distinct ethnic groups. In addition, it was either blessed or cursed with an extraordinarily large and complex system of mass media. The postcommunist Commonwealth of Independent States was also a case study of the reemergence of culture as a basis for conflict.

Leninism in Practice

Given Lenin's emphasis on the press as an instrument of propaganda, agitation, organization, and control, it is not surprising that the development of mass media was a priority for him and his successor, Josef Stalin. Under Stalin particularly, the media were expanded rapidly and assumed the character that Americans came to associate with the communist concept. The media were filled with the glorification of the party leadership and wildly optimistic assessments of the march toward communism. Party slogans, which guided editorial content, were chosen months or even years in advance. Front pages were laid out several days before publication. The news was predictable, dull, and even incredible. Television was worse. No news program was complete without statistics of agricultural or industrial progress, accompanied by stock and sometimes faked footage, and endless shots of Stalin himself as leader of the nation and international communism.

Like Western Kremlin-watchers, the Soviet public learned to read between the lines and to pay as much attention to what was not reported as to what was. Despite government efforts to jam the signals, foreign short-wave radio provided a "reality check" for those who were not satisfied with the official party interpretation of the world.

Remember that there was no private property in the pre-*glasnost* Soviet Union. Every aspect of the economy was determined by directives from government and party authorities, not demand from the public. The same was true for the social system. Control was centralized and exercised by a massive bureaucracy that numbered in the tens of millions. The result was widespread inefficiency and lethargy and a hierarchy of privilege that allowed some people to circumvent the queues and shoddy goods according to their political class. Mass media were part of the system at all levels.

The Soviet Media System

At the top were *Pravda* ("Truth"), published by the Central Committee of the Communist Party, and *Izvestia* ("News"), published by the Council of Ministers, roughly equivalent to the U.S. Cabinet. An old joke had it that there was no truth in *Pravda* and no news in *Izvestia*. Western critics could point out that the "truth" in *Pravda* failed even before you got to the news. A line above the nameplate in every issue proclaimed that the paper was founded by Lenin on May 5, 1912. In fact, Lenin was actively involved in the Bolshevik conference in Prague that approved the decision to start the paper but was back in exile in Paris on May 5. His first contribution appeared in the 16th issue, his second in the 63rd.[5] After the 1991 attempted coup, the line was changed to "Founded

---

[5] Angus Roxburgh, *Pravda: Inside the Soviet News Machine* (New York: George Braziller, 1987), pp. 14–15.

at the Initiative of V. I. Lenin." Other traditional features such as the reproduction of party prizes awarded to the paper and the slogan "Workers of All Nations, Unite" were dropped.

Of the two central papers, *Pravda* was more important because the party rather than the government determined policy. It was also the prototype for papers published by lower echelons of the party. Because there was a party organization at every level of Soviet society—all-union or national, republic, regional or provincial, city, even factory or collective farm—some form of the party "truth" was produced down to the smallest cell. Some, such as *Komsomolskaya Pravda,* an organ of the party youth organization, or *Moskovskaya Pravda,* published by the capital city party, were influential papers in their own right and widely distributed. At lower levels, some papers reprinted parts of the national *Pravda* and added their own local information. Others were simple mimeographed sheets tacked to bulletin boards in factories or housing blocks.

Other elements of the vast bureaucracy also published a range of media, including 10 daily papers that were distributed throughout the Soviet Union. Several were among the largest circulation papers in the world. *Krasnaya Zvezda* ("Red Star") was a daily published for the military, *Trud* ("Labor") for the labor unions, and *Selskaya Zhizn* ("Rural Life") for the farm workers. In all, the Soviet Union claimed it produced more than 8,000 newspapers with a total circulation of nearly 200 million and more than 5,000 periodicals. There were fewer than 200 daily papers but circulation of the eight largest totaled nearly 70 million copies.[6]

All of the papers and periodicals were published by elements of the party or government or by government-approved organizations. Independent or unofficial journalism existed only in the clandestine and illegal *samizdat* (self-published) sheets that were usually individually typed and passed from hand to hand. The *samizdat* carried information about the government's suppression of dissidents as well as unauthorized, and therefore officially unpublishable, literature. Through Leonid Brezhnev's years in power, government suppression of these publications and their authors was relentless though never completely successful.

Controlled Radio and TV

Broadcasting was controlled by a state committee directly under the Council of Ministers. This would be comparable to the U.S. networks being run out of the White House. Content and politics aside, broadcasting faced formidable obstacles. The country covered 11 time zones, but much of it was so sparsely populated that traditional ground transmitters were impractical. It was so far north that the stable, geostationary satellites 40,000 kilometers over the equator didn't work. Just getting a signal to Soviet living rooms was difficult enough. Then there was the problem of language. Russian was an official language throughout the country, but each of the 14 non-Russian republics had at least one other official language,

---

[6] Thomas F. Remington, *The Truth of Authority: Ideology and Communication in the Soviet Union* (Pittsburgh, PA: University of Pittsburgh Press, 1988), p. 100. Most of the figures are from the mid-1980s.

and collectively the number of languages spoken totaled more than 200. Fifteen languages were used in television, and several dozen were heard over radio.

Until the late 1980s, your hotel TV in the major cities, which were the only places foreigners were allowed, would have brought in two national channels in Russian and one or two local channels that, depending on the location, could have been in other languages. In parts of the Russian republic, one or two local or regional channels were also available. Outside the big cities, local authorities often inserted local programming into the national channels for some local content. Muscovites also received the local Leningrad channel, one of five available in the capital.

Until *glasnost,* programming was predictable and dull. Sports and children's programs were the main release from a steady diet of movies about World War II and the triumphs of socialism, political indoctrination, and, for the minority who liked it, top-quality high culture. The main news program was *Vremya* ("Time"), in prime time at 9:00 P.M., which, despite its lack of credibility and production values, attracted an audience of up to 150 million. Here is a *New York Times* reporter's description of a typical *Vremya* program, circa 1970:

> The average 30-minute nightly television newscast consists of a long feature on grain harvesting by "our outstanding collective farmers" at the Dawn of Communism Collective Farm in the Ukraine, a report that the shockworkers at the Magnitogorsk Metallurgical Combine have pledged to fulfill this year's economic plan three weeks ahead of time, and an interview with a Lebanese Communist who managed to answer one question in a nonstop, five-minute recitation that varies only minutely from the latest *Pravda* commentary on the Middle East. These anchor items lead into riot pictures from Ireland, demonstrators outside the American Embassy in Greece, miscellaneous Soviet sports news, and weather reports. Accompaniment for the main items consists of stock newsreel shots of grain pouring into railroad cars, harvest combines in carefully staggered phalanxes rolling across fields, and steelworkers pouring molten steel into troughs or white-hot ingots sliding toward the camera. The themes and pictures are unvaried day in and day out and seem to have very little connection to the date on which they are shown.[7]

Radio was an especially difficult medium for Soviet authorities because it represented a window to the outside world that often conflicted with the official version of reality. For pragmatic reasons, short-wave capability was built into most radio receivers. This meant listeners could tune into Western services such as the BBC, Voice of America, and U.S.-financed Radio Liberty as well as to the domestic services that had to use the medium to reach across the vast Soviet land mass. At various times, Soviet authorities experimented with use of wired receivers that provided good quality reception but only to the approved stations; extensive jamming of the outside broadcasters, which never worked very well; and

---

[7] Hedrick Smith, *The Russians* (New York: Quadrangle, 1976), pp. 365–366.

competition to foreign stations by offering popular programming designed to entice the audience away from the outside influence.

The Failure of Monopoly

The communist concept of mass media includes an information monopoly controlled by the governing elite who are part of the dictatorship of the proletariat, guiding the people toward true communism. Despite the use of mass media as tools of propaganda and agitation and the massive efforts to maintain an information monopoly, the system never worked. People tuned in to Western broadcasts despite jamming. Outside newspapers and periodicals got into the country despite searches of visitors and mail. And the illegal *samizdat* newsletters kept a network of dissidents informed despite the secret police. The speed with which journalism changed after Gorbachev took power and the enthusiasm of journalists for reform are evidence that Lenin's belief in the power of persuasion was misplaced.

One aspect of the Soviet information system we know very little about was the vast army of party propagandists and agitators who worked, in many cases, full time to fulfill the mandate of Lenin's principle of communication. At local "agitation points"—something like neighborhood education centers— to full-fledged universities of Marxism-Leninism and party "higher schools," millions of party activists studied, lectured, and promoted the party cause. Propaganda/agitation was a career specialty for some party members—although not a very popular one—and a temporary assignment for many others.

Figures are difficult to come by and to interpret, but it is known that enrollment in various party schools totaled more than 20 million in the late 1970s. In the mid-1980s, more than 60 million were involved in various kinds of political study programs. Occasional lectures, discussions, and films were part of the routine at all work sites, reinforcing the media's uniform and repetitious messages.

Information as Power

To the Western visitor, one of the most puzzling aspects of the Soviet Union was the obsession with secrecy. It started with the media, of course, but included even what seemed to be the most harmless information. Airports and trains would not give out schedules or announce delays. Even information about accidents was kept from families of the victims. Smith tells of one family whose daughter simply disappeared on a trip to Moscow. All inquiries were met with silence until one bureaucrat whispered that she had been killed in a plane crash that had never been acknowledged.[8]

Libraries—even the famous Lenin Library, one of the world's largest—had a double card-catalog system, one available to the public and the other accessible only with special permission. Most books and documents were stamped to indicate who could have access to them. Frequently a stern librarian would demand to know why you wanted a particular book. Photocopy machines, of course, were

---

[8] Hedrick Smith, *The Russians* (New York: Quadrangle, 1976) pp. 345–346.

unavailable or controlled as though they were atom bombs. In 1978, I was shown the international newspaper library of the prestigious Moscow University School of Journalism. It included a few communist papers published in Europe, which were available to all students. Media such as the *New York Times* and *Time* magazine were kept in a locked vault, and access to the vault required the permission of the dean of the school.

The system also included a multitiered media system. Beyond the predictable public media were various publications whose candor was proportional to restrictions on access. In addition to the material distributed for public consumption, the Soviet news agency TASS ("Telegraph Agency of the Soviet Union") published a daily "White TASS" file running to several hundred pages of factual information from home and abroad that was available only to party officials. An even more rarefied "Red TASS" (named for the color of the cover sheet) went to the highest-ranking journalists, party officers, and government ministers. It contained not secret intelligence but the kind of information found in ordinary newspapers in the West.

Gorbachev's Revolution

As we have noted earlier, everything that had been associated with the Soviet Union—especially its mass media—began to change when Gorbachev took power in 1984. By the end of the 1980s, little in the old system was recognizable, but change proceeded two steps forward and one step back.

The legal status of *glasnost* was still insecure, but a law passed in 1990 gave private organizations the right to start their own publications. Until then, only approved elements of the party or government could publish. The government censorship organization, *Glavlit,* remained alive, however, and government retained the right to prohibit publication of material that "threatened" state security. The rights of journalists and the limits of government control of information were still untested in a judicial system that was only beginning to view law as a restraint on government power.

Broadcasting was in an even more uncertain limbo. It had led the way in exposing the worst of the abuses and failures, but party functionaries still controlled the airwaves and what went out on them. At one point, Gorbachev, ostensibly making broadcasting independent of the government in the model of Western European systems, actually installed a close ally as its director. Some of the more daring programs were toned down and others were openly censored.

With the disintegration of the Soviet Union, broadcasting entered an even more insecure state. Each former republic moved to establish its own system with varying degrees of political control and commitment to independence. Private entrepreneurs established commercial stations that met audience interests in news and entertainment but often operated without legal sanction and flirted continually with financial collapse. Of course, the first years of the 1990s saw all of the former communist empire of Central and Eastern Europe walking a narrow line between Western-style modernity and political and economic chaos. The fate of media emerging from the communist concept was tied with the larger fortunes of the countries themselves. With easy public access to the global information network and journalists still in the forefront of the effort to replace the creaky Soviet system, a return to the pre-*glasnost* days seemed remote. But a resurgence of ethnic animosities, fed by economic collapse, did not.

Although the media were intended to be an ally in Gorbachev's economic reforms, they became an independent force that often criticized him as vigorously as they found fault with the stagnant Soviet economy and unmoveable bureaucracy. They also played a key role in the rise of nationalism in the non-Russian republics that finally brought about the collapse of the union itself. By the end of 1990, the two main advocates of press independence, Foreign Minister Eduard Shevardnadze and Politburo member Alexander Yakovlev, were out of the government, and Gorbachev himself was calling for the repeal of the law that granted an independent press a legal basis.

Two actions were significant in Gorbachev's turnabout, both symbolically and practically. The first was an attack by Soviet troops on the TV headquarters in Vilnius, Lithuania, on January 13, 1990, as part of a broader Soviet occupation to counter the small republic's declaration of independence. Fourteen civilians were killed in the attack. A week later, journalists seemed to be a special target when forces staged a similar attack in the capital of Latvia.

Two months earlier, Gorbachev had replaced the head of Gostelradio—the central broadcast system—with a party hard-liner, Leonid Kravchenko. Supposedly the change came when broadcasting was transferred from the central government to a public corporation, but, in fact, it allowed Kravchenko, who answered directly to Gorbachev, to cancel a number of critical programs and to fire some of the most aggressive journalists. First to get the ax was *Vzglyad* ("Viewpoint") described as "a massively popular, two-hour Friday night magazine that mixed embarrassing exposes of the Soviet Army with Soviet rock; gyrating, sexy MTV videos with sharp-tongued discussions censuring Stalin, Lenin, and Gorbachev."[9] One interesting challenge to the newly tamed Soviet broadcasting was a television service run by the Russian republic, which, curiously enough, rented transmitter time and facilities from Gostelradio. Some of the fired broadcasters moved to Russian Television, which continued to operate until the attempted coup. After the failed coup, Russian Television came back on the air, stronger than ever, but beholden to Yeltsin as Gostelradio was to Gorbachev.

The campaign to control the media in 1990 and 1991 failed because many of the journalists were able to outmaneuver the censors and because alternative voices—both foreign and domestic—were readily available. The Leninist notion of a monopoly press used as an instrument of propaganda, agitation, organization, and control was never very effective even when the communist concept of the media was the model for more than a dozen countries. Modern communication technology destroyed the possibility of implementing the communist press concept, and the Soviet experience in 1990 and 1991 destroyed the concept's remaining legitimacy.

---

[9] *1991: The Soviet Media's Year of Decision* (New York: Committee to Protect Journalists, 1991), p. 7.

The Coup and After

The failed coup against Gorbachev in August 1991 was the stake in the heart that killed Soviet communism and the communist concept of journalism. For four days, Gorbachev was held prisoner in his vacation *dacha* in the Crimea while Yeltsin, who had emerged as the most powerful of the reformers, holed up in the Russian parliament building protected from tanks by massive crowds of supporters. At one point, he climbed on one of the tanks to shout his defiance. The moment, carried around the world live on CNN and repeated in a thousand newspapers, became an instant visual icon of Soviet communism's last gasp.

The "emergency committee" of hard-line communists who staged the coup allowed only nine politically reliable papers to publish and seized both the Russian broadcast facilities and several independent stations. However, several of the banned publications used desktop publishing systems and photocopiers to put out simple newssheets. The main broadcasters, too, undermined the coup by broadcasting details of protests and especially Yeltsin's opposition.

For reasons not clear at the time, both domestic and international telecommunication lines were not cut as they were in China after Tiananmen Square. After four days, facing domestic opposition and international condemnation, the emergency committee capitulated, and Gorbachev, looking tired but vigorous, returned to Moscow in triumph. Now the positions reversed, and the hard-line papers were temporarily banned, while new life was breathed into the independent media. Many of the loyalists Gorbachev had installed in the party media were tossed out. The new heroes were the independent journalists who had defied the coup.

The coup, of course, was a dramatic visual event that seemed made for television. Live coverage brought it to homes around the world. Whether mass media made the coup itself possible or made its failure inevitable is a topic for Chapter 11. For everyone who watched, listened, and read—the millions within the Soviet Union and probably several billion around the world—the power of global communication was evident in three vignettes that captured several of the trends we have encountered throughout our armchair media tour.

1. The emergency committee that staged the coup claimed that Gorbachev had been temporarily removed from power for undefined medical reasons. When he heard this, Gorbachev made a videotape with a home camcorder to document his good state of health and to denounce his detention. He planned to smuggle the tape to supporters who would distribute it as a high-tech *samizdat* publication.
2. When the coup-controlled state radio and TV refused to broadcast Yeltsin's denunciation of the takeover, he faxed a copy to Washington, D.C., with a request that it be forwarded to the Voice of America (VOA) and broadcast back to the Soviet Union. It was, and the emergency committee's attempt to silence Yeltsin failed.
3. After the coup, Gorbachev explained that he and advisers detained with him had rigged up a short-wave antenna and listened to the BBC, VOA, and Radio Liberty. He said the BBC was the best,

although it was not clear from his remarks whether he was referring to reception quality or coverage. In all three incidents, modern communication thwarted an effort to maintain a monopoly on information. In the second two, the global power of Anglo-American media was again underscored.

In the twenty-first century, the political entity that follows the Soviet Union will have to contend with another of the global trends—the rise of nationalism as a source of conflict—in addition to finding a way to move from communism to democracy. In the aftermath of the attempted coup, the remnants of the Soviet Union still faced the ordeal of shifting to a market economy and a workable democracy. Media, especially those cut adrift from the party, had to look for financial support in a shrinking economy. They were even more dependent on the West for technology, which had to be paid for with nonexistent hard currency. Although some progress was made in creating a system of law that guaranteed press freedom, independent journalism's financial and political position remained precarious. The "end of history" produced a whole new set of problems, which neither communism nor twenty-first-century Western capitalism had solved.

With easy access to the global information network and journalists still in the forefront of the effort to dismantle the Soviet system, a return to the pre-*glasnost* days seemed remote. However, one country had demonstrated in 1989 that you could put the genie back into the bottle. If nothing else, China was an argument that the end of history had been postponed.

CHINA

Cultural Factors

China is a country of extremes. Its population of more than 1 billion includes every fifth person in the world. Despite an appearance of cultural uniformity to outsiders, China includes a range of ethnic minorities and diversity within the broad Chinese culture. The written language, for example, is understandable to all Chinese, but the spoken version is not. This is possible because the Chinese characters stand for ideas or objects rather than phonetic sounds. A Mandarin speaker from Beijing and a Cantonese speaker from Hong Kong would both recognize a language character but pronounce it differently. To Tibetans, of course, either dialect would be a foreign language. They would prefer their own language in a country free of Chinese domination.

The Chinese culture is one of the oldest and most sophisticated in the world. Gunpowder and printing with moveable type were invented there while Europeans were running around in animal skins. Yet today, China is one of the poorest countries in the world (although with the fastest growing economy), and its future is a bigger question mark than that of the former Soviet Union.

The West and particularly the United States have had a love-hate relationship with China for two centuries. In the nineteenth century, the United States developed a paternalistic attitude toward China, something like that between Britain and India. Christian missionaries and businessmen flocked there by the hundreds to "civilize" one of the oldest civilizations in the world without asking the Chinese whether they wanted to be Westernized. After the communist revolution of 1949, the two countries turned their backs on each other and refused to speak for two decades.

Mao Zedong's 1949 victory over the U.S.-backed Nationalists was the second great victory for communism and the first in what was becoming known as the third world—the great majority of newly independent and about-to-be independent countries that belonged neither to the capitalist West nor to the communist East. Could economically undeveloped countries nourish a system that Marx had said could emerge only out of advanced capitalism? Did the principles of propaganda and agitation developed to foment a revolution against an autocratic European monarchy apply to a country like China? Was some form of Marxism the solution to the gap between the prosperous, stable West and the poor, volatile third world? In the later decades of the twentieth century, a lot of people thought it was and looked to China as the vanguard of the twenty-first century.

Depending on your point of view, China under Mao—"Red China," as it was called during the 1950s—was either the best example of the power of indoctrination applied to evil ends or the best example of the truth of Marxism-Leninism when given a chance. One side pointed to the small group of U.S. prisoners-of-war in Korea who denounced their country after being "brainwashed" by Chinese captors. This, they said, was evidence of the power of modern propaganda and reason enough to sustain the cold war. Through the occasional glimpses behind the closed doors of China, we saw what appeared to be a monolithic people responding, in robot-like fashion, to the power of Maoist propaganda and agitation. Surely these things were evidence of the dangers of "Chicom agi-prop."

A few others—mostly Western academics—looked at the same images and decided that China was the future: One of the poorest countries in the world had forged an enviable system of equality and prosperity—and had done it alone, without intrusion from the West. What better evidence could you ask for of the natural fit between communism and the emerging third world?

Of course, the larger truth lay somewhere in between these two extremes. Progress in economic and social development was impressive, but the price in human lives and personal freedom was high. No one knows the price because a short-lived period of openness and reform after Mao's death ended in 1989. For the West, China remains a fascination and a puzzle. In the topsy-turvy world of the 1990s, a conservative Republican administration was attacked by liberals for failing to condemn a Chinese government committed to maintaining a traditional communist regime.

Chinese Media Theory

In adapting the broad outlines of communism to China, the Mao government made several changes to the communication system that had developed in the Soviet Union. These included (1) insulation of the people against the outside world,

(2) repetition of simple themes contained in a single message, and (3) reinforcement of mass media messages with interpersonal communication. Each of them requires further discussion.

China's isolation from the communist revolution to the 1970s was a product of both its own choice and U.S.-led policy. Extensive use of community loudspeakers and wired radio, combined with jamming of foreign short-wave broadcasts, gave the Chinese authorities a near monopoly on information that the communist regimes in Europe could never achieve. Few foreigners were allowed in, and those who were were tightly controlled. A largely illiterate population could not read outside material even when it was smuggled in. China during this period was one of the most isolated countries in modern times.

The use of simple agitation slogans was more extensive than in the Soviet Union. Mao himself once said that even a simple slogan like "Down with imperialism!" could be more powerful than modern weapons. In practice, the social environment of the Chinese people was a constant bombardment of slogans. On trains, in local markets, at work, and on the street, loudspeakers played martial music interspersed with political announcements and the omnipresent slogans. Even in private homes, wired radios carried the same programs. The off button provided the only relief.

The use of interpersonal reinforcement of mass media messages has some support in modern psychology. In all cultures, public ceremonies are used to acknowledge and reinforce a commitment to marriage, a church, or a public office. Public affirmation promotes internalization of the message and makes it difficult to recant. In China, the technique was used extensively. People in a factory or commune lived together, too, so their common experience was total. After work, a group might get together to hear the latest slogans and to have them explained by the work unit party agitator. After discussion, individuals were expected to commit themselves to the implementation of the slogans at work or to "confess" how they had failed to carry out the dictum in the past. Promotions at work, access to living quarters, and even the right to marry and have children were sometimes tied to the enthusiasm with which one responded to the indoctrination.

Indoctrination was used extensively in a series of mass campaigns that were designed to catapult China from poverty to modernity with little more than ideology as propellant. The two best known were the Great Leap Forward in the late 1950s and the Cultural Revolution a decade later. The first came after Mao broke with the Soviet Union and tried to assert leadership in a separate, third-world communist movement. The second came when an aging Mao tried to restore vigor to the country by sending legions of radical young Red Guards rampaging across the country and exiling most of the leadership to the countryside. In both cases, the result was social disruption and economic chaos, not quick progress toward the goal Marx had promised a century earlier.

Chinese Media

Like Lenin, Mao started with an underdeveloped country and a primitive media system. He created a media system much like that of the Soviet Union. It included a national party newspaper, *Renmin Ribao,* usually identified by its English-language translation as the *People's Daily,* and supporting media for various segments of the party and society. Radio was given special emphasis because of its value in spreading information quickly from the party headquarters to a huge and largely illiterate population. Until the economic reforms after Mao's death, television was given little attention, and few Chinese families could afford to buy a TV set. Despite rapid growth in both radio and television, China remains one of the most media-poor nations.

Like the Soviet Union and other communist countries, China had a dual information system. Media for public consumption were carefully controlled and edited to reflect party priorities and views of the world. However, insiders had access to a wider range of information that was often culled from Western news media.

The Chinese version of the system included three levels of secret information. The first was called *Reference News,* a four-page tabloid containing reports about world affairs and outsiders' coverage of China. Circulation was about 10 million, twice that of the *People's Daily.* It was available by subscription to most Chinese but not to foreigners.

Above *Reference News* was a twice-daily digest of foreign material called *Reference Material.* It was apparently assembled by Xinhua, the Chinese news agency, for party members above a certain rank. Higher officials had access to several internal reference reports that were frequently candid and critical of domestic affairs. Only the Central Committee members and highest-ranking military commanders had access to *Cable News,* which was apparently designed to keep the leaders instantly in touch with major developments at home and abroad.[10]

Post-Mao China

China started toward *perestroika* and *glasnost* before the Soviet Union made the rest of the world familiar with the terms. After Mao's death, pragmatic reformers instituted a program of "Four Modernizations," which encouraged private entrepreneurship and foreign investment and increased contact with the rest of the world. Changes in mass media included the introduction of limited Western advertising and programming on TV, loosening of the tight control on print media, and the occasional unauthorized but tolerated independent medium. These included giant wall posters criticizing the government (an update of a traditional medium), a few racy tabloids, and one serious newspaper, the *World Economic Herald,* published in Shanghai.

The *Herald,* founded in 1979, served a function like that of *Ogonek* and *Moscow News.* At first the paper focused on global economic affairs, but soon it became a forum for advocates of reform. Despite harassment from government officials and occasional threats, the *Herald* prodded and nagged and exposed. Circulation reached 300,000. After the crackdown on the prodemocracy movement, the *Herald* was one of the first targets of government suppression. All media

---

[10] Fox Butterfield, *China: Alive in the Bitter Sea* (New York: Bantam, 1982), ch. 18.

were quickly brought back under control of the party, although links with the outside world through short-wave radio and business and personal contacts made a return to the information isolation of the 1960s impossible.

The collapse of communism in the Soviet Union left China and a few other outposts of Marxism outside the global information system but not insulated from it. Teenagers in China, Cuba, and North Korea knew as much about the latest Western rock stars and movie idols as their counterparts in the West—even more, in some cases. Their parents probably could keep up with world events almost as well as people with their own satellite dishes and 100-channel cable TV systems. Whether communism as a political system can survive even in a handful of isolated countries against the force of a global information age is a question that remains to be answered.

MAIN POINTS

1. The communist concept of media is the opposite of the Western concept. It derives from a different theory of history and assigns very different responsibilities to the mass media.
2. Marx provided the intellectual background to the communist idea of mass media, but Lenin was the first to define specific media functions: propaganda, agitation, organization, and control.
3. Under Gorbachev, *glasnost,* or openness, replaced the traditional tight, centralized control over mass media. Journalists were encouraged to support economic restructuring, or *perestroika,* and became important allies of Gorbachev in his effort to reform (or dismantle) communism. The collapse of the Soviet Union destroyed the legitimacy of the communist concept of journalism.
4. Reforms in China also included the rise of independent, critical media. The military attack on protesters demanding radical reforms in Tiananmen Square in 1989 was followed by a reimposition of censorship and party control over mass media.

FOR MORE INFORMATION

Books on the communist concept of the media divide neatly into pre-*glasnost* and post-*glasnost* groups. Among the former are Saul K. Padover, ed., *Karl Marx on Freedom of the Press and Censorship* (New York: McGraw-Hill, 1974); *Lenin about the Press* (Prague: International Organization of Journalists, 1972); Angus Roxburgh, *Pravda: Inside the Soviet News Machine* (New York: George Braziller, 1987); Hedrick Smith, *The Russians* (New York: Ballantine, 1976); and several other journalistic memoirs written before the mid-1980s.

Post-*glasnost* books (and a couple that straddle the Gorbachev revolution) are Hedrick Smith, *The New Russians* (New York: Random House, 1990); Walter Laqueur, *The Long*

Road to Freedom: Russia and Glasnost (New York: Scribners, 1989); Ellen Mickiewicz, *Split Signals: Television and Politics in the Soviet Union* (New York: Oxford University Press, 1988); David Wedgewood Benn, *Persuasion and Soviet Politics* (Oxford: Basil Blackwell, 1989); Thomas F. Remington, *The Truth of Authority: Ideology and Communication in the Soviet Union* (Pittsburgh, PA: University of Pittsburgh Press, 1988); Martin Walker, *The Waking Giant: Gorbachev's Russia* (New York: Pantheon, 1986); Dusko Doder and Louise Branson, *Gorbachev: Heretic in the Kremlin* (New York: Viking, 1990); and Brian McNair, *Glasnost, Perestroika and the Soviet Media* (London: Routledge, 1991).

Material on Chinese media—especially contemporary accounts—is more limited. For a start, see Robert L. Bishop, *Qi Lai! Mobilizing One Billion Chinese: The Chinese Communication System* (Ames: Iowa State University Press, 1989); Godwin C. Chu and Francis L. K. Hsu, eds., *Moving a Mountain: Cultural Change in China* (Honolulu: University Press of Hawaii, 1979); Godwin C. Chu, *Radical Change through Communication in Mao's China* (Honolulu: University Press of Hawaii, 1977); Jay Mathews and Linda Mathews, *One Billion: A China Chronicle* (New York: Ballantine, 1983); and Fox Butterfield, *China: Alive in the Bitter Sea* (New York: Ballantine, 1982).

Studies of post-Gorbachev Russia and some preliminary analyses of the collapse of the Soviet Union are available. Many include assessments of the role of mass media. For a tour of communism's outposts, written just before the revolution of 1989, see Anthony Daniels, *Utopias Elsewhere: Journeys in a Vanishing World* (New York: Crown, 1991). A journalistic assessment of Cuba after the collapse of the Soviet Union is Tom Miller, *Trading with the Enemy: A Yankee Travels through Castro's Cuba* (New York: Atheneum, 1992). Pico Iyer's *Falling off the Map: Some Lonely Places of the World* (New York: Knopf, 1993) includes visits to Cuba, North Korea, and Vietnam.

An unusual, detailed assessment of communist censorship in action is Jane Leftwich Curry, ed. and trans., *The Black Book of Polish Censorship* (New York: Vintage, 1984).

FOR DISCUSSION

1. Watch Russian TV news programming, which in early 1993 was broadcast daily on C-SPAN and on SCOLA and is available on many college campuses via satellite dishes. Compare it with U.S. coverage for content and techniques.

2. Compare the influence of international mass media in the attack on protesters in Tiananmen Square with that in the attempted coup in Moscow, noting how efforts to control foreign journalists differed.

3. Write a memo outlining the type of media system you recommend for the former communist states. You could argue for a traditional European-style system (partisan newspapers and public service broadcasting), the U.S. system (nonpartisan, watchdog newspapers and mostly private broadcasters), some combination of the two, or something entirely new created using new technologies.

4. Write a letter to Professor Hachten, advising him how you believe he should treat the communist concept of the press in the next edition of his book: historical artifact, blueprint for the future, utopian ideal but practical impossibility, or mask for government control.

DATA BASE

I. Availability of communications media from communist and formerly communist countries (number per 100 population).

Country	Newspaper Circulation	Radio Sets	Television Sets	VCRs	Phone Lines
Albania	4	18	9		2
Bulgaria	27	56	36	6	19
China	3	26	13		1
Cuba	13	34	21		3
Czechoslovakia	35	61	51	5	14
Hungary	27	81	47	8	9
North Korea	N/A	13	2		N/A
Poland	18	52	39	3	8
Romania	16	38	34	3	13
Soviet Union	47	41	38	1	10
Vietnam	N/A	10	4		0
Yugoslavia	10	47	27	7	15

SOURCE: Newspaper circulation figures are mid- to late-1980s and from UNESCO figures and other sources; phone line data are from American Telephone & Telegraph's (AT&T) *The World's Telephones,* 1991, and the International Telecommunication Union's (ITU) *Yearbook of Common Carrier Telecommunication Statistics* (18th ed.). Radio, TV, and VCR data from *World Radio and TV Receivers,* ed. by Carol L. Forrester. Copyright © 1991 IBAR-BBC World Service. Reprinted by permission.

II. Circulation figures for the leading papers of some communist countries:

Soviet Union's 10 All-Union Dailies	Circulation
Izvestia ("News")	10,500,000
Komsomolskaya Pravda	18,500,000
Krasnaya Zvezda ("Red Star")	2,000,000
Pravda ("Truth")	9,664,000
Selskaya Zhizn ("Rural Life")	9,000,000
Socialist Industry	1,500,000
Sovetskaya Russiya	4,221,000
Sovetsky Sport	3,900,000
Trud ("Labor")	20,202,000
Gudok ("Whistle")	500,000

NOTE: The Soviet *Union,* or *Union* of Soviet Socialist Republics was, in theory, a voluntary union of sovereign republics or nations. The 10 dailies that circulated throughout the USSR are called *all-union.* The same term is used for anything that referred to or encompassed the entire country. "National," on the other hand, refers to Russian, Latvian, etc., and also means ethnic group within a republic. A national paper serves one nation—Russian, Moldavian, Hungarian, German, etc. *Pravda* was one of 10 all-union papers.

China	*Ed/Pub 1992*	*Benn's Media Directory 1992*
People's Daily	4,000,000	5,000,000
China Daily (English)	70,000	150,000
Reference News	N/A	3,600,000
Economic Daily	2,250,000	1,591,000
China Youth Daily News	N/A	3,000,000

NOTE: All figures and political groupings from pre-1989–1990 revolutions.
SOURCE: Robert U. Brown, ed., *Editor & Publisher International Yearbook 1992* (New York: Editor & Publisher, 1992), and *Benn's Media Directory International 1992* (Tonbridge, UK: Benn Business Information Services, 1992).

III. Estimates of circulation of some Soviet publications in 1990 and 1991:

Ogonek	3,200,000
Moscow News	1,916,000
Argumenti i Fakty	23,840,000
Literary Gazette	1,200,000
Pravda	3,201,000
Izvestia	4,700,000
Soviet Russia	1,900,000
Red Star	2,500,000
Labor	18,900,000

Vremya, the prime-time Gostelradio program, was renamed *TV-Inform* after the failed coup.

Vzglyad reappeared after the failed coup.

SOURCE: From *The Soviet Media's Year of Decision* (New York: Committee to Protect Journalists, 1991). Copyright © 1991 Committee to Protect Journalists. Reprinted by permission.

IV. Estimates of subscriptions to selected Russian newspapers in early 1993, with changes from 1992:

	93 Subscriptions	*Change (%)*
Argumenti i Fakty (weekly)	8.9 million	−65.5
Komsomolskaya Pravda (daily)	3.4 million	−73.7
Trud (daily)	3.1 million	−66.4
Selskaya Zhizn (daily)	1.2 million	−66.6
Izvestia (daily)	800,000	−73.3
Sovetsky Sport (daily)	495,000	−74.2
Pravda (daily)	472,000	−52.4
Moskovsky Novosti (weekly)	452,000	−12.2
Sovetskaya Rossiya (daily)	404,000	−52.5

SOURCE: Celestine Bohlen, ''Few Russian Papers Thriving with the New Press Freedom,'' *New York Times,* January 26, 1993, p. 1.

CHAPTER 9

Authoritarian Media

ABOUT THIS CHAPTER

The authoritarian concept of the press is both the oldest type of media system in the world and still the most common today. It has links to the communist system, which we have already examined, and to the development system, which we consider in Chapter 10. Even the most democratic governments indulge in some of the practices we associate with authoritarianism.

At the end of the twentieth century, authoritarian media systems are common in Latin America and in parts of Asia. Some of the countries in Central and Eastern Europe seem to be moving from communism toward traditional authoritarianism. Their media systems, too, reflect this dramatic change.

INTRODUCTION

History

The authoritarian concept of mass media was all-powerful government's response to the second communication revolution, the invention of printing with moveable type. The history of mass media as we know the term begins with authoritarianism.

Fred Siebert, who wrote about authoritarianism in the original formulation of the *Four Theories of the Press,* concluded that authoritarianism was (and presumably still is) the most pervasive media system in the world. He added:

> It is the theory which was almost automatically adopted by most countries
> when society and technology became sufficiently developed to produce
> what today we call the "mass media" of communication. It furnishes

the basis for the press systems in many modern societies; even where it has been abandoned, it has continued to influence the practices of a number of governments which theoretically adhere to libertarian principles.[1]

Today, of course, every country has some system of mass media that is large and pervasive by standards of even a few decades ago. Even the poorest country in the 1990s has a communication system beyond the imagination of kings and bishops of the fifteenth and early sixteenth centuries, when printing spread across Europe. The reaction of governments today to the threat from technological innovation, however, is similar. Why does a media theory developed by autocrats in response to an invention of three centuries ago still hold sway?

To get to the answer, we should first recall the discussion of various media theories. You will remember that the first distinction all of them make is the relationship between media and government. The Western concept begins with the assumption that media function best when they are independent of government. Usually there is an implicit assumption that mass media should function as some kind of check on government. In extreme cases, media can be used to overthrow existing governments, which is the core of the revolutionary concept.

Although the argument that media and government should remain separate is popular among journalists and political speech makers, the opposite view is more widely observed in practice. Government influence can take the form of denying mass media the power to threaten government authority or of mobilizing mass media as an instrument of social change. The former is the traditional authoritarian concept of mass media. The latter is the basis for both the communist concept and the development concept, which we consider in Chapter 10. In both cases, independent, critical journalism is difficult at best and often impossible.

In Anglo-American textbooks, we tend to read the works of those who established the libertarian concept of mass media. U.S. heroes are those who fought for this concept. The pantheon includes the familiar names of John Milton, John Locke, Thomas Jefferson, and John Stuart Mill as well as gutsy journalists and printers such as Thomas Paine and John Peter Zenger, who put the inspiring words of libertarianism to the test.

We often forget, however, that the Western tradition also includes a strong current of suspicion of individual liberty and a parallel current recognizing government as the legitimate and appropriate embodiment of a culture or nation. Even Plato proposed expelling those who were offenders of rigid codes of behavior and argued in favor of requiring poets to submit their work to authorities. Later political philosophers such as Niccolo Machiavelli, Thomas Hobbes, and especially Georg Hegel supported the notion of the right—even responsibility—of the state to control power and, therefore, information.

Hegel, whom we have met both as the intellectual father of Marxism and the source of today's "end of history" argument, believed the individual found freedom through the state but dismissed the notion that individuals had any inherent *right* to participate directly in government. As he put it:

---

[1] Fred S. Siebert, Theodore Peterson, and Wilbur Schramm, *Four Theories of the Press* (Champaign: University of Illinois Press, 1963), p. 9.

In it [the State] freedom attains to it the maximum of its rights; but at the same time the State, being an end in itself, is provided with the maximum of rights over against the individual citizens, whose highest duty it is to be members of the State.[2]

A recent interpretation of the varieties of freedom notes that in societies where discipline, divine authority, and protection in a social order are paramount cultural values, freedom can mean being outcast, lost, or abandoned. In many cultures in history, freedom has meant the freedom to rule others.[3] Keep this in mind as an aid to understanding cultures that talk about freedom but embrace what we would call authoritarianism, such as Islam and some regimes in Central Europe. Without putting too much emphasis on it, an argument could be made that the difference in attitudes toward mass media between the English-speaking countries and the continental European countries is a reflection of the difference between Locke and Jefferson, on the one hand, and Machiavelli and Hegel, on the other.

Methods of Control

Historically, authoritarian governments kept the revolutionary technology of cheap, fast printing under control with a mixture of carrot and stick incentives. The carrots included licenses to operate printing plants and permission to publish specific works. The sticks included harsh legal penalties for those who published without authority, especially printers who dared to use their powerful new medium to challenge the power of the establishment.

Most of the early printers were private entrepreneurs who were as interested in profits as in politics. Then, as now, technological innovation offered the lure of riches. Religious books, scholarly treatises, and, of course, the flood of vernacular literature all contributed to the rapid development of the new publishing industry. For most printers, journalism was a small part of their activities and for many probably a relatively unimportant one. Money could be made from government printing contracts as well as from publishing noncontroversial materials. Printers had good reasons to use their new power cautiously and to avoid running askew of the greater power of the state.

AUTHORITARIANISM TODAY

Most of the characteristics of early authoritarian media systems apply today as well. Authoritarian media are usually privately owned and have commercial interests as well as political. They tend to be found in countries that are already relatively well developed or well along the road toward economic development. And like the early printers in Britain and the United States, media proprietors in authoritarian regimes maintain a symbiotic relationship with their governments.

---

[2] Quoted in Fred S. Siebert, Theodore Peterson, and Wilbur Schramm, *Four Theories of the Press* (Urbana: University of Illinois Press, 1963), p. 14.

[3] Orlando Patterson, *Freedom in the Making of Western Culture* (New York: Basic, 1991).

They often come from the same elite classes and share many social and economic goals. At the same time, however, journalists who challenge authoritarian governments include some of the world's bravest men and women. In many countries, they are the only voices challenging the power of brutal regimes.

The five concepts we are using to classify the world's media systems are not always precise, and specific countries do not always fit neatly into any one concept. This is particularly true when we consider the overlaps among Western, authoritarian, and developmental media systems. Most Latin American countries can be classified as having authoritarian media systems. So, too, can several Asian/Pacific nations, especially the economic "tigers" of Taiwan, Singapore, South Korea, and Hong Kong. A few countries in the eastern Mediterranean and Middle East could be included as well.

How can a government at the end of the twentieth century justify authoritarian controls over its national media, especially when a wave of freedom is washing over most of the world and modern communication technology makes efforts to control information largely futile? The traditional defense of authoritarianism is often invoked: the existence of threats to the nation sufficiently grave to justify the suspension of a right enshrined in virtually every written constitution on earth. Usually full freedom is promised to be restored once the existing dangers are removed. The dangers, real or imagined, can be internal guerrilla insurgencies or the threat of invasion from belligerent neighbors. Sometimes, of course, the danger is real, although regimes in power can tend to confuse themselves with the nations they represent and to interpret simple criticism as sedition. It is easy to invoke the mantra of national security to avoid the inconvenience of open government; the tendency to do so is universal.

An insidious element of authoritarian control is that it can include shadowy acts and threats that governments can later deny. Sometimes governments themselves are powerless to protect media from threats by nongovernment sources. During the military dictatorship in Argentina between 1976 and 1983, more than 100 journalists were assassinated or simply disappeared.[4] Most assume that government officials sanctioned the murders even if many were carried out by private paramilitary groups. Sometimes the bodies were found, sometimes not.

In the 1980s, a Colombian drug cartel attacked several newspapers and murdered journalists. The Colombian government was unable to provide protection or to prosecute those responsible. Freedom House counts about 1,000 instances of attack and harassment of journalists each year. To be sure, not all of them take place in authoritarian countries, but many do.[5] If General Karl von Clauswitz were around to see the symbiosis of global communication and politics at the end of the twentieth century, he might argue that war is now an extension of journalism, or vice versa. He probably would not be surprised to learn of the large number of casualties among journalists in the rubble of Yugoslavia.

---

[4] *Information, Freedom and Censorship: The Article 19 World Report, 1988* (London: Longman, 1988), p. 63.

[5] "Press Freedom: Struggle and Toll—1990," *Freedom Review,* vol. 22, no. 1, 1991, p. 58.

A new argument justifying authoritarian control of mass media is that the nation is too fragile to permit the scrutiny of a critical press. Western-style media independence, it is argued, may come later, after goals of economic development and political stability have been achieved. The argument—absolutely true—is that Western countries took several centuries and a long history of horrible wars to reach their present state of stability and prosperity. Developing countries are trying to do the same thing in a few decades and need the cushion of controlled media. This argument is consistent with Siebert's assertion that authoritarianism is the route most countries use to progress from traditional society to modernity.

Current examples of this kind of influence include government control of broadcasting and prohibitions on critical reporting in most third-world countries. Usually there is not open censorship but rather a combination of lack of access to information, an absence of legal remedies, and stiff penalties for violators. The developmental media concept rests largely on this argument, but it applies to the authoritarian concept as well.

Authoritarianism versus Totalitarianism

Jeane Kirkpatrick, the U.S. ambassador to the United Nations during the Reagan administration, once made a distinction between totalitarian and authoritarian regimes. She advocated cooperation with authoritarian governments, which, she believed, could reform themselves into democracies, but not with totalitarian regimes, which could not.[6] The argument was controversial. Critics said it belonged to the cold war and the U.S. tradition of support for any regime that was sufficiently anticommunist, regardless of its abuses of citizens' liberties.

Soon after the collapse of communism in Central and Eastern Europe, Ambassador Kirkpatrick acknowledged the novelty of a totalitarian regime evolving, more or less peacefully, into something less threatening but maintained her position on support for unpalatable authoritarian governments. Given the Siebert principle, perhaps it is not surprising that the Soviet Union and its former European allies moved toward authoritarianism rather than directly to Western-style democracy. There may be hope for China as well.

Economics versus Politics

For nations moving out of the shadow of communism or third-world dictatorships in the 1990s, a basic question is how to move toward democracy while avoiding slipping back into the abyss of chaos or totalitarianism. In words made famous by the Gorbachev revolution in the Soviet Union, a basic policy decision is to choose *glasnost* or *perestroika*. In more traditional language, the choice for authoritarian governments determined to move toward democracy is whether to emphasize (1) political democracy on the assumption that openness (*glasnost*) leads to economic growth or (2) economic reform (*perestroika*) on the assumption

---

[6] Jeane J. Kirkpatrick, "Dictatorships and Double Standards," *Commentary,* November 1979, pp. 34–45.

that stable democracy will follow. This question is central to the developmental media concept we encounter in Chapter 10. In the twenty-first century, much of the world will constitute a global experiment of different paths toward the economic and political stability the West takes for granted. The experiment will include a test of what role—if any—communication can play in the great crusade.

With a few admittedly arbitrary classifications, an argument could be made that a majority of the world's people today live in an authoritarian media environment. First, we accept Jeane Kirkpatrick's argument and put the former Soviet Union and most of the no-longer-communist Central European nations into that category; same for China, which is more old-fashioned totalitarian than communist but leaning toward authoritarianism. We recognize the dramatic movement toward democracy in Latin America in the 1980s but remember that significant tensions between government and media remain. We note the movement toward multiparty democracy in Africa. Finally, we acknowledge the strength of India's tradition of press freedom but keep in mind government influence, especially on broadcasting.

If all these classifications are accepted, then a majority of the planet's people know firsthand the authoritarian media concept. The oldest press theory is still the most common at the end of the twentieth century. We can hope that the twenty-first century will see the truth of the Siebert hypothesis and an evolution toward greater press freedom.

AUTHORITARIANISM'S FUTURE

All of the countries profiled in this chapter—and the list could include many others, among them the postcommunist nations of Central and Eastern Europe—face the ordeal of creating stable, prosperous democracies in conditions where chaos and repression thrive. From the secure perspective of the West, it is easy to argue that press restrictions in the name of state security are a fig leaf covering government incompetence and corruption and that the timidity of media reflect an unhealthy connection between public authority and private greed.

This may be, but we need to remind ourselves of the long, painful history that got us where we are today and the imperfections remaining in Western media systems. Authoritarianism at least holds open the possibility of evolution toward the ideals of democracy. In the 1990s, two opposite pressures seem to be at work in authoritarian media systems. The outcome of the tussle between the two will influence the nature of news media in many countries during the twenty-first century.

One trend is the growing assertion of independence and critical reporting by journalists. Throughout the dictatorship years of the 1970s and 1980s in Latin America, journalists were among the few voices challenging military governments, and often they were the only voices. The pattern continues in Asia and is taking hold in Africa. The collapse of communism in the Soviet Union and the attack on the prodemocracy movement in China destroyed the legitimacy of the communist press concept but not the power of governments to control information. The development media concept, as we will see, was also discredited as a plausible alternative to the Western tradition. Ironically, as former dictatorships of both the Right and the Left struggle toward democracy via authoritarianism, journalism is both their ally and their enemy.

It is an ally because journalists are often in the front lines of the battle against dictatorship. It becomes an enemy when the temporary coalition that brought about the revolution breaks down and the government that emerges from the revolution begins to cope with the intractable problems of economics, politics, and possibly ethnic unrest. At that point, the scrutiny of critical journalism becomes first embarrassing and then threatening. The temptation is to buy off, intimidate, or mobilize critical news media in the name of national unity.

The second trend is an increasing willingness by governments to use their power to stifle media criticism. Perhaps noting the effective control of information by the British and U.S. governments during the Falklands/Malvinas war, the invasion of Panama, and the Persian Gulf War, authoritarian governments seem more willing to deal with their critics by silencing them. Although modern technology has made a true government monopoly of information impossible, it has not eliminated the attractiveness of government control. At home, it is still easy for authoritarian governments to influence what gets reported and how. Abroad, global media can sometimes be controlled. Almost always they can be kept at bay or ignored. To see what might be ahead for much of the world now moving toward democracy, case studies in Latin America and Asia are instructive.

BRAZIL

Overview

By almost any global standards, Brazil is a ''major-league'' country. It ranks sixth in the world in population (150 million in 1990, half the total population of South America). Its two major metropolitan areas are both among the 10 largest urban centers in the world. Physically, it is the world's fifth largest country, nearly as large as the United States, and contains the world's second longest river and its largest rain forest. It is the world's tenth largest economy and the second largest consumer market in the Western Hemisphere. Brazil also has the developing world's largest foreign debt and one of the world's highest inflation rates.

In media, too, Brazil is a nation of superlatives. It has more TV sets than the rest of Latin America combined. Its multinational, multimedia TV conglomerate, Rede Globo, is, by most measures, the world's fourth or fifth largest network. Its regular prime-time audiences of 60 million to 80 million are the largest of any network in the world.

It is easy to forget that Brazilians speak Portuguese, not Spanish. Because of the size of Brazil, the presence of Portuguese-speaking countries in Africa, and lingering remnants of the Portuguese Empire in Asia, the language can claim status as a second-tier international language. It is spoken by some 140 million people, putting it in the same league as German, French, and Arabic and not far from Spanish and Hindi. The relationship between Brazil and Portugal is similar to that

Authoritarian government influence on mass media is usually subtle and indirect, but after a state of emergency was declared in Bangkok following antigovernment demonstrations in May, 1992, the Bangkok *Post* appeared with clear evidence of censorship.

between the United States and Britain: The offspring has outgrown the parent and, to mix a metaphor, has become the tail wagging the dog.

In spirit, the Brazilians tend to reflect their multicultural population. In language, too, "Brazilian"—a simplified form of Portuguese and a product of multicultural New World influence, especially North American English—has emerged as the global standard, much to the chagrin of Portugal.

Media

Relations between government and media are typical of those in authoritarian countries at the end of the twentieth century. The media are privately owned, heavily entertainment oriented, and nonthreatening. During the period of military rule from 1964 to 1985, the government ruled with less violence and brutality than in many other Latin American dictatorships. Brazilian media were at best respectful and restrained in urging a return to civilian rule. They offered no serious challenge to the military regime. In return, they were given the freedom to prosper.

Newspapers in the two great cities of Rio de Janeiro and São Paulo were—and are—fat with advertising. Dailies—more than 200 are published in the country—range from the serious and internationally recognized *Jornal do Brasil, O Estado de São Paulo,* and *O Globo* to splashy tabloids. Although press runs are small by European standards and circulation is only 62 per 1,000 people, most dailies are professionally edited and printed on modern presses. The array of papers for sale in the big cities, bulging with ads and columns of sophisticated political reporting, belies both the economic problems of this supernation and the cozy ties between the media and government.

It is in television, however, that Brazil has achieved a global reputation and even significant global influence. Brazilian television is essentially one network and one man. Though not as well known internationally as the BBC or Rupert Murdoch, TV Globo and its creator, Roberto Marinho, belong in the dubious pantheon of modern global media moguls. In 1926, Marinho founded the Rio de Janeiro daily *O Globo,* which was the base for an empire that now extends from media to agriculture, real estate, and manufacturing. Media holdings include radio, records, video, telecommunication, regional papers, and other publications. But television is the core of the empire.

TV Globo dominates Brazilian television, attracting 80 percent or more of the prime-time audience with slickly produced soap operas and glitzy variety shows that are also exported to more than 40 other countries. The 80–90 percent share of the Brazilian audience represents the single largest audience for any one network in the world. By most criteria of audience size, money, and programming, TV Globo ranks just behind the three U.S. commercial networks.

The technical sophistication and production values of TV Globo are striking, even for someone used to the fast pace of U.S. commercial television. Computer-generated graphics are a specialty. In Brazil, U.S. imports appear only at the periphery of the TV schedule and seem dull by comparison to local productions.

In between the two prime-time soap operas is Globo's main newscast, *Jornal Nacional,* which is said to have as much influence in the country as the Catholic church. Because of the importance of television in a country of high illiteracy and the enormous audiences who watch *Jornal Nacional* as a break between entertainment programs, the program is probably the single most important political forum in the country. Marinho is not bashful about his influence on the program and frequently dictates content and play. In 1987, he told a reporter:

> We give all necessary information, but our opinions are in one way or another dependent on my character, my convictions, and my patriotism.[7]

Marinho himself was influential in persuading the military government to step down in 1984 and in electing the opposition party candidate for president.

---

[7] "The World According to Globo," *The Economist,* July 4, 1987, p. 44.

The president-elect, Tancredo Neves, died before he took office, so the new vice-president, José Sarney, became Brazil's first elected president in 20 years with Marinho's blessing and support.

In the new civilian government, the minister of communications was a Marinho friend, ally, and business partner. Not surprisingly, the new constitution omitted any reference to regulation of broadcasting. Marinho's—and Globo's—real clout, however, came in the presidential election in 1990 to replace Sarney.

Rise and Fall of Collor

After five years of the conservative Sarney, Brazil was saddled with hyperinflation, the third world's largest foreign debt, and growing labor and social unrest. The 1990 campaign pitted the head of a leftist labor party against a young, attractive landowner/politician who rose from nowhere in the polls with the help of—surprise—TV Globo. Fernando Collor de Mello, 40 at the time, came from a wealthy, landed family whose holdings included a newspaper, several radio stations, and—surprise again—a local affiliate of TV Globo. Brazil entered the age of TV politics, and with a combination of extensive, slick political advertising on TV and the network's blatant support, Collor—a Kennedy-like personality campaigning on a populist reform platform—became president.

Collor's populist, reformist politics were popular for a while but had limited success in coping with Brazil's hyperinflation, bloated bureaucracy, and stagnant and inefficient economy. Rumors of corruption by family members and political cronies nagged him until specific charges involving the theft or misappropriation of more than $20 million led to his impeachment at the end of 1992. A major factor in the impeachment was the relentless investigative reporting of *Veja,* an independent weekly news magazine that operated in the tradition of the Watergate-era *Washington Post.* Collor stayed in office despite the impeachment—the approval of the indictment by the legislature—but resigned a few hours before the trial was to begin.

Although an obvious embarrassment to Brazilians and a big setback to the nation's hopes for the 1990s, the Collor affair was both a shining example of democracy in action in a part of the world not known for such success and a reminder of the transitory power of mass media. The Globo empire could not keep Collor in office and could not prevent public opinion from turning against him when evidence—unearthed and publicized by the key elements of any democracy, opposition politicians and an opposition press—began to build. Nor could it counter the weight of a persistent voice of journalistic opposition when that voice built its case on documentable facts.

Getting elected with the help of the Globo empire was easier than coping with the massive problems facing the South American colossus. Brazil in the twenty-first century will be a test case of the durability of Latin American democracy and of Ambassador Kirkpatrick's prediction about the evolution from authoritarianism to democracy. Mexico is our next stop.

MEXICO

U.S.–Mexican Relations

In Mexico, an old joke goes, "Poor Mexico! So far from God and so close to the United States." Relations between the colossus of North America and its southern neighbor have always been difficult. Wars, very different cultural traditions, and stubborn problems ranging from foreign investment to illegal immigration have built a legacy of misunderstanding that sometimes seems impossible to overcome. Even today, despite Mexican commitment to a North American free trade pact and an administration in Washington, D.C., more sensitive than many of its predecessors, mistrust remains.

The border between the United States and Mexico, like that between the United States and Canada, is open. It is the only national border between a first-world and a third-world country and reflects the disparities and incongruities that exist between these two worlds.

From the north, one fear of those who advocate English as an official language in the United States is that a third "nation" will emerge along the border, neither Mexican nor Yankee and not quite at ease with either language or either culture. The result could be, as in so many trouble spots around the world, a permanent cultural conflict. On the other hand, Mexicans and other Latin Americans who use Mexico as a stepping stone to the United States could be the vanguard of the transformation of the United States into what Ben Wattenberg calls the first "supernation," or a true nation of nations.[8] In demography, economics, and culture, Mexico looms large in the future of the United States.

Mexican influence is growing more rapidly than that of any other immigrant group. In a century or two, North America may be a single entity, shading from a small French enclave to the dominant English region and then to Spanish. National borders may be nonexistent or unimportant. Even if a single North America fails to emerge, Mexico will remain one of the largest and fastest-growing countries in the world, the largest source of immigrants to the United States, and the United States' third largest trading partner.

Media Background

We often forget that Mexico (along with much of the rest of Latin America) was colonized by Spain a century before English settlers began arriving in large numbers in Virginia and Massachusetts. As a result, the New World's first university and first printing press were in Mexico City, not Jamestown or Boston. However, despite a century and a half of political independence, Mexico can claim an imperfect democracy and a poor record of economic and social development.

---

[8] Ben Wattenberg, *The First Universal Nation: Leading Indicators and Ideas about the Surge of America in the 1990s* (New York: Free Press, 1990).

Like Brazil, Mexico at first seems to resemble other developing countries: crowded, polluted cities; a big gap between rich and poor; and the icons of Anglo-American pop culture overlaid incongruously on a culture that seems at odds with them. But unlike many other developing countries, Mexico is media rich. Mexico City offers a diversity of newspapers, most fat with commercial advertising, that rivals Paris and London. Television is everywhere, glitzy and fast moving, with more commercials than prime time in the United States.

Mexican media, rivaled only by those in Brazil in wealth and sophistication, represent both the strengths and the weaknesses of authoritarian systems. On the plus side, the best papers—*Excélsior* in Mexico City is often compared to the *New York Times*—have an intellectual quality comparable to that of the best European papers. They are, on occasion, also an effective voice of opposition in a country that is run by a corrupt and often ruthless one-party government. On the negative side, media owners are part of the rich governing elite with a strong personal and business interest in maintaining their privilege. Both the watchdog function and the educational-cultural function of Western media systems are weak to nonexistent.

In Mexico, the ties between newspapers, broadcasting, and government are particularly strong. Newspapers are concentrated in a half dozen chains that typically include both national dailies published in Mexico City and smaller papers published outside the capital. Romulo O'Farrill, Jr., for example, owns *Novedades,* published in Mexico City, and seven other papers. He is also chairman of the board of Televisa, the broadcasting conglomerate that is virtually a Mexican monopoly and one of the largest broadcasters in the world.

Government influence on the media is varied but seldom subtle. The first level is self-censorship by journalists themselves, who understand the boundaries of permissible reporting. When that fails, the reporter can be offered bribes (a common practice) or threatened with violence (frighteningly common as well). When a reporter is beaten up or murdered, as happens regularly, other journalists also get the message. Journalists are notoriously underpaid and are expected to accept payment either for printing a story or for suppressing it. One estimate is that 90 percent of all journalists accept some kind of payoff; the other 10 percent are considered stupid.[9] Many of the papers also follow an old practice of printing what are essentially advertisements or PR releases as news stories in return for cash that arrives with them. In fact, government advertising accounts for about two-thirds of all advertising, and it is awarded with patronage and influence, not circulation or markets, in mind. Much of it appears as news stories without identification of source or purpose.

Most Mexican newspapers are uncritical supporters of the government. This is a product both of the common economic interests of the owners and political leaders and of a system that makes cooperation lucrative and opposition dangerous. Until 1990, the government maintained a monopoly on imported newsprint and continues to control importation of printing technology and

---

[9] *Information, Freedom and Censorship: The Article 19 World Report 1988* (New York: Longman, 1988), p. 102.

domestic communication satellites. If the economic pressures fail, various legal pressures can be applied. As a last resort, mobs can be rallied to attack presses and newsstands.

Scherer and *Proceso*

An exception to the pattern of Mexican journalism is Julio Scherer García.[10] He became editor of *Excélsior* in 1968 shortly before bloody student riots disrupted Mexico City as they had done in Europe and in the United States. Several hundred were killed, and many survivors were jailed. Under Scherer, coverage of the massacre and subsequent crisis was unsparing and critical. Luis Echeverría, who became president of Mexico a few months later with promises of reform and openness and rhetoric that initially pleased Mexico's substantial intellectual Left, tried various means to silence the paper.

These included the usual threats, an advertising boycott, and, finally, an internal coup that forced Scherer and some of his staff out of the paper. According to one U.S. journalist, "the paper that had become the best Spanish-language newspaper in the world under Scherer became safe and tame again. It remains so today."[11] Scherer, however, established a feisty weekly news magazine, *Proceso,* that became, despite government opposition, "the most fearless, most respected publication . . . the best single source of what is really going on in Mexico."[12]

Each new national president, hand-picked by his predecessor, promises reform and moves the country a little toward multiparty democracy and openness. Several newspapers, especially in the north, have joined Scherer in producing the critical investigative reporting that is part of the Western press tradition. Broadcasting, however, remains a government lapdog, not a watchdog.

Broadcasting

Television resembles Mexican newspapers as a predictable source of bland, pro-government information. Beyond that, the medium influences the country to a degree that is notable even from the perspective of the media-saturated United States or Japan. The pervasive medium seems to dominate the lives of people in even the poorest barrio in Mexico City and the most remote village with a diet of consumer advertising, imported action, and Mexico's own unique contribution, the telenovella. The novellas, syrupy and crude soap operas, fill hour after hour of prime time and are exported to most other Latin American countries. Like Rede Globo productions from Brazil, they found audiences in the rapidly expanding commercial markets around the world in the 1990s. For a time, a Mexican novella became the hottest program on Russian TV, forcing factories

---

[10] Latin practice is to use the mother's maiden name as we would use a middle name but to put it after the family name. Sometimes only the initial is used, as in Julio Scherer G.

[11] Patrick Oster, *The Mexicans: A Personal Portrait of a People* (New York: William Morrow, 1989), p. 188.

[12] Patrick Oster, *The Mexicans: A Personal Portrait of a People* (New York: William Morrow, 1989), p. 189.

and stores to adjust their activities around viewers who put the daily telecast ahead of work and business.

Alan Riding, long-time *New York Times* correspondent in Mexico, decried the government's generous subsidy of traditional arts but failure to prevent the debasing of the country's popular culture because it turned a blind eye to a steam-roller of North American imports and domestic clones:

> Thus, while Mexican culture is well preserved in museums, galleries and bookstores, traditional values are being decimated in the country's homes by the revolution in mass communications. Rather than serving as an arena for Mexican creativity, popular entertainment has become a broad avenue for cultural penetration by the United States.[13]

Riding's concern was widely shared by Mexican intellectuals, but this was not strong enough, as we will see, to bring about reform. Mexican broadcasting developed in the shadow of the United States as a privately owned, commercial system with minimal social obligations built into oversight laws that were never enforced. The commercial U.S. networks were active in establishing Mexican radio and television but have been without direct involvement for a generation. Several commercial networks evolved into Televisa, a unique conglomerate that captures virtually all of the country's TV viewers. Riding describes Televisa (it also created the Spanish International Network, or SIN, in the United States, which was sold to Hallmark Cards in 1988 and renamed Univision) as Mexico's Ministry of Culture, Ministry of Education, and Ministry of Information.

His indictment of Televisa is familiar (and echoed by Mexican intellectuals who see it as a prime example of Yankee cultural imperialism): "It is changing consumption patterns, social models, daily language, and political opinions"[14]—all with the passive approval of a government that is concerned with keeping the potential challenge of the medium at bay. A weak public system offers little competition to Televisa's dominance. Control of information is handled as it is through the print media, through a combination of shared interests, financial incentives, and intimidation.

Riding's complaint is not just that the authoritarian system in Mexico eliminates the possibility of a significant role for broadcasting in the political life of the country but also that the cheap entertainment that fills the screens hour after hour debauches the real popular culture of the country. Unlike Western Europe, where, as we have seen, broadcasters compensate for timidity in political reporting by asserting leadership in promotion of the national culture, Mexican television combines the worst of the public service and the commercial models. Even the one unique Mexican contribution to the medium—the telenovela—along with its print equivalent, the fotonovela, depends on lowest-common-denominator

---

[13] Alan Riding, *Distant Neighbors: A Portrait of the Mexicans* (New York: Vintage, 1986), p. 445.

[14] Alan Riding, *Distant Neighbors: A Portrait of the Mexicans* (New York: Vintage, 1986) p. 453.

appeal and a predictable set of characters and plots. They reinforce the traditional subservient role of women, domestic violence, passive acceptance of one's fate and, of course, consumerism. Efforts to reform the system have failed.

Broadcast Reform[15]

Not surprisingly, the Mexican broadcast system has been the target of frequent criticism, particularly from liberal intellectuals who see it as part of a global communication system that was created by the powerful North to maintain countries such as Mexico in a state of dependence and at the periphery of global power. In the 1970s, concurrent with the New World Information Order (NWIO) debate in the United Nations, the Mexican government undertook a series of actions that were supposed to tame the powerful broadcast industry and harness it to the development needs of the country. The goals and problems encountered could provide a guide book for other nations moving toward democracy.

The proposed reforms included changes in broadcast regulations to reorient the media toward the European public service model and to implement parts of the undefined NWIO. Some goals were vague and general, such as defining radio and television as "vehicles for national integration and enrichment of life through cultural, recreational, and economic activities." Others were specific. They required 10 percent of radio and 30 percent of TV programming to be live and allowed advertising to 18 percent of TV time and 40 percent of radio time.

In the 1970s, national plans, which are general planning documents rather than specific proposals, also adopted much of the rhetoric of the NWIO debates, including a collective right to communicate, social responsibilities of the media, and harnessing of the media to support development. At the end of the decade, a government-sponsored committee of scholars and experts proposed even more radical changes. Among the recommendations—never officially made public but reported in Scherer's *Proceso*—were proposals to require a minimum of 50 percent domestic TV programming and 25 percent live or in-studio radio programming, a temporary ban on reception of foreign satellite broadcasts, and tightening of the old law—never enforced—that required stations to give the government 12.5 percent of their broadcast time in lieu of taxes.

The committee also proposed creation of citizens' advisory committees to influence broadcast content and policies and recommended several restrictions on the print media. These included identification of all sources of information and a ban on distribution of information from foreign news services directly to customers in Mexico. Dispatches presumably would be routed through a national agency, a practice common in many third-world countries.

The government's proposals for information policy reform produced a flurry of media reaction—almost all negative—but little else. In the end, the various recommendations and goals were forgotten, and the traditional media system

---

[15] See P. Dale Gardner, Jr., and Robert L. Stevenson, *Communication Development in Venezuela and Mexico: Goals, Promises, and Reality,* Journalism Monographs No. 108 (Columbia, SC: Association for Education in Journalism and Mass Communication, 1988).

remained. The Mexican vision could be taken as a case study of what several countries tried to do during the NWIO debates. Almost all failed. Why?

Mexico undertook a radical reform of a powerful and entrenched media system when it was flush with oil revenues and looking for a major role on a global stage. President Luis Echeverría (president from 1970 to 1976) had aspirations of becoming the secretary-general of the United Nations and winning a Nobel Peace Prize. Reform of the media represented the kind of bold break with the old system that global leadership required. He also had the strong support of intellectuals, who had joined with others from Latin America to define the popular theories of cultural imperialism and information dependency that were the basis of the NWIO debate. However, by the end of his term, oil prices had collapsed, and Mexico's ambitious development program had turned into one of the world's largest foreign debts. Echeverría left office, as many Mexican presidents have, in a cloud of failure and scandal.

The Mexican plan also challenged one of the most powerful institutions in the country and one that had close ties with the government. Both the media and the government benefited from the old system, and public opinion supported the status quo. Without public outrage, even in a democratic country, which Mexico is not, serious reform is difficult, often impossible. As a result, Mexican media are still powerful allies of the government and still channels for the growing invasion of information, pop culture, and influence from the United States. Neither Brazil nor Mexico so far provides much assurance that the evolution from authoritarian to democratic politics and media is easy or even guaranteed. Perhaps other parts of the world can offer different experiences.

SINGAPORE

Singapore is an improbable country but one that shares many of the problems of the postcolonial era. It is a multinational state with no indigenous culture and no logical geography except for the obvious boundaries of its relatively small and resource-poor island. It is one of the smallest countries in the region. It is also one of the fastest-growing economies in the world and is usually classified with Hong Kong, Taiwan, and South Korea as a newly industrialized country (NIC) or one of the "four tigers" of Asia. By no realistic economic or social standard can Singapore still be considered third world.

Cultural Anomalies

Singapore was founded as a British trading colony in 1819. Its strategic location at the tip of the Malay Peninsula and its deep-water harbor ensured prominence for the tiny colony before independence and courting by the world's trading nations after. Singapore, which first joined and then separated from Malaysia to become fully independent in 1965, however, is staunchly anticommunist. Like its fellow tigers, it pursues capitalism with vigor and determination that set a new standard for nations of the Pacific Rim. Compared to the chaotic state of Bangkok or Hong Kong, Singapore is breathtakingly clean, modern, and efficient, but it is often devoid of the spontaneity and unpredictability that can delight the traveler elsewhere. By only one criterion—an authoritarian government—does it fit the usual definition of a third-world developing country.

At independence, Singapore faced a problem similar to that of other former colonies: how to take the disparate cultures and overlay of European influence that colonialism had created and to weave them into a modern state. Like the United States, Canada, and Australia, Singapore was spared the problem of traditionally hostile indigenous cultures bound together by unnatural modern state boundaries, with the consequent problems of tribalism and distribution of power. But Singapore also faced the absence of a natural set of shared cultural values and traditions that it could use as the building blocks of a modern nation-state.

Singapore is three-quarters Chinese, with minorities of Malays, Indians, and a few Arabs. Singapore's crowded island supplied few natural resources and no place for expansion. From the beginning, growth has gone up rather than out, giving Singapore the appearance of a tidy, tropical Manhattan. Turning a multi-ethnic colony into a cohesive nation was more difficult than creating a super-clean, super-efficient modern state.

Singapore's prime minister until 1990, Lee Kuan Yew, tried. He adopted cultural policies that were attacked, ridiculed, and occasionally copied by leaders of other newly independent countries. They included strict enforcement of codes of public behavior, use of English as both a socially integrative as well as commercial language, and formal development of a national ideology built around cultural tolerance and commitment to the nation. As in neighboring Malaysia, racial, religious, and ethnic conflict was suppressed and exorcised from the news.

Lee could look at the rise of cultural and ethnic hostility in other parts of the world, especially in other countries moving away from colonialism, and argue that the only alternative was a strong central government that could overcome the natural pressures to splinter states into their component antagonistic parts. The occasional opposition to his policies was suppressed with little visible protest from Singaporeans or from the domestic media, which he largely controlled. His quarrels with foreign media, however, made him a symbol of the clash between modern authoritarianism and independent journalism. Although Lee was unsympathetic to the New World Information Order debate—he joined Britain and the United States in withdrawing from UNESCO—some of his complaints about foreign journalists were identical to those voiced in Paris. He took more action against them than most other third-world leaders.

Foreign Media

Singapore was a favorite regional base for international media. Its strategic location, efficient transportation and communication system, and high standard of living made it preferable to chaotic Bangkok, crowded Tokyo, and unstable Hong Kong for reporters assigned to cover the vast region of Asia. As in other regional centers that attracted foreign journalists, such as Nairobi, there was an unwritten rule that reporters were left alone as long as they avoided critical coverage of their host country. Sometimes this system worked. Many reporters saved up their notes until they were about to be reassigned and then wrote a long series that left the Singaporean government irate but unable to do much about it. Other reporters covered events as they occurred and hoped for the best.

Singapore in the 1970s and 1980s became known for its scuffles with foreign media, which the media almost always lost. The government of Singapore used its Internal Security Act, which dated to its years as a British colony, and new legislation to charge various foreign media with vague antigovernment activity, including sedition, interfering in domestic politics, and—shades of the NWIO—failure to honor a national right of reply. Media that ran afoul of the government included *The Economist, Far Eastern Economic Review* (largely owned by Dow Jones), *Asiaweek* (Time, Inc., has an interest), and, most notably, the *Asian Wall Street Journal.*

Singapore began with a British tradition that allowed considerable government action in the name of national security. This allowed the government to take over domestic media and to act occasionally against foreign publications. However, a law passed in 1986 gave the government authority to act against outside media that "engaged in the domestic politics of Singapore." This was defined to include

> publishing material intended to generate political, ethnic and religious unrest; indulging in slanted, distorted or partisan reporting; or persistently refusing to publish government rejections to mis-reporting and baseless allegations.[16]

The law was used against several of the publications noted above, which usually refused to publish apologies and the long statements the government demanded as part of its national right of reply. Under the law, the government then could reduce the publication's circulation in Singapore. *Time*'s circulation was cut from 18,000 to 2,000 in 1987. The *Asian Wall Street Journal,* which battled Lee and his government repeatedly, was cut from 5,000 to 400 copies a day. The *Far Eastern Economic Review* stopped distributing in Singapore in 1988 after its circulation was cut from 10,000 to 500. In 1990, the *Wall Street Journal,* too, announced that it was suspending distribution. Curiously enough, at the same time that circulation of critical foreign publications was nearly eliminated, the government allowed photocopy reproductions of such publications, minus ads and any payment to the publications, to be circulated widely.

The Singapore government also used other tactics against foreign publications. It expelled several foreign correspondents, denied visas and residency permits to others, and brought other legal action, such as libel suits. By the 1990s, several major foreign media had moved their operations to less efficient but more tolerant locations. Journalists who had hoped for more elbow room when Lee retired in 1991 were disappointed. One of the last legislative acts under his regime was

---

[16] *Information, Freedom and Censorship: The Article 19 World Report 1988* (London: Longman, 1988), p. 165.

a law requiring foreign periodicals circulating in the country to get an annual license and to post a bond, the amount to be determined by the government, against legal liabilities and costs of litigation.

Lee's retirement from office seemed to do little to change the authoritarian character of the Singapore government. At the beginning of 1992, it outlawed the sale of chewing gum because of the cost of cleaning it off the city's still-immaculate streets. Other Big Brother–like control of public and private life continued as well, suggesting that the new national ideology had found a good fit between traditional Confucian cultural values and the needs of modern capitalism. Troubles with foreign media diminished, but control of domestic newspapers and broadcasting remained in the firm hands of the government. As in other Asian economic dynamos, complaints came more from outside than from within.

MAIN POINTS

1. The authoritarian media concept arose as government's response to the challenge of new printing technology in the sixteenth and seventeenth centuries. At its core, the authoritarian concept prohibits mass media from challenging government authority or threatening its power.

2. Since the invention of modern printing, authoritarian media systems have been—and still are—the most common type of media systems. Even present-day democratic governments practice some elements of authoritarianism. These include efforts to control access to information, to manipulate coverage, and to use the media to mobilize public support for national policies.

3. In authoritarian countries, the media are typically privately owned and allowed to flourish as long as they pose no challenge to the government. Often, media and government officials come from the same narrow elite social strata and share cultural values, financial interests, and political purposes.

4. In the 1990s, the authoritarian concept is likely to gain strength as countries move from communist and development media systems. A common belief—not universally accepted—is that authoritarian systems can evolve into democracies.

FOR MORE INFORMATION

Most current surveys of authoritarian countries contain some references to mass media and their role. The best comparison of the postcolonial experiences of mass media in Africa and Asia is William A. Hachten, *The Growth of Media in the Third World: African Failures, Asian Successes* (Ames: Iowa State University Press, 1993). Several chapters in *Transnational Communications: Wiring the Third World,* edited by Gerald Sussman and John A. Lent (Newbury Park, CA: Sage, 1991), apply critical analysis criteria to telecommunication policies of authoritarian countries.

An extensive body of scholarly literature is devoted to media and communication practices in Latin America, much of it reflective of the leftist "media dependency" school. As an example, see Elizabeth Fox, ed., *Media and Policies in Latin America: The Struggle for Democracy* (Newbury Park, CA: Sage, 1988). A largely descriptive survey of Latin American media is Michael B. Salwen and Bruce Garrison, *Latin American Journalism* (Hillsdale, NJ: Lawrence Erlbaum, 1991). See also their chapter in John C. Merrill, ed., *Global Journalism: Survey of International Communication,* 2nd ed. (White Plains, NY: Longman, 1991). For a discussion of problems generated by cultural differences between the United States and Mexico, see John C. Condon, *Good Neighbors: Communicating with the Mexicans* (Yarmouth, ME: Intercultural Press, 1985).

Singapore's rancorous relations with the foreign media are reported in the media affected, particularly the Anglo-American news magazines and global newspapers. Check any of the computer- or CD-ROM-based indexes of these periodicals for an update.

FOR DISCUSSION

1. Debate Ambassador Kirkpatrick's assertion about the distinction between authoritarian and totalitarian regimes, emphasizing whether and how Western media should support their professional colleagues in authoritarian political systems.

2. Do Western and authoritarian media represent distinct concepts, or are they opposite ends of a continuum of government influence?

3. Assume that you are the leader of a relatively prosperous but politically unstable nation, such as Brazil, Mexico, or Singapore. Prepare a speech for a group of visiting Western journalists, justifying various limits on press freedom that they want you to eliminate.

DATA BASE

Most media systems contain elements of the authoritarian media concepts. Government influence depends less on ownership and direct influence than on legal tradition, informal control, and professionalism of journalists. For these reasons, classification of media systems as authoritarian rather than development or Western is sometimes arbitrary. For simplicity, countries in Latin America and the Caribbean as well as those in Asia and the Pacific that are clearly not part of the Western first world or communist second world are included here. Data are listed as numbers per 100 population.

Countries in the Middle East and Africa are treated as examples of the development concept and are included in the Data Base of Chapter 10. Remember that a good number of countries here have media that are independent, professional, and critical; a few have media that are more Western than those of some of the countries listed in Chapter 7. Generalizations are useful but dangerous if carried too far.

Country	News-paper Circu-lation	Radio Sets	Tele-vision Sets	VCRs	Phone Lines
Latin America and Caribbean					
Argentina	17	65	26	2	10
Bahamas	14	77	33		24
Barbados	15	85	26	4	30
Belize	0	51	26	15	8
Bolivia	5	34	11		3
Brazil	5	44	27	3	7
Chile	7	35	20	2	5
Colombia	N/A	21	13	3	7
Costa Rica	9	26	15	1	9
Dominican Republic	4	15	8		4
Ecuador	6	31	10	2	5
El Salvador	5	34	10	1	2
Guatemala	5	23	7	1	2
Guyana	8	39	6		3
Haiti	1	13	0		1
Honduras	4	22	8		7
Jamaica	5	51	20		4
Mexico	13	35	16	2	6
Nicaragua	5	24	7		1
Panama	7	40	21	6	9
Paraguay	N/A	25	15	1	2
Peru	3	25	14	3	2
St. Lucia	6	53	14		7
St. Vincent/Granadines	0	53	14		10
Suriname	10	52	14		9
Trinidad/Tobago	11	55	28		12
Uruguay	N/A	59	23	2	13
Venezuela	19	53	19	5	8
Asia and the Pacific					
Afghanistan	1	10	1		2
Bangladesh	1	4	1		0
Bhutan	0	2			3
Brunei Darussalam	0	26	18	8	12
Cambodia	N/A	13	1		3

Country	News-paper Circu-lation	Radio Sets	Tele-vision Sets	VCRs	Phone Lines
Asia and the Pacific (cont.)					
Fiji	11	56	3	3	5
Hong Kong	N/A	67	38	16	40
India	3	9	4		1
Indonesia	2	17	7	1	1
Laos	2	14	1		0
Malaysia	34	20	17	6	8
Maldives	1	11	3		2
Mauritius	7	32	13		5
Mongolia	9	14	4		4
Myanmar	2	8	0		0
Nepal	2	6	2		0
Pakistan	6	9	6	1	1
Papua New Guinea	2	9	1		1
Philippines	6	16	6	1	1
Singapore	29	61	33	10	4
Solomon Islands	0	15			1
South Korea	16	55	28	7	28
Sri Lanka	4	17	3	1	1
Taiwan	10	39	32	5	29
Thailand	9	17	11	2	2
Tonga	6	57			4
Vanuatu	0	26	6	6	2
Western Samoa	N/A	44	3		3

SOURCE: Newspaper circulation figures are mid- to late-1980s and from UNESCO figures and other sources; phone line data are from American Telephone & Telegraph's (AT&T) *The World's Telephones,* 1991, and the International Telecommunication Union's (ITU) *Yearbook of Common Carrier Telecommunication Statistics* (18th ed.). Radio, TV, and VCR data from *World Radio and TV Receivers,* ed. by Carol L. Forrester. Copyright © 1991 IBAR-BBC World Service. Reprinted by permission.

CHAPTER 10

Development Media

ABOUT THIS CHAPTER

If you watched *Sesame Street* as a child or belonged to a 4-H club, you experienced a development media system. In this chapter, we look at how the idea of using media to promote social change moved from the heartland of North America to the emerging third world and, finally, to the United Nations Educational, Scientific and Cultural Organization (UNESCO), where it became part of a global controversy whose effects are likely to be felt well into the twenty-first century.

INTRODUCTION

The developmental concept of the mass media is the newest of the five semi-theories of media systems we are using to guide our global armchair tour. However, its roots are much deeper and originate in what may seem a surprising place. In the past three decades, numerous developing countries adopted parts of the developmental media model, but few now can point to persuasive evidence that it has contributed significantly to national development, regardless of how development is defined.

Like the communist theory, the developmental concept lost legitimacy in the 1980s, to the point where one can question whether it exists as a distinctive category of national mass media systems. However, one key element of the developmental concept emerged from the 1980s with renewed vigor. It is the belief that communication—mass media and especially telecommunication—can stimulate economic growth and political stability, the core of modern Western culture. We return to this aspect of the developmental concept later.

MASS MEDIA AND DEVELOPMENT

The terms *development communication* and *development journalism* were closely associated with the New World Information Order (NWIO) debate that centered in UNESCO in the 1970s and early 1980s. The argument that mass media could be mobilized to guide social change originated long before UNESCO, however. It derived in large part from the experience of the United States and a few other Western countries early in the twentieth century. These countries created a variety of government programs to promote development in rural areas. In the United States, a large bureaucracy called the Agricultural Extension Service was established to administer these programs. The "county ag agent" and "home agent" are still fixtures in rural courthouses around the country, still working to improve agricultural production and rural life in general. Local radio shows and weekly newspaper columns prepared by the ag extension office are part of life in many rural areas of the United States. It was thought that this experience could be used to tackle some of the dreadful problems facing the newly independent nations of Asia and Africa in the 1950s and 1960s.

This supposition was the basis of a small field of communication research activity that became known as communication development, development-support communication, development information, and, finally, development journalism. All of the terms, which often are used interchangeably and usually are used imprecisely, refer to the simple idea that social change (progress, development) can be facilitated by change agents and that the work of change agents can be multiplied by mass media.

An ag extension agent in the 1930s might explain to a farmer in the U.S. Midwest how to improve crop yields or prevent soil erosion. For the home agent, the topic could be food preservation, nutrition, or even basic infant care. The agent could work with farm families individually or in small groups but could also print pamphlets, write a column for the local newspaper, or produce a radio program. With mass media, the efforts of the local county ag agent and home agent could reach dozens or hundreds, possibly thousands. If coordinated nationally, such programs could reach millions and transform the nation.

Much of the work of agricultural extension in the United States was carried out at the large land-grant state universities, especially in the Midwest, where third-world students began arriving in large numbers in the 1950s and 1960s to learn skills they hoped would guide their countries toward the modernity they found all around them in the West. Harnessing mass communication to multiply the efforts of individual change agents, incorporating mass media into ambitious national development plans, and using communication to compress the centuries of Western development into decades all were part of the knowledge a generation of new teachers, scientists, and bureaucrats carried home. The work of three scholars was especially important in creating the academic specialty of communication and development.

Rostow and History

W. Walt Rostow, an economic historian then at Harvard University, published a book in 1960 that tried to explain the development of the Western economic system over many centuries. In *The Stages of Economic Growth*,[1] he argued that change in Europe had evolved slowly until a critical mass of people and resources reached a takeoff point, at which time economic growth became self-sustaining. The modern West—rich, economically stable, growing—began at that point. This, of course, was exactly what the developing countries needed to replicate in their first decades of independence. Their goal was to accelerate the Western experience while avoiding the political catastrophes that marred most of Western history.

Rostow's book appeared just as the Kennedy administration arrived in Washington, D.C., with an inflated confidence in its ability to influence world events and enthusiasm for an active U.S. leadership in world affairs. The book served as a guide for the administration's development assistance programs, and its author became a close advisor to the president.

Lerner and Communication

About the same time—the late 1950s and early 1960s—an MIT social scientist's study of change in the Middle East emphasized the importance of communication. Daniel Lerner carried out one of the first scientific public opinion surveys in seven countries that formed an arc around the eastern end of the Mediterranean. While compiling the results of the survey, Lerner was struck by the evidence of rapid change taking place in those very traditional societies and by the apparent influence of mass communication. He found some of the same patterns Rostow had described in Europe, but with a difference. Mass media seemed to be accelerating the change and replacing some of the traditional agents of cultural influence.

Lerner's book[2] sketched out the elements of a semi-theory of the role of mass communication and development that became known as the "dominant paradigm." The phrase *semi-theory* indicates that Lerner nowhere systematically laid out and tested all of the component parts of a theory. Instead, after the original data focusing on public opinion were collected in personal interviews all over the region, he began to see evidence of the influence of mass media that he had not expected. His theory emerged from data already collected and some additional fieldwork. Lerner's book was record of this discovery and its elaboration. The dominant paradigm was the theoretical model of how mass communication could stimulate social change. It guided a generation of change agents in the third world.

---

[1] W. Walt Rostow, *The Stages of Economic Growth* (Cambridge, UK: Cambridge University Press, 1960).

[2] Daniel Lerner, *The Passing of Traditional Society: Modernizing the Middle East* (Glencoe, IL: Free Press, 1958; paperback edition, 1964).

The argument went like this. Traditional societies evolve over centuries and tend to do things the same way earlier generations did them. The resulting strong culture provides stability but makes change difficult. The key to cultural change is the ability to imagine different ways of doing things, a future that differs from the past. Empathy—a key element in Lerner's formulation—is the ability to imagine what might be, not just what is.

Traditionally, people learned empathy by occasional physical contact with other cultures that had evolved differently, but mass media now provide a vicarious contact with the rest of the world. Even in the 1950s when Lerner wrote, newspapers and radio had ended the centuries of isolation that kept those parts of the Middle East essentially the same for centuries. These mass media, along with urbanization and literacy, produced the critical mass of "modernity" that brought developing countries to the takeoff point of self-sustaining economic and social growth. The process was similar to what Rostow had described in the West, but mass media accelerated it. It appeared that mass media could be a tool to speed and guide development.

When Lerner wrote about modernization, he defined the goal of development in political terms: Western-style democracy. His argument was not that democracy as we know it was inherently superior to the traditional, tight-knit but rigid, authoritarian governments of the Middle East but that only democracy could accommodate the accelerating change that was engulfing the modern world. Without the adaptability and flexibility of political democracy, traditional societies would be vulnerable to radical, even violent, change, the argument went. It is a prediction that recent events have validated.

Development was originally defined in political terms, but most development efforts were directed toward economic growth. The term came to be defined in measurable economic terms, often as gross national product (GNP) per capita or average per capita income. The explication of economic development goals came from many scholars and practitioners, but especially from one of Lerner's contemporaries and later colleagues, Wilbur Schramm.

Schramm's "Great Multiplier"

Schramm was associated with third-world development through much of his academic life but is best known for a book published in 1964 that became both a technical manual for communication development and a bully pulpit for advocating the use of mass media as a key component of development programs.[3] In it, he summarized how mass media had been used to speed development—social change toward political stability and economic growth—in many countries and outlined how communication could be put to work in the newly independent countries of the third world.

Here is his list of what media can do: be social watchdogs and broaden horizons, focus attention and raise aspirations, create a climate for development,

---

[3] Wilbur Schramm, *Mass Media and National Development* (Stanford, CA: Stanford University Press, 1964).

feed interpersonal channels of communication and confer status, and enforce social norms and help form tastes. He also cautioned that media can help only indirectly to change strongly held attitudes or valued practices. In other words, mass media could be a valuable tool to help promote change, but they could not change traditional cultures overnight or substitute for basic economic and political changes that traditional governments often resisted.

Schramm's inventory of media contributions was a mixture of research findings, practical experience, and common sense. It was elegantly written and full of optimism. At first it was not controversial. Nor was his spirited call for mobilization of modern communication in support of rapid development:

> This is the really exciting question: how much could we increase the present rate of development, how much could we smooth out the difficulties of the "terrible ascent," how much further could we make our resources go, how much more could we contribute to the growth of informed, participating citizens in the new nations, if we were to put the resources of modern communication skillfully and fully behind economic and social development?[4]

The phrase "terrible ascent" had been coined by Julius Nyerere, president of Tanzania, to describe what the newly independent nations were going through as they struggled to reach the level of wealth and stability the West had achieved only after centuries of effort. Could mass media really make the struggle easier or faster?

Paradigm Attacked

Strangely enough, even those who bitterly attacked the United States for its "cultural imperialism" in the 1970s believed communication could accomplish this. So did Lenin. A key element in all of these concepts of media as agents of social change was that media could be multipliers of (usually) government efforts to change long-held attitudes and behavior, the core of cultural identity. All great leaders have a vision of what they want their nation to be, what they hope their people will become. To anyone with any contact with modern mass media, it seems reasonable—beyond question, really—that mass media can be a powerful resource to help people reach those goals.

However, despite its common-sense appeal, the evidence to support that belief was never overwhelming and often nonexistent. The speed with which people in communist and authoritarian countries in the 1980s turned away from the kind of systems their governments had tried to create with the help of mass media is a good reminder of Schramm's caution that even powerful modern communication cannot reshape deeply held cultural values.

---

[4] Wilbur Schramm, *Mass Media and National Development* (Stanford, CA: Stanford University Press, 1964) p. 271.

Even though it guided communication development for several decades, the dominant paradigm outlined by Lerner and Schramm came under attack almost as soon as their books appeared. Criticism came first from those who saw the dark side of modern Western life—social alienation, pollution, inequality—and then from those who saw it as a device to maintain the old colonial world of dominance of nations at the periphery of the global system by a handful of powerful nations at the center. We now often hear about "North-South" issues or disparities. The term refers to the big gap in development between the industrialized nations, which are mostly in the Northern Hemisphere, and the emerging third-world nations, which are mostly in the Southern Hemisphere. It acknowledges that the hopes for communication as a development tool to narrow the gaps were overly optimistic, perhaps even misplaced.

When the dominant paradigm came under attack from a chorus that included a new generation of scholars and researchers, third-world political leaders, and UNESCO delegates, the criticism reflected the failure of the first decades of political independence in Africa and Asia to lead to prosperity and stability and the radical rejection of the dominant paradigm as an instrument of neo-imperialism. The argument was that under the guise of development aid and training, Western governments were really using the increasingly powerful mass media to maintain themselves as the center of an emerging world system and keep the developing nations at the periphery, still dependent on the nations at the center. Mass media had replaced the colonial armies of the eighteenth and nineteenth centuries as the spearhead of influence and control. It was an argument that appealed to governments committed to the use of media as an instrument of rapid development, particularly those that rejected the Western model of journalism as an independent, critical force. If the media were mobilized to support a vision of development that included disengagement from the Western-dominated global system, news would be very different from the blend Americans read, see, and hear every day.

DEVELOPMENT NEWS

Development information was originally technical material that promoted national development goals such as literacy, health, and agriculture. It was helpful tips to improve life supplied by a knowledgeable neighbor. When the definition of development itself changed, development information became development news. These terms are now used differently by different authors, but it is important to remember the two different ideas behind them. What we'll call *development communication*—or *development support communication,* as it is also called— refers to information that is distributed to promote education, agriculture, public health, nutrition, or family planning. It is usually technical and noncontroversial. Development information communicators, like the county ag and home agents, theoretically are there to improve life for everyone, not to promote a political agenda. Usually development communication programs are directed toward rural areas, but urban slums are increasingly the targets of such information.

Communication is often considered the "great multiplier" of social change and is used in situations as varied as the rural United States, Marxist states, and especially the developing nations of the third world. Here radio is used for "distance learning" in Africa, extending the teacher's influence to many remote classrooms.
SOURCE: United States Agency for International Development.

Development journalism or *development news,* in contrast, is a modern adaptation of development information to support political development. This includes identification with a state rather than a tribe or traditional culture, recognition of a political leader as a symbol of the state, and mobilization of a nation's mass media to support political change. The movement of development communication/news from the Great Plains of North America to the halls of UNESCO in Paris is a complicated story.

When Lerner talked with isolated villagers at the eastern end of the Mediterranean in the 1950s, who were living as their ancestors had lived, he posed "what-if" questions: "What would you do if your were village chief?" "What would you do if you could change the way you live?" The responses, not unlike those the ag extension agents heard, often reflected incredulity. "But I'm not the village chief." "But we've always done it this way. The future will be like the past."

Lerner concluded that occasional personal contact with other cultures—seeing different, sometimes better ways of doing things—traditionally had provided the spark to ignite social change. The ag extension agent was really a planned encounter with new ideas, but his or her ability to influence people was limited. In the modern age, however, mass media could multiply change agents' influence and speed development. The media were the magic multipliers of planned social change.

From the first interest in the role of communication in third-world development in the late 1950s and early 1960s through the early stages of the NWIO debate in the 1970s, "development" was assumed to be Western. The "underdeveloped" or "developing" nations—what we now usually call the third world—were trying to become like the "developed" countries of the West. Development was defined politically as Western democracy and economically as wealth derived from market capitalism. The goal of development programs was to speed and smooth the process of becoming like the West.

During this period, the development-related messages of the mass media were technical and apolitical. However, the definition of development changed gradually in the 1970s and, with it, the role of communication changed, too. Development communication in many countries became development journalism, a concept of journalism you can encounter in many third-world countries today.

Many third-world countries that gained political independence in the 1960s and 1970s were artificial products of European colonialism that overlaid arbitrary boundaries on complex traditional cultures. The problem was particularly acute in Africa and the Middle East but less so in Asia, where cultures were stronger and better aligned with political boundaries. Some new countries contained tribes traditionally hostile to each other, whose presence under the same new flag virtually guaranteed civil strife. In the Indian subcontinent, of course, the British decided Hindu-Muslim animosity was so great that they split the great colony into Hindu India and Muslim Pakistan. The decision did not prevent massive bloodshed at independence or several wars later. In other areas, coherent cultures were split between two countries (as in east Africa) or minority tribes ended up controlling the government (as in most of the Middle East). Most new countries also contained minority tribes or cultures that began agitating for autonomy or independence.

Imagine yourself as leader of a newly independent third-world country in the late 1960s. You inherit a patchwork quilt of cultures and subcultures, languages, religions—all of the things that make for conflict and civil war. People think of themselves as Ibos or Yorubas, as Shias or Sunnis or Kurds, not Nigerians or Iraqis. These groups never liked each other very much and are now threatening secession. A prime obligation—perhaps your single most important task as president or prime minister—is to hold the nation together. You have to create a sense of nationhood where none exists. You have to get people to think of themselves as Nigerians or Iraqis first, Ibos or Shiias second. The history of Europe even today, of course, is a chronicle of this sort of conflict.

To avoid repeating the European experience, leaders of many newly independent countries tried to become symbols of their new, fragile nations. Without a 1,000-year-old monarchy or 200-year-old presidency to embody the national culture, the regime was the only symbol of nationhood. The regime was embodied in the person of a powerful leader, who more often than not was in office as the result of a coup. The goal of national development was no longer economic growth or political stability but simply survival as a nation. Democracy could come later.

Back to your role as such a leader. The first goal of national development is to create a sense of identity with the nation rather than the tribe. You modestly conclude that you are the most appropriate symbol of the nation. In fact, you may be the only symbol. Among the tools available to you to promote national identity are the mass media. People need to see you symbolically representing the nation. They need to know of the nation's progress toward modernity. They need information that will help them transfer their loyalty from tribe to nation. Enter development news and its offspring, protocol news.

History

The term *development news* or *development journalism* goes back to the Philippines in the 1960s. Then it meant technical information in the extension agent tradition that helped people improve their economic productivity and, with it, their lives. Later, as the goal of development changed from economic and political change to identification of the regime in power with the nation, development news changed, too. It became more blatantly identified with the regime. It excluded criticism and negative information. It emphasized the positive aspects of social change, the slow climb toward modernity that the Western media, with their focus on disruption and disaster, ignored. Development news centered more and more on the symbolic actions of the leader. Coverage of ceremonial events was called protocol news, which can be thought of as an extension of development news.

You can find examples of modern-day development news or protocol news in the news media in many countries. Check a paper from Kenya or Zambia or any of the Arab countries in the Middle East. Chinese media, too, tend to emphasize development and protocol news. If you can, watch a TV newscast from one of these countries. Even without knowing the language, you can understand most of what is going on.

Development News in Practice

China Daily is an English-language newspaper edited in China and printed there and in the United States for an international audience. It is modern in appearance and thorough in its coverage of world affairs, for which it relies mostly on the Western news agencies. Coverage of China is restrained compared to the obsequious fawning over the "great leader" in the *Pyongyang Times* published in North Korea, but it clearly emphasizes positive developments. Here are a few samples of what you would have learned from the paper in August, 1993.

> The drastic economic and social changes of the last decade have presented a great challenge to the traditional method of supporting the elderly.

For centuries, old people have been looked after by their families.

But now, says a recent article in *People's Daily,* China should explore a new system which uses support from both society and the family. (August 12, 1993, p. 4)

The State Council plans to reduce the country's illiteracy rate to under 10 percent of the population by 2000. . . . New amended regulations made public yesterday included the provision to expand the target of the compulsory literacy campaign to cover all Chinese people above the age of 15. (August 11, 1993, p. 1)

Chinese scientists pulled off a major breakthrough in infra-red technology in May.

They successfully produced an infra-red free electron laser putting them on a par with their colleagues in the United States, the Netherlands and France. (August 13, 1993, p. 5)

China's satellite communications industry will get a big boost next year.

A Chinese-made telecommunications satellite is due to be launched into orbit. (August 12, 1993, p. 1)

You won't find much coverage of domestic unrest, disruption, and decline in *China Daily.* Problems are covered with an emphasis on progress toward solutions, and the bizarre "events" that titillate readers of the popular Western tabloids are ignored. The paper's editors would argue that their coverage documents China's progress in development, which Western media ignore, and contributes to it.

Protocol News

At its extreme, development news becomes protocol news. Protocol news is the comings and goings of national leaders; the syrupy toasts and communiqués of friendship and cooperation; and the airport arrival ceremonies with lots of flags, bands, and motorcades. Of course, Western media cover these events, too, but there is usually an opposition politician or skeptical reporter to remind the audience that *frank discussion* translates as *argument* and that vague communiqués can paper over harsh disagreements. A lot of protocol news appears in third-world media. Often the president's daily protocol activities take up half of the evening telecast or front page. Many events are covered without any indication of what actually happened. Check some newspapers from Africa or the Middle East for examples of this kind of coverage. Even better is television news coverage, which you can usually understand without knowledge of the language.

Here in exaggerated form from the English-language weekly *Pyongyang Times* is protocol news. The top story in the July 17, 1993, edition—not atypical by any means—started off this way:

President Kim Il Sung of the Democratic People's Republic of Korea on July 10 signed the "Statement on Population Stabilization" to be issued jointly by the heads of state or government of the non-aligned countries on the occasion of world population day, the statement sent to him by President Suharto of the Republic of Indonesia, Chairman of the NAM.

President Kim Il Sung sent a letter to President Suharto in reply to the latter's letter to him.

Other stories, all focusing on Kim ("the great leader") or his son, Kim Jong Il, heir apparent and "dear leader," included these leads:

President Kim Il Sung on July 6 sent a message of greetings to Manuel Esquivel upon the victory of the United Democratic Party of Belize in the general elections and his assumption of office as Prime Minister.

Bagneux City in France awarded a medal to the great leader Kim Il Sung on the occasion of the 40th anniversary of the victory of the Korean people in the Fatherland Liberation War.

A message was sent to President Kim Il Sung of the Democratic People's Republic of Korea by Lansana Conte, President and Head of State of the Republic of Guinea, in connection with the Month of International Solidarity with the Korean people.

Recently the Foreign Languages Publishing House of the DPRK has published in book form the dear leader Comrade Kim Jong Il's celebrated work "Let Us Prepare the Young People Thoroughly as Reliable Successors in the Revolutionary Cause of Juche," a speech delivered to the senior officials of the Central Committee of the Workers' Party of Korea on January 17, 1990.

In hearty response to the call issued by the Central Committee of the Workers' Party of Korea to mark the 40th anniversary of victory in the Fatherland Liberation War (June 25, 1950–July 27, 1953), the people working in agricultural production have concentrated their efforts on achieving a rich harvest. They have launched a wide range of initiatives for making systematic use of scientific processes in sowing seeds and transplanting seedlings at the right time. These activities and measures have provided a good crop in all paddy and non-paddy fields.

The *Pyongyang Times* is a fringe newspaper, of course. It is a heavy-handed international propaganda sheet for one of the world's few surviving Stalinist regimes. However, it is a lot like pre-*glasnost* media in the Soviet Union and only marginally different from media in some developing countries today.

News for Separate Development

To the Western eye, development journalism looks a lot like the kind of journalism practiced under the communist concept. The two concepts do overlap, but some defenders of the development concept argue that it is temporary, an expedient needed to bridge the necessarily turbulent and difficult leap from underdeveloped colony to stable, prosperous nation. A Western media system is a luxury that follows from development, not a tool to promote development. In authoritarian media systems, criticism of the regime is usually proscribed, but otherwise, the media can print or broadcast pretty much what they want. In the development concept, media are mobilized by the government as agents of change. In that way, the development media concept is more like the communist system than the authoritarian concept. Most advocates of development journalism argue that government control can evolve into something resembling the Western concept. But not all agree.

A more radical interpretation of development journalism is that authentic third-world development requires disengagement from the dominant, Western-dominated communication system and that Western cultural values are at best irrelevant to the third world, at worst dysfunctional for it. Mustapha Masmoudi, former Tunisian secretary of information and one of the principal architects of the New World Information Order, put it this way:

> By transmitting to the developing countries only news processed by them, that is, news which they have filtered, cut and distorted, the transnational media impose their own way of seeing the world upon the developing countries. . . . Moreover, [they often] present these communities—when indeed they do show interest in them—in the most unfavorable light, stressing crises, strikes, street demonstrations, putsches, etc., or even holding them up to ridicule.[5]

What was needed, he argued, was a definition of journalism appropriate to third-world needs, and if Western journalists dismissed it as merely government-controlled puffery disguised as nation-building information, that was their problem. The New World Information Order was supposed to give developing countries the resources to create their own media systems and their own definition of news, free from the irrelevant, disruptive journalism of "coups and earthquakes."

Certainly, development and protocol news were—and are—mainstays of much third-world journalism. Although it is easy to dismiss the endless coverage of airport arrivals, wreath-laying, and speeches, it is important to remember that symbolism is important, especially to nations that lack the deep cultural roots of most Western countries. It is also true that Western coverage includes a lot of development and protocol news.

Compromise

The attack on Western media was part of the larger NWIO broadside against Western dominance in all areas of global communication, but it linked the seemingly benign tradition of the ag extension service to the political wrangle that occupied UNESCO for so long. Finally, in 1978 a compromise declaration

---

[5] Mustapha Masmoudi, "The New World Information Order," *Journal of Communication,* vol. 29, no. 2, 1979, pp. 172–185.

on the role of mass media was reached at UNESCO, and the radical alternative interpretation of communication development began to lose support. In return for dropping some of the more odious demands—control over all information leaving or entering a country as part of cultural sovereignty, international right of reply, licensing of journalists—Western representatives promised to increase technical assistance to developing countries, whose media systems were often hopelessly inadequate and outdated. The compromise goal of a "free *and* balanced" flow of information between media-rich North and media-poor South was to be reached, so everyone hoped, by improving the ability of the third world to speak for itself, not by silencing the powerful West.

If you look at the news around the world, you find frequent use of mass media to support national development. Most nations still rely on mass media to promote various kinds of social change, particularly education, and most media in the developing world still give heavy, flattering coverage to the national leaders. However, the UNESCO debate did renew interest in the question that is at the core of any development media system: Can communication promote, support, speed, or multiply social change?

COMMUNICATION AND DEVELOPMENT

Throughout the history of modern mass media, a common assumption has been that the media are powerful agents of influence. That's why Western governments court them, why authoritarian governments control them, and why many developing countries mobilize them to support development. Whether the goal of development was the rich, democratic West or some "authentic" non-Western model, development advocates assumed that communication was a magic multiplier of change. In fact, the evidence to support such a belief was never overwhelming and often completely lacking. The UNESCO debate revived interest in the original Lerner–Schramm theory, but in the 1990s, emphasis is on telecommunication rather than mass media as a tool of development.

Assessing Development

Researchers who want to assess the impact of communication as a development tool can do it in two ways. One, a microlevel approach, examines the influence of specific development projects on their target audience. Sometimes the research is as conceptually simple as Lerner's study, which looked at the statistical relationship between exposure to mass media and "modernity" as measured by knowledge of the world, empathy, attitudes toward change, and so on. If people who have a lot of contact with the media tend to be more knowledgeable, empathetic, or positive toward change than those who don't, the argument is plausible that the media produced that difference—plausible, but not proved. Even with high-powered statistics that sort out the influence of other factors, the correlation between exposure to modern mass media and "modernity" is small.

A more sophisticated approach is to survey a target audience before a campaign is undertaken and again after the campaign or to match the target audience with similar people in a different village or region who are not exposed to the development campaign. Differences between the experimental "test" group and "control" group strengthen the argument of the media's effect, but social scientists are always cautious about attributing cause and effect to anything outside the carefully controlled laboratory experiment.

In fact, even a simple before-after assessment is complicated in execution. Often it is impossible because the researchers are not brought in until the project is underway or because bureaucrats running the project want to avoid a critical assessment of their work. Even if you can demonstrate that a development project increased the proportion of villagers using birth control or a recommended farming practice from X percent to Y percent, there is no evidence that a corresponding change in population growth or per capita GNP will follow.

For that reason, some researchers prefer to study development at a macro level, using national-level statistics such as literacy rate, infant mortality, and per capita GNP as indicators of economic development and newspapers, radios, or TV sets per capita as measures of a nation's level of communication development across a wide range of countries, and often the entire world. The statistical relationships between one group and the other are calculated for an entire continent, region, or even the world. Until recently, data for many developing countries were missing, and any definitive analysis was impossible. Even now, with better data and more sophisticated techniques of analysis, it is still difficult to answer the simple question of how—or whether— communication can be the great multiplier of social and economic change.

Communication's Contribution

It is also difficult to summarize the hundreds and hundreds of studies of thousands and thousands of development projects that used modern communication in one way or another. However, the massive body of research suggests these general conclusions:

1. Mass media can be useful in programs to promote education, rural development, and some kinds of social change, such as health and nutrition. However, these programs do not seem to lead to measurable changes in aggregate measures of development, such as literacy, GNP, or infant mortality. In short, development support communication can be a useful part of a long-range development program, but don't expect economic or social growth to follow automatically or quickly from such programs. Nor can communication transform long-held cultural values, as Schramm warned and communism demonstrated.

2. At the aggregate level, the number of radios and TVs per capita is unrelated to (or even negatively related to) the level of economic development. This seems to be a product of two factors: the sharp

decline in cost of sets, which made it easier for people in the poorest countries to buy them, and the strong demand for them among the poorest people in the world. As a result, the most rapid growth in radio and television now is in the poorest countries.

3. The level of newspaper circulation is positively related to economic development, although the mechanism through which it leads to economic growth is not clear. In fact, the number and circulation of newspapers in the third world have fallen steadily in the past 20–30 years. As a result, newspapers may inevitably become less important as tools of development-support communication projects.

4. Democracy, which was one of the original goals of development, seems to be more a product of media (and economic) development than a spur to it.

5. Telecommunication—telephones and the other media that use the same technology—does seem to have a demonstrable power to promote economic growth. In the 1990s, interest in communication and development was clearly in telecommunication rather than in radio, television, or newspapers.

For once, with telecommunication, both individual-level and aggregate-level studies pointed in the same direction. In fact, the NWIO debate reinvigorated interest in communication and development and led, if only indirectly, to a call for increased investment in telecommunication as part of the third world's development strategy in the twenty-first century.

TELECOMMUNICATION AND THE 1990s

Three important studies in the early 1980s focused attention on the potential power of telecommunication to do in the 1990s and beyond what a similar interest in mass media had failed to do in the preceding decades. The World Bank's unofficial 1983 study was the most cautious of the three but concluded that, at a minimum, demand for telecommunication services in the third world should be met and, where possible, service should be extended to rural areas.[6] Because demand was increasing rapidly throughout the world—and costs were dropping and new technologies were rapidly evolving—even that cautious approach implied a substantial increase in telecommunication investment. An increase in economic growth was assumed to be concomitant.

A report by the Organization for Economic Cooperation and Development (OECD, the "rich nations' club" in Paris) and the International Telecommunications Union (ITU, an agency of the United Nations in Geneva) was less circumspect about the importance of telecommunication to economic growth.[7] Case studies

---

[6] Robert J. Saunders et al., *Telecommunications and Economic Development* (Baltimore, MD: Johns Hopkins University Press, 1983).

[7] William Pierce and Nicolas Jequier, *Telecommunications for Development* (Geneva: International Telecommunications Union, 1983).

examined in the report showed cost-benefit ratios as high as 100 to 1 in a wide range of economic enterprises when telecommunication was improved. A hypothetical calculation concluded that one simple satellite earth station connected to telephones over nine years could contribute from $4,000 to $15,000 to the gross domestic product of a relatively wealthy developing country with a minimal telephone system in place. In a rural area, the return was estimated to be from $167,000 to $496,000.

The authors of this study, unlike the cautious social science researchers who could never satisfactorily sort out cause and effect in Lerner's and Schramm's time, argued that the direction of the arrow linking telecommunication and growth was clear—and, in fact, opposite of what earlier research had suggested. The secretary-general of the ITU, Richard Butler, noted the conventional wisdom that telecommunication growth followed economic development and was a luxury that a developing country could afford only after other needs were met. Now, he noted in a preface to the report, it appeared that telecommunication produced important benefits across the whole spectrum of development activities and should be at the core of development programs, not at the periphery. This was clearly a different way of thinking about development than the earlier emphasis on one-way, vertical mass media of the 1950s and 1960s.

A third report added another voice to the growing chorus favoring investment in telecommunication as a key to third-world development.[8] This one was produced by an international commission headed by Sir Donald Maitland, a British diplomat. It was organized by the ITU, which clearly had taken the leadership in global communication from a weakened UNESCO.

In the spirit of the hard-headed 1980s, the commission recognized the importance of shifting available resources to telecommunication—including a small tax on international calls to finance third-world development—rather than to massive new investment programs. The goal, it said, should be to make basic telecommunication service available to everyone on earth by the early twenty-first century. That was defined as putting a telephone within a day's walk. Foolish idealism, perhaps, but the plan was no more visionary than the goal for distribution of radio receivers—traditionally the preferred medium for development purposes—that UNESCO had set a generation earlier, a goal that had been reached without fanfare in the late 1980s.

Both the ITU/OECD and the Maitland Commission reports offered the outlines of specific but expensive ideas for implementing their conclusions. The former argued in favor of a GLOBDOM (for *global* and *domestic*) system, comprising four satellites with global coverage linking a network of ground stations, with a total cost of $1.26 billion. The goal would be telephone service to all the rural regions of the developing world, for an initial investment cost comparable to that of the telephone service of the industrialized countries.

The Maitland Commission recommended establishment of a global center for telecommunication development. Its major task would be to come up with

---

[8] *The Missing Link* [Maitland Commission Report] (Geneva: International Telecommunications Union, 1984).

$12 billion a year for investment needed to reach the ambitious goal the report called for. The center was established, although donor-country enthusiasm for massive aid to support telecommunication development did not follow. The $12 billion figure seemed less fanciful when one remembered that the developing nations were already investing $8 billion a year in telecommunication in 1983 and that unit costs were dropping rapidly as new technologies found their way from the telephone-rich North to the telephone-poor South.

Many assumed that telecommunication remained the province of the elites in third-world countries and an instrument of their power, but in one of his last research efforts, Ithiel de Sola Pool showed how even the poorest and most isolated villagers in rural Egypt benefited from telephones.[9] Government and private bureaucracies functioned more efficiently, prices rose when farmers could check several regional markets, and individuals saved money and nonproductive time away from work when a telephone call could replace personal emergency visits to neighboring villages or cities. Telecommunication, as the quantitative analyses had indicated, seemed to be a rising tide that raised all boats. It is certain to get more attention from development programs in the twenty-first century than the usual 5–10 percent allocated to communication and transportation (mostly the latter) in the last decades of the previous century.

COMMUNICATION DEVELOPMENT DURING THE 1990s

The goals of third-world development during the 1990s—economic growth and political stability—were the same as they had been when Rostow, Lerner, and Schramm tried to find a simple way to get there decades earlier. The early promise of communication as a magic multiplier of efforts to bridge the gap between the rich, stable North and the poor, unstable South was weakened but not entirely discredited. If anything, the explosive growth of communication in the West and the dazzling technology it produced provided a new incentive for communication-minded development planners to harness satellites and computers as well as radio, television, and newspapers.

The collapse of the communist media concept discredited much of the development concept. Not all third-world countries, however, had opted for a system that mobilized mass media to support national development, and most that did turned toward more independent media systems in the early 1990s. Two case studies are instructive of the state of the development media concept at the end of the twentieth century.

---

[9] Ithiel de Sola Pool and Peter M. Steven, ''Appropriate Telecommunications for Rural Development,'' in Indu B. Sing, ed., *Telecommunication in the Year 2000* (Norwood, NJ: Ablex, 1983), pp. 150–157.

NIGERIA

In Nigeria, you can see most of the complexities, problems, and possibilities of the great African continent. It is not a microcosm of Africa; Nigeria represents the single largest piece of the continent and is one of the largest countries in the world. At times, it is the world's fourth largest democracy. Nigeria could become the engine that pulls black Africa into modernity.

Nigerian media are often described as "lively" and sometimes as "combative," despite restrictions imposed by a military government. Except for South Africa, Nigeria has more daily newspapers and more radio and TV stations than any other African country. The enthusiasm for democracy seems stronger here than in other parts of the continent. The media system is classified here with the developmental concept, but it contains elements of both the authoritarian and Western concepts as well. Nothing about Nigeria is simple.

Begin with the country itself. With more than 100 million people and a birth rate that may take the population to more than 300 million in the twenty-first century, Nigeria comprises one-quarter to one-fifth of all Africans. Oil made it ambitious for rapid development in the 1970s, but the early promise was destroyed by the collapse of oil prices and the failure to create either sustained economic growth or political stability, the two traditional development goals.

Nigeria shows clearly the imprint of the three great influences on African cultures: indigenous cultures, the Islamic invasion, and later European colonization. Some 400 mutually unintelligible native languages are spoken by 250 or so tribal groups in Nigeria. In the north, Islam is dominant in religion and politics; the south is mostly Christian. The national borders and use of English as the national language are the product of British colonizers who supplanted Portuguese slave traders in the eighteenth century and made Nigeria a colony in 1861. Independence from Britain came 99 years later.

The current political structure is modeled on that of the United States rather than the British Parliament: a loose confederation of states (including local kings and Muslim mullahs) organized into a federal union. At the top, power would be separated among three branches if a stable civilian government takes power.

Nigerian newspapers evince a U.S. investigative and adversarial tone, even though the names and lineages run back to the British journalists who followed the Union Jack around the world in search of adventure and profits. The media seem to reflect a spirit that is both a special characteristic of Nigeria and a product of the U.S. education of many Nigerian journalists and journalism instructors. In comparison to most other African countries, the dozen-plus dailies are the core of a substantial media industry. But they have to serve a country massive in both population and land mass. When the half million total daily newspaper circulation is divided into the more than 100 million population, the media poverty of the country is apparent.

The same is true for broadcast media. Despite explosive growth, Nigerian radio and television are well developed only in comparison to other African countries. Against the standard of the West and even some parts of the third world, Nigeria, like all of black Africa, is media poor.

Background

Nigeria's first newspaper was published in 1859 in English and Yoruba by a British missionary. It started a tradition of independent journalism that survived periodic colonial suppression and continues to the present. Nigerian journalism is also strongly African, a contrast to other countries where European ownership, management, and influence are still the norm. At independence, Nigerians published more than 100 papers. Journalism was an important factor in the drive for independence and is a persistent voice for return to civilian rule.

Nigerian journalists face a daily struggle beyond the imagination of most Western journalists. Not the least of their problems is the government, which is a military regime that came to power in a coup in 1985. The civilian governments that ruled after independence and between coups were, like the military governments, corrupt and incompetent although nominally less physically threatening. The tradition of intimidation is as old as the nation. Throughout its independence, Nigeria has endured periodic ethnic violence, especially a bloody civil war in the 1960s. Domestic conflict, common to most African countries, interferes with progress toward stability and slows economic growth.

Less than a year after independence, a local journalist called the "Thomas Paine of Nigeria" was convicted of sedition for publishing a pamphlet that included the sentence, "The common man in Nigeria can today no longer be fooled by sweet talk at election time only to be exploited and treated like dirt after the booty of office has been shared." In the years after, the degree of criticism tolerated by government authorities varied, but the trend in the 1980s was toward repression.

A military government decree in 1984 established heavy penalties for publication of unauthorized information about public officials. Three months later, two journalists were jailed for a year for publishing a story about possible changes in Nigeria's foreign service. Just before a coup the next year that replaced the harsh general in command of the country, at least 12 journalists were in prison, and military authorities threatened to close any papers that were too critical. Still, Nigerian journalists operate with vigor and independence that is missing from most other African countries.

A military dictatorship is one obstacle to the development of an adequate media system, but not the only one. Other problems, typical of the third world, are especially acute in Africa. Among them:

1. Lack of communication infrastructure. Journalism depends on moving information quickly, but most developing countries lack reliable telephone service. Calling across town or from one city to another can be impossible. Simple teletypes and fax machines that use the same lines are also silenced for days or weeks. In a country more than twice the size of California, the frequent collapse of internal communications makes routine news gathering and dissemination impossible.
2. Inadequate financial base. Journalism is an expensive business. Revenues to pay for it come from three sources: consumers,

advertisers, and/or governments. In countries such as Nigeria (annual per capita income of $800), purchase of a daily newspaper, weekly magazine, or radio or TV set can exceed the budget of most people. Nor can the local economy generate enough advertising to pay for the production of even modest newspapers and broadcasts. For that reason, some kind of government support of media is almost inevitable.

Another financial problem is the lack of "hard" foreign currency to pay for technical equipment, almost all of which must be imported. TV cameras, videotape machines, printing presses, and editing systems all come from the West and require payments in U.S. dollars, German marks, or Japanese yen. Even newsprint must be imported and represents a hard currency outlay every time the presses roll.

3. Physical barriers. Lagos itself was a traveler's nightmare when oil revenues in the 1970s turned the dull capital into an immense metropolis that teetered perpetually on the verge of physical collapse. Getting from one side of the city to another could take half a day. Distributing newspapers and magazines outside the capital with even a hint of timeliness could be impossible. Even getting them from the printing plant to newsstands was a daily ordeal.

In many of the larger African countries, roads end at the edge of the capital city. Railroads are nonexistent. Only an inadequate and unreliable air network ties the country together. The result is that print media are often limited to the capital and large regional centers. Broadcast, too, particularly television, is concentrated in the urban areas. Countries like Nigeria have a double information gap. Even the limited media serve mostly the urban elites. The problem of inequitable distribution of wealth and resources between the urban and rural areas and between the elites and ordinary people within the urban centers adds to the problem of mobilizing the media to support development.

Development Policies

The British roots of Nigeria's media philosophy gave it both a respect for individual liberty and mechanisms for effective government control. The military governments used various methods—both within and outside the law—to stifle media criticism, but the notion that national media had a positive responsibility to promote development is woven throughout Nigeria's independent history. In 1973, for example, the Federal Radio Corporation of Nigeria (FRCN), which operates one network of radio and TV stations, issued a set of policy objectives that included the following:

To provide efficient broadcasting services to the whole Federation of Nigeria based on national objectives and aspirations; to external audiences in accordance with Nigeria's foreign policy;

To provide a professional and comprehensive coverage of Nigerian culture through broadcasting; to promote cultural growth through research into the indigenous culture, and to disseminate the results of such research;

To contribute to the development of the Nigerian society, and to promote national unity by ensuring a balanced presentation of views from all parts of Nigeria.[10]

The News Agency of Nigeria (NAN), founded in 1976 in the shadow of the NWIO debate, also was mandated a positive role by the military government that authorized it:

To uphold the integrity of the Federal Republic of Nigeria. . . . To ensure that news and comments emanating from the agency are truthful, honest and fair but do not jeopardize peace and harmony in the country.

Not to act as an institutional opponent to any government or interests; but where it is in the public interest to report criticism of public policy, it must do so in a restrained and objective manner;

Not to be neutral in matters that affect the sovereignty or unity of Nigeria.[11]

Patriotism is not inherently hostile to honest journalism, and most Western journalists would argue that, by criticizing their governments, they are acting in the tradition of great patriots. Nor is an obligation to promote the development of Nigeria necessarily at odds with the professional values of most Nigerian journalists. The problem comes at the gray area between "truthful, honest, and fair" reporting and acting as "an institutional opponent to any government or interest." Any story, especially one critical of the regime, can fall into either category, depending on your perspective. What is good, professional reporting to the journalist is often hostile to nation-building in the eyes of the government official.

Nigeria had run its share of traditional development projects supported by communication—rural radio programs and newspapers, TV programs devoted to education and traditional cultures—but overpowering evidence that they had contributed significantly to development goals was hard to come by, as it often is. After 30 years of independence, the traditional development goals of political stability and economic growth remain elusive.

The country itself was never closely identified with the attack on the Lerner–Schramm model of communication or with the NWIO debate that sought to end Western dominance in the third world. It was, however, a model of the new style of development media, which failed in Nigeria as it did in other countries where mass media were supposed to be the engines of rapid change.

---

[10] From Frank Ugboajah and Idowu Sobowale, "The Press in West Africa: A Comparative Analysis of Mass Media Trends," in John A. Lent, ed., *Case Studies of Mass Media in the Third World, Studies in Third World Societies No. 10* (Williamsburg, VA: College of William and Mary, 1980), pp. 133–151.

[11] Ibid.

INDIA

India stands out as a remarkable exception to the dismal history of most postcolonial nations. Although poor and threatened by possibly the largest babel of languages and cultures in the world, the country (with one exception) has remained democratic since its independence from Britain in 1947. As in similar countries, the colonial experience left its imprint in language, political institutions, and mass media. As in most other former British colonies, there is a strong tradition of press independence and public service broadcasting. Both clash regularly with the concept of development media.

As is true with most of the countries highlighted in our armchair tour, India could be classified into more than one media concept. It is the world's largest democracy, which includes an independent press that could qualify it for inclusion among the Western media. The government, however, maintains enough influence over television—and periodically in newspapers—that the Indian media also could be considered part of an authoritarian system. By virtue of a long tradition of government control over broadcasting and extensive use of the media, especially broadcasting, to promote a range of development projects, India is included here as a case study of the development press concept.

Background

Like Nigeria, India inherited aspects of the British media system. These include several newspapers called *The Times* (*Hindustan Times, Times of India,* etc.), a noncommercial broadcast system vulnerable to government control, and an enthusiasm for democracy. Unlike Nigeria—and most other former British colonies—India has held on to democracy, despite ethnic violence, political assassinations, and failure to keep pace with other parts of Asia in economic development. With more than 1,000 daily papers and 20,000 weeklies and periodicals published in almost 100 languages, India can boast a media diversity matched only by the former Soviet Union.

However, when matched to India's 800-million-plus population, the figures reveal a media-poor country that is belatedly experiencing the exponential growth found in other parts of the developing world. Until Rajiv Gandhi took power in 1984 after his mother, Prime Minister Indira Gandhi, was assassinated, the country had followed a policy of economic self-reliance. This meant, among other things, that the transistor and microchip revolution bypassed India. Domestic production of radio and TV sets was low priority, and a 300 percent import duty on Panasonics and Sonys discouraged imports. That changed when the younger Gandhi became prime minister, and the country entered the last decade of the twentieth century in a feverish explosion of modern communication hardware and software. It included the usual array of Walkmen, CD players, and multistandard VCRs (so people could play videotapes sent by family members in Britain and North America) found in every other country in the world, as well as some unique Indian inventions. One was a monthly videotape news magazine modeled on *60 Minutes* that was sold on newsstands. *Newstrack* dealt with issues the government-controlled TV avoided. Its 11,000 copies (commercials included) were seen by up to 3 million viewers a month. Others followed, with tapes specializing in business and general news in Hindi, which provided a potential audience much larger than for English-language tapes. During the Gulf War, satellite dishes sprung up throughout the country, many plugged into informal (and illegal) neighborhood cable systems that exposed middle-class Indians to CNN and other Western news services.

Media Policies

Indian media shared one characteristic with most other third-world countries, especially those that embrace the development concept, but also differed in one key area. The common characteristic is control of broadcasting. The exception to the third-world pattern is a long-standing commitment to an independent, vigorous, critical press.

India's press freedom began at independence in 1947 and continued except for a two-year period in the 1970s. That occurred when Prime Minister Indira Gandhi declared a national emergency and suspended the constitution after she was found guilty of electoral fraud. More than 250 journalists were arrested, and newspapers, traditionally the most independent mass medium, were muzzled or shut down. Other methods of controlling criticism included withholding of government advertising—a major source of revenue for smaller papers—and control of distribution of newsprint.

The state of emergency lasted two years. By then, the Indian Supreme Court had cleared Gandhi of the fraud charges, but her Congress party lost a general election. The papers returned to their traditional independence, although possibly with a new respect for the power of even a democratic regime to suppress dissent. Broadcasting remained firmly in the hands of the controlling party, where it had always been.

All-India Radio (AIR) and Doordarshan (the TV system, which means "Televiewing") resemble their equivalents in other developing countries. A large part of their programming is devoted to development information. This includes special material for farmers and even soap operas with development-related messages of family planning and health. Most programming is geared toward the three-quarters of India's population still living in traditional villages. It also includes a good dose of development and protocol news, showing the prime minister at great length and rarely with a hint of criticism. Bad news is ignored, delayed, or softened to the point that AIR was sometimes called All-Ind*ira* Radio, and later Doordarshan became known as Rajiv-darshan.

Rajiv Gandhi came to power after Indira's assassination as a thoroughly modern young man addicted to technology and free of most of his mother's autocratic tendencies. However, tolerance of critical broadcast media was not one of his strengths, and he kept a tight rein on both radio and TV. He also proposed—and later withdrew in the face of vigorous press opposition—a defamation bill that would have given the government broad new powers to suppress investigative reporting and prosecute noncompliant journalists.

Rajiv Gandhi's political career was short-lived. From a landslide victory following Indira's assassination, his party fell from power after accusations of corruption and failure to deal with India's growing ethnic conflict. He was trying to make a political comeback at the time of his own assassination in 1991. India survived the deaths of both Gandhis, but the world's largest democracy was stretched thin by the kind of ethnic violence that has plagued so much of the third world and by its failure to make the leap to modernity. Mass media, which became a window to the world from even the most remote Indian village, seemed to produce not the revolution of rising expectations that Lerner said would boost developing countries to wealth and stability, but a revolution of rising frustrations that threatened to tear the nation into a dozen warring factions.

Communication Development

It is probably impossible for a North American to imagine life in one of India's thousands of villages. Old-timers can talk about recent change, but to the outsider, life seems to go on as it has for centuries, with its mixture of good and bad. There is little starvation but some hunger. The caste system still prescribes each individual's place in the rigid social hierarchy. As in Lerner's Turkish village of Balgat, people are born to a life their grandparents and great-grandparents would find familiar and live out their days in a village that changes little from their birth to their death.

But there are changes, and, as in Balgat, mass media represent one of the big ones. A series of anthropological studies of Indian villages in the early 1980s help us understand the changes.[12] The village of Podapadu in the coastal region of Andhra Pradesh in southern India contained about 1,000 residents, a mixture of Hindus (nine castes) and Muslims. Agriculture was the main occupation of villagers, but some people made cotton webbing for cots. The village was largely self-contained, but larger villages only a few kilometers away provided a post office, medical clinic, railroad, and small shops that supplied ordinary consumer goods.

The village depended on travelers and mass media for information. Five copies of two regional newspapers were delivered to the village, but only two people were regular readers. Forty-six radio sets were in the village. The reach of the media was larger than the numbers suggest, however, because of pass-along readership and the placement of radios in public places. Two-thirds of the heads of households, in fact, were exposed more or less regularly to AIR broadcasts. Interpersonal communication—the conversation exchanged in daily village life—extended the media's message to most of the villagers.

The papers contained material written especially for rural development, and the AIR programs were also oriented toward agriculture and other development interests. Some villagers found the material useful, but much of it seemed unrelated to their daily lives. Innovations that had been adopted—better varieties of seed,

---

[12] Paul Hartmann, B. R. Patil, and Anita Dighe, *The Mass Media and Village Life: An Indian Study* (Newbury Park, CA: Sage, 1989).

use of fertilizers—were based on personal recommendation and experience. The big obstacle to further change was usually not a lack of information but lack of land or money or the strict caste system that determined how everyone would spend his or her life.

Other villages in the study showed different levels of exposure to mass media, but patterns of availability and use were similar. By Western standards, the villages were isolated and media poor. Could India, which missed the industrial revolution, use the power of modern communication to help these villagers make the "terrible ascent" to the twenty-first century?

An experiment in the mid-1970s suggested that the answer might be yes. It was enough to encourage India to develop its own satellite system in the 1980s. The full effect of the system will not be known until the twenty-first century, but many other developing countries are watching the Indian experience with interest.

Satellites

The Satellite Instructional Television Experiment (SITE) involved a U.S. satellite that was moved to a stationary orbit over India for a year in 1975–1976. The experiment—certainly the most ambitious communication development test ever carried out—was to use the satellite to broadcast a variety of school and adult programs directly to 2,400 villages that were equipped with specially built community TV sets. The signals were received at each site through receivers similar to backyard satellite dishes. Programming consisted of special educational broadcasts during the day and broadcasts for adults at night. On average, about 100 children watched each set during the day, and a similar number of adults watched in the evening.

Probably no experiment in development support communication was evaluated as thoroughly as SITE. Everything that a generation of research and practice had learned went into the development of the program and into an evaluation of it. At the end, results were mixed. Schoolchildren who watched the programs showed more interest in science, a major subject of daytime programming, than similar children not participating in the experiment, but overall achievement was about the same. Among the adults, changes in knowledge of and attitudes toward new ideas in health, agriculture, and family planning were modest and often inconsistent. Technical failures knocked many villages out of the program and demonstrated the difficulty of adapting high-tech hardware to difficult third-world environments. At the end of the experiment, no one was sure whether the results from SITE could translate into the kind of national change that would move India from the bottom of the list of countries in development indicators such as literacy, infant mortality, and agriculture to, say, somewhere in the middle.

The Indian government decided that high-tech development was its best chance to leapfrog into the future and authorized an ambitious program based on an Indian-built satellite system, INSAT. The first satellite, INSAT-1A, was launched in August 1982 but failed after a few months. INSAT-1B, launched the next year, was a success. Ironically, one of its first social missions was to help the giant nation share the grief of Indira Gandhi's assassination and funeral.

Like the SITE satellite, INSAT had the capability of transmitting television signals directly to receiving dishes in villages throughout the country. It also contained the electronics to monitor the weather—valuable information in the storm-prone subcontinent—and ordinary telephone circuits. After a decade, INSAT is still controversial in India. Its critics see it as either an instrument of political control, an extension of All-Indira Radio, or as a frivolous example of high tech engineering in a country that lacks clean water, roads, and schools.

In fact, in the 1990s, the Indian satellite experience parallels that of other developing countries. The TV service, which was the showcase of the system, is becoming relatively less important as a more reliable and flexible terrestrial network expands, and the ordinary telephone circuits are proving to be of great value in overcoming Indian government bureaucracy and in piecing together modern business information networks that leapfrog an outdated and crumbling infrastructure inherited from colonial Britain.

Other forces are also at work that portend great changes for India and other practitioners of the development media concept. These include an inevitable trend toward expanded and commercial broadcasting, cheaper and more accessible printing technology, and an end to any government's power to mobilize the media for whatever purposes it chooses. Any system that defines mass media as a legitimate element of government—the authoritarian, communist, and development concepts—is in trouble. For them, modern communication, almost by definition, is a threat because it cannot be controlled. Challenges come from inside and outside the system and threaten the power of the information monopoly. Almost by definition, modern communication technology is revolutionary. In Chapter 11, we consider the revolutionary media concept and how it challenges many of the media systems we have looked at so far.

MAIN POINTS

1. The development concept of the press assumes that media can function as multipliers of national development efforts. The concept dates to the use of mass media to promote rural development in Western countries and includes elements of the communist and authoritarian concepts.

2. Development was traditionally defined as economic growth and stable democracy. However, some argued in the 1970s that authentic third-world development should reject the Western model and accompanying integration into the Western-dominated global system.

3. The New World Information Order (NWIO) debate included an effort to legitimize the development media theory and to expand the concept of "communication support information" into "development news" (the positive elements of third-world change) and "protocol news" (the ceremonial aspects of national leadership).

4. Although mass media can be used to support traditional development activities, research has failed to demonstrate that communication alone can multiply economic or political growth.

5. The NWIO debate produced a new interest in communication and development, particularly in the use of telecommunication as an important tool of national development.

6. The collapse of communism severely damaged the development concept of the press. Development news and protocol news now lack credibility. The global communication system has made a government information monopoly impossible.

FOR MORE INFORMATION

William A. Hachten's *The Growth of Media in the Third World: African Failures, Asian Successes,* cited in Chapter 19, is the only book that considers the experience of the development concept of the press in detail. It compares success of the largely authoritarian Asian media with the failure of the largely developmental African media.

No full-length book on the development concept of the press has appeared, but books about media in regions where the concept is practiced include William A. Rugh, *The Arab Press: News and Media and Political Process in the Arab World,* 2nd ed. (Syracuse, NY: Syracuse University Press, 1987); Graham Mytton, *Mass Communication in Africa* (London: Edward Arnold, 1983); and John Barton, *The Press of Africa: Persecution and Perseverance* (London: Macmillan, 1979). General works on the regions include Sanford J. Unger, *Africa: The People and Politics of an Emerging Continent* (New York: Simon & Schuster, 1985); David Lamb, *The Africans* (New York: Random House, 1982); David Lamb, *The Arabs: Journeys beyond the Mirage* (New York: Random House, 1987); Allister Sparks, *The Mind of South Africa* (New York: Ballantine, 1990); Charles Glass, *Tribes with Flags: A Dangerous Passage through the Chaos of the Middle East* (New York: Atlantic Monthly Press, 1990); and David K. Shipler, *Arab and Jew: Wounded Spirits in a Promised Land* (New York: Penguin, 1987).

Overviews of the role of communication and development include Robert C. Hornik, *Development Communication: Information, Agriculture, and Nutrition in the Third World* (New York: Longman, 1988); Srinivas R. Melkote, *Communication for Development in the Third World* (Newbury Park, CA: Sage, 1991); and Robert L. Stevenson, *Communication, Development and the Third World: The Global Politics of Information* (New York: Longman, 1988). All contain extensive bibliographies.

FOR DISCUSSION

1. Debate Hachten's conclusion about Asian successes and African failures in building stable, relatively prosperous regimes and the role of mass media.

2. Examine copies of third-world newspapers or broadcast news for evidence of development news and protocol news. Argue whether this kind of information (1) promotes or (2) retards social and economic change.

3. Review some of the key studies referred to in Hornik's book (or any of the other reviews of communication and development) for evidence that communication can promote

technical change, such as family planning, health, or agricultural practices. How important should such programs be in third-world countries today?

DATA BASE

See note in the Data Base of Chapter 8 for explanation of selection of countries and statistics. Data are given in numbers per 100 population.

Country	Newspaper Circulation	Radio Sets	Television Sets	VCRs	Telephone Lines
Africa					
Algeria	2	21	15	3	3
Angola	1	9	1		1
Benin	0	9	1		0
Botswana	2	11	2		2
Burkina Faso	0	5	1		0
Burundi	0	7	0		0
Cameroon	1	16	5	1	0
Cape Verde	0	14	0		2
Central African Republics	N/A	7	1		0
Chad	1	9	0		0
Comoros	N/A	11			1
Congo	1	13	1		1
Côte d'Ivoire	1	14	7	1	2
Cyprus	13	60	29	11	32
Djibouti	0	9	4		1
Egypt	4	32	14	3	2
Equatorial Guinea	2	25	1		N/A
Ethiopia	0	8	0		0
Gabon	1	19	5	4	2
Gambia	1	16			1
Ghana	3	27	2		0
Guinea	0	7	1		1
Guinea-Bissau	1	5			2
Kenya	1	20	2		1
Lesotho	3	14	1		1
Liberia	1	19	2		0
Libya	2	23	10		7
Madagascar	1	19	1		0
Malawi	0	14			0

Country	Newspaper Circulation	Radio Sets	Television Sets	VCRs	Telephone Lines
Mali	0	7	2		0
Malta	16	63	38		35
Mauritania	N/A	14	2		0
Morocco	N/A	29	13	3	1
Mozambique	1	5	0		0
Namibia	1	5	2		4
Niger	0	6	1		1
Nigeria	2	15	7	1	0
Rwanda	0	6			0
São Tomé/Principe	0	22			2
Saudi Arabia	2	35	25	16	9
Senegal	1	15	8	8	0
Sierra Leone	0	21	1		1
Somalia	1	6	1		2
South Africa	5	32	11	2	9
Sudan	1	16	8		0
Swaziland	7	15	3		2
Tanzania	1	10	0		0
Togo	0	14	1		0
Tunisia	4	25	15	2	3
Uganda	0	11	1		0
Zaire	0	10	3		0
Zambia	1	11	4		1
Zimbabwe	2	13	4	1	1

SOURCE: Newspaper circulation figures are mid- to late-1980s and from UNESCO figures and other sources; phone line data are from American Telephone & Telegraph's (AT&T) *The World's Telephones*, 1991, and the International Telecommunication Union's (ITU) *Yearbook of Common Carrier Telecommunication Statistics* (18th ed.). Radio, TV, and VCR data from *World Radio and TV Receivers*, ed. by Carol L. Forrester. Copyright © 1991 IBAR-BBC World Service. Reprinted by permission.

CHAPTER **11**

Revolutionary Media

ABOUT THIS CHAPTER

In the midst of the third communication revolution, the world at the end of the 1980s witnessed great political changes: *glasnost* in the Soviet Union helped bring about the collapse of communism in Central Europe; cracking of one-party regimes in Africa and even, apparently, the beginning of the end of apartheid in South Africa; and transfer of political power from generals and colonels in Latin America to civilian governments.

The suppression of protesters in Tiananmen Square, however, reversed China's march toward democracy and was a reminder that political change is not inevitably in one direction. Still, the trend is clear. Is there a connection between global political change at the end of the twentieth century and the emergence of global communication systems transmitting unlimited packets of digitized text, sound, and pictures all over the planet? This question is the theme of this chapter.

INTRODUCTION

Each of the three communication revolutions to date has led to a drastic restructuring of power in the cultures to which they were introduced. This is why we have used the term *revolution,* which means exactly that. *Webster's Collegiate Dictionary* includes these definitions: "a sudden, radical, or complete change . . . a fundamental change in political organization . . . activity designed to effect fundamental changes in the socioeconomic situation (as of a racial or cultural segment of the population).''

Written language ended the power monopoly of the elders who preserved and passed on the oral sagas and poems that contained the accumulated knowledge of preliterate tribes. Inexpensive printing with moveable type challenged the authority of church and crown and allowed the flowering of vernacular languages and, eventually, democracy.

Our political definition of the word *revolution* is a product of this change. At the end of his life in 1543, the early astronomer Nicolaus Copernicus published a book titled *On the Revolution of the Celestial Spheres* that challenged the Catholic church's official dogma that the earth was at the center of the solar system. A century later, in defiance of the Vatican, Galileo Galilei published a book, *Dialogue on the Great World Systems,* that pitted an earth-centered system against a sun-centered system. He clearly favored the latter and was brought before the Inquisition for questioning the official version of reality. Galileo was convicted and put under house arrest for life, where on his death-bed he was said to have muttered, "but still it revolves."[1] The doctrine that the sun revolved around the earth stayed in place officially until 1992, when a commission belatedly acknowledged what the rest of the world had accepted three centuries earlier.

Our political meaning of the word *revolution* derives from Copernicus's book and Galileo's run-in with an absolute power that didn't appreciate questions of its authority. The book was truly revolutionary: It challenged the church's monopoly of information, its monopoly of truth, and changed the world forever.

We are at the beginning of the third communication revolution—the creation of global networks exchanging exponentially increasing volumes of digitized text, sound, and pictures—and cannot predict how national and global power may shift as a result. Already books have been written about the evolution of "information societies" in the United States, Japan, and Western Europe and about how information has become the dominant element of politics and economics.[2] Some authors talk about the gap between North and South in terms of information rather than traditional political and economic power and use this gap to account for continuing Anglo-American influence in spite of sharply diminished economic and political strength.[3] However, the revolutionary concept of the press is less concerned with the rise of information as a replacement for political and economic power than with its utility as a tool in old-fashioned political revolutions. We can look backward in history and around the world today for several useful examples.

---

[1] See J. Bronowski, *The Ascent of Man* (Boston: Little, Brown, 1973); and Marie Boas Hall, "Nicolaus Copernicus," in *Makers of Modern Thought* (New York: American Heritage, 1972).

[2] Wilson P. Dizard, *The Coming Information Age,* 3rd ed. (New York: Longman, 1989); Joseph S. Nye, Jr., *Bound to Lead: The Changing Nature of American Power* (New York: Basic, 1990).

[3] Herbert I. Schiller, *Who Knows? Information in the Age of the Fortune 500* (Norwood, NJ: Ablex, 1981).

INFORMATION AND REVOLUTION

To begin, let us consider the role of information in the great revolutions of the eighteenth century that were a product of the second communication revolution. Was information a key element in the American and French revolutions? To be sure, information played a role. An early action in the British American colonies was to establish Committees of Correspondence, whose job was to keep revolutionary committees apprised of activities in other colonies. Thomas Paine's pamphlets helped fan the sparks of rebellion and, of course, the Declaration of Independence itself was written as much to justify the revolution to the world as to seal the bond among the rebels.

Revolutionary Eighteenth Century

The American Revolution inspired rebels in France, but in neither revolution was information unambiguously an essential element. The founding fathers of the new republics did not use mass media to challenge established authority, to rally public opinion, or to consolidate power after seizing power. Nor did the rest of the world witness these upheavals. Compared to our own time, even news of the great events traveled slowly. King George III noted in his diary that nothing important happened on July 4, 1776.

Revolution Today

Modern revolutions are different. We learn about them instantly and follow them live on television. It seems—proof is difficult to muster, but it seems—that the global media system is itself part of the revolution as much as its witness. Perhaps this is so, but the answer is not as clear-cut as it sometimes appears. We can argue that modern communication can aid, support, encourage, help, and assist modern revolutionaries, but it is probably not sufficient by itself to make revolution inevitable and certainly not successful. What can communication do?

Ending Government Monopoly.   Modern communication can end a government monopoly on information. At one time it was possible for a government to maintain close to an information monopoly. As we have seen, government control is part of the traditional authoritarian and modern communist media concepts. Something close to government monopoly is also part of the development concept.

Government control, if not total monopoly, was possible at one time if the government was willing to isolate itself. Twentieth-century examples include China and Cambodia after their revolutions and Albania until its communist government was overthrown. Now probably only North Korea qualifies, and cracks are growing in its wall around itself. However, even in these countries, control was imperfect. Short-wave radio, which has been available for most of the twentieth century, crosses even the most heavily guarded border. *Samizdat* literature found its way into the Soviet Union, and Iranian police were never able

Rebel forces from Burma watch videotapes in a camp near the Thai border. Modern communication technology can undermine a government's monopoly on information but, by itself, probably lacks the revolutionary power often attributed to it.

SOURCE: Harunart Prapanya/Time Magazine.

to intercept the smuggled audiocassettes that helped undermine the shah's regime. Even early in the twentieth century, revolutionary tracts published abroad and smuggled into Russia aided in the overthrow of the tsar.

Such revolutionary information usually reaches a small elite of people sufficiently motivated to seek it out or willing to take the chance of getting caught passing it on, but that can be enough. Most revolutions are put together by small groups of elites. Majority support comes later, if at all. A few illegal fliers, a handful of audiocassettes, or snatches of foreign short-wave newscasts can set off ripples that engulf governments if the fliers, audiocassettes, or newscasts reach the right people.

The colonial printers who defied British authority helped unite the small band of men and women who later defied the king. Their modern counterparts include Chinese students in the late 1980s bombarding the handful of fax machines in China with news summaries and Czechs traveling from village to village to share videotapes banned from government-controlled television. Even at the end of the twentieth century, a sizable club of ex-presidents, ex-kings, and ex-generals can attest that a little knowledge in the right hands can be a big threat. With modern media—small, cheap, and ubiquitous—the threat to absolute power has never been greater.

Organizing. Modern communication can allow insurgents to organize. Revolutions are spearheaded by small groups of individuals who need to be mobilized and directed against the weak links of strong regimes. In response, governments try to attack the insurgents by dividing and isolating them. The assumption is that a revolutionary threat will die if denied solidarity and publicity. The tactic was widely used in the pre-*glasnost* Soviet Union, which maintained an extensive domestic archipelago of prison camps where dissidents were kept in isolation. One key function of illegal *samizdat* publications was to keep families and supporters of political prisoners informed about prisoners' location and status. Isolation and ignorance are powerful tools to demoralize both revolutionaries and their supporters.

In the old days, the standard tactic of revolutionaries was to attack the palace and then run up their flag and proclaim victory. In the communication age, a first target is often the newspapers and broadcasting facilities. The assumption is that when these modern instruments of power are controlled, opposition will end. Sometimes it works, but not always.

In August 1991, instigators of the coup against President Gorbachev suspended independent media and took over key newspapers, radio, and TV. However, through oversight or general incompetence, they failed to control international telecommunication. Supporters of the besieged Russian President Yeltsin sent faxes directly to Washington, D.C., urging that his statements condemning the coup be broadcast back to the Soviet Union on the Voice of America and the U.S.-financed Radio Liberty. Internal telecommunications were maintained as well, with the result that people throughout the Soviet Union knew what was going on in Moscow. However, before the relative strengths of the media of the two sides could be tested, the coup collapsed.

The situation was different in China, where authorities pulled on the plug on international television and took over domestic communication before the tanks were ordered into Tiananmen Square. Even there, though, enough links with the outside world were maintained that people outside of China and many in the country knew what was happening.

Destroying Legitimacy. Modern communication can destroy the legitimacy of a repressive government. This has two effects, one international and one domestic. The Chinese government demonstrated in Tiananmen Square in 1989 that tanks are still an effective—if bloody—way of dealing with popular protest. In that case, even though Chinese officials stopped use of international television circuits, some still photos and videotape did record the massacre. As a result, the Chinese government became an international pariah and global symbol of dictatorship in a world moving rapidly away from dictatorships.

Domestically, the influence of communication is different. China demonstrated that dictatorship is still possible if a government is willing to pay the price in international public opinion. However, if a government blinks before the

cameras when confronted with massive opposition, the fear of dictatorship—
and hence its power—disappears.

In the dramatic revolutions in Central Europe, this happened in several
countries. The effect was particularly clear in Romania, where a staged mass rally
supporting President Nicolae Ceauçescu unexpectedly turned against him. The
live telecast was interrupted but not until viewers had seen the crowd sentiment
and Ceauçescu's incredulous, stunned reaction. Something similar may have
happened in the Soviet Union in 1991.

It was not clear at the time whether the armed forces refused to attack the
thousands of people surrounding the Russian "White House," where Yeltsin was
leading opposition to the coup, or whether the instigators of the coup never
ordered an attack. Knowledge that cameras were on hand to send live pictures
around the world must have been a consideration. Once people lose their fear
and government loses its nerve to use force, the collapse of totalitarianism is
inevitable. When one side blinks, modern media can show it in close-up.

Bringing Down Governments.   Modern communication can bring down
governments. Here we must use lots of caution signs because it is not at all clear
that mass media alone or in the hands of revolutionaries are powerful enough
to destroy dictatorship. If the government has enough guns and is willing to accept
world condemnation, it can prevail. China is the most recent example, but others
could be cited: Warsaw Pact forces invading Czechoslovakia in 1968, the Khmer
Rouge genocide in Cambodia, even the Iraqi invasion of Kuwait. For more than
20 years, the Berlin Wall kept East Germans home and their ugly regime in power
despite full access to West German television.

The world is generally tolerant of countries that do terrible things to their
own people at home but less so when one country attacks another. For the former
reason, the dramatic pictures of civil war in the former Yugoslavia, the attacks
on Chinese protesters, and the genocide victims in Cambodia do not stir an international response. Modern communication brings these tragedies to our living
rooms as well as to the debating chambers of the United Nations, but the response
is restrained. The last two examples are also reminders that a television camera
does not always have more power than a tank. In the televised revolutions of
1989–1991, communication acquired the status of a key element. Whoever controlled
the minicams, the argument went, won. Perhaps this is so, but a closer examination
of the role of mass media in recent revolutions may help us sort out their real
influence from the myth of omnipotence they have acquired in recent years.

SAMIZDAT IN THE SOVIET UNION

Tradition of Suppression

The Soviet Union emerged from an autocratic monarchy with no tradition of
liberty. Except for a brief period of chaos following the Russian Revolution, a
government monopoly on information as envisioned by Lenin was the standard

practice until the introduction of *glasnost*. However, the monopoly was never complete, and the degree of control varied. Limited literary and political independence were possible under Lenin, who tolerated some criticism. Under his successor, Joseph Stalin, there was none, and the media and arts became a hymn of constant adulation that today is seen only in North Korea.

The pendulum swung back toward literary openness under Nikita Khrushchev, who was party chief from 1953 until he was removed in 1964. Khrushchev was a peasant who made no effort to hide his disdain for modern arts, but he permitted—at times even encouraged—artistic license that was without precedent in Russian and Soviet history. During his tenure, Alexander Solzhenitsyn's stark novel of life in a prison camp during the Stalin era, *One Day in the Life of Ivan Denisovich,* was published. Authorized periodicals such as *Literary Gazette* and *Novy Mir* ("New World") published a wide variety of material that was, by Soviet standards, bold and critical. Through novels and poetry, a generation of writers was able to nibble away the edges of the secrecy that surrounded Soviet history.

Khrushchev's successor, Leonid Brezhnev, embraced a policy of accommodation abroad but matched it at home with a renewed crackdown on literary and political dissent. While he traveled around the world promoting détente, or relaxation of tensions between East and West, his police at home imprisoned thousands of individuals for what in the West would be considered mundane political and literary activity. However, the more the government cracked down, the more the resistance grew. Brezhnev, a crude peasant something like Khrushchev, will be remembered for his photo-opportunity embraces of U.S. presidents and for a Russian word that entered the global vocabulary during his regime—*samizdat*.

The *Samizdat* Tradition

The word *samizdat* means "self-publishing" in Russian and refers to a wide range of documents published independently (and therefore illegally) in the Soviet Union. They became particularly visible during the domestic crackdowns of the Brezhnev years, but they had existed even during the tsarist era.

The early *samizdat* emphasized mostly literature and religion, but after the Soviet government began its attack on writers in the mid-1960s, they became more political. The most famous of the *samizdat* publications was *Chronicle of Current Events,* which documented arrests, secret trials, and the lives of imprisoned dissidents for more than a decade. The *Chronicle* was remarkable because it maintained a regular bimonthly publication schedule and because it was, like all *samizdat* publications, produced by individuals who typed every issue, six or eight copies at a time, and distributed them from person to person. The usual forms of production, such as printing presses and photocopy machines, were tightly controlled by the government.

It is hard to imagine the circumstances under which the *samizdat* were produced and distributed. The government's policy was to destroy the informal networks of dissidents, who depended on the comfort and support of one another.

Separation from friends and isolation in a mental institution or the massive prison system Solzhenitsyn called the "gulag archipelago" left one alone and vulnerable, often with the despair of not knowing whether friends and family were even aware of one's predicament. A major goal of the *samizdat* was to make sure this isolation didn't happen.

Typically, small groups of "journalists" gathered periodically in an apartment to prepare material for the *samizdat,* then typed multiple copies on onionskin paper. Most aspects of the process—collection of information, distribution of the copies—were handled like an intelligence network. No single person knew more than a few of the links, to prevent the police from destroying the network if one of the participants collaborated or confessed. The police and KGB were always a threat. Once the KGB arrived at the *Chronicle* editor's apartment when an issue was laid out on her kitchen table. She threw the papers into a pot of soup, which a friend calmly stirred throughout the search.[4]

Samizdat Accomplishments

Despite massive efforts by authorities to destroy the *samizdat* network, hundreds—probably thousands—of publications were produced. They served several purposes both within the Soviet Union and internationally.

1. They provided an outlet for literature and journalism the Soviet authorities tried to prohibit. Many of them were later published in the West. Some were smuggled back into the Soviet Union or broadcast over Western short-wave stations. The smuggled copies or broadcasts captured on audiocassette spread the *samizdat* to a much wider audience.

2. They required Soviet authorities to acknowledge the crackdown on dissidents and occasionally to respond to international pressure. Secrecy and silence are the strongest allies of dictatorship. Public administration of even a corrupt legal system brings pressure for reform. In a few instances, Soviet authorities were forced to temper their suppression of dissenters. The actions of brave *samizdat* writers, political activists, and *refusniks* frequently forced the government to open legal proceedings and kept a weak but steady searchlight on government activities.

3. They linked the dissident movement in the Soviet Union to a global audience through the small band of Western correspondents in Moscow. Moscow correspondents regularly received copies of the *samizdat* and were frequently offered material from dissidents. They had to be careful because the offers occasionally were government plants and used as a pretext for expelling aggressive Western

---

[4] Joshua Rubenstein, "The Enduring Voices of the Soviet Dissidents," *Columbia Journalism Review,* September–October, 1978, pp. 32–39.

reporters from the country.[5] Even the legitimate *samizdat* writers were using the Western media as a mechanism for global publication and sometimes for protection, which raised ethical problems for the Western reporters. However, the global impact of a story in the *New York Times* or on the BBC World Service was great enough—and the resistance itself a big enough story in the West—that the symbiotic relationship between Soviet dissidents and the Western press remained an important part of the *samizdat* movement.

In February 1974, Hedrick Smith, a *New York Times* correspondent, was summoned to Solzhenitsyn's Moscow apartment and given the last part of *Gulag Archipelago,* which brought Solzhenitsyn's exposé of the Soviet system right to Brezhnev himself. Earlier sections had already been published in the West to the great annoyance and embarrassment of the Soviet government. The next day, Solzhenitsyn was arrested and later forced into exile in the West while Smith had a story that made headlines around the world and helped him win the Pulitzer Prize. Fifteen years later, *Novy Mir* serialized the complete *Gulag,* a symbolic triumph of *glasnost* that made the *samizdat* obsolete.

Soviet dissidents in the 1970s were denied much of the communication technology that was credited with the great revolutions of the 1990s. However, even at the time, dissidents were demonstrating that modern media could be used effectively to challenge a government monopoly on information. Curiously enough, this happened next door to the Soviet Union.

POLAND

Background

A glance at a map of Northern Europe will show you why geography destined Poland for trouble. Located on a low plain between Russia and Germany, Poland inevitably got caught in conflicts between the traditional European superpowers. For much of modern history, it did not exist as an independent nation. Poland was obliterated as a state in the late 1700s and mandated to the tsar of Russia. It surfaced briefly as an independent nation between the world wars and, after enduring the worst of Hitler's and Stalin's armies, was annexed to the post–World War II Soviet empire.

On the positive side, Poland is a shining example of the triumph of culture, especially language and religion, over political adversity. More than any other country that took part in the great communication revolution of 1989, Poland demonstrated that a strong nation, aided by modern communication, can survive an alien regime and defeat it. Poland is an unusual case study because we have

---

[5] This happened as late as 1986 when Nicholas Daniloff, a reporter for *U.S. News & World Report,* was set up and briefly imprisoned before being expelled. Nicholas Daniloff, *Two Lives, One Russia* (Boston: Houghton Mifflin, 1988).

a record of communist censorship in the years before the revolution and because the country developed a virtual parallel underground culture that challenged and eventually replaced the official regime imposed by the Soviet Union after World War II.

Polish Censorship

We know from our consideration of the communist concept of the press that Lenin considered the media as legitimate instruments of government propaganda, agitation, organization, and control. We also know that information is treated as a monopoly of the regime. We do not know very much about the day-to-day operations of the censorship apparatus of communist regimes—although *glasnost* is changing that—because the directives and operations of the censors are themselves highly classified. Very little was—and is—known about the shadowy *apparatchiks* who made and enforced the intricate rules of what could be made public and what could not.

Poland is an exception because in 1977 a Polish censor—No. C-36 of the Krakow Main Office for Control of Press, Publications, and Public Performances—traveled to Sweden on vacation.[6] His real goal was defection, and he carried, strapped to his body in plastic bags, some 700 pages of documents that he had secretly collected in the two preceding years. The documents, all highly classified, of course, included specific instructions about what could and could not be published, training materials for novice censors, and lots of examples of censorship in action. The censors kept careful records of their activities, even publishing a biweekly bulletin with examples of material that had been removed from publications or changed to conform to guidelines that changed frequently.

Existence of the censorship operation was itself classified, but strangely enough, most of the censors were low-level bureaucrats who couldn't get better jobs. No. C-36 got his job through a well-placed brother in the Krakow city administration. The sloppiness of his fellow censors allowed him to collect the documents he smuggled to the West.

Some of the proscribed topics—anything to do with the Warsaw Pact, anything critical of the Soviet Union—were obvious, but the censors' instructions, which changed frequently, included some surprising topics. Prohibited were statistics on Poland's meat exports to the Soviet Union; expressions of sympathy with Ethiopian rebels; plans by General Idi Amin, the Ugandan dictator, to erect a statue of Adolf Hitler; stories on plant and cattle disease in Poland; figures on water consumption by one textile company; and announcements of the purchase of a U.S.-made computer for the Nuclear Research Institute.[7]

Also on the list was any mention of environmental pollution originating in Poland, although problems from pollution originating in Czechoslovakia (and

---

[6] Jane Leftwich Curry, ed. and trans., *The Black Book of Polish Censorship* (New York: Vintage, 1984).

[7] Anna Husarska, "Up from the Underground in Poland," *New York Review of Books,* October 8, 1989, p. 1.

affecting Polish rivers) could be reported. At the time, the issue seemed relatively minor, but as Poles discovered after the collapse of the communist regime, environmental degradation in Central Europe was among the worst in the world and represented one of the most glaring failures of the communist regime.

Publication of the Polish "Black Book" showed in detail how the government had tried to use the media to create an illusionary world of great accomplishment and no failure. It was a world that was so at odds with what Poles saw every day that it lacked credibility. Pictures of protocol triumphs make little impression on people who have to cope daily with empty shops. In every country now and especially in Poland in the 1970s, the official media's version of reality was contradicted, first by media outside the country and, then, by a network of underground domestic media. These Polish *samizdat* created a parallel culture that was significant and perhaps decisive in the collapse of the communist government. Together they represent a good test of the proposition that modern mass media can undermine an undemocratic regime.

Solidarity

In 1980, the communist government of Poland, continually challenged by the Catholic church and the closely knit Polish people, was shaken by a series of strikes that produced unauthorized independent trade unions. The head of the unions' coordinating committee, Solidarity, was a shipyard worker, Lech Walesa. Walesa was an improbable candidate for the fame and power that led eventually to a Nobel Peace Prize and the presidency of the first postcommunist government. Slightly overweight, with a droopy mustache and unfashionably large family, Walesa himself became a celebrity around the world in large part because of television. At home, a sophisticated but illegal communication network allowed him to develop Solidarity into a shadow government that eventually rivaled and challenged the official regime. Under a decree of martial law that lasted two years, Solidarity was banned and an invasion by Soviet armed forces seemed imminent. Solidarity persisted, however, and in the year of revolutions, 1989, was overwhelmingly elected to power in an open contest against the hapless communist party. As Poland joined its neighbors in one of the most remarkable political transformations in history, the question arose whether modern communication made the collapse of communism possible or inevitable or whether global media merely recorded the events.

Poland's geographic position, which made it a frequent battlefield, also protected it against the information monopoly that the censors tried to enforce. From the earliest days of the cold war, the Iron Curtain (as Churchill called it) dividing Europe was never soundproof. Radio Free Europe, a U.S.-financed short-wave service intended to represent a media watchdog, albeit from exile (more discussion in Chapter 14), broadcast a strong signal to Poland. It was joined by short-wave services of the BBC, Voice of America, and others to provide virtually all Poles with a steady stream of information that was usually at variance with the official media. In later years, illicit receiving dishes snatched TV news from Western satellites as well. Solidarity married unofficial information with modern technology to a degree that was not possible in either the Soviet Union, other Central European countries, or China. What worked for Poland was an extraordinary bond of people against their own government plus access to information and technology that was denied to the operators of the Soviet *samizdat* networks.

The underground media movement began spontaneously when martial law was imposed. One leader put it this way to a *New York Times* reporter: "Once resistance had meant taking up a gun. Now, people instinctively took up typewriters."[8] For Poles in the 1980s, the resistance expanded from typewriters to a vast network of clandestine printing presses, photocopiers, audiocassettes, and videocassettes—the whole range of modern communication technology. Sometimes materials were prepared abroad and smuggled into Poland. Domestically the underground network included even clandestine radio and TV services.

Stefan Bratkowski, president of the Polish Journalists' Association and long identified with opposition, underground, and Solidarity newspapers, estimated that up to 200,000 people were involved in a distribution network for more than 2,000 issues of 700 titles published during the years from the imposition of martial law to the collapse of the communist government in 1988.[9] Another source estimated that at the peak in 1982, 766 periodicals were being printed regularly from more than 160 illegal publishing houses.[10] The leading weekly, *Mazowsze,* was printed in 12 to 20 separate locations in press runs that ranged from 40,000 to 80,000 copies. Many of the other papers and magazines maintained regular publication and distribution even though the police made the destruction of the underground media networks a high priority. Ninety percent of Poles imprisoned during martial law and after were connected to the clandestine media system.

Even more threatening to the government's media monopoly was the underground use of modern electronic media. Bratkowski himself pioneered the use of audiocassette newspapers. One-hour information-oriented cassettes were duplicated and passed on. In some cases, up to 25,000 copies of the original spread the Solidarity message to even the most remote corners of the country. Similar networks in and out of the country produced and distributed videocassettes, although on a smaller scale.

Solidarity also operated its own clandestine radio and television transmitters, which served both as a source of unofficial information and a symbolic thumbing of the nose at authorities. The system allowed Solidarity to maintain a fast and reliable national communication network even when the regular telecommunication and mail system was suspended in a futile effort to break up the network. The *New York Times*'s Michael Kaufman once was taken to a Warsaw suburban apartment and told to expect a surprise. A few minutes after the regular TV evening news began, the words "Solidarity lives" appeared briefly over the news

---

[8] Michael T. Kaufman, *Mad Dreams, Saving Graces* (New York: Random House, 1989), p. 87.
[9] Stefan Bratkowski, "Poland, Solidarity, and the Press: the Difficulties of Returning from the Moon," Annual Harold W. Anderson Lecture, sponsored by the Center for Strategic and International Studies and the World Press Freedom Committee, December 6, 1989.
[10] Leila R. Gray, *Polish Media in the Age of Solidarity,* paper presented to the Association for Education in Journalism and Mass Communication meeting in Minneapolis, MN, August, 1990.

announcer's head. Later "Listen to Radio Solidarity in half an hour" appeared, along with the frequency of the broadcast.

Kaufman's hosts told him that the clandestine transmitter had a range of perhaps a mile and could produce a ghost message visible to only a few thousand people. Although using the system to publicize radio frequencies was less risky than dropping leaflets, its real value was in challenging the authorities. "It's driving the police crazy," one of the perpetrators said. "They can't believe we can penetrate their television."[11]

THE TECHNOLOGY OF REVOLUTION

Whereas both previous communication revolutions were built on new technology—written language and modern printing—the third revolution is the product of a wide range of innovations that make communication faster, easier, cheaper, and harder to control. The tsar's secret police had to worry about underground printing presses and bundles of smuggled leaflets. Today's dictator must contend with home computers, fax machines, photocopiers, and, most dangerous of all, hand-held video cameras, whose pictures can end up being shown around the globe on CNN. The technology of the communication revolution at the end of the twentieth century is worth a closer look.

Short-Wave Radio and Audiocassettes

Short-wave radio is the oldest of the modern international electronic media and still one of the most important, though it is largely unknown to North Americans. Chapter 14 describes the medium in some detail; here we need only note that a short-wave radio signal quite literally can bounce off the ionosphere and be received around the world from the transmitter. Short-wave was used a little in World War I, helped keep European empires in touch after the war, and came into its own in World War II. The British Broadcasting Corporation (BBC)—and later the Voice of America (VOA) from the United States—learned that broadcasts to occupied Europe had a large and loyal following, even though listening at times was punishable by death. The BBC especially developed a reputation for thoroughness and accuracy that defeated any propaganda value in programs controlled by the occupation forces of Germany and Japan.

After the war, the United States established short-wave services to the Soviet Union (Radio Liberty) and Central Europe (Radio Free Europe). Their mission was to be a watchdog-in-exile to countries whose domestic broadcasters were used to support their communist regimes. The BBC's External Services (now World Service) and VOA continued as well and were joined by other countries to fill the crowded frequencies assigned to short-wave with a cacophony of competing interpretations of world events and versions of truth. A good short-wave receiver is still relatively expensive but a good investment for the tourist or armchair

---

[11] Michael T. Kaufman, *Mad Dreams, Saving Graces* (New York: Random House, 1989), p. 85.

traveler who wants to see the world from different perspectives. In countries where governments still try to monopolize information, a short-wave radio is a must.

Radio Free Europe (RFE) and Radio Liberty (RL) were ostensibly financed by contributions from the U.S. public and operated independently of the U.S. government. However, during the uprising in 1956 in Hungary that was put down by an invasion of Soviet forces, resistance fighters claimed that the Hungarian service of RFE promised U.S. intervention. As a result, the U.S. government began exercising some oversight of RFE and RL broadcasts. A greater embarrassment came in 1971 with the disclosure that most of RFE and RL operating funds came, in fact, from the U.S. government and were channeled through the Central Intelligence Agency, not from public contributions. As a result, government funding was made overt and administered by a presidentially appointed Board of International Broadcasting.

Short-wave broadcasting—especially the services operated directly by governments—came to symbolize the propaganda aspect of the cold war. Ads soliciting contributions to RFE/RL reminded us that "the Iron Curtain isn't soundproof," and communist officials seemed to reinforce the point by complaining regularly about foreign broadcasters. They also tried to prevent the signals from reaching listeners by broadcasting interference on the same frequencies, spending several times as much money trying to jam as the broadcasters spent producing the signals. Jamming was never effective, and governments that required a monopoly on information as part of their media philosophy failed.

When the rhetoric of the cold war receded in the 1970s, a popular argument was that short-wave radio—certainly openly provocative services such as RFE and RL—belonged to an outmoded era of propaganda. One of the arguments of the New World Information Order debate was that uninvited foreign voices violated a nation's cultural and information sovereignty.

When the communist regimes in Europe collapsed, a lot of people were surprised to find out how popular short-wave radio had been and how important some of the new democratic leaders still considered it. Strong endorsements came from Lech Walesa and Czechoslovakia's first postcommunist president, Vaclav Havel, among others, along with pleas not to shut down Radio Free Europe, whose mission seemed to have ended with the collapse of the Iron Curtain. In the short-lived coup in the Soviet Union in 1991, President Gorbachev listened to the BBC, VOA, and RL on a system rigged by one of his aides who was imprisoned with him.

Globally, VOA and BBC operate in a class by themselves. Although most countries have some kind of international short-wave service, VOA and BBC have the transmitting power (from transmitters at home and around the world), the language services, and the broadcast hours to justify a claim to be a global service. In most but not all countries where statistics are available, BBC has an edge in audience and credibility.

In China, VOA became part of the popular revolution that preceded the attack in Tiananmen Square. Its correspondents became celebrities and were occasionally mobbed when reporting demonstrations. Television reporters are used to celebrity status, but radio reporters are usually anonymous. For VOA reporters, with semiofficial status as government employees, the situation was both exhilarating and disconcerting. VOA Chinese-language newscasts were frequently recorded on audiocassettes and rebroadcast through loudspeakers at rallies throughout China. The linking of short-wave and audiocassettes extended the influence of a relatively old medium.

The use of short-wave in China was extensive but not unprecedented. Earlier in the Soviet Union, "magnetizdat"—audiocassettes recorded from external short-wave or smuggled in from abroad—had begun to supplement the traditional written underground publications. Several of Solzhenitsyn's banned works were read over foreign short-wave and recorded by hundreds of listeners, copied, and passed along to others just as the traditional written *samizdat* had been.

Audiocassettes alone were credited with a significant role in the overthrow of the shah of Iran in 1979. For several years before the revolution, Ayatollah Ruhollah Khomeini, in exile in Paris, had rallied a small group of fellow Shiite Muslims with sermons of the sort that are common to the culture of Islam. Followers of Khomeini began recording them and smuggling copies into Iran where they were used to recruit and inspire a network of supporters that eventually overthrew the regime in power.

The shah's police knew of the audiocassette smuggling—and a smaller campaign using videocassettes—but were unable to stop it. Cassettes were small and easily routed through a complex network of international trade and travel that even the government's massive security apparatus could not monitor. Khomeini's triumphant return to Tehran aboard an Air France 747 was interpreted as evidence of the power of the new, compact, and easily hidden audiocassette.

Fax Machines and Electronic Bulletin Boards

The facsimile—or simply fax—machine came into common use in the 1980s. It is something like a photocopier, which is barely a decade older as a part of ordinary business offices, but transmits an electrical signal over ordinary telephone circuits to produce a copy of the original document across town, across the country, or on the other side of the world.

Faxes as a revolutionary medium of communication came into their own in China but also were used to undermine earlier regimes. When the head of Panama's armed forces (and later the country's president), General Manuel Noriega, shut down the country's independent papers in 1987, Panamanian journalists in exile established a news center in Washington, D.C., that relied extensively on the then-new fax technology. Stories from U.S. papers were translated and printed with Spanish headlines and the center's logo. Contributors in Europe and exiled journalists occasionally added material to what we would today call an early example of desktop publishing. The resulting "newspaper" was then faxed to about 20 machines in Panama, where collaborators would retransmit the papers to other machines and photocopy the material for local distribution as one-page fliers.

One Panamanian journalist in Miami recalled talking to a acquaintance in Panama at 10:00 A.M. and mentioning a *New York Times* story from that day's paper. "We've seen it already," the acquaintance said, adding that photocopies were being distributed throughout downtown Panama City. At one point, as many as 30,000 copies of fax/flier/newspapers were distributed each day.[12]

The fax system reached maturity of sorts during the protests before and after Tiananmen Square. Groups of the 40,000 Chinese students studying in the United States coalesced at several campuses to collect and exchange information. They also compiled lists of about 1,500 fax machine telephone numbers in China and began to produce news fliers, much like those the Panamanian journalists had used earlier. They then bombarded the known fax machines in China with their fliers, wire photos showing the protests, and other materials. Many incoming faxes presumably were confiscated and destroyed, but as in Panama, some—no one knows how many—got added to the mix of fliers, posters, and rumors that outflanked the government-controlled media.

The Chinese students also relied on computer network bulletin boards. These are public files accessible to personal computer users who use modems and ordinary telephone lines to connect their computers to other PCs anywhere in the world. Global networks are in common use in universities and part of the routine activity of most academic researchers. Chinese students scattered throughout North America and Europe used the networks both to exchange information among themselves and to pass information on to the limited number of academics in China who had access to the systems. As with the fax, the technique was informal: pack as much information as possible into the system with the hope that some of it would emerge at the other end and let the well-developed Chinese rumor society take care of final distribution.

Fax and computer networks were also used in the abortive Soviet coup of 1991. For three days, the coup leaders controlled the traditional mass media and silenced independent media, but as in Panama and China, they overlooked the new technologies using the telecommunication system. At one point, people with Boris Yeltsin who were barricaded in the headquarters of the government of the Russian republic sent his condemnation of the coup by fax to Washington, D.C., with a plea that it be forwarded to the Voice of America for broadcast back to the Soviet Union. The appeal worked. Within the Soviet Union, Interfax, an unofficial news agency based on facsimile distribution technology, and some opposition papers continued to operate, using the combination of fax machines and photocopiers to produce simple emergency editions of their publications. Word-of-mouth distribution carried the information to a large audience. A fax-based news distribution system modeled on the Russian Interfax debuted in Mozambique in 1993, demonstrating that modern communication technology represents a potential challenge in any part of the world.[13]

---

[12] Susan Benesch, "Getting the Fax into Panama," *Columbia Journalism Review,* January–February 1988, pp. 6–8.

[13] Bill Keller, "By Pluck and Fax, Tiny Free Press," *New York Times,* March 1, 1993, p. C6.

Several Soviet professors used computer networks to contact colleagues in the West. In a few cases, they pleaded for help; in most, they offered details of events that were eventually fed into the global news accounts of the coup.

In all three examples—and in other similar circumstances in the 1980s and 1990s—government officials (or would-be officials) seized the traditional media but overlooked new forms of communication. As a result, information monopoly was lost and, with it, possibly the crucial difference between victory and defeat. Was the failure ignorance, oversight, or technical incompetence?

Probably a little of all three. Panamanian and Chinese officials may not have understood the technology of fax machines and bulletin boards and certainly did not understand the power of these relatively unknown technologies to undermine an information monopoly. They and the Soviet conspirators may have been prepared to accept the international outcry that accompanies a coup or near-coup and to expel the Western reporters who send the words and pictures to the rest of the world. But they may well have underestimated the power of the point-to-point technologies to circumvent the domestic mass media monopoly they needed to support their actions.

The question of technical incompetence is difficult to assess. Because personal computers and fax machines operate on electrical power and use ordinary telephone circuits, it ought to be easy for governments or insurgents to interrupt them. When the Polish government declared an emergency in 1981 in the face of growing support for Solidarity, one of its first acts was to disconnect the country's entire telecommunication system. Although the country is much larger and the system more complex, the Soviet coup leaders probably could have done the same in 1991. Perhaps they and the Chinese authorities before them felt they needed to maintain domestic and international telephone links for their own purposes, or perhaps they did not know how to pull the plug on the nation's telecommunication system. When the histories of the revolutions of 1989–1991 are written, there are likely to be chapters on the new telecommunication media.

Television

Even though attention is now often focused on the new communication technologies, the relatively old medium of television is still a major player in revolutionary politics. It comes in two packages: the traditional over-the-air television service that is frequently the first objective when tanks attack the capital and the newer mixture of miniature camcorder and VCR that gives anyone the power to challenge an ''official'' version of reality.

Television is still the textbook for revolutionaries. Timothy Garton Ash, a British scholar who witnessed much of the collapse of communism in Central Europe in 1989, put it this way:

In Eastern Europe, one could actually see people learning revolution from television reports of their neighbors' experiments: This is what a huge spontaneous crowd looks like; when you get up on a balcony, you make a V-for-victory sign; and here is a Round Table. In the window of the striking students' building in Prague, they played an American videocassette of Tiananmen Square in Beijing. I gather (from television reports) that protesters in Azerbaijan say that the frontier dividing them from their brothers and sisters in Iran should be opened "like the Berlin Wall." Where did they see the opening of the Berlin Wall?[14]

Television instructs the new generation of revolutionaries, but it also becomes an instrument with which to challenge the old regime. A picture may not always be worth 1,000 words, but television pictures of events contradicting official media are always compelling. In Prague, Czechoslovakia, student groups were active for a year before the protests coalesced into a series of mass demonstrations in November 1989. Official coverage was hesitant. One day, the first edition of the official party newspaper, *Rude Pravo,* carried the headline about 200,000 demonstrating in Wenceslas Square; the second edition said 100,000. Protesters prepared posters of the two together to demonstrate the official medium's lack of credibility. Then television added to the confusion. Live coverage of one mass demonstration was interrupted and programming switched to light music. Then the program inexplicably switched back to the demonstration. This hesitancy may have been the first sign of the government's vulnerability. At the next day's demonstration, an even larger crowd chanted "Live transmission! Live transmission!" Within a few days, Czech broadcasting swung unabashedly in favor of the protests, and the communist regime's days were numbered.

Students also made videotapes of the demonstrations—along with other snippets of information such as an interview with Ivan Lendl, the émigré tennis star. The videotapes played over and over at the headquarters of Civic Forum, the umbrella opposition group that eventually brought down the government, and, with photocopied newssheets and posters, were distributed through the countryside. A party official, asked about the next day's demonstration, advised a foreign journalist to check Civic Forum's videotape.

The official media, wavering between support of the government version of events and open reporting, finally sided with the demonstrators. As Ash notes, the mass demonstrations and general strike in Czechoslovakia were effectively declared a success by the television reporting of them.

In Poland, too, a key point in negotiations between the Solidarity trade union and the communist government over free elections (which Solidarity won decisively) was control of television. According to a Solidarity leader, a party official said during the negotiations, "We'll give you the Zomo (riot police) before we give you the TV." "And he's quite right," the Solidarity man said. "I'd much rather have the TV."[15]

The collapse of the communist government in Romania was even more closely tied to television. A mass demonstration orchestrated by the Ceauçescu

---

[14] Timothy Garton Ash, "The Third Superpower," *World Press Review,* March 1990, p. 72. From the *Independent* (London).

[15] Timothy Garton Ash, *The Magic Lantern: The Revolution of '89 Witnessed in Warsaw, Budapest, Berlin, and Prague* (New York: Random House, 1990), p. 26.

regime spontaneously turned against him—while live television carried the unheard-of antiregime chants and his incredulous reaction. After the Ceauçescus fled the capital, the television broadcast facility became a center of conflict between the army, which protected the broadcasters, and Ceauçescu's personal security police. Several skirmishes and the establishment of the provisional government took place live before the nation. The *New York Times* described it like "watching live coverage of the storming of the Bastille or the Battle of Yorktown, interspersed with debates from the Constitutional Congress."[16]

Control of television may not be sufficient to topple a dictatorship but it often seems to be necessary. In each of the great revolutions of 1989, the outcome was uncertain until television fell to the insurgents. Then the weight of public opinion swung toward the revolutionaries.

MAIN POINTS

1. Each communication revolution has produced a political revolution, a radical change in the nature and control of power. Today's communication revolution—the effect of the convergence of satellites, computers, and digitized information—is also changing global power.

2. Global communication does not always prevent a regime from maintaining a monopoly of power but it destroys the regime's domestic and international legitimacy. A government monopoly on information—never possible in the past—is now even more precarious.

3. Modern communication technology aids insurgents to mobilize support, maintain contact, and challenge authority more efficiently and more effectively.

4. The revolutionary concept of the press was an important factor in the collapse of communism in the 1980s and in the discrediting of the authoritarian and development concepts.

FOR MORE INFORMATION

Information on mass media is included in several books about the revolutions of 1989 to 1991 that are cited in this chapter. Most of the books about the Soviet Union noted in Chapter 8 also consider the influence of mass media. New books on the revolutions in Eastern Europe and China appear regularly, and many discuss the role of mass media.

See also Lawrence C. Soley and John S. Nichols, *Clandestine Radio Broadcasting: A Study of Revolutionary and Counterrevolutionary Electronic Communication* (New

---

[16] John Kifner, "The Airwaves: Rumanian Revolt, Live and Uncensored," in Bernard Gwertzman and Michael T. Kaufman, eds., *The Collapse of Communism* (New York: Random House, 1990), p. 341.

York: Praeger, 1987), for information up to the mid-1980s. Studies of the early phases of *glasnost* and the role of mass media during the Gorbachev era are in Ellen Mickiewicz, *Split Signals: Television and Politics in the Soviet Union* (New York: Oxford University Press, 1988); and Brian McNair, *Glasnost, Perestroika and the Soviet Media* (London: Routledge, 1991).

The role of technology in current global politics is discussed in two books by Ithiel de Sola Pool: *Technologies of Freedom* (Cambridge, MA: Harvard University Press, 1983); and *Technologies without Boundaries: On Telecommunication in a Global Age* (Cambridge, MA: Harvard University Press, 1990); and in Leonard R. Sussman, *Power, the Press and the Technology of Freedom: The Coming Age of ISDN* (New York: Freedom House, 1989).

FOR DISCUSSION

1. Debate the following proposition: Without modern communication, the political revolutions of 1989 would have failed. If you prefer, argue the opposite: Modern communication was a spectator of the 1989 revolutions but not a participant.

2. Interview people who have lived in a totalitarian society, such as Chinese students or recent immigrants from Central and Eastern Europe, about their use of foreign or illegal domestic media. Were they able to keep up with events at home and abroad? If so, how?

3. Search a computerized data base of current news media for examples of revolutionary media. Use search terms such as FAX, BULLETIN BOARD, PHOTOCOPY, and COMPUTER with REVOLUTION. You may want to add geographic references such as CHINA, CENTRAL EUROPE, and AFRICA.

DATA BASE

I. Many unauthorized (and therefore illegal) publications appeared in China after the assault on Tiananmen Square.

Xin Xi ("Information") is a monthly 12-page digest published in Hong Kong since October 1990.

Democratic Discussion and *Iron Currents* focused on demands for reform of the communist system. Several students connected to them were arrested in 1990–1991 and sentenced to jail terms for "counterrevolutionary propaganda."

All of Us was founded by a study club with more than 200 members at the People's University in October 1990. The first two issues—each more than 50 typed pages—included essays on the compatibility of socialism and human rights, criticism of "ultra-left" cultural theory and practice, and a discussion of the role played by intellectuals in China.

Poetry publications include *Sichuan Modern Poems, Wild Grass, Herb of No Name,* and *Fracture.* Most of the authors and publishers were arrested.

Phenomenon on Earth (Wan(g)Xiang) emphasized plays on words, including the corrected title, which, uncorrected and with the crossed-out but visible "g" in the Roman transcription, means "daring, unrealistic ideas."

In June 1991, university students began wearing T-shirts with slogans such as "I'm terribly depressed," "Life is meaningless," "I fear not suffering, I fear not death, I fear not YOU either," and "Cleanse the world of all evil beasts." At the end of the month, the shirts were seized and banned.

SOURCE: Lau Kin Chi, *"Samizdat* and Designer T-shirts," *Index on Censorship,* September 1992, pp. 31–33.

II. The Soviet *samizdat* tradition continued after the revolution. Leading publications included *Glasnost,* published in Russia; *Russkaya Mysl'* (*La Pensee Russe*), published in Paris; and *Novoye Russkoye Slovo,* published in New York City. Typical examples:

Letter From a Sverdlovsk Prison, by Sergei Kuznetsov, who was arrested in 1988 and charged with resisting arrest. "Valera (last name not known), age 25, from Tavatui village, sat in Post 22, cell –13. He was put away while still very young, and hasn't been out since he was 14. Complaints regarding the sentence were declined, and the result was the same in the Supreme Court. He has been denied newspapers, radio, parcels and visits with relatives. He protested by opening up his veins three different times and without being given any medical help—indeed it led to nothing—he was tossed into the cooler for doing so. On death row (it turns out there are such places)—cells Nos. 28 and 29—all the walls are splashed with blood and covered with writing. The graffiti is life-affirming: 'Long live the 71st Anniversary of Soviet Power! Hurrah!' They could be shot any day. . . .

Homeless Mother Is Deprived of Her Children. On April 18 [1989], Moscow's Red Guard Court gave a May Day present to Ludmila Bykonia: it deprived her of maternal rights and took away her children. She has four children; the oldest is nine, and the youngest girl is still a baby.

The grounds, as always, were very convincing. A Frenchman sired one of the children, which meant that the mother must be a prostitute. During a search, the police found an empty bottle, which means that the mother 'uses alcoholic beverages.' The mother believes in God, which means that she must be ruining her children.

Such false grounds were adduced to hide the real reason for the reprisal: the Bykonia family had no home. They were wandering the streets, and their plight had become a scandal for the authorities. . . .

The Baltic Path; 1939–August 23–1989. Tallinn, August 22. The mood in the city and in the republic on the eve of the 50th anniversary of the signing of the Molotov-Ribbentrop pact is calm. The political strikes of the "Intermovement" and the United Council of Labor Collectives have been suspended.

On City Hall Square the collecting of signatures for the call to a referendum for the sovereignty of Estonia continues. The signatures are being collected by the Estonian Democratic Movement (EDM-88). The only question which is being proposed to bring out in the referendum: Will Estonia remain in the USSR? As of August 23, around 30,000 signatures have been collected. . . .

On Work Conditions; To the International Labor Organization. I have appealed to Soviet law enforcement branches and to the Office of the Public Prosecutor, and I got the typical threat—that they'll put me in a psychiatric hospital. Therefore I am compelled to appeal to your organization, not seeking help, since I understand how things are, but I want to testify on the basis of my own story (and there are thousands and thousands of others like mine) to the absurd, unprotected position of the worker in the USSR. . . .

An Open Letter to Mikhail Gorbachev from Andrei Sakharov. Most Esteemed Mikhail Sergeyevich: I have decided to appeal to you regarding our two most acute nationality problems at the present time: the return of the Crimean Tatars to the Crimea and the reunification of Nagorno-Karabakh with Armenia. In both cases, the question is one of rectifying injustices committed against two of the peoples of our country.

SOURCE: *The Samizdat Bulletin,* issues of 1989 and 1990, published in San Mateo, CA. The *Bulletin* ceased publication in winter, 1990.

III. The following are clandestine radio stations that were on the air from 1981 to 1985. The ideology and source location are indicated in parentheses.

Voice of Oman (PFLOAG, from South Yemen)

Voice of the Free Sons of South Yemen (Islamic, anti-Marxist)

Voice of Iranian Kurdistan (Iranian Kurdish Democratic party)

National Voice of Iran/Radio Iran Toilers (Tudeh party)

Free Voice of Iran (Oveissi/CIA)

Radio Iran/Radio Vatan (Bakhtiar's National Resistance Movement)

Voice of the Iranian Communist Party (antifundamentalist, Maoist)

Radio Salvation Iran (Neqab, constitutional monarchist)

Radio Free Iran/Voice of Iran (monarchist)

Voice of the Mujahedin (Mujahedin e-Khalq)

Voice of the Fedayin (Fedayin e-Khalq)

Ahvaz Voice of Al-Qadisiyah, Iran (Arab Front of Ahvaz, from Iraq)

Voice of the Iraqi Islamic Revolution (Islamic fundamentalist, from Iran)

Voice of the Iraqi People (Iraqi Communist party)

Voice of Iraqi Kurdistan (Kurdish Democratic party of Iraq)

Voice of the Iraqi Revolution (Patriotic Union of Kurdistan)

Voice of Palestine/Voice of the Palestine Revolution (PLO factions)

Voice of the Revolutionary Movement for the Liberation of Tuknisia/Gafsa Radio (from Libya)

Voice of Arab Syria (from Iraq)

Voice of Egypt of Arabism (from Iraq, rejectionist)

Voice of the Egyptian People (from Libya, rejectionist)

Voice of the Libyan People (from Egypt)

Voice of Free Sahara/Radio of the Saharan Democratic Arab Republic (POLISARIO)

Radio Bardai (FROLINAT, Libyan-backed)

Voice of the Sudanese People's Liberation Army (Garant's forces, from Ethiopia and Libya until 1985)

Voice of Eritrea/Voice of the Eritrean Revolution (Eritrean Liberation Front)

Voice of the Broad Masses of Eritrea (Eritrean People's Liberation Front)

Voice of the Tigre Revolution (Tigrean People's Liberation Front)

Radio Kulmis/Radio Halgan (Ethiopian-supported, to Somalia)

Voice of the Western Somalia and Abo Liberation Front (Somalian-supported, to Ethiopia)

Voice of Namibia (Southwest African Peoples Organization)

Radio Freedom (South Africa) (African National Congress)

Voice of Resistance of the Black Cockerel/Voice of Truth (Angola) (UNITA/South Africa)

Voice of Free Africa (Mozambique) (National Resistance Movement/South Africa)

Radio Truth (Zimbabwe) (from South Africa)

Our Radio/Voice of the Turkish Communist Party (Turkish Communist party)

Radio Solidarity (Poland) (Solidarity Trade Union)

Radio Free Suriname (Liberation Council of Suriname)

Radio Macondo (Colombian M-19 Organization)

Radio Maquisaria (Colombia) (Fuerzas Armadas Revolucionarias)

Voice of Chilean Resistance (Allendist, via Radio Algiers)

Radio Magallanes (to Chile) (Allendist, via Moscow)

La Voz de Cuba Independienta y Democratica (anti-Castro/CID)

Radio Libertad Cubana (Commander David, from United States)

Radio Cuba Libre (Democratic Christian Movement of Cuba)

La Juventud Progresista Cubana (anti-Castro, from United States)

Radio Antorcha Martiana (Cuba) (Marti Insurrectional Movement)

Radio Mambi (Cuban Patriotic Junta, from United States)

La Voz de Alpha 66 (anti-Castro, from United States)

Radio Abdala/Radio Trinchera/Cuba al Dia/Radio Caiman/La Voz de la Esperanza/Radio Giron

Radio Quince de Septiembre (Nicaraguan Democratic Forces, from Honduras)

Radio Miskut (anti-Sandinista/Miskito, from Honduras)

La Voz de Libertad (anti-Sandinista)

La Voz de las Fuerzas Especiales de la Guerrilla Anticommunista (anti-Sandinista, Cuban exile)

Radio Monimbo (anti-Sandinista)

La Voz de Sandino (Sandino Revolutionary Front)

La Voz de Nicaragua Libre (Nicaraguan Democratic Movement)

Radio Revolucionaria del Pueblo (El Salvador) (People's Revolutionary Army)

Radio Veneceremos (El Salvador) (People's Revolutionary Army–FMLN)

Radio Liberacion (El Salvador) (antigovernment, FMLN from Nicaragua)

Radio Farabundo Marti (Popular Liberation Forces–FMLN)

Radio Guazapa (Armed Forces of National Resistance–FMLN)

Radio Unidad (Revolutionary party of Central American Workers–FMLN)

Radio Soberania Nacional/Radio Venceremos (black) (anti-FMLN)

Voice of Tamil Eelam (Sri Lanka) (Tamil Separatist)

Voice of the Islamic Revolution in Afghanistan (Islamic fundamentalist, from Iran)

"Free Konar" Radio (anti-Soviet, to Afghanistan)

Radio Free Kabul/Voice of the Afghan Mujahedin/Voice of the United Muslim Fighters of Afghanistan (antigovernment/anti-Soviet, Afghan resistance)

Radio Kawthulay (Burma) (Karen)

Patriotic Youth Front Radio/National United Liberation Front Radio/Patriotic Voice Radio (anti–Ne Win/Burmese United Front)

Voice of the People of Burma (Burma Communist party)

Voice of the People of Thailand (Communist party of Thailand)

Vietnam Resistance Radio (anticommunist/National United Front)

Voice of Democratic Kampuchea/Voice of the National Army of Democratic Kampuchea (anti–Heng Samrin/Khmer Rouge)

Voice of Khmer/Voice of the Joint Resistance/Voice of the People of Cambodia (exiled coalition government, noncommunist factions)

Central People's Broadcasting Station (black) (Black Versions of Beijing Government Domestic Services)

Voice of the PLA/Radio Spark/Radio October Storm/Contingent of Proletarian Fighters (Taiwan/CIA, to China)

First August Radio (to China) (black, USSR-sponsored)

Voice of Hope (from South Korea to North Korea)

Voice of the Revolutionary Party for Reunification/Voice of National Salvation (from North Korea to South Korea)

Voice of the Malayan Revolution/Voice of Malayan Democracy (Malayan Communist party)

Voice of the People of Malaya/Voice of the People of Malaysia (Malayan Communist party)

SOURCE: Lawrence C. Soley and John S. Nichols, *Clandestine Radio Broadcasting: A Study of Revolutionary and Counterrevolutionary Electronic Communication* (New York: Praeger, 1987), Appendix B. "Black" means stations disguised as broadcasts from another source. "Clandestine" means the stations are not registered with the ITU or publicly licensed by any government.

CHAPTER 12

Global News Flow

ABOUT THIS CHAPTER

Depending on your age, some or all of these events are etched permanently in your memory: the assassination of President John F. Kennedy in 1963, the first manned flight to the moon in 1969, the opening of the Berlin Wall in 1989, the air attack on Baghdad in 1991. In all cases, what we knew about these events— our vicarious participation in them—came from the mass media. Usually it was television that took us there first and most dramatically.

In this chapter, we look at the global news system and how it operates. We also take a quick snapshot of how the world looks from different perspectives and consider the assertions that the system is controlled by Anglo-America. Western, and especially Anglo-American, dominance of global news is at least as controversial as its dominance of popular culture. This dominance fostered the global debate over a New World Information Order that led, in part, to the withdrawal of the United States and Britain from the United Nations Educational, Scientific and Cultural Organization (UNESCO) in the 1980s.

INTRODUCTION

In the age of instant global communication, it sometimes seems that events do not take place unless the media are there to record them. The famine in Africa in the 1980s captured the world's attention only when pictures brought it to our living rooms. The Khmer Rouge genocide in Cambodia in the 1970s passed largely unnoticed, at least in part because there were so few words and pictures of the horror. As we saw in Chapter 11, dictators still try to isolate themselves from the global media, usually with only limited temporary success.

The television pictures from around the world are the most dramatic evidence of the third communication revolution. The revolution touches everyone. It is still possible to find parts of the world where modern media do not intrude routinely, but in the media-rich West we are so surrounded with news that we take it for granted. We expect the cameras to be there—live and in color—and we assume that the morning paper will have the details and probably full-color maps and graphics as well. The problem is to avoid drowning in a flood of information coursing through a global system that reaches from St. Petersburg, Russia, to St. Petersburg, Florida. Despite virtually constant contact with the global news system, most of us know little about it.

THE GLOBAL NEWS SYSTEM

The Big Four, Plus or Minus One

The handful of global agencies that supply most of the news for the world are relatively unknown. They are also, by the standards of multinational trade, surprisingly small and increasingly adjuncts to larger enterprises linked to information societies. They are also almost entirely Western and mostly Anglo-American.

Most studies focus on the "big four" news agencies because they all operate globally and supply about half of the international news that shows up in most newspapers. Even for broadcasters, the four—the Associated Press (AP), United Press International (UPI), Reuters, and Agence France Presse (AFP)—are essential sources. For all news operations, they are the war horses, the services that provide, day after day, the summaries of routine government activities, the stock market reports, and sports scores. When coups and earthquakes briefly bring some hidden part of the world into the global spotlight, it is usually the big four that report first. Here are thumbnail sketches of them and one other service that is sometimes included in the group of global elites. Recent statistics are in the Data Base of Chapter 1. Remember that statistics vary because the agencies' operations change rapidly, and studies often measure different aspects of complex operations.

The Associated Press.   AP is possibly the largest news organization in the world. It is a nonprofit cooperative owned by newspapers and broadcasters in the United States and Canada. Virtually every media outlet in these countries uses its services. The huge domestic base gives the agency most of its revenues and its claim of being first among the giants. As of about 1990, the AP served 15,500 subscribers in 112 countries. It maintained 617 full-time foreign correspondents in 67 countries outside of the United States and transmitted news in five languages.[1]

United Press International.   Unlike the AP, UPI is a private, profit-making corporation. Like the AP, it relies on North American customers to maintain a global operation. It is the basis for the "minus one" in the above subheading

---

[1] These figures, circa 1990, are from Mark D. Alleyne and Janet Wagner, "Stability and Change at the 'Big Five' News Agencies," *Journalism Quarterly,* vol. 70, no. 1, Spring 1993, pp. 40–50.

because its future is uncertain. For decades, UPI was profit making only in theory. It finally filed for bankruptcy in 1991 while maintaining more or less normal operations and hopes of resuscitation in an increasingly competitive business. Its sale in 1992 to an organization that produces TV programs for the Middle East raised eyebrows and questions of editorial independence, but its short-term future was assured.

Despite its financial difficulties and status as the second U.S. news agency, UPI issued 14 million words a day to 6,000 customers in 100 countries. It maintained 105 correspondents in 81 countries outside the United States.

Reuters. A British organization, Reuters operated strictly as an international news agency until 1984. It was owned by a handful of London newspaper proprietors and the British domestic Press Association. Then it became a public corporation whose shares you can buy on the NASDAQ exchange and expanded rapidly into the growing field of financial information. Most of its revenues now come from that part of the operation, especially Reuters Monitor, a service that provides instant information on currency prices worldwide. The information is fed to more than 170,000 computer terminals in 120 countries where the minute-by-minute fluctuations of the dollar, mark, and yen mean lots of dollars, marks, and yen for the savvy dealer. Since 1981, the Reuters Dealing service allows buyers and sellers around the world to complete their deals directly.

Reuters is the largest supplier of financial information around the world but maintains a large news operation as well. Unlike the other global giants, Reuters is strictly an international news agency. It covers Britain as it does any other country. The serious London papers have their own foreign correspondents and also buy directly from Reuters and the domestic Press Association, which also supplies the regional papers. At the start of the decade, Reuters maintained 968 correspondents in 74 countries and sold news to 29,310 subscribers in 131 countries. It produced 1.5 million words a day.

Agence France Presse. AFP is the only non-Anglo-American member of the exclusive club of global news services (except for TASS, the question-mark "plus one" agency). Like the AP and UPI, AFP operates a large domestic service that provides a market for its international operations. AFP receives a large part of its revenues from the French government through the sales of its news services to French embassies and subsidized sales to third-world media. The financial dependence of any news medium on its government typically makes Western journalists nervous, but AFP maintains an international reputation for independence and professionalism. By some criteria—such as number of countries in which bureaus are maintained and news is sold—AFP is larger than either the AP or Reuters. The agency maintained 550 full-time correspondents in 150 countries and served 12,500 subscribers in 144 countries. It produced three million words a day.

TASS, the Telegraph Agency of the Soviet Union. TASS is the "plus one" agency. Until the collapse of communism, it operated like other Soviet media as an arm of party and state. It can be considered one of the major global agencies on the basis of number of countries in which correspondents are stationed, number of languages in which news is distributed, and number of words disseminated. However, on the basis of influence and even use by news media, TASS was never competitive. Except in the old Soviet Union itself and a handful of Soviet client states, it was invisible as a source of news. After the failed coup of 1991, TASS announced that it would be reorganized as an independent, Western-style agency. Then in early 1992, it changed its name to Information Telegraph Agency of Russia and announced that its dispatches would be tagged ITAR-TASS. The "TASS" part seemed likely to be short-lived. ITAR-TASS's future was also dependent on the world's ability to support five competing global agencies offering essentially the same product.

Prerevolution statistics showed it maintaining 150 foreign correspondents in 127 countries and serving 5,100 subscribers in 93 countries. It produced 4 million words a day. Postrevolution statistics are a mixture of guesses and hopes.

Global Dominance

The big four, plus or minus one, all have the size and influence that puts them in a class by themselves. With UPI lagging behind, all maintain bureaus or correspondents in 100-plus countries, all distribute news in a half dozen or more languages, all process several million words a day, and all maintain the global communication networks that can flash bulletins around the world in seconds. For the blockbuster events that dominate the news every day in every country, the global agencies have the human and technical resources to get to the story when and where it happens and then to get it out to newspapers and broadcast outlets around the world while it is still news.

Reasons for the dominance of the big four are the subject of debate and are discussed later in this chapter. Implications of this dominance are also controversial. One common third-world complaint, however, is not supported by an examination of the global news system. It is the contention that the big four monopolize news flow, that they constitute a "de facto hegemony and a will to dominate," as one important critic put it.[2] Although it is true that the big Western agencies are uniquely influential in global news flow, other players are also important.

THE REST OF THE ELEPHANT

The story of the three blind men describing different parts of an elephant has parallels in any examination of the world news system. From one perspective, you see only the global giants that have the resources to dominate global news flow. If you look more closely, however, you will see other parts of the system that make issues of Western dominance more complex than Masmoudi suggests.

---

[2] Mustapha Masmoudi, "The New World Information Order," *Journal of Communication,* vol. 29, no. 2, Spring 1979, pp. 172–185.

In the West, smaller services and specialized and alternative agencies provide news with a different perspective for the small audience with the determination and resources to seek them out.

In the third world, the flood of information is less overwhelming, but even the poorest newspaper or broadcast station (or national news agency that supplies it) in the developing world receives many times more information from a variety of sources than it can ever use in its publication or newscast. Driving the global news system, of course, as we have just noted, are the big four that supply news of daily events that make up the core of every medium's news diet. But they are not the only players.

Second-Tier Western Agencies

Operating in the shadow of the big four are about a half dozen Western agencies that operate much like their giant competitors but on a smaller scale. They include dpa (Germany), ANSA (Italy), efe (Spain), Kyoto (Japan), and a few that technically are not Western, such as Tanjug (former Yugoslavia) and MENA (Egypt). They put out news in almost as many languages, operate actively in perhaps 50 countries (instead of 100), and transmit daily files numbering tens or hundreds of thousands of words (instead of millions). Usually they put out a general bulletin—perhaps a little heavy on news from the home country—and several regionally oriented services. The larger ones offer economic or feature services, and several have services tailored to specific geographic regions, just like the big four. In some areas of the world—particularly Latin America and Asia—these services contribute significantly to the information mix.

Specialized and Supplementary Agencies

New and different news sources proliferated in the 1970s and 1980s, a product of both technological innovation and complaints of big-four dominance. The specialized sources include agencies such as Inter Press Service (IPS), Depthnews, Gemini, and South-North News, all of which are oriented toward third-world and development issues; Women's News Service; and the nearly invisible Non-Aligned News Agencies pool (NANA), which transmits material supplied by agencies of members of the Non-Aligned Movement. The supplementary agencies are mostly produced by Anglo-American newspapers: the *New York Times* news service, *Washington Post–Los Angeles Times* service, *Guardian* news service, and so on. Their emphasis is on feature and background material, but a few—particularly the *New York Times* service—compete with the traditional news agencies.

Use of material from these sources varies. Most media still rely on the major news agencies for the bulk of their international information, but stories from the specialized sources do show up in feature pages and occasionally are incorporated into news agency copy. Specialized publications, of course, are a major outlet for their material. In the third world, where criticism of the Western giants was the strongest, the alternative services have had little impact. The modest amount of international news appearing in most third-world media still comes from the big four, usually via national agencies.

National Agencies

A focus of media development efforts during the NWIO debates was establishing national news agencies for the handful of countries that lacked them and strengthening those already in operation. By the 1990s, virtually every country in the world had its own national agency. They range from MENA and Tanjug that operate globally and offer modest competition, to the big four, to impoverished government-run offices that crank out a mimeographed daily bulletin. In between are about 150 national agencies that operate under all of the five media concepts we have examined and with financial and technical resources that range from lavish to pathetic. Most fall on the modest end of the scale, combining small amounts of international news gleaned from the global agencies and regional exchanges with domestic stories they produce themselves. Frequently they are the only source of news for the country's feeble newspapers, broadcasters, and government agencies.

The national agencies, particularly in third-world countries, serve several functions. Most concentrate on reporting and disseminating news within the country. The larger ones have a correspondent or two in a neighboring country or regional center but rely on the big four or supplementary or specialized services for information about the rest of the world. The daily product is something like a regional or state service of the Associated Press that small U.S. media receive. It is a mixture of a few international stories, perhaps a feature or two, and a lot of local news. In many developing countries, the national agency has a monopoly on all incoming information and can select from a dozen or more services. It probably receives 10, 20, even 100 words from outside for every word that gets into the domestic file.

The agency also represents an important link between the country and the rest of the world. The daily domestic file is usually exchanged with neighboring national agencies and is often transmitted to a major agency in a "my-news-for-yours" exchange agreement. In many places, journalists working for the national agency are also part-time stringers for the global agencies.

Regional Exchanges

When journalists and politicians looked critically at the global news system in the 1970s, the most conspicuously weak link was regional exchange. Why, many third-world leaders asked, do we have to depend on global agencies with headquarters in New York City, London, and Paris, to find out what our neighbors are doing? At the time, several regional exchanges were operating with various degrees of success. Now even more are in business, flying a wide range of political/media banners.

In the 1990s, all parts of the world have at least one regional exchange, and most have several. The Caribbean News Agency (CANA) and Pacnews in the South Pacific islands operate largely independent of governments and enjoy modest success filling in gaps in coverage supplied by the global agencies. Others, particularly the Pan-African News Agency (PANA) and the global Non-Aligned News Agencies pool (NANA) operate on the NWIO principle that every nation should speak for itself (or remain silent if it chooses) and carry only material supplied by member national agencies. As we have seen in previous chapters, news in communist, authoritarian, and development media systems often lacks credibility and audience appeal. Development and protocol news—a mainstay of these systems—is rarely exportable. PANA, NANA, and others patterned after them carry on but contribute very little to the tide of information that swirls through the global news system. Though often run by people of good intention and technical skill, they stand as living examples of the difficulties of competing with the dominant Western services and the global appeal of the Western concept of news.

BROADCAST NEWS

Even though we seldom see them in action or know how they operate, the names of the major Western news agencies are fairly well known. The reporter from Reuters or the AP shows up often enough in old movies that the public has some sense of how the system operates. Not so with broadcast news. Except for Cable News Network (CNN), which is a highly visible newcomer to the world stage, the very small number of TV news agencies operate anonymously as wholesalers to broadcast news operations around the world. Note again the Anglo-American dominance.

International Agencies

Two global organizations are the film equivalent of the Western big four. The larger was Visnews, headquartered in London, which was established by Reuters and the BBC with links to other Anglo public service broadcasters, NHK in Japan, and the U.S. commercial network NBC. At the end of 1992, Reuters bought the outstanding stock of Visnews and renamed it Reuters TV. As we will see, two U.S. networks' international news operations are closely linked to Reuters TV and its competitor, Worldwide Television News (WTN). Reuters TV claims a daily global audience of 1.5 billion viewers. The figure is hard to prove or disprove, but the organization clearly is the largest and most influential of the small group of global TV news services.

Somewhat smaller in volume, bureaus, and so on is WTN, also located in London. Until the mid-1980s, WTN was known as UPITN. The letters represented its original organizers, UPI and ITN (for Independent Television News, the news unit of Britain's commercial TV service). In the late 1980s, controlling interest in WTN was bought by ABC News, inspiring rumors that the ABC's news operations and WTN might be merged. They weren't, but WTN and ABC cooperate in international coverage, usually with CNN as a partner.[3]

Both Reuters TV and WTN operate much like the print services, supplying what is essentially wholesale material to a wide range of "retailers." In most cases, these "retailers" are national or local broadcasters, although they also work with regional exchanges, such as Eurovision. The footage usually emphasizes actuality coverage of events with natural sound and enough background information so the end user can write a script. Sometimes, of course, local broadcasters will show identical film with dramatically different explanations of what's going on. One country's freedom fighters are another country's terrorists, and domestic television, even more than newspapers, usually reflects the prevailing national worldview.

Global wholesalers of information—both print and film—have to supply a product that is maximally adaptable to different uses and interpretations. This is why Reuters TV and WTN emphasize the pictures and the sounds, not political interpretations that are better left to retail end users, and it is why politically prepackaged services are generally unsalable.

Global television news is a creature of the global telecommunication network, which was born in the 1960s but grew to maturity in the 1980s. Many people cite the Vietnam War as the watershed in global news coverage, but they often forget that the first "living-room war" was not covered live. The technical system at the time lacked the capacity for live global transmission, so film and videotape were flown to Hawaii or Los Angeles and edited for broadcast there. Live coverage is a decade newer, and the live extended coverage of unfolding events we associate with the Gulf War and Soviet coup date back only to the 1980s. That kind of coverage is still the specialty of CNN, not Reuters and WTN, which are the pack mules routinely supplying the raw material for the regularly scheduled evening news.

The Networks

Like the Hollywood studios, the commercial U.S. networks evolved as domestic institutions with little interest in marketing their products overseas. When the networks had what seemed to be unlimited budgets and a monopoly on the ratings, the newsrooms at ABC, CBS, and NBC saw the rest of the world as something to be reported to U.S. viewers. Budget cuts and shrinking audiences changed that operating principle significantly, first, by forcing the networks to curtail their news operations both at home and abroad and, second, by forcing them to think of global markets and partnerships.

NBC's international activities were closely tied to Visnews, but ABC and CBS sold news to a variety of international customers. These included weekly videocassettes of packaged highlights of daily newscasts that were sold to U.S. embassies and occasionally shown at libraries and cultural centers. News specials and

---

[3] Jeremy Tunstall, "Europe as World News Leader," *Journal of Communication,* Summer 1992, pp. 84–99.

magazine-format public affairs programs, too, are marketable overseas. Packaged correspondent reports, mixing actuality and "sound bites" from several sources, graphics, and the familiar reporter's sign-off, are less attractive to international customers than the raw footage of Reuters TV and WTN for both linguistic and sometimes political reasons. Most services now carry their logo at the bottom of the screen. Even in countries where you don't understand the language, you can carry out your own analysis of TV news flow by keeping track of logos and other telltale signs of origin.

The tough 1980s sent the networks in search of international partners as a solution to budget squeezes.[4] NBC acquired 38 percent of Visnews (Reuters maintained 51 percent), and Visnews began to report international events Western style. Meanwhile, ABC stopped syndicating its services while increasing its ownership of WTN to 80 percent. In both cases, the global services began to operate more like U.S. networks, and the networks increased their reliance on their international partner for material shown on their domestic network news programs.

CBS—the old Tiffany Network—announced an agreement in 1990 to merge its field coverage with Tokyo Broadcast Service (TBS), one of the Japanese commercial networks. At first the binational activity was limited to behind-the-camera activities, but at some point, Japanese correspondents—probably doing their reports in English—could be expected to show up on the *CBS Evening News.* CBS correspondents probably would cause less of a stir in Japan, where foreign news programs are shown routinely and where even the domestic network news programs are broadcast with an English soundtrack in one stereo channel. For the Japanese, partnership with U.S. broadcast journalism on a global basis seemed to be more practical than direct competition, which was also considered.

Both the BBC and ITN are also major international suppliers of broadcast news. In 1991, the BBC began a global TV service that mixed hourly newscasts with entertainment programming. The newscast also appeared on an English-language cable service distributed on the Continent. Initially, the BBC service was fed into a few cable systems and to scattered customers with their own satellite dishes. Later it was transmitted via an Asian satellite that give it a theoretical potential audience of more than a billion viewers. The working assumption—and hope—was that people in former British colonies would find the BBC style and accent more familiar and appealing than CNN. BBC World Service Television started slowly—and only after the British government refused to fund it as an extension of the short-wave radio World Service—but could develop into the world's first full-service global network.

Global networks, however, are not likely to replace traditional domestic services. Most people want to watch the world news at a regular time in their own language in a familiar setting. The exception is the unfolding of a few blockbuster events that are the specialty of the upstart service that modestly calls itself "the world's most important network."

---

[4] Adam Clayton Powell III, "The Global TV News Hour," *Gannett Center Journal,* vol. 4, no. 4, Fall 1990, pp. 119–127.

Cable News Network

When Ted Turner, the Atlanta entrepreneur and one-time defender of the America's Cup whom *Time* magazine called "the prince of the global village," announced the founding of a 24-hour-a-day cable news channel, there must have been snickering in the newsrooms of the big three commercial networks. Turner should have been taken more seriously, however. He had invented the "superstation" by using a satellite to distribute the signal of his weak, independent station in Atlanta to a national cable audience (and largely creating the current U.S. cable system in the process). And he was both rich and unimpressed by convention and tradition. In fact, he seemed to thrive on being described as an upstart, brash challenger to conventional and traditional broadcasters.

It took most of the 1980s for Cable News Network (CNN) to achieve acceptance as a legitimate network. By the end of the decade, however, CNN, with two domestic round-the-clock services in the United States, a global service pieced together from the two plus some additional material and a part-time Spanish-language service for Latin America and the North American Spanish-language market, had grown in scope and influence enough to justify its own promotional slogan. The network staffed more overseas bureaus than any of the U.S. commercial networks, signed agreements with more than 100 broadcasters around the world for use of CNN material and earned a reputation for importance without precedent in the history of global communication. Everybody who was anybody watched CNN: George Bush, Margaret Thatcher, King Hussein of Jordan, King Fahd of Saudi Arabia, Mikhail Gorbachev, Saddam Hussein, Fidel Castro of Cuba, and most of the rest of us as well.

Besides broadcasting to an audience of world leaders and several million ordinary viewers outside of the United States, the latter mostly in hotel rooms and scattered cable systems, CNN was a fixture in newsrooms and government offices around the world. Nobody could match it for extended live coverage of the dramatic events that seemed to draw the world together in dread, hope, and amazement. World leaders, knowing that counterparts were also watching, used it to send messages to one another. It also became a showcase for U.S.-style journalism, an important contributor to what was called, in Chapter 1, the triumph of independent journalism.

The genius of CNN was that it combined the drama of unfolding world events with a unique ability to cover them with the hardware of the global telecommunication system and unlimited air time. When something big happens anywhere in the world, most of us expect to find live coverage, running hour after hour if necessary, as near as our TV. With 19 overseas bureaus and working relationships with virtually every broadcaster in the world, CNN turned the promise of real-time global communication into something close to Marshall McLuhan's famous "global village."

CNN World Report

The network also contributed modestly to a broadening of the narrow U.S. perspective on the world. Early on, Turner forbade the use of the word *foreign* on the air. Events could be international, but in the global village CNN created, nothing was foreign. And for the first time in history, a national news center was created outside of New York City and Washington, D.C.

Turner also responded to complaints of U.S. dominance in global information flow by inviting every broadcaster in the world to send in a weekly three-minute report on any topic of its choosing. He promised to run them without change and in the process to challenge the Anglo-American standards of global TV journalism.

The result was *CNN World Report,* more than five hours a week of material submitted by 100 broadcast organizations, some professional and critical, some amateurish puffery. CNN sent tapes of the entire production to organizations that could not watch it live, creating the world's largest school of broadcast journalism. Contributors were encouraged to circumvent the Anglo-American dominance of global news by using material from the program for their own broadcasts, but almost no one did. Advantages accruing to CNN included occasional breaking stories that could be added to its regular programming and news production teams around the world that could be called on as needed in places where the competition had no resources.

The real suppliers of international news are often difficult to identify. Some media, as a matter of principle, remove any reference to the original source. Others edit each incoming dispatch a bit and credit it to themselves. As a result, you may not be able to tell whether a story in the Lagos, Fiji, Pakistan, or Tico *Times* came originally from Reuters, PANA, or the paper's own correspondent. TV news has the same problem, but the handful of major suppliers now usually run the network logo in the corner. That way, if some other broadcaster, with or without permission, uses the material, the original source is at least identified.

Tracking the flow of information through the global news network is detective work. Some media make it easy by identifying their sources, but others don't. If you find yourself in a hotel room in another country—especially one where the language is not one you understand—buy a couple of newspapers and turn on the TV set. See how much you can learn about that country's window on the world from the cues you can interpret. Even without knowing the language, you can probably sense the Anglo-American dominance, and you may even understand a little of why news practices you take for granted have stirred such anger abroad.

NEWS FLOW

In his witty and insightful book on the global news system, *Coups and Earthquakes,*[5] Mort Rosenblum describes how a correspondent covers his first foreign assignment—the rebellion in West Malaria. Rodney Permapress encounters many of the problems experienced two generations earlier by William Boot, the hero of Evelyn Waugh's hilarious novel, *Scoop.* They include bad communications, deceitful government officials, unreasonable editors back home, and locals willing to do and say anything if the price is right. Despite obstacles that would challenge the faith of a saint, Rodney and his zoo of colleagues get the story and get it out into

---

[5] Mort Rosenblum, *Coups and Earthquakes: Reporting the World for America* (New York: Harper & Row, 1979).

While covering Pope John Paul II's visit to Angola, AP Rome Bureau Chief Dennis Redmont stays connected to the global communication system with laptop computer, telephone, and the Pope's "white line," his ever-present portable satellite link to the Vatican that was made available to reporters.

SOURCE: Associated Press.

the global news system. We wake up to the details of the rebellion from the reassuring voice of a TV breakfast-news anchor.

Mort Rosenblum is no Rodney Permapress. A long career with the Associated Press has taken him to wars, rebellions, and triumphs of democracy all over the world and given him unique insight into global news flow. He knows where the critics of Western dominance are right and where they are wrong. His solution for what ails the current global news system is not to replace it—as some advocates of the New World Information Order argued—but to make it work better.[6] Doing that requires an understanding of how news of the West Malaria rebellion now gets into your local newspaper and on your radio station.

The System

The global news system is both surprisingly large and surprisingly small. It is large because it covers—or so it seems—the entire planet. There are very few countries, very few rebellions that are permanently outside the scrutiny of the system. Of

---

[6] Mort Rosenblum, "Special Correspondent Quixote," *Gannett Center Journal,* vol. 3, no. 4, Fall 1989, pp. 1–15.

course, reporting resources are unevenly distributed. Most agencies are in the industrialized North and democratic West and put their resources where their revenues and customers are. Even in the remnants of the communist sphere and in the third world, reporters gravitate toward the more liveable spots, cities with good telecommunication and air travel links, and countries with strong links to their home country.

The system is surprisingly small because no news agency operates in every country of the world and none operates primarily as a collector and disseminator of international news. The AP and UPI rely on their huge domestic base, AFP relies on its home market and government subsidy, and Reuters is dependent on its technical, financial, and economic services. Even the biggest agencies count overseas reporters in the dozens or low hundreds (not thousands) and budgets in a few million dollars (not tens of billions). On a scale defined by Sony, Exxon, and Phillips, the news agencies are small business.

At the Malaria Arms hotel, reporters from the big four dominated the group of 61 Western reporters who had flown in to cover the rebellion in West Malaria. Most of the world would learn about it from them. Most of us learn about global events from the same sources, which do supply about half of the foreign news in most newspapers around the world. Broadcasters, too, rely heavily on the news agencies for day-to-day coverage of the world.

The input end of the global system, however, is more complex than the West Malaria rebellion suggested. In addition to the full-time correspondents stationed abroad (or parachuted in from regional bureaus), the larger news agencies rely on part-time "stringers," who are usually local journalists, Western freelance writers working for several media simultaneously, or the local media themselves. Even a "bureau" may be one correspondent, working out of his or her apartment. The daily routine includes reading the local papers, making a few follow-up phone calls, then filing the main stories into a computer data base that is edited at a regional center such as Paris or Bangkok or Mexico City.

A particular story may end up in a regional service sent back to the national news agencies and some media in the region. Remember that all operate regional services abroad and that most of the information they generate stays in the region, just as most of the stories an agency produces at home stay in the local network. On the other hand, the story may bounce around the world several times and end up in newspapers and newscasts around the world, including your local paper. The same system, operating pretty much the same way, can get a story from your hometown to readers in Lagos, Lisbon, or Lima.

Covering the World

Foreign correspondents rarely cover their beats to the same depth that reporters do at home. They can't. There aren't enough of them, and their areas of responsibility can include several hundred million people in a dozen countries. The brace of correspondents that descended on West Malaria is characteristic of the handful of blockbuster events that briefly bring one part of the world into the media spotlight but not typical of the daily routine of international reporting. Around the world—as in Washington, D.C., London, and Paris—most "bureaus" consist of one or two people and most "reporting" consists of rewriting the local media.

Nevertheless, the global news system produces a staggering amount of information. The total amount available to the newspaper or broadcast station in just about any part of the world is 10, 20, or 100 times the amount that gets into the paper or on the air. And it comes from a variety of sources. Most third-world media (or national news agencies, which are often monopolies supplying all of the domestic media's news) get a regional service of the big four, one or more second-tier and specialized services, and probably exchanges from neighboring national agencies. Their services are exchanged or monitored by the larger players, especially in countries where the global agencies do not maintain their own correspondents. Even in the mid-1970s, the Ghana News Agency, one of the most impoverished in a media-poor continent, had access to 12 separate news agency files: 5 Western, 5 socialist, and 2 North African. In 1982, the News Agency of Nigeria received copy from AFP, TASS, dpa, OPECNA (OPEC News Agency), IPS, Reuters, UPI Economic Service, and, occasionally, Tanjug and the NANA pool.[7] In both cases, a flood of information washed up against the national news agency gatekeeper, which passed only a trickle to domestic media.

In the United States, few small and medium-size papers take more than the AP plus one or two supplementary services. Even from these, however, they get thousands of words—probably tens of thousands—of international news. The Western agencies fill computerized data banks that are constantly updated and rewritten for different customers. A small radio station in the mountains of North Carolina can subscribe to the AP hourly broadcast service edited in Raleigh that combines state and national news with a handful of headline briefs from the rest of the world. A major paper in Raleigh or Charlotte can aim its rooftop receiving dish to the AP satellite and plug into the full data bank, including probably the Spanish-language services that go to Latin America. If not enough news is still a problem in some parts of the third world, the problem in the West is too much— so much flowing into newsrooms, so much flowing into our homes and lives, that the temptation is to turn our back on all of it. Citizens of the global culture need to resist that temptation.

It is difficult to measure the total volume of news flow because some stories circulate through the system several times, whereas others never get out of a small regional wire that serves one state or region. A large part of the material in the international region stays only in that part of the system. At various points, key editors determine whether each story will passed to higher or lower parts of the system. Summaries of major stories are transmitted regularly to help editors plan upcoming editions or newscasts. These gatekeepers have as much influence on what finally ends up in your local paper as Rodney Permapress, who sets the process into motion.

A recent study estimates that the big four together produce about 33 million words a day, figures that vary somewhat from those cited in Chapter 1 and in

---

[7] Robert L. Stevenson, *Communication, Development, and the Third World: The Global Politics of Information* (New York: Longman, 1988), pp. 136–137.

this chapter.[8] This breaks down to 17 million for the AP, 11 million for UPI, 3.4 million for AFP, and 1.5 million for Reuters. In contrast, some of the leading second-tier and special agencies measure their output in thousands of words, not millions: dpa (Germany, 115,000), ANSA (Italy, 300,000), efe (Spain, 500,000), Tanjug (Yugoslavia, 75,000), and IPS (development-oriented Inter Press Service, 100,000). Of course, no single AP customer receives 17 million words, a figure that includes the same story rewritten many times for various services and languages. Even dpa's "mere" 115,000 words represent 10 to 100 times the amount of coverage most of its customers can or choose to carry. The total of *original* material is considerably less than these figures suggest. The total volume processed and distributed around the world is greater.

NEWS VALUES

Every issue of a newspaper and every newscast represent a snapshot of the world on one day. Editors do not worry about having enough news to fill the space or time available for the planet's daily photo. Their problem is always deciding what must be left out, never what should be included. News is not a random sample of all the people and events in the world. Some people, some events, and some parts of the world are more likely to get through the complex global news system than others.

All sorts of people make decisions that influence the focus and texture of the picture that appears in your local media. At the beginning point, Rodney Permapress (or his boss) has to decide to cover the West Malaria rebellion rather than the opening of a new hospital in a neighboring country. A series of editors— especially if Rodney is working for a news agency—decides whether his story is more "newsworthy" than other stories from other reporters. If all of the gate-keepers make the right decision, the story will end up in your local paper or newscast, and you will know—briefly—something about West Malaria. Then probably the rebellion will be won or lost (or the government will expel the Western reporters), and Rodney will move on to the next trouble spot. West Malaria will disappear from sight and mind.

From our discussion of different media theories, we can reasonably expect to find a lack of agreement on what kinds of people, places, and events ought to be singled out as newsworthy. The communist journalist sees news as the unfolding of history as Marx predicted and would dismiss the rebellion as a mere event, unless it was a war of liberation against Western imperialism, which would be newsworthy. The development journalist would say the opening of the hospital was news but the rebellion was not. The Western journalist, of course, would turn the two around. Because of the unique influence of Western media around the world, it is usually the Rodney Permapress version that gets into print and on the air around the world, not just in your all-American hometown.

---

[8] Hamid Mowlana, *Global Information and World Communication* (New York: Longman, 1986), p. 28.

Structural Factors

People who study the global news system often distinguish among factors that influence who and what get reported and how. One set of factors focuses on characteristics of the news system itself and the political-economic environment in which it operates. These include the following:

1. Distribution of news-gathering resources. Reporters report from where they are assigned, and they are assigned to specific locations on several criteria: big countries where lots is happening, countries with good air service and telecommunication, often countries that are pleasant to live in. Most correspondents and resources are in the North, few in the South. The skewed distribution of sources reflects income and customers, of course, but occasionally the phenomenon that one can cover a country or region better from outside.

2. Importance to the host country. News tends to flow to and from neighboring countries, among countries with extensive trade and cultural links, and between countries that threaten each other. This accounts for the relatively generous coverage of Britain, Japan, and the former Soviet Union in the U.S. media and, depending on the moment, coverage of Vietnam, Central America, and the Persian Gulf countries. Nothing explains the lack of visibility of Canada and Mexico.

3. Ease of reporting. We get news from places where news is easy to get. Some of the factors in #1 apply here, too, but add a tolerant government and reliable media, common language, and efficient infrastructure. An old joke was that news agency coverage of Latin America pretty much followed the route map of Braniff airlines. Braniff is history, but the complaint continues—with some justification.

Gatekeeper Values

We can also look at the content of the news itself to consider why one event ends up on front pages around the world while others remain in darkness. This is often called the gatekeeper approach, a reference to the people throughout the global news system who open or close the gate as each story passes through. The small selection of international stories that end up in a paper or on a newscasts— out of the hundreds that are reported daily—reflect the gatekeepers' cumulative assessment of what is "newsworthy" and what is not. Some criteria are:

1. Violence and disruption. Although the news generally contains less disruption than critics contend, the unusual event is more newsworthy than the usual one. The old cliché is that it's news when a man bites a dog but not when a dog bites a man. The same applies internationally. Coups and earthquakes are news, but the routine lives of ordinary people are not. You don't expect to pick up a newspaper in the morning with a story that starts, "500 planes landed at the airport yesterday, almost all of them safely." At the international level,

the headline is not "Most Governments Were Not Overthrown," "Country X Did Not Invade Country Y," "Life Was Normal Throughout Region Z."

2. Magnitude. A large event, involving many people, in a large country is more likely to get past the gatekeepers than a small one, involving a few people, in a small country. Journalists sometimes engage in ghoulish discussions of how many people have to be killed in country X to be newsworthy in country Y. This is an extension of the principle that all news is local. One person killed in a highway accident is big news in a small-town newspaper, but it takes several deaths to make the news in the next state and even more when those deaths occur in a different country.

3. Personal and human interest. Events that touch some emotion in audiences are usually newsworthy, often way out of proportion to their real importance. Stories of whales trapped in the ice or children trapped in wells seem to make front pages regardless of any realistic assessment of their newsworthiness. Dramatic symbols of major events such as the eyewitness to Iraqi atrocities in Kuwait who turned out to be an official's daughter and real or alleged mistresses of public officials are always good for headlines and air time.

4. Prominence. Celebrities, according to Daniel Boorstin, are people who are well known for being well known.[9] For reasons that defy common sense, celebrities are newsworthy around the globe. And for reasons that are perfectly logical, prominent people in prominent nations are also newsworthy, more newsworthy than leaders of less prominent nations. The British royal family and Hollywood royalty are media stars throughout the world. On the global popularity scale, the Beatles probably were—as they themselves claimed—more popular than Jesus Christ.

These factors account for some of the reasons why the world we see through the media is not a cross-section of the real world. And although the Western news agencies supply much of the raw materials that end up forming the media world in most countries, gatekeepers outside the dominant Western nations have the power to form the raw material into a picture of the world that matches their sense of newsworthiness, their media philosophy, their political-cultural-economic environment. The Data Base in this chapter provides a snapshot of that effort.

THE WORLD OF THE NEWS

Some news values seem to be universal and can be found in the media of almost every country. But others are unique, and the snapshots of the day assembled by different national media can be very different. On the whole, the news system

---

[9] Daniel J. Boorstin, *The Image: A Guide to Pseudo-Events in America* (New York: Atheneum, 1971).

itself and the gatekeepers who operate it produce a daily picture of the world that reflects some common sense of what is important. Although it is misleading to suggest that the *New York Times* and the old-fashioned *Pravda* had much in common, at one level their pictures of the world were similar.

1. Politics and economics. The largest comparative study of international news, completed in the late 1970s, found that politics and economics dominated international news around the world, not "coups and earthquakes," the shorthand phrase for disruptive or violent events.[10] News makers tend to be the presidents and prime ministers, and news is what they say and do.

2. Proximity or regionalism. If you draw a map of the world in which each country or region is represented in size in proportion to the amount of attention it receives in the media, a curious phenomenon emerges. In virtually every country, the immediate region emerges as the center of the world. In Latin American media, Latin America is a giant; in African media, news from and about Africa dominates; and so on. Considerably less dominant but still prominent are usually the United States and Western Europe. Least visible are countries and regions with few economic, political, or cultural ties to the immediate region: Latin America in African media and vice versa, for example. Also invisible in most regions until recently were the Soviet Union and Eastern Europe.

3. National involvement. Not surprisingly, interest in other parts of the world increases when we have some personal or national linkage. At the personal level, knowing someone from a different country, living there, or even visiting usually sparks an interest in international news. A national involvement can be political, economic, military, geographic, or cultural. Check your local paper for headlines of the sort: "Local Man Safe in Earthquake Abroad" or "Local Company Signs Contract for Foreign Sale." Local reporters and editors, on rare trips abroad, often complain of having to cover great events from the perspective of Milwaukee or Memphis. However, the Society of Professional Journalists argues that it is good journalism to show how world events affect Greenville, Mississippi, Richmond, Virginia, and La Crosse, Wisconsin—and vice versa. It sponsored a program to improve international coverage by stressing local links to the world.[11]

4. Elites. Let's face it: Some people are more newsworthy than others. The news focuses on politicians, business movers and shakers, celebrities, and criminals. The rest of us are lucky—or unlucky—to

---

[10] Annabelle Sreberny-Mohammadi et al., *Foreign News in the Media: International Reporting in 29 Countries,* UNESCO Reports and Papers on Mass Communication No. 93 (Paris: UNESCO, 1985).

[11] John M. Hamilton, *Main Street America and the Third World* (Cabin John, MD: Seven Locks Press, 1986).

make even the local news a few times in our lives. Big and powerful nations also make the global news more than small and weak ones. The presidents of the United States and Russia are more newsworthy than the prime minister of Denmark, and the flow of news from Moscow and Washington, D.C., to Copenhagen is inevitably greater than the reverse. The prime minister of Tuvalu (look it up!) is unlikely to make the news of any country outside of the immediate region and probably rarely even there.

5. Disruption. As we remember it, news seems to be an endless litany of crime, violence, and disasters. In fact, politics and economics account for a much greater part of the news hole than coups and earthquakes, but the latter tend to make a greater impact. Except for the discredited communist and development press concepts, exceptional events—coups, earthquakes, accidents, disasters, scandals—are universally newsworthy. And, if readership surveys and ratings are to be believed, of interest to readers and viewers as well. While we can decry the excesses of the worst tabloids and sleazy television, it's good to keep in mind Senator Daniel Moynihan's observation that where the papers are full of good news, the jails are full of good men.

6. Skill in using media. Although not a news value in the usual sense, the ability of some people, groups, and nations to use the global news system to their advantage is reflected in the world picture that emerges from it. Some things are obvious: a shared language or political culture, good telecommunications, openness, and access to officials. Others, however, reflect a sensitivity to news values and the way the system operates.

As noted in Chapter 11, modern revolutionaries learned quickly how to stage media events—even to signs in English—for the benefit of the world press. It takes more than fluency in English, clever sound bites, and good visuals to rise above the flood of words and pictures that flow through the global news system, but they help.

CONTROVERSIES

Kent Cooper, executive manager of the Associated Press, wrote a book in 1942 that described global news flow in an earlier age when the big three of the time—British Reuters, French Havas, and German Wolff agencies—divided the world and operated it as a cartel. Reuters was responsible for covering the United States:

So Reuters decided what news was to be sent from America. It told the world about Indians on the war path in the West, lynchings in the South and bizarre crimes in the North. The charge for decades was that nothing creditable to America ever was sent. American businessmen criticized The Associated Press for permitting Reuters to belittle America abroad.[12]

A generation later, very similar complaints were made about the global news system and the way it covered the emerging third world. Now, of course, the AP was on the other side, an object of criticism in a global debate that few North Americans ever heard of and few Western journalists understood.

Third-World Complaints

In one sense, third-world complaints reflected a shift to a global information economy in which traditional wealth and political power diminished as sources of international influence while information—language, pop culture and, of course, news—increased. The result was a world still dominated by the developed nations of the North and one increasingly at variance with traditional cultures in the developing world.

One of the most influential bills of indictments against the Western news media was prepared by Mustapha Masmoudi, a Tunisian who served as ambassador to UNESCO. His long statement was presented to the MacBride Commission, a special committee appointed by the director general of UNESCO in 1976 to consider the "totality of the problems of communication in modern society." This extensive quote captures both the substance and the strong emotion of third-world complaints:

A flagrant quantitative imbalance between North and South . . . created by the disparity between the volume of news and information emanating from the developed world and intended for the developing countries and the volume of flow in the opposite direction . . . [resulting in] a veritable *de facto* monopoly on the part of the developed countries.

A de facto hegemony and a will to dominate . . . evident in the marked indifference of the media in the developed countries, particularly in the West, to the problems, concerns and aspirations of the developing countries. . . . They are exercised above all through the control of the information flow, wrested and wielded by the transnational agencies operating without let or hindrance in most developing countries and based in turn on the control of technology, illustrated by the communication systems satellites, which are wholly dominated by the major international consortia. . . . By transmitting to the developing countries only news processed by them, that is, news which they have filtered, cut, and distorted, the transnational media impose their own way of seeing the world upon the developing countries. . . . Moreover, [they often] present these communities—when indeed they show interest in them—in

---

[12] Kent Cooper, *Barriers Down* (New York: Farrar & Rinehart, 1942), p. 12.

the most unfavorable light, stressing crises, strikes, street demonstrations, putsches, etc., or even holding them up to ridicule. . . .

The present-day information system enshrines a form of political, economic, and cultural colonialism which is reflected in the often tendentious interpretation of news concerning the developing countries. This consists in highlighting events whose significance, in certain cases, is limited or even non-existent; in collecting isolated facts and presenting them as a "whole"; in setting out facts in such a way that the conclusion to be drawn from them is necessarily favorable to the interests of the transnational system and of the countries in which this system is established. . . . Even important news may be deliberately neglected by the major media in favor of other information of interest only to public opinion in the country to which the media in question belong. Such news is transmitted to the client countries and is indeed practically imposed on them, despite the fact that readers and listeners in these countries have no interest therein.[13]

Prelude to NWIO

This sweeping indictment of Western journalism captured both the substance and emotion of the debate over Western dominance of the global news system and the rejection (by some) of the whole Western concept of the press. Even from this excerpt, several of the key arguments of what became the New World Information Order debate are clear:

1. The global information system is a reincarnation of the old imperial economic/political system that kept smaller, weaker nations at the periphery, dependent on the powerful nations of the center.
2. Information is used by the nations of the North as an instrument of domination, a twentieth-century equivalent of the colonial armies that had conquered so much of the world in earlier centuries.
3. Cultural values inherent in Western news are inappropriate for the third world and dysfunctional to its development.
4. Authentic development is possible only when third-world nations disengage from the global information system and establish their own, based on their needs, their cultural values, and their traditions, not on a pale imitation of the West.
5. Postcolonial equity requires a massive transfer of resources from the rich nations to the poor nations as compensation for past exploitation.

---

[13] Mustapha Masmoudi, *The New World Information Order,* Document No. 31, submitted to the MacBride Commission (Paris: UNESCO, 1978). Extensive excerpts are printed in L. John Martin and Ray Eldon Hiebert, eds., *Current Issues in International Communication* (New York: Longman, 1990), pp. 311–320.

This is how to achieve a balanced flow of news and other types of information among all nations.

THE NEW WORLD INFORMATION ORDER

At its extreme, the NWIO debate was a rejection of the Western concept of mass media in favor of a mixture of the new development concept and elements of the communist and authoritarian concepts. However, behind some of the more strident rhetoric—Masmoudi's statement, for example—was a plea for help. Although dissatisfaction with Western media coverage was (and is) nearly universal, third-world journalists started to squirm when NWIO rhetoric got hot. The speakers were invariably government officials, and journalists everywhere like to operate independently as critics of government, not extensions of it. The power of Western journalists, especially with the memory of the Vietnam War and Watergate fresh in mind, was a strong card that the West finally played successfully.

From NWEO to NWIO

The New World Information Order debate itself was a product of a broader debate that took place primarily at UNESCO in the 1960s and 1970s. The debate focused on the large and growing gap between the rich industrialized democracies of the North and vast poor nations of the South. Why was one part of the world rich and the other poor? The socialist bloc that had dominated the older East-West struggle was a minor player in this debate. It provided rhetoric and a few case studies of alternative development—mainly Cuba, Tanzania, and China—but the debate on this question was between the North, rich in both traditional wealth and information, and the South, poor in both.

Much of the rhetoric for the NWEO/NWIO debate came from the global theory of dependency or the Spanish *dependencia,* which acknowledges its Latin American origins. According to *dependencia* theorists, the global economic system was set up by the colonial powers to their advantage. A symbolic example was the British colonial rule that required Indian cotton, to be shipped to British mills that turned it into finished products that were then sold back to the Indians. Domestic manufacture was prohibited. A symbol of Gandhi's fight for independence was a centuries-old hand spinning wheel that he used every day in defiance of British colonial rules. A modern variant was the reporting of world coffee prices in terms of how much the North American consumer would pay at the grocery store. That was fine—if parochial—for the North American paper, but in some places, coffee prices determined the nation's economic fortunes. The Northern housewife's cheaper cup of coffee was the Southern farmer's economic disaster.

Two concepts are important in the *dependencia* argument. One is the center or core versus the periphery. The handful of colonial powers constituted the center of the global system. They periodically fought each other but operated essentially as a global cartel, dividing the great land masses of Africa and Asia among them and keeping them at the periphery of the system. The Monroe

Doctrine, which declared Latin America off limits to European colonizers after independence from Spain and Portugal, was interpreted as the U.S. declaration of dominance over most of the Western Hemisphere.

Dependency Theory

The second concept is dependency itself. According to the theory, the system was designed to make the core nations powerful and rich while keeping the nations at the periphery poor, weak and dependent on the core for protection, investment and inspiration.

By the 1970s, when *dependencia* became popular with some of the UNESCO crowd, the dismantling of the old European empires was virtually complete. The first decade of independence had not brought wealth or stability, however, and the use of mass media as magic multipliers of development in the shadow of the West was under attack. The first need was a massive shift of economic resources from the North, which had become rich through the colonial system, to the South, whose poverty was a product of that system.

In 1975, UNESCO passed a resolution calling for a New World Economic Order (NWEO) based on the arguments of dependency theory. Like all such resolutions, it had no provision for enforcement, and the Western nations paid little attention. The United States was preoccupied with the aftermath of the Vietnam War and with Watergate. Dependency theory itself seemed obsolete because virtually all former colonies were independent, and the wealth and power of the West were showing signs of crumbling. The biggest transfer of wealth in history—exactly what the NWEO called for—was already taking place. Wealth was flowing not from North to South, of course, but from everywhere to the handful of nations that exported oil.

In an age that defined wealth more and more by information and the technology that controlled information and less and less by money, manufacturing, and raw materials, the leap from the NWEO to the NWIO was relatively easy and, to many at UNESCO, obvious. But in the end, the goals of the NWEO and NWIO were never realized, and even the rhetoric disappeared. In the 1990s, the New World Information Order is mostly an artifact of history, seldom invoked even by critics of Western dominance and submerged in the recent global triumph of Western journalism.

MAIN POINTS

1. Western agencies dominate global news flow. The big four—AP, UPI, Reuters, and AFP—provide about half of the international news in most countries. However, a wide range of supplementary, alternative, and national news agencies is available and has some influence on regional flow.

2. A similar group dominates TV news around the world. It includes Western agencies with close ties to the U.S. networks, CNN, and the BBC.

3. Although small by standards of international business, thin in most spots, and unevenly distributed, the global news network can bring information from any point on earth to any other almost instantly.

4. The picture of the world that emerges from global news flow is influenced by structural factors and decisions of numerous gatekeepers. Coverage emphasizes politics and economics, neighbors and national involvement, disruption, and prominent nations and people.

5. Even in the age of global communication dominated by the West, the picture of the world that emerges from media of various countries differs greatly according to media philosophy, resources, news values, and national interest.

FOR MORE INFORMATION

A major theorist of the center-periphery argument is Immanuel M. Wallerstein. See his *The Modern World System* (New York: Academic Press, 1974), and *Geopolitics and Geoculture: Essays on the Changing World System* (New York: Cambridge University Press, 1991). The cultural imperialism argument is advanced in a number of books by Herbert I. Schiller, ranging from *Mass Communication and American Empire,* 2nd ed. (Boulder, CO: Westview, 1992) to *Culture, Inc.: The Corporate Takeover of American Expression* (New York: Oxford University Press, 1989). Other theoretical interpretations include Mike Featherstone, ed., *Global Culture: Nationalism, Globalization and Modernity* (Newbury Park, CA: Sage, 1990); and Roland Robertson, *Globalization: Social Theory and Global Culture* (Newbury Park, CA: Sage, 1992).

The New World Information Order debate is described in Howard H. Frederick, *Global Communication and International Relations* (Belmont, CA: Wadsworth, 1993); Johan Galtung and Richard C. Vincent, *Global Glasnost: Toward a New World Information and Communication Order?* (Cresskill, NJ: Hampton, 1992); Thomas L. McPhail, *Electronic Colonialism: The Future of International Broadcasting and Communication,* 2nd ed. (Beverly Hills, CA: Sage, 1987); and Robert L. Stevenson, *Communication, Development, and the Third World: The Global Politics of Information* (New York: Longman, 1986). The UNESCO controversy is described in William Preston, Jr., et al., *Hope and Folly: The United States and UNESCO 1945–1985* (Minneapolis: University of Minnesota Press, 1989); and C. Anthony Giffard, *UNESCO and the Media* (New York: Longman, 1989).

For studies of the global news agencies, see Oliver Boyd-Barrett, *The International News Agencies* (Beverly Hills, CA: Sage, 1980); Jonathan Fenby, *The International News Services* (New York: Schocken, 1986); and Donald Read, *The Power of News: The History of Reuters* (Oxford: Oxford University Press, 1992). A listing of smaller agencies and their activities is in Oliver Boyd-Barrett and Daya Kishan Thussu, *Contra-Flow in Global News: International and Regional News Exchange Mechanisms* (London: John Libbey, 1992). Activities of the U.S. government promoting information policies after World War II are described in Margaret A. Blanchard, *Exporting the First Amendment: The Press-Government Crusade of 1945–1952* (New York: Longman, 1986).

Comparative studies of international news, in addition to the UNESCO monograph cited, include Peter Golding and Philip Elliott, *Making the News* (London: Longman, 1979); Roger Wallis and Stanley Baran, *The Known World of Broadcast News* (London: Routledge, 1990); and Robert L. Stevenson and Donald Lewis Shaw, eds., *Foreign News and the New*

World Information Order (Ames: Iowa State University Press, 1984). The International Institute of Communications study excerpted in the Data Base is unusually comprehensive.

FOR DISCUSSION

1. Examine newspapers from different parts of the world for sources of information. How much is supplied by the big four, how much by smaller, regional agencies, how much by the papers themselves? If you have access to SCOLA or other international satellite services, do a similar study of TV news.

2. Compare coverage of one day's news or a major world event in the media of as many countries as possible. Look for evidence that supports or refutes the generalizations about the nature of news in this chapter.

3. Interview a local newspaper, radio, or TV editor about sources of international news available to him or her, criteria for selection of material, and estimates of audience interest.

DATA BASE

I. Each year, *World Press Review* surveys leading journalists about the top ten stories of the previous year. Results are compared with similar surveys carried out by AP and UPI at home and by AP abroad.

Associated Press (domestic)
1. Bill Clinton elected U.S. president.
2. Riots in Los Angeles following acquittal of policemen in the Rodney King beating.
3. Hurricane Andrew hits Florida.
4. U.S. troops intervene in Somalia.
5. Civil war rages in Yugoslavia.
6. The lingering U.S. recession.
7. Former Soviet republics make transition to independence and ethnic violence and Russian President Boris Yeltsin's reforms.
8. Supreme Court abortion ruling limits states' control.
9. Lebanese kidnappers release last Western hostages.
10. Jeffrey Dahmer pleads guilty to 16 murders in Milwaukee.

AP International Poll
1. Yugoslavia.
2. U.S. elections.
3. Former Soviet republics' transition; ethnic violence and Yeltsin's reforms.
4. EC friction over unity.
5. Famine hits war-torn Somalia and other countries.
6. Germany plagued by neo-Nazi attacks on refugees.
7. Earth Summit focuses attention on environment.
8. South Africa's rocky road to ending apartheid.

9. Race riots hit L.A. and other cities in the U.S.
10. Mideast peace efforts.

Asiaweek, Hong Kong

1. "Ethnic cleansing" in Bosnia-Herzegovina.
2. The emergence of a strong market economy in China.
3. Election of Clinton.
4. Prodemocracy forces triumph in Thailand.
5. Europe's crises over currency union and growing racism.
6. International mission to Somalia.
7. Riots across South Asia after destruction of mosque in India.
8. In Cambodia, UN undertakes its toughest and biggest mission.
9. Britain and China clash over Hong Kong's future.
10. L.A. race riots.

La Nación, San José, Costa Rica

1. Xenophobia and racial violence in Europe.
2. The North American Free Trade Agreement.
3. Election of Bill Clinton.
4. International trade talks, disputes.
5. Breakup and violence in Yugoslavia.
6. Starvation in Somalia.
7. Russian turbulence.
8. Fall of Brazilian President Fernando Collor de Mello.
9. The new Roman Catholic catechism.
10. The "self-coup" in Peru and capture of Shining Path rebel leader Abimael Guzmán.

Newswatch, Lagos

1. Struggles for democracy in Africa.
2. Dismemberment of Yugoslavia.
3. Somalia.
4. Triumph of Clinton.
5. Religious riots in India.
6. Arab-Israeli talks.
7. Africa's economic crisis.
8. The Liberian war.
9. Europe's unification efforts.
10. Separation of Prince Charles and Princess Diana.

SOURCE: Barry Shelby, "The Top 10 News Stories of 1992," *World Press Review,* February 1993, pp. 8–9.

II. The International Institute of Communications in London captured news from 87 TV newscasts, global and regional news services, and 63 newspapers on November 19 and 20, 1991. Sample TV headlines follow, in the order they were presented.

Ethiopian TV, Addis Ababa: President Arap Moi's visit to Ethiopia; Talks between President Moi and President Zenawi; Three-day meeting on plant genetics - Africa Hall; Ali Mahdi tried to reverse the takeover of General Haideed; two heads of the government-controlled media dismissed by the new Zambian government; two hostages freed in Beirut; President Mitterand opens summit of Francophone countries in Paris.

NTA, Nigerian TV, Lagos: President Babangida in Madrid; Federal capital territory minister announces move to Abuja; census arrangements; Lagos judge agrees on hearing for gubernatorial aspirant; release of Terry Waite.

NHK, Tokyo: Stock market manipulation revealed; sumo news: Konishik on top; earthquake hits Tokyo; more than 1,000 killed in Timor after confrontation with Indonesian army; stock exchange broker manipulated prices; Japanese economists worry about trade imbalance.

Channel 9, Bangkok: Kenyan ambassador visits Princess Somdej Prathep; parliament and senate speaker join together; costs of chicken eggs at "big roundabout"; fire in Udon Thani; hostage release in Lebanon.

Channel 1, New Delhi: Congress increases tally in Lok Sabha by-elections; winter session in Parliament to begin tomorrow; nation celebrates 74th birth anniversary of Indira Gandhi; two new national commissions on women announced; Soviet women beat South Koreans in Indira Gandhi Memorial Gold Cup Hockey.

Channel 5, São Paulo: Killing of slum children in Rio; giant traffic jam in Rio; two youngsters paint graffiti in Corcovado, Rio; Brazil seeks buyer for Chernobyl meat; campaign for protection of street kids; violence against children in Brazil; Shevardnadze back to ministry.

TV Caracas [Venezuela]: serious student demonstrations in Caracas; President Perez announces constitutional reform while visiting Brazil; Shevardnadze new minister of foreign affairs; Bush says USA coming out of recession.

KTV, Kuwait: Sheikh Jaber the Emir orders national team of firefighters to have medical checks; arrival of the Emir in Italy; Emir meets Italian officials; Emir sends greetings to President of Austria; Soviet president affirms views on POWs; National Assembly meets today.

Channel 11, Kingston, Jamaica: stock market; PNP executive accuses JLP of mischief making; foreign exchange market criticized; union woes at Eastern Banajna Co.

XEW-TV, Mexico City: freight train ran off rails in Tehuacan City; world's summit in favor of infancy; process of government-clergy relationship; government's income law for next year; government companies for sale; Mexican Constitution reform; Diego Riviera sold for record sum in New York.

ABC, New York City: Sutherland and Waite released; armed resistance eliminated in Croatia; stock market going downhill; loan scams in Georgia Loan.

BBC 1, London: Terry Waite flies to Britain; survivors come out of cellars in Vukova; recession technically over.

TF 1, Paris: capitulation of Croatians; return of Shevardnadze to Gorbachev government; opening of conference of French-speaking communities; agricultural income falls; Interallie Prize to Sebastien Japrisot.

III. Geographic location and subject matter were calculated for each broadcast region. Coverage is shown in percentages of stories. (Stories can be counted in more than one region.)

	Southern Africa	Latin America	North America	Western Europe	Eastern Europe
Australia & New Zealand	0%	0%	0%	0%	0%
China	0	0	0	0	1
Western Europe	19	4	20	63	21
Eastern Europe	5	8	20	23	80
Japan	0	0	0	0	3
Latin America	0	92	7	1	1
Middle East	8	2	16	19	8
North Africa	5	0	7	1	1
North America	6	7	80	11	12
Other Asia	2	1	1	9	0
Polar	0	0	0	0	0
South Africa	80	0	9	3	0

	Japan	China	Middle East	Other Asia	Australia & New Zealand
Australia & New Zealand	4%	0%	0%	0%	56%
China	5	64	2	3	0
Western Europe	0	12	43	12	20
Eastern Europe	6	14	28	12	4
Japan	78	10	0	2	2
Latin America	0	7	0	2	0
Middle East	0	19	85	5	19
North Africa	0	6	17	0	0
North America	1	17	13	5	14
Other Asia	8	21	8	80	10
Polar	0	0	0	0	0
South Africa	0	7	1	1	0

	Southern Africa	Latin America	North America	Western Europe	Eastern Europe
Conflict	11%	5%	27%	42%	37%
Crime	6	17	3	7	3
Destruction	1	10	9	1	0
Economics	34	32	22	12	26
Environment	8	2	3	2	0
Health	9	17	25	4	3
Culture	0	3	4	5	7
Politics	34	38	49	33	38
Sport	8	9	0	4	10
Technical	1	1	8	2	1
Values	25	18	27	8	1

	Japan	China	Middle East	Other Asia	Australia & New Zealand
Conflict	5%	11%	31%	13%	29%
Crime	17	0	10	1	7
Destruction	9	0	4	1	0
Economics	34	36	17	27	14
Environment	10	7	0	7	3
Health	12	13	0	3	8
Culture	1	2	0	1	2
Politics	20	47	80	43	15
Sport	9	0	0	9	19
Technical	0	11	0	3	5
Values	7	17	3	11	15

SOURCE: "The Global News Agenda," *InterMedia,* January–February and March–April, 1992. A summary is in "Each Man an Island," *The Economist,* February 18, 1992, p. 94.

CHAPTER 13

Technology of Communication

ABOUT THIS CHAPTER

The communication revolution we encounter every day is based on three technical innovations of the late twentieth century. They are communication satellites, computers, and digitization. The first two are already vaguely familiar even to those of us who claim to be fully ignorant of modern technology. Most of us use digitized information every day even if we don't know it. For the moment, we can define digitization as the transformation of any text, sound, or pictures into a stream of ones and zeroes that can be transmitted from any point on earth to any other point via almost any medium. Its use in global communication is closely linked to both computers and satellites.

In this chapter, we look at the three innovations that will have an even greater impact on global communication on the twenty-first century than they already have had on the last years of the twentieth century.

INTRODUCTION

Technology is the mother of communication revolution. Each of the three revolutions to date—including the one we are now in the midst of—was the direct result of a technological innovation. We know nothing of the history of the first revolution—the development of printed language—and not very much of the history of the second—the development of printing with moveable type in Europe in the 1400s. However, we can surmise that the inventors-discoverers-revolutionaries in both cases worked without any conscious intention to disrupt the established order and certainly with no prescience of the forces they were setting loose. To the extent that we can draw inferences about events long ago from sketchy evidence, we can conclude that the two earlier revolutions involved one or two key innovations along with the insight to marry them to existing technology to produce powerful new applications.

Imagine any one of many simple cultures about 35,000 years ago. It could be in almost any part of the world but probably was in southern Europe, the eastern Mediterranean, or northern Africa. It had a spoken language of limited vocabulary and grammar but no written form. A member of the tribe needs to leave a message for another member. Perhaps there is danger ahead, or safety, or food. He draws a crude symbol of an animal or cave in the mud along a river bank or sketches it on a rock with the end of a stick from the fire. The symbol might have been a variation of a drawing the tribe already used to decorate its cave home.

A few tribal members coming along the trail understood the danger, safety, or opportunity ahead. The message was crude but effective. Over years, decades, or centuries, the list of symbols members of the tribe understood and used expanded and became more stylized. At some point, the nuances of grammar and vocabulary of the spoken language got adapted to written form, and the first communication revolution was complete. The preservation of the written language was assured when someone discovered permanent, portable media such as clay tablets and papyrus. That, too, may have been the accidental product of a message left in a drying mud puddle or the discovery that crushed reeds took the carbon from a burned stick easily and were portable as well.

Sumerian cuneiform and Egyptian hieroglyphic writing—largely pictographic—developed about 3000 B.C. The Phoenician syllabary, from which modern alphabets of Europe and the Middle East evolved, came along about 2,000 years later. Paper and the use of brush and ink date to a few centuries before the birth of Christ, although papyrus was known in Egypt around 3000 B.C.

By the time Johannes Gutenberg turned to printing in the Rhine city of Mainz in the 1400s, cultures were much more complex, thanks in large part to the long-term effect of written language. It allowed monasteries and noble houses to collect, preserve, and pass on the accumulated knowledge not only of Christian Europe but of other great civilizations as well. Alas, making a single copy of a single book could be the work of years. Of necessity, access was limited, but the long-term collective influence of the great libraries was to give birth to the Renaissance and to modern Western culture.

Even in the medieval era, knowledge—the record of cultural experience—was no longer limited to memorized sagas and songs passed from one generation to the next. It could expand indefinitely and cross barriers of time and space. People in one culture could vicariously share other cultures by studying their languages. Monks along the Rhine in Germany could immerse themselves in the civilizations of the ancient Greeks, contemporary Muslims, even the oldest cultures of the eastern Mediterranean. But, of course, access to this knowledge was limited because the manuscripts themselves were rare and precious, and the abbots, princes, and university rectors who owned them must have had some sense of their potential power. Truth was still very much imposed by authority. There is no evidence that Gutenberg himself was a troublemaker or chafed under the authoritarianism of medieval Germany. He was interested in solving a technical problem.

By the mid-1400s, printing was well established, but each page had to be carved in reverse from a single block of wood. Getting even a simple cartoon picture with a few words right was difficult enough. The work of days or weeks could be ruined when the cutting knife slipped or when too much pressure on the press split the finished page block.

Such an accident was said to be exactly what gave Gutenberg the idea of carving each letter separately, then binding them together to form full lines and whole pages. As a goldsmith, he was familiar with the technique of casting metal in molds and presumably came up with the idea of using a mold to cast unlimited supplies of identical letters. That was a major contribution to the second communication revolution. Several other adaptations of existing technology, such as using winemakers' presses and changing ink to adhere to metal type, resulted in a new technology that, with minor improvements, lasted until the middle of this century.

Within two decades, the new technology had spread throughout Europe with all of the political implications noted in Chapter 11—development of vernacular languages, challenges to the authority of the church and crown, the birth of modern democracy. Gutenberg lived long enough to see technology established across Europe but died before its impact on the political establishment became clear. Like many other innovators, he failed to make money from his invention and apparently died deeply in debt.

The third revolution—the establishment of a global communication system built on computers, satellites, and digitization of text, sound, and pictures—also followed from the confluence of technologies rather than the creation of a single revolutionary technology. No single individual is associated with this revolution. Arthur C. Clarke is credited with describing the geosynchronous orbit that makes communication satellites practical, but credit for the development of several generations of computers and satellites in the years between World War II and today belongs mostly to the anonymous workers at International Business Machines (IBM), AT&T, and numerous government agencies who pieced together the new technologies at what, in retrospect, was startling speed. To understand the current revolution, we need to know a little about the natural phenomena and technologies that made it possible.

COMMUNICATION SATELLITES

Modern science is based on figuring out natural laws of the universe. Some of them—a round earth orbiting the sun—now seem obvious. Others—such as the genetic code and the ultimate subatomic particle—are still puzzles to be unraveled by future generations of scientists. Global communication exploits both relatively old science and some of the latest discoveries.

Electromagnetic Spectrum

Electromagnetic radiation is produced when charged particles are accelerated. When fields of electromagnetic radiation reinforce each other, waves are produced. The electromagnetic spectrum is defined by the frequency with which the waves vibrate or pulse. The spectrum of radiated energy includes the household electricity that powers a TV (50–60 cycles per second) and visible light (10^{14}–10^{15} cycles per second). In between are the frequencies that carry radio and TV signals from transmitters through the air to receivers in your living room and the frequencies that carry your voice from the telephone in your living room to a satellite in space and back to a friend halfway around the world. Give a cheer for the electromagnetic spectrum! Without it, life—if it existed at all—would be drab.

Knowledge that the electromagnetic spectrum includes more than visible light goes back more than a century. Just about a century ago, Heinrich Hertz, a German scientist, proved the existence of the spectrum and demonstrated how you could transmit waves of electromagnetic energy. In his honor, we use the word *hertz,* usually with a prefix meaning *many,* to designate the specific frequency of each point along the spectrum. Household current is described as 50 or 60 hertz. Ordinary AM radio operates in the range of 600 to 1600 kilohertz (kHz, or thousand cycles per second). FM radio uses 88 to 108 megahertz frequencies (mHz, or millions of cycles per second) and is surrounded by frequencies allocated to TV sound and short wave radio. Satellites operate with frequencies of billions of cycles per second (gHz, or gigahertz). Beyond them, electromagnetic waves become infrared, visible, and ultraviolet light and then cosmic rays.

For practical as well as scientific reasons, someone has to decide how to use this unique global resource. You couldn't broadcast TV in the visible light spectrum, for example, or use the frequencies of household current for radio. Even among the possible frequency ranges, someone has to decide how to use a specific frequency and who is going to get access to it. Basic decisions are made by the International Telecommunications Union (ITU), an agency of the United Nations. Additional control is exercised by national governments, such as the U.S. Federal Communications Commission (FCC).

In most cases, the world's engineers and politicians can make reasonable decisions, but there are always controversies. Should certain frequencies be given to CB radio or commercial broadcasters? Who gets to use short-wave frequencies, which are used to broadcast from one country to another? Manufacturers need to know how to build equipment, and users—like broadcasters—need to agree on rules to avoid turning the spectrum into a new Tower of Babel.

Sometimes the various interests clash. A technical decision may not be politically palatable, and a political solution may make no sense economically. Issues of access to the spectrum and control of its future use are all part of global communication. Controversy also extends to a new resource, in use only three decades, that is part of the current global revolution in communication.

Geosynchronous Orbit

Imagine for a moment that you are the strongest person in the world, a real-life Superman. You throw a baseball so high and so far that when it comes back to earth, it misses the earth. What would happen to it?

Okay, you're not Superman. A more realistic experiment would be to put that baseball at the tip of a rocket. Then when the rocket reached some appropriate height and speed, you could fire the baseball off into space. The same question applies. What would happen to it?

The answer is, it depends. It depends on two forces that determine whether the ball will sail off into space, perhaps even escaping the solar system, or fall back to earth. Inertia—the force that keeps any moving object moving in the same direction—would push up and away from the earth. Gravity, however, would pull it back to earth. Without the super strength of Superman or a properly directed rocket, the force of gravity would win easily, and the ball would arch into the air and fall back to earth. Even a shot fired from a gun would follow the same trajectory.

But suppose you hired a clever engineer and built a rocket to release the ball at some point several hundred kilometers above the earth. At exactly the right distance above the earth and at exactly the right speed, the force pushing the ball away from the earth would match the force pulling it back to earth. At that point, the ball would enter an orbit around the earth and circle the planet forever—at least that's the theory. And the practical basis for the hundreds of satellites that now circle the earth.

If the orbit is exactly 35,800 kilometers away from the earth's surface and is directly over the equator and is spinning in the same direction as the earth, then something truly exciting happens. In this orbit, a satellite takes exactly 24 hours to complete one orbit of the earth. From the perspective of the earth, the satellite appears to stay in one spot. While it is really whirling around the planet at 11,000 kilometers per second, it appears to hang in the sky, never varying from its parking place over the equator. This is called the *geostationary* or *geosynchronous* orbit and is used by virtually all of the communication satellites in use today. Without it, you could not phone a friend on the other side of the world, and you could not watch the live TV pictures that are a routine part of the nightly news. The geosynchronous orbit is at the heart of the third communication revolution.

The unique importance of the geosynchronous orbit was first pointed out in the 1940s by Sir Arthur Clarke, the science fiction writer and futurologist who wrote the novel *2001: A Space Odyssey* and sequels. He noted that three communication satellites equally spaced around the geosynchronous orbit acting as relays for radio signals would produce a system capable of sending a message from any point on earth to any other. You could send the signal to one satellite, which could then bounce it to another, and then back to earth. Just bouncing it off a single satellite could get it back to any point in a "footprint" covering one-third of the earth.

Once you use the satellite as a relay, traditional barriers to broadcast and telecommunication development become irrelevant. Distance is the most important factor that becomes irrelevant but so do construction costs and time. Alaska and Florida can be linked by a single up-down circuit as easily as Miami and Miami Beach, and messages can move back and forth just as quickly. The traditional difficulties of building and maintaining terrestrial systems over rough real estate are eliminated.

It took just two decades to put Clarke's idea to the test. The first successful communication satellite was *Sputnik* ("Fellow Traveler") launched by the Soviet

Union in 1957. By 1990s standards it was a puny, low-flying ball that transmitted radio beeps back to earth but did nothing useful. However, it represented a technological and political triumph for the Soviet Union (and a big blow to U.S. self-confidence). The beep-beeps were heard around the world and set off a superpower competition in space that lasted, more or less, until the first American astronauts landed on the moon in 1969.

Since then, the number of communication satellites has grown with the same accelerating exponential growth we have seen in other aspects of global communication. By 1990, more than 3,300 had been launched.[1] Many were low-flying, special-purpose birds that did not need the unique stability of the geosynchronous orbit. However, Clarke's orbit was home to several hundred communication satellites, becoming—in Singleton's elegant phrase—a "gossamer string of pearls [encircling] the earth."[2] Jeweler of the celestial pearls is the International Telecommunications Satellite Organization (Intelsat).

Intelsat

Intelsat is a consortium of 120 nations of the world that was founded in 1964 at the initiative of President Kennedy. His goals were both to realize Clarke's vision of global communication and to make sure that the United States maintained leadership of the system. Its first satellite, Early Bird, operated from 1965 to 1969 over the Atlantic. It offered 240 voice/data circuits or a single TV channel. In contrast, the Intelsat system today includes 15 satellites (plus backups) over the Atlantic, Pacific, Indian oceans, covering the entire planet except the poles. The Intelsat VI generation of satellites, first launched in 1989, each carries 24,000 voice/data circuits (multiplied to 120,000 through engineering) and three TV circuits.

Throughout its short history, the capacity of the Intelsat system increased exponentially, while cost to national PTTs decreased at the same rate. This is why you can pick up a phone today and dial Hamburg or Hong Kong and easily as Hartford, Connecticut, at the cost of a short-distance domestic call a few years ago.

Intelsat is close to a global monopoly, but not quite. Intersputnik was created by the Soviet Union in 1968. It served a dozen Soviet allies but was a casualty of the collapse of communism. Inmarsat, founded in 1979, is similar to Intelsat but serves ships at sea. Most geographic regions have their own satellites and satellite organizations and so do a number of individual countries.

The string of pearls in geosynchronous orbit is actually a strange collection of robot-like machines, each hundreds of kilometers from its nearest neighbor. It includes satellites owned and operated by all the players of modern communication, the global and regional organizations, national satellite administrations, and—mostly in the United States—even satellites owned and operated by private

---

[1] Heather E. Hudson, *Communication Satellites: Their Development and Impact* (New York: Free Press, 1990), p. 7.

[2] Loy A. Singleton, *Global Impact: The New Telecommunication Technologies* (New York: Harper & Row, 1989), p. 33.

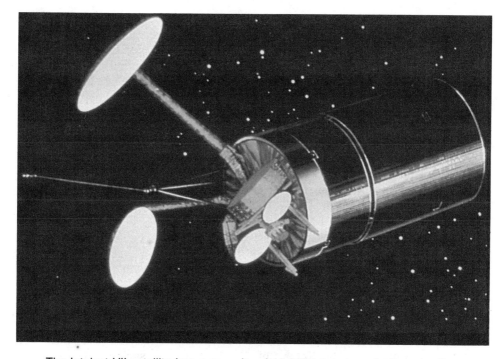

The Intelsat VII satellite has a capacity of 18,000 telecommunication circuits and three TV channels, which can be expanded to 90,000 circuits. The confluence of digitization, satellites, and computers has led to the third communication revolution, producing, among other effects, an exponential growth of global communication capacity.

SOURCE: Intelsat.

companies. Subject to minimal international and national oversight, orbital parking spaces are filled mostly on a basis of who gets there first. So far, there is room for all, but some developing countries want to claim orbital slots for their future use. It is one of several controversies involving the fast-growing global satellite system, to which we will return.

COMPUTERS

Satellites are useful to connect two telephones in different parts of the world, but the real value of the global communication system is linked to the explosive power of computers. More telecommunication circuits are now used by computers to exchange data than by people to exchange business tips or gossip. However, computers really show their muscle when they are used as traffic cops to keep the various satellite circuits pumping as much information through the system as possible.

As we will see shortly, when you call Hamburg or Madrid, you don't get exclusive use of an Intelsat satellite circuit. In most cases, your voice will be digitized and mixed with other conversations, text, and even pictures to form a stream of information that is sent pulsing through the global system. Your question about the weather over there can go through one route, while the answer comes back through through another. Big computers keep track of everything. Without them, the global communication system could not operate.

DIGITIZATION

Until recently, most U.S. schoolchildren learned a poem by Longfellow that included these lines:

> One if by land, and two if by sea;
> And I on the opposite shore will be,
> Ready to ride and spread the alarm
> Through every Middlesex village and farm.

The poem commemorates the famous midnight ride of the Boston silversmith and patriot Paul Revere who rode to warn the Minutemen militia waiting outside Boston that the British forces were landing. The signal was lanterns hung in the steeple of the Old North Church. When Revere saw the two lights, he set off to alert the local militia with the cry that has sounded through U.S. history for two centuries: "The British are coming! The British are coming!" You know the rest of the story.

What, you may well ask, does the midnight ride of Paul Revere in the eighteenth century have to do with global communication in the twenty-first century? The answer lies in the signal he devised. One lamp meant a land attack, two a sea attack. He needed only that one piece of information, and a simple signal gave it to him. In modern parlance, we'd call it a "bit" of information, a BInary digiT that contains two values: yes/no, on/off, 0/1. Revere needed two lamps because the "off" or "zero" value couldn't be distinguished from an ambiguous "no answer." The course of the American Revolution might not have been much different if Revere had not devised his simple binary code, but the communication revolution we're in now depends on something similar. We need to learn something about how it works.

We usually express binary codes as a series of zeroes and ones, but, in fact, they can be anything. In modern communication systems, they are usually different frequencies of electromagnetic energy, pulses of electrical current, even flashes of laser light. The extraordinary thing about binary codes is that they can be extended to accommodate unlimited values of text, sound, and light.

Number Systems

Our number system is a decimal system, that is, there are 10 distinct values, not just the two in the lamps in the Old North Church. But, of course, we are not limited to numbers from zero to nine. We can also write and understand numbers such as 4,215 and 1,476,204. Take a closer look at the first example, 4,215, and think of it this way:

$$4 \times 10^3 = 4000$$
$$2 \times 10^2 = 200$$
$$1 \times 10^1 = 10$$
$$5 \times 10^0 = 5$$

If you've forgotten your basic algebra, it may be useful to note that any number raised to the first power is the number itself ($10^1 = 10$) and any number to the zero power is one ($10^0 = 1$). We can go beyond the original 10 digits available in a decimal system by taking advantage of the power of exponents.

There's no reason we have to use a number system based on ten. It's just tradition and simplicity, possibly function of the number of fingers and toes that served as simple early calculators. Suppose, for example, that the sample number were in base eight. Then it would "translate" into the following:

$$4 \times 8^3 = 2,048$$
$$2 \times 8^2 = 128$$
$$1 \times 8^1 = 8$$
$$5 \times 8^0 = 5$$

In this example, 4,215 in base eight would represent 2,189 in our familiar decimal system. To repeat, there's no rule that says numbers have to be base ten. In fact, another system might have important advantages. Consider a binary system, that is, one that has only two values, 0 and 1. Such a system can be transmitted as pulses of electricity, beeps of sound, or lanterns in a church tower.

Take the binary number 10101. We can translate the binary digits like this:

$$1 = 2^4 = 16$$
$$0 = 2^3 = 0$$
$$1 = 2^2 = 4$$
$$0 = 2^1 = 0$$
$$1 = 2^0 = 1$$

Voila! 10101 is *really* 21. Or at least in the number system we take for granted. The number of possible combinations in any system is equal to the base raised to the power of the number of digits used to construct a multiple-digit number. So if you start with the base ten and use two digits, you can come up with 10^2 or 100 possible combinations—00, 01, 02, and so on. All very simple, although possibly not the way you thought of numbers.

Bits and Bytes

Let's go back to the binary system where only zeroes and ones are allowed. We'll extend the system to eight digits with combinations from 00000000 to 11111111. Our little rule tells us that there are 2^8 or 256 combinations, more than enough for the set of uppercase and lowercase letters in the Latin alphabet, with combinations left over for digits and various symbols. Combinations also can be set aside for letters with various diacritical marks used in other languages with which English shares the Roman alphabet. Non-Roman languages can use the same system as long as they don't exceed 256 letters.

Eight-bit (or sometimes seven-bit) binary numbers are known as *bytes,* a word familiar to even the most computer-illiterate. Bytes are simply the way that computers, which internally can process only tiny impulses of electricity, digest letters and decimal numbers. As long as computers agree that 00000001 is really *a,* they can make sense out of what you type on the keyboard. A computer on the other side of the earth can also understand the same message if it uses the same code as yours. This is why standardization is important and often politically charged.

If the world accepts one system to the exclusion of others, the accepted standard accrues advantages that extend beyond technology. Most of the world uses either a system known as ASCII (American Standard Code for Information Interchange) or the newer ANSI (American National Standards Institute), which are written for the Roman alphabet. Because so much of modern computer technology—and especially the software applications that make it run—was developed in the United States, most computers "speak" a form of American English. This both reflects the Anglo-American communication dominance that earlier chapters described and reinforces it. Of course, even the technical jargon of computer-speak is rarely translated, with the consequence that words such as *software, hard drive,* and *byte* itself have become part of a global vocabulary.

Perfect Sound

If digitization only allowed computers to do the prodigious number- and text-crunching we take for granted, it could still claim credit for unleashing the world's third communication revolution. There's more to it than that, however, and you probably have an example at home, maybe even in your backpack right now. The ordinary compact disc (CD) player is part of the digital revolution along with the personal computer (PC) and in one way is even more dramatic.

Recorded sound has been around for a century, but the CD is as different from the familiar cassette or LP as the laser printer is from Gutenberg's then-revolutionary moveable type printing system. Until the CD arrived, sound recording was based on a system of analog recording. The idea is simple enough but the application is complex. It works like this.

Any sound you hear comes from a single wave. It doesn't matter if the sound is the relatively simple tone from a human voice or the complex cacophony of a symphony orchestra. The single sound wave moves through the air until it reaches your ear and sets your eardrum vibrating. The ear then transmits the impulses to the brain where it is interpreted as a friend asking about tomorrow's assignment or the latest hit from your favorite heavy metal band that sends your parents off the deep end.

Traditional recording devices mimic the ear by using an electronic device to translate the sound wave into minute vibrations. The vibrations then are converted into a weak electrical current that reproduces the original wave. The current produces an analog of the sound wave, that is, if you could see them both, the pattern of the current would look very much like the original sound wave. The electrical current can be transferred to a permanent storage system for later playback. In LPs, the tiny squiggles in the groove of the record represent the analog of the original sound wave. With a magnifying glass, you can see them. In cassette tapes, the pattern is formed by magnetically aligning invisible particles of metals and don't exist in any visible form.

In both cases, the sound is reproduced by reversing the process. The phonograph needle vibrates as it rides along the groove and translates the squiggles into a weak current. The playback head of the cassette player does the same thing with the patterns recorded on the tape. At some point, the electrical current drives a device that converts the current back to a physical vibration. You then hear a remarkably accurate reproduction of the original sound through your earphones or loudspeaker, even though you are separated from the source by time and space.

The ability to preserve sound is a noteworthy achievement, almost equivalent to the invention of written language, which was a revolution in communication in its own right. Imagine life 200 years ago when the only music people heard was what they made themselves. Even a modest collection of tapes and LPs today contains more and better music than Thomas Jefferson—one of the most sophisticated people of his generation—heard in his lifetime. With an inexpensive radio in an ordinary city, you have access to more and better music—well, at least more—than the richest and most powerful people in the world had a few generations ago.

Today's analog systems are good, but why are the CDs so much better? Digitization. In a digital system, the sound waves are picked up by microphones and converted into electrical signals, but the comparison with analog systems stops there. Instead of capturing the analog electrical signals in some permanent medium, the digital system divides the sound wave into tiny segments—44,000 per second, if you can imagine such tiny sound bites—and converts each one into a digital format that captures the characteristics of the sound wave at that precise moment. In most systems, four bytes are used to represent each of the sampling points, two for each of the two stereo channels. The digital format is more accurate than traditional analog media and not subject to deterioration. Each snippet of the original sound wave is stored permanently as a set of digital bytes of information that is used to reconstruct the original sound with virtually flawless fidelity to the original.

In theory, you can play a CD indefinitely without loss of quality because the information is "read" by a laser, not a needle that scrapes the grooves. You can also copy it with perfect fidelity for all your friends if you and they have DAT (digital audio tape) systems, a prospect that sends the popular music industry into a cold sweat.

It's hard to imagine your favorite Michael Jackson hit as nothing but a series of zeroes and ones, but that's what the CD would look like if you could see it the way you can see the grooves on an LP. If you think about it, it's also difficult to imagine music as a long squiggle in an LP groove. Actually, the CD uses a series of microscopic pits to represent the bits of information. Our representation of any binary system as 0s and 1s is itself a convention that appeals to our understanding of the system, not an accurate description of what's really happening inside the CD player or a personal computer.

Perfect Pictures

Pictures, like sound, can be reproduced by modern analog systems. You see the product of this technology every day in newspaper photos and every time you turn on the TV. The system is much like that used in analog sound systems, but, of course, with differences because the basic data are visual rather than audio. In both your TV and the newswire photo system, the picture is divided into a series of fine horizontal strips. In the TV, the picture consists of 525 horizontal lines in the U.S. NTSC system, 625 in the European PAL or SECAM systems.[3] A photoelectric sensor scans the picture or image registered on the TV camera, line by line, and produces a weak electrical current that is *analogous*—remember that word?—to the values of light and darkness you would see if you looked at the picture the same way.

The scan is repeated 60 times per second in the NTSC system, 50 in PAL and SECAM. Either system produces a continuous signal that overlaps enough that you see it as a reasonably steady and reasonably high resolution moving picture when the process is reversed in your TV set. In the TV set, an electron gun scans the inside of the picture tube, while the fluctuating electronic signal activates tiny dots of the screen into varying shades of brightness. If you get close enough to the picture tube, you can see the tiny dots that fuse into a single picture at normal viewing distance.

The signal gets from the source to your local newspaper office in much the same way. At the end, however, instead of converting the analog signal into a moving TV picture, a laser "burns" tiny dots of varying intensity into a piece of paper. They, too, merge into a reasonably accurate analog of the original photo.

To shift the process of analog picture transmission into a digital system, something similar to the process used in the compact disc is used. First you have to divide the electrical signal that represents the picture into a series of discrete points of light of varying value. Each point of light—called a pixel—is then translated into a digital equivalent. A conventional byte can express any one of 256 shades. Color filters can separate an image into its basic hues, which can be reassembled into a color image on the printing press or TV screen.

Compared to text, digitized photos require a lot of bytes. There are no standards, but simple digital cameras now available require 100,000 bytes to capture

---

[3] NTSC stands for National Television Systems Committee (or sometimes facetiously "Never Twice the Same Color"). It refers to the cheap but admittedly inferior technical system used to produce color TV in the United States and other countries, such as Canada, Japan, and most of Latin America. PAL (phase alternate line) is widely used in Western Europe and former colonies, and SECAM (sequential couleur à mémoire) is used in France and its former colonies and in the Soviet Union and its satellites. The systems are incompatible, which is why you get nothing but snow (and sometimes sound) when a friend in Britain, Africa, or the Middle East sends you a home videocassette.

the detail of a single photo. High-resolution scanners can take 6 million bytes or more. Such masses of data strain the capacity of today's desktop publishing systems and telecommunication networks. Today's television pictures cannot cope with the billions and billions of bytes per minute that real-time transmission of high-quality digital moving pictures would require. The best today's telecommunication system can handle is the slow-scan picture phone and "pixelator," a gadget that can transmit TV pictures one frame at a time.

Technological obstacles are overcome quickly, however, and a true digital HDTV system is likely to be operational by the end of the century. Political and policy questions are as important as technical questions and more difficult to overcome. One hope is that a single technical standard will be adopted globally to avoid the problems of incompatibility that plague the conventional systems.[4] The world moved closer to that goal in 1992 when several full-digital high-definition TV (HDTV) systems were demonstrated in Washington, D.C. The FCC then ordered the several consortia that proposed the various HDTV systems to work together on a single system that could be operational within a decade without massively disrupting the existing allocation of frequencies. The plan was to select a single standard, then give each existing station a new HDTV frequency and several years to switch. If the broadcaster didn't, the HDTV frequency would be sold or awarded to another applicant.

The marvel of the proposed HDTV systems was twofold. One was a giant technical leap forward in compressing the amount of data needed for HDTV into the limited segments of the electromagnetic spectrum already allocated to individual channels. The popular assumption was that a terrestrial system might reduce by half or more the number of HDTV channels that could operate in any market. That possibility had seemed to restrict HDTV to optical fiber cable systems or direct broadcast satellites until the competitors in the 1992 demonstration used the existing public TV transmitter to send up to 60 billion bits of digital information per second to HDTV receivers in the Capitol.

The second was the unexpected leap of the United States into global leadership of HDTV technology. Of the three major global players—Japan, Europe, and the United States—only the United States had left the development of HDTV up to private initiative, while both Japan and Europe had already spent millions of dollars on prototype systems that instantly became obsolete. Both the European Community and Japan announced in 1993 that they would cooperate in developing the new U.S. standard rather than continuing work on their own systems. A single global standard for second-generation HDTV might finally eliminate the problems of the incompatible NTSC/PAL/SECAM first-generation systems.

HDTV is somewhere in the not-too-distant future, but digital still photos are already all around you. The Associated Press's "electronic darkroom" transmits digitized photos to newspapers all over the country. Editing is done on a TV monitor. Several news services also distribute charts, maps, and other graphics

---

[4] Philip Elmer-Dewitt, "The Picture Suddenly Gets Clearer," *Time*, March 30, 1992, pp. 54–55.

the same way. They can be stored for later retrieval on the same kind of PC disks most students use routinely for class exercises.

Merging Information

If analog sound systems were acceptable for a century and analog picture systems for more than half a century, why all the excitement about CDs and digital photos? Two reasons are important. One is obvious, the other not.

The obvious reason is apparent when you switch from a Walkman tape cassette system to a CD player. The quality of the sound is improved dramatically, of course, and the full complexity of the original sound is reproduced exactly as you would have heard it at the concert. Perhaps even better because the recording and mixing process balances the various pieces of the source better than even the orchestra conductor hears it. The phrase ''perfect reproduction'' is often used when talking about digital sound. It is not far off the mark. An added advantage is that digital media do not deteriorate if played repeatedly or copied.

The second reason for the importance of digital recording is that any form of communication—text, sound, pictures—can be converted to a common code and transmitted over all conventional media with perfect fidelity. These include telephone line, satellite, conventional over-the-air broadcasting, conventional cable, and optical fiber. An ordinary compact disc can store massive quantities of digitized data and doesn't care if they represent the complete works of Shakespeare, the latest hit from today's pop star, or a video of him or her in action.

We're beginning to see the merger of text, sound, and picture and the emergence of the compact disc as the preferred medium for both serious research and pop culture. Your library probably has a fast-growing collection of CDs that have replaced many traditional references. CD or laser disc systems integrating pictures, sound, and text are on the market for PCs and accommodate rock videos, the NASA space archive, or a highlights of the Gulf War with equal ease. New ''multimedia'' CD systems that resemble a hybrid of video games and electronic encyclopedias are also on the market.

In fact, the integration of text, sound, and picture already happens every day. You participate in this third communication revolution when you pick up the telephone, try one of the new picture phones, or use a modem to connect your PC to a mainframe across the country.

ISDNs

ISDN stands for integrated services data network and refers to what passes through the global telecommunication system with ever-greater frequency. A hundred years ago, when you called someone in a neighboring city, a weak electrical analog of your voices traveled along one of the copper wires looped from your house to his or hers. Now what we routinely call ''telephone lines'' carry streams of digitized data cascading around the world up to one satellite, back down to earth and up to a second one, then down again on the other side of the earth at the speed of light. Even when you're used to it, you can be startled at the quality of sound when you talk to a friend in Tokyo, Paris, or Sydney. Often you can talk with equal clarity to someone in Nairobi, Lima, or Bombay. When the signal fades or disappears in static and interference, the problem is in the last few kilometers of the antiquated local system, almost never in the tens of thousands of kilometers of the global ISDNs. Global and national systems are moving rapidly toward ISDNs. Early in the next century, digital communication will become the standard for all telecommunication. About the same time, radio and television broadcast signals will be digital as well, bringing the startling clarity of a CD player to every radio and theater-screen clarity to digital high-definition TV (HDTV) that may well be a huge, flat screen covering one wall of your home's "media room."

Integration

The miraculous part of modern ISDNs is not that they extend the clarity of CDs to global telephone service—ordinary conversations could be almost lifelike if better technology and more of the frequency spectrum were utilized. The real wonder is that all forms of digitized information—text, sound, pictures—can be integrated into a single data stream and sent through the satellite system in a cascade of routine business transactions between computers, phone calls between friends, and even occasionally photographs. Computers at the front end switch packets of information from one stream of outgoing data to another to keep them operating at full capacity. At the receiving end, the packets are put back into the right order, and the reassembled messages are sent off to ordinary telephones, computers, or fax machines.

It is not too far from reality to say that the spaces between the words in your phone call back home from overseas are stuffed with pieces of credit card bills and fax messages. If you could grab a small sample of the data stream and translate the ones and zeroes back into something intelligible, you would find scraps of text, sound, and pictures. Global communication at the end of the twentieth century no longer distinguishes among them.

CONTROVERSIES

You'd think that most people would stand in awe of the new technology, either waiting like a child at Christmas for the newest products from Sony and Panasonic or grumbling about how everything was fine the way it was and who really needs these new contraptions anyway. Most of us, of course, fall somewhere between the trend-setting TAFies (technologically advanced families, as marketing people refer to them), anxious to be the first on the block when some new gadget hits the market, and the laggards who still think the old black-and-white television works just fine and would be satisfied with a vacuum-tube radio if they could still get the replacement parts.

At the international level, however, controversies about communication technology and technological innovation are bigger than whether you should keep up with the TAFies. A basic question for developing countries that we have already explored is whether modern communication can be a tool for national develop-ment or whether it merely disrupts traditional cultures without bringing them any closer to the goals of political and economic stability they desire.

Closely linked to this question in the New World Information Order debate was the inequitable distribution of the world's communication resources between the information-rich North and information-poor South. Check back in the Data Bases of several recent chapters to see the size of this information gap. If infor-mation is the wealth of the information age and, therefore, its power, the handful of information-based economies that produce both the hardware and software of global communication maintain a level of influence over the rest of the world comparable to that of the empires of the past. And like traditional colonial powers, they tend to acquire and keep a lion's share of the information resources as well. The NWIO defined a more equitable distribution of information resources as one of its goals. Whether that should be achieved by transferring resources from North to South or by helping the South improve its own capabilities was one of the flash points of the UNESCO debate. One thing is clear, however: To be a poor nation in the twenty-first century is to be one poor in information. Different issues arise at different times, but controversies in the early twenty-first century are likely to include several problems of inequity and control.

Radio Spectrum

The ITU allocates frequencies for specific uses but, contrary to widespread belief, does not assign them to individual countries. Countries register their intention to use frequencies with the ITU and then assign them to domestic users. In most cases, the system works efficiently, but there are some flash points, usually involving radio and TV broadcasting.

A problem can occur near national borders where broadcasters on one side can interfere, deliberately or accidentally, with broadcasting on the other side. Examples include powerful commercial and religious broadcasters in northern Mexico aiming at audiences in the United States, the Reagan administration's experiments beaming a powerful domestic AM frequency to Cuba, and pirate stations operating in international waters.

Usually these problems can be worked out, but short-wave radio presents special difficulties. Because of its unusual propagation characteristics, it is used mostly for international broadcasting. At this point, the frequencies allocated to short wave are crowded and are largely registered to the Western nations that got into the business well before many of today's third-world countries even existed. Although relatively unimportant in industrialized countries, short wave remains a major player in global communication.

Technical and political solutions to the problem of short-wave frequency overcrowding are possible but not likely. Major broadcasters such as the BBC and VOA could release some frequencies they claimed years ago but probably won't because they are expanding operations. Broadcasters could switch to single sideband (SSB), which splits the signal into separate halves, effectively doubling the capacity of each frequency. This would require replacing all existing short-wave receivers, a prospect appealing to Sony and Grundig but not to the rest of us. Direct broadcasting from satellites could utilize the existing frequencies more efficiently with better directional transmission and less scatter of errant signals.

Technology can also improve receivers. Expect technical improvements in transmission and reception and perhaps replacement of terrestrial transmission using the ionosphere as a reflector by direct satellite broadcasting. Despite these innovations, short-wave is likely to remain a noisy, overcrowded but vital part of global communication.

Orbital Slots

When the potential of the geostationary orbit became clear, some countries that had missed the rush for short-wave frequencies were determined not to lose out again. The New World Information Order debate included two arguments related to slots in the geosynchronous orbit. One was that national sovereignty extended into space. For the countries astride the equator, this meant that they could claim ownership of the strip of the geosynchronous orbit overhead and either use it themselves or sell it. The argument applied only to a handful of countries—none of them capable of defending territory in space—and was never an important part of the NWIO debate. Most satellites were over oceans, which, by tradition, belonged to everyone.

A second argument was that countries should be able to reserve specific orbital slots for future use, even though they lacked the current technical capability to launch or utilize a satellite. Early in the space age, this seemed important because the first satellites had to be separated by as much as three or four degrees. This meant that the entire orbit could accommodate only 90 to 120 satellites. Intelsat and the handful of national space powers were filling them up fast.

The Western nations adopted the position that technology would solve technical problems and that a reservation system would impede the development of the resource for everyone. In fact, each generation of satellites had greater capacity and was more efficient than its predecessors, and early limits vanished. Capacity and diversity of the global system grew faster than demand for services, which was one reason for the dramatic drop in costs in the 1980s. Reservation of orbital slots as an international political issue died in the 1980s along with the NWIO debate itself.

Information Sovereignty

Electromagnetic waves pulsing through the atmosphere or beaming down from a satellite don't stop for a passport check at national boundaries. Short-wave radio programs directed to other countries frequently irritate governments on the receiving end but never became an international political issue because virtually every country in the world engages in the practice. During the cold war, communist regimes, claiming an information monopoly as part of their media philosophy, frequently tried to jam incoming signals but were never very successful. They couldn't make too much fuss at international organizations because they never asked permission before sending their short-wave signals around the world.

Television was different, however. Although transmission of TV signals directly from satellites to sets in other countries was never technically or politically realistic, several international regulatory agencies—ITU, UNESCO, the United Nations itself—debated the issue during the 1960s and 1970s. At one point, the Soviet Union announced that it was prepared to shoot down any satellite intended to serve as a TV version of a BBC or VOA short-wave service. Ironically, in the 1980s, concern shifted from the information and cultural sovereignty of communist and third-world nations to protection of commercial broadcasters' rights against pirating of signals and protection of Western public service broadcasting against the intrusion of commercial multinational conglomerates.

THE FUTURE

Prophecy in global communication is a risky business. Ask anyone who bought a Betamax VCR or eight-track cartridge tape system. Communication in the twenty-first century will change as much as it has in this one. Predicting how it will change is as difficult as anticipating ISDNs in 1890 when radio was a scientific curiosity and television and personal computers beyond imagination. Still the outlines of several new technologies that your grandchildren will take for granted can be seen in the 1990s.

Digitization

Digital communication has so much going for it that the old-fashioned analog systems are like dinosaurs. Digital is more efficient and flexible, produces higher quality, more accurate reproduction, and squeezes more information into less space. In every comparison of text, sound, or picture storage, transmission, and reproduction, digital is light years ahead of the analog alternative.

The demonstration of digital HDTV in 1992 instantly made the only existing analog system obsolete. The Japanese NHK analog system, which had been in experimental operation for about a year, was abandoned along with the EC's semi-HDTV proposal. The capacity of the digital systems was staggering, even by standards of other digital media. Each frame of an HDTV picture—repeated 60 times a second—contained a billion bits of information. Engineers created demonstration systems that could compress that quantity of information into a standard over-the-air signal with help from a computer inside the receiver. Transmission of data or CD-quality sound over the air using the same technology would give virtually unlimited capacity to over-the-air frequencies allocated to such purposes and speed the development of services such as global call-forwarding, paging, positioning, and, of course, Dick Tracy–style wristwatch phones.

Compression of digital information also made the picture-phone possible and led to the introduction of a new generation of compact disc recorders and players the size of a paperback book. At some point, a bit may be represented by a single electron of electricity or photon of light.

The most dramatic example of the digital revolution remains high definition television. Even if a single technical standard emerges, however, several questions dealing with policy, marketing, and technology remain. How fast will HDTV be introduced and who will do it? Will the system be tied to direct-broadcast satellites, traditional over-the-air frequencies, or made part of a second-generation optical fiber cable system that will plug your home into the twenty-first century world of digital information? Can the world avoid the problem of competing incompatible standards that plagued traditional television? Check today's paper for recent developments and speculation about what's over the horizon.

Integration

The CD is a good example of what happens when information is digitized. The medium developed for music shows up in the library replacing reference books, and then in a personal computer replacing the floppy disk. The CD player adds video to its perfect audio, and the text of PCs and library CD-ROMs is surrounded by pictures and sound. The "nonprint" section of most libraries is expanding rapidly; a century from now, visitors may examine curiosities in a small "non-electronic" section. It will contain what today we call "books."

Something similar is happening to the telephone line and cable TV. When you can use a personal computer connected to a distant data base via telephone modem to check the moment's sports scores or order a pay-per-view movie on cable TV, then the old functions of media are changing. Each medium seems to have a natural life cycle of birth, expansion, and replacement. At maturity, it can evolve into something new or disappear. Network radio and television and mass appeal magazines are examples of old mass media that have disappeared or are barely clinging to life. Newspapers are accelerating down the slippery slope.

In the coming years, a big debate will be over control of, access to, and content of a second generation cable that could replace both the telephone and cable TV. It will determine how we plug into the global information system. At stake are huge sums of money and the fate of entire industries. And, of course, global influence.

Miniaturization

Computers have already reached one practical limit—keyboards so small that human fingers can barely find the keys. Each decline in physical size is matched with an increase in capacity. Underneath the tiny keyboard of a notebook computer is more computing power than a mainframe had two generations ago. As the ability to pack more and more technology and information into a smaller and smaller space continues, one generation's fixed installation becomes the next generation's suitcase and the next generation's pocket gadget.

Miniaturization means privatization and mobility of technology. When the first radio arrived, it was common property, and the entire family—in some parts of the world, the whole community—gathered around to listen. Your parents may remember when there was one television set in the house, and everyone had to watch the same program. Of course, with only one or two channels, the choice wasn't too difficult. Then, as receivers became smaller and cheaper, multiple sets appeared. They became a part of each person's private world. The decision of when to watch and what to watch was made by the individual, not the family or community. Watching and listening became private behavior, not part of a group experience.

Then, of course, miniaturization freed the individual from the tether of the electrical cord. Sony gave us the Walkman and the Watchman, and we now can go anywhere on the earth—literally—plugged into whatever part of the electronic environment we choose.

Recycling of Media

Parallel to the process of miniaturization is a "recycling" of media themselves into different functions. Until a few years ago, most of us would have accepted as obvious and inevitable that the telephone would be connected to a wire and radio and TV signals would come over the air. Now, of course, we take cellular phones in the car and on the street, and we can call from trains and planes. If necessary, we can carry our own suitcase phone, which allows to call from anywhere on the planet. In contrast, most of us watch TV programs—and often listen to radio signals—delivered by cable. Pay-per-view/listen options and almost unlimited cable capacity turn these old mass media into individually tailored information environments. These changes reflect both an evolution of mass media into individual media and a change in delivery systems.

A similar shift is taking place at the global level. Optical fiber cable is replacing various point-to-point telecommunications circuits, especially the satellite-based systems that have revolutionized global communication. In addition to eliminating the annoying half-second lag in international telephone conversations, the change frees old media for new uses. Satellites and terrestrial broadcast can be used in areas of the world not connected to the cable grid.

Examples of innovations now under development or technically possible include a global portable telephone system, short-wave radio via direct broadcast satellite, and satellite-based global positioning and messaging systems built into vehicles and hand-held units. Many of these exist in primitive form. Remember the devices U.S. forces used in the Gulf War to navigate the desert and the suitcase phones reporters used to send text, pictures, and sound from the isolated corners of the battlefield. Commercial versions are already available and getting smaller, cheaper, and more accurate.

Inevitably innovations get better, cheaper, smaller, and more accessible. It is not too hard to imagine getting into your car in a few years and punching in the location of your friend's house across town or across the country and letting a "smart" onboard system plot the route, including warnings of traffic jams and detours. Your friend could follow your progress on a home information system and pass along a request to you to pick up ice cream at the supermarket around the next corner. Of course, you already would have dialed up the evening's entertainment of movies, videos, or whatever, to be shown on a wall-size flat screen in the "information room." Friends in other cities or countries might join you via picture phone.

The changes represent more than the "gee whiz" of real-world technology outrunning the imagination of science fiction. Technology drives innovation, which, in turn, comes together on rare occasions to change the nature and structure of power. When that happens—when people learned to write down ideas; when printing dispersed them widely; and when computers, satellites, and digitization created a global information system—then we can speak of a true global revolution and be pleased that we are there to witness it.

MAIN POINTS

1. Today's communication revolution is based on computers, communication satellites, and the transformation of any type of text, sound, and pictures into a common digital code.
2. Satellites orbiting 35,800 kilometers above the earth's surface appear to hover in one spot. This geosynchronous or geostationary orbit is particularly important to global communication.
3. Miniaturization allows portable equipment to transmit information from any point on earth to any other, using a geostationary satellite as a relay point.
4. Technology promotes integration and recycling of media. The digital compact disc is emerging as a basic medium for storage and use of digital text, sound, and pictures, while a new generation of optical fiber cables may replace current domestic telephone and cable TV and global satellite telecommunication. Satellite-based technology may provide access to the global communication grid in areas not served by fixed cable and to moving vehicles.

FOR MORE INFORMATION

It is almost impossible to separate technical aspects of communication technology from political aspects. And almost anything in book form is at least partially outdated by current events. Useful overviews with minimum technical emphasis include Loy A. Singleton, *Global Impact: The New Telecommunication Technologies* (New York: Harper & Row, 1989); Heather E. Hudson, *Communication Satellites: Their Development and Impact* (New York: Free Press, 1990); Irwin Lebow, *The Digital Connection: A Layman's Guide to the Information Age* (New York: Computer Science Press, 1991); Wilson P. Dizard, Jr., *The Coming Information Age,* 3rd ed. (New York: Longman, 1989); Raymond Akwule, *Global Telecommunications: The Technology, Administration, and Policies* (Boston: Focal Press, 1992); Jarice Hanson and Uma Narula, eds., *New Communication Technologies in Developing Countries* (Hillsdale, NJ: Lawrence Erlbaum, 1990); and Michael M. Mirabito and Barbara L. Morgenstern, *The New Communications Technologies* (Boston: Focal Press, 1990).

An emphasis on political and cultural aspects of the same issues can be found in George H. Quester, *The International Politics of Television* (Lexington, MA: Lexington Books, 1990); W. J. Howell, Jr., *World Broadcasting in the Age of the Satellite* (Norwood, NJ: Ablex, 1986); Gerald Sussman and John A. Lent, eds., *Transnational Communications: Wiring the Third World* (Newbury Park, CA: Sage, 1991); and Ithiel de Sola Pool, *Technologies without Boundaries: On Telecommunications in a Global Age* (Cambridge, MA: Harvard University Press, 1990).

FOR DISCUSSION

1. Debate one side of the following proposition: developing countries should embrace modern communication technology as a means of overcoming the gap between the information-rich North and information-poor South; or developing countries should resist modern communication technology because it perpetuates a state of dependency and destroys traditional culture.

2. Find someone with a satellite dish and log the various international services available, paying attention to both the video channels and audio subcarriers. Discuss with the local cable operator why more are not available on the local system.

3. Visit a local newspaper and TV station to examine the technical systems they use to receive information. Interview gatekeepers about how decisions are made; note how the technology itself has changed the kind of information from abroad that gets into the paper and on the air.

DATA BASE

I. The entire electromagnetic spectrum ranges from 1 hertz (cycle per second) through visible light and into cosmic waves (10^{21}–10^{22} cycles per second). The part that can be used for electronic transmission (radio frequency spectrum) runs from about 30,000 cycles per second (kilohertz, or kHz) to about 300 billion cycles (gigahertz, or gHz). Frequencies up to 300 gigahertz are allocated, although the higher frequencies are not used.

VLF (very low frequency): below 30 kilohertz; not used for broadcast.

LF (low frequency): 30–300 kilohertz; long-wave broadcast.

MF (medium frequency): 300–3,000 kilohertz; AM radio, maritime and air communication, ham radio.

HF (high frequency): 3–30 megahertz; short-wave radio, ham radio, and CB radio.

VHF (very high frequency): 30–300 megahertz; VHF-TV, air navigation, public safety radio, FM radio.

UHF (ultra high frequency): 300–3,000 megahertz; public safety radio, UHF-TV.

SHF (super high frequency): 3–30 gigahertz; commercial satellites, radar, microwave, air navigation.

EHF (extremely high frequency): 30–300 gigahertz; research, experimental, and military satellites.

SOURCES: W. H. Howell, Jr., *World Broadcasting in the Age of the Satellite* (Norwood, NJ: Ablex, 1986), p. 6; Loy A. Singleton, *Global Impact: The New Telecommunication Technologies* (New York: Harper & Row, 1989), p. 20.

II. Major commercial satellites used in North America by name, location, and major services:

SpaceNet 2—69° West: USIA Worldnet, CSPAN, AFRTS, SCOLA

Satcom F2—72° West: WRAL (Raleigh), WABC (New York), WXIA (Atlanta)

Galaxy 2—74° West: occasional feeds; no regular services

Satcom 4R—82° West: Sports Channel, Playboy Channel, International Channel

Telstar 302—85° West: CBS affiliate feeds, HBO and Cinemax tests

SpaceNet 3—87° West: WSBK (Boston), KTVT (Dallas), WPIX (New York), KTLA (Los Angeles), HTS

Galaxy 3—93.5° West: Fox, Weather Channel, QVC, VH1, MTV, Nickelodeon, C-SPAN I and II

Telstar 301—96° West: CBS, ABC

Galaxy 6—99° West: several religious broadcasters

SpaceNet 4—101° West: CNN/Telemundo

Anik E2—107.3° West: various Canadian services

Anik E1—111.1° West: various Canadian services

Morelos 1—113.5° West: various Mexican services

Morelos 2—116° West: various Mexican services

SpaceNet 1—120° West: PBS, Univision

Westar 5—122.5° West: various sports, CNN Headline News, Group W

Telstar 303—125° West: TVN, Showtime

Satcom F1—131° West: American Movie Classics (AMC), Learning Channel, USA Network, HBO, Cinemax, BET, Home Shopping Network

Galaxy 1—133° West: TNN, WGN (Chicago), Disney, ESPN, CNN, CNN Headline, TMC, A&E, WWOR (New York), Showtime, TNT, WTBS (Atlanta), Discovery Channel, HBO

Satcom C1—137° West: KUSA (Denver), SportsChannel, KMGH (Denver), KCNC (Denver), KWGN (Denver), Prime Sports Network

SOURCE: "August 1993 Satellite TV Channels," *Orbit,* August 1993.

III. Number of Intelsat channels in use by region and year:

Year	Atlantic	Pacific	Indian	Total
1965	150	—	—	150
1970	2,633	1,312	314	4,259
1975	8,862	1,926	2,581	13,369
1980	27,530	4,676	8,409	40,615
1985	49,707	12,025	19,298	81,030
1990	71,477	22,200	28,229	121,906

SOURCE: Annual Report, 1990–1992 (Washington, D.C.: International Satellite Consortium, 1992).

IV. Current and future Intelsat spacecraft:

Intelsat V
First launched: 1980

Prime contractor: Ford Aerospace

Launch vehicles: Atlas Centaur, Ariane 1, 2

Lifetime: 7 years

Capacity: 12,000 circuits and 2 TV channels

Intelsat V-A
First launched: 1985

Prime contractor: Ford Aerospace

Launch vehicles: Atlas Centaur, Ariane 1, 2

Lifetime: 7 years

Capacity: 15,000 circuits and 2 TV channels

Intelsat VI
First launched: 1989

Prime contractor: Hughes

Launch vehicles: Ariane 4, Titan

Lifetime: 13 years

Capacity: 24,000 circuits and 3 TV channels (up to 120,000 circuits with digital circuit multiplication equipment, DCME)

Intelsat K
First launched: 1992

Prime contractor: GE Astro Space

Launch vehicles: Atlas IIA

Lifetime: 10 years

Capacity: 16 54-megahertz Ku-band transponders; can be configured to provide up to 32 high-quality TV channels

Intelsat VII

First launched: 1993

Prime contractor: SS/Loral (formerly Ford Aerospace)

Launch vehicles: Ariane 4, Atlas IIAS

Lifetime: 10–15 years

Capacity: 18,000 circuits and 3 TV channels (up to 90,000 circuits with DCME)

Intelsat VII-A

First launch: 1995

Prime contractor: SS/Loral

Launch vehicles: To be determined

Lifetime: 10–15 years

Capacity: 22,500 circuits and 3 TV channels (up to 112,500 circuits with DCME)

SOURCE: Annual Report, 1990–1992 (Washington, D.C.: International Satellite Consortium, 1992).

CHAPTER 14

Persuasive Communication

ABOUT THIS CHAPTER

The global communication system of the twenty-first century will offer unparalleled opportunity to reach a global audience. It will come as no surprise that governments, advertisers, and occasionally even private citizens use the technology of modern communication to attempt to influence attitudes and behavior of people around the world. International politics via CNN is a current example of the use of public communication for political ends, but the practice is older and wider.

In this chapter, we consider "public diplomacy"—a modern term for old-fashioned political propaganda—and advertising as the major players in the global marketplace. Then, as we complete our armchair tour of global communication at the turn of the twentieth century, we try to organize our souvenir snapshots into a coherent picture of global communication at the end of a century that has been transformed by new media, new technology, and new ideas.

INTRODUCTION

For most of the twentieth century, social scientists have been trying to figure out what kind of influence—if any—mass media have on us. We have already seen how several generations of development specialists used communication to try to speed social change and how Lenin and those he inspired mobilized mass media to help create a Marxist society. Did it work? Do modern propaganda and advertising work?

Mass or Limited Effects?

A simple answer to a complex question is always wrong. In this case, it's hard to know what a simple answer is, or even a reasonable answer. Communication scientists generally divide themselves into two camps. One group is identified with "mass effects" theories that posit the kind of overwhelming media influence on modern life that popular writers and occasionally common sense support. But an equally large camp of researchers argues for "limited effects" theories that see mass media as facilitators and magnifiers of change but with little inherent power to overcome the permanent forces of culture, economics, and politics.

You could cite the following in support of a "mass effects" theory: Hitler's use of propaganda and the "great lie" technique in World War II, the success of China and perhaps Cuba in using communication in the revolutionary restructuring of their countries, modern political campaigning and commercial advertising, and the influence of news media in international relations.

On the other hand, from the perspective of limited effects, you could point to the failure of most new commercial products and political candidates, advertising not withstanding; the tenacity of traditional cultures, including the nasty component of war; and perhaps most dramatically, the failure of communism. Anyone who watched the revolutions of 1989 was struck by the vigor and anger with which masses of people scorned and occasionally attacked the media that had bombarded them with a singular message for anywhere from 40 to 70 years.

If nothing else, modern communication isolates events and magnifies them, often out of proportion. A terrorist attack in an airport overseas, starving children in Somalia, or the savagery of war in Bosnia fill the small television screen day after day to the point where we can forget that they are news, exceptional events, outside the lives of most people in most places most of the time. In the past, wars raged and children starved, but most people didn't know about them. The picture of the world that filtered through the primitive global communication system was slow and sketchy, subject to multiple censors, and missing the impact of live television. Now it seems that we know of every tragedy instantly. It's useful to remind ourselves occasionally of what doesn't make the news: most airplanes don't crash; most governments are not overthrown; most people are not threatened by war and starvation.

It is also true, however, that even the "limited" effects of modern communication can have profound implications. In most democracies, elections are won or lost by the shift of a tiny segment of the electorate. Advertising campaigns are judged successes if only the smallest part of the target audience responds. And a public relations campaign—propaganda campaign, if you prefer—aims for minute shifts in public opinion. These shifts, of course, lead to important changes in the distribution of wealth and power.

Modern Communication

The modern global communication system—CNN, the BBC World Service, the news agencies flooding the planet with words and pictures around the clock—adds a dimension to modern life that was missing to earlier generations. Part of it is the volume and immediacy of information that illuminates, however briefly, parts of the world that would have escaped notice in the past. Part of it is a new set of limitations and opportunities for persuasion.

Common wisdom is that long, traditional wars such as the Korean War and the Vietnam War are not possible in democracies in the age of television. Only wars like those in the Falklands/Malvinas, Grenada, and the Persian Gulf—short, militarily decisive, with the pictures temporarily controlled by the government— are possible. After the initial burst of support, public opinion falters and then demands a conclusion. Drawn-out wars with daily pictures of the casualties and destruction but lacking evidence of progress toward resolution—exactly what the Vietnam War was to most Americans—apparently cannot be sustained even by the most media-sophisticated government. Outside media-saturated Western democracies, however, the story may be different.

Wars continue in many parts of the world, often encouraged by leaders who use whatever communication they have available to fan old passions. The magnifying lens of modern media can add to the layers of ethnic antagonism and fuel new conflict. Sometimes it can force outside reaction. Common wisdom is also that pictures of warring and starving Somalis and Bosnians eventually produced some kind of international response. In the past, the dark side of culture was equally common—and probably even more frequent—but the rest of us remained in happy ignorance. Now the international community occasionally can be goaded or shamed into action. When it fails to act, we are left with the burden of seeing the pictures day after day and the knowledge of what is going on. The innocent ignorance of the past is gone.

Modern media, of course, can be used to call attention to grievances, real or imagined; to call for help; or to reach an international audience. Staging events for the global media is now part of international relations and adds a dimension that was missing in previous generations: the ability to force attention, to demand reaction, to set the political agenda. Choreographed demonstrations directed to governments and TV viewers on the opposite side of the earth, reinforced with English-language signs and timed for the evening news, are pseudo-events, of course. Depending on your sympathies toward the sponsors, they can be an affront or a legitimate persuasion tactic. Compared with other ways of attracting global attention—hijacking airplanes and blowing up buildings, for example—using the media for persuasion has a lot going for it. Everyone does it—political groups looking for attention, but advertisers and governments as well.

PERSUASIVE COMMUNICATION

When in the Course of human Events, it becomes necessary for one People to dissolve the Political Bonds which have connected them with another, and to assume among the Powers of the Earth, the separate and equal Status to which the Laws of Nature and of Nature's God entitle them, a decent Respect for the Opinions of Mankind requires that they should declare the causes which impel them to the Separation. . . . To prove this, let Facts be submitted to a candid World.

We don't usually think of the Declaration of Independence as international propaganda, but it served both to commit the founding fathers and mothers to the struggle for independence and to solicit support from the rest of the world. Most of the declaration is a litany of complaints against British rule, for which King George III was held personally responsible:

> He has plundered our Seas, ravaged our Coasts, burnt our towns, and destroyed the Lives of our People. He is, at this Time, transporting large Armies of foreign Mercenaries, to complete the works of Death, Desolation, and Tyranny, already begun with circumstances of Cruelty and Perfidy, scarcely paralleled in the most barbarous Ages, and totally unworthy the Head of a civilized Nation.

These were dangerous things to say about your king, especially when he still wielded a big stick. Although it didn't immediately stir Europeans to arms, the document is largely responsible for the king's reputation as a foolish monarch whose incompetence lost the American colonies. His descendant, the current Prince of Wales, thinks he got a bum rap. The declaration was a brilliant success as an exercise in international propaganda as well as core document of Western democracy.

Propaganda

In most Western languages, the word *propaganda* has a pejorative connotative meaning. In a few countries, the word or its equivalent can be translated neutrally as "public relations" or even "advertising," but in most, the social meaning includes some element of deceit, falsity, or subterfuge. This seems to come from two uses we have already encountered.

The first was the Catholic church's "Congregation for the Propagation of the Faith"—*Congregatio de propaganda fide* in Latin—that was established in 1622 to counter the Protestant Reformation. It led to the Inquisition, whose members were, to say the least, unsympathetic to independent-minded skeptics such as Galileo. The second was Lenin's definition of propaganda as a legitimate function of the party media. From both sources, we get the idea that we ought to be alert for propaganda and suspicious of anyone who is out to win our hearts and minds.[1]

If propaganda is defined, minus the historical baggage, as an effort to inform and persuade, it takes on a less sinister connotation and embraces a range of activities that we consider normal and reasonable. In most cases, other words are preferred to describe these activities: *public relations, public information,*

---

[1] Garth S. Jowett and Victoria O'Donnell, *Propaganda and Persuasion,* 2nd ed. (Newbury Park, CA: Sage, 1992). The authors define propaganda as one-sided, furthering only the aim of the propagandist as distinguished from persuasion.

even *education* and *advertising*. Our focus here is on government activities designed to reach and influence people in other countries. In a few countries, it is still called propaganda, but most prefer the modern term *public diplomacy*.

Public Diplomacy

Public diplomacy differs from other kinds of international political, economic, and military relations because it represents the efforts of one *government* to influence the *people* of another country. Most official information between nations flows from embassy to foreign ministry, but the public diplomats—official propagandists, if you prefer—are a direct link to the public. Every nation engages in public diplomacy of some sort. Smaller countries may necessarily limit themselves to an occasional press release and embassy spokespersons who respond to public and journalists' inquiries among their other duties. In addition, almost all countries also operate short-wave radio services that are beamed to listeners in other countries. More about them later.

The larger (and wealthier) countries also sponsor a range of activities that fall within the domain of public diplomacy. They include libraries and cultural centers, educational exchanges, regular publications distributed overseas, and even get-acquainted tours of the homeland for VIPs. The United States operates one of the largest public diplomacy programs in the world at an annual cost to taxpayers of about $1 billion. While the program varies somewhat from those of comparable nations such as Britain, Germany, and Japan, it represents a good case study of public diplomacy in the 1990s. Curiously enough, while American government public diplomacy (or propaganda) activities are virtually unknown at home, initials such as USIS and VOA are almost as well known as IBM and MTV in most parts of the world.

UNITED STATES INFORMATION AGENCY

Origins

The United States Information Agency (USIA) is an independent executive agency that traces its roots to two activities in World War II and one that started at the end of the war. Worried that Germany might try to get Latin American countries into the war as allies, President Roosevelt appointed Nelson Rockefeller to establish an educational and cultural program that would keep Latinos neutral and sympathetic to the United States if not outright allies. The Germans in both wars had tried actively to get Latin America mobilized as an ally, and the thought of a pro-Nazi government south of the Rio Grande was unsettling. The appointment was not as strange as it now seems because the Rockefeller family had been instrumental in developing Latin American oil, and the name was well known and identified positively with Yankee know-how.

Rockefeller's program included promoting personal exchanges between citizens of the United States and Latin Americans and establishment of binational cultural centers in many Latin American countries. Both activities were models for programs in Germany and Japan after the war and became part of USIA when the government's public diplomacy activities went worldwide.

The second activity was a short-wave radio broadcast service to Germany and occupied France that went on the air in 1942, using transmitters and other facilities borrowed from several commercial and private broadcasters. It was part of a larger international information program headed by the playwright Robert E. Sherwood. The style of the Voice of America, as the service was known, was set largely by John Houseman, who had produced the famous Orson Welles *War of the Worlds* radio broadcast in 1938 and ended a distinguished theatrical career a half century later as Professor Kingsfield in *The Paper Chase.*

Intelligence reports had demonstrated that the British Broadcasting Corporation's broadcasts to Germany and occupied countries had a large audience even though listening, in some cases, was punishable by death. The broadcasts were an integral part of the British war effort and demonstrated that it was possible to reach citizens even of enemy regimes that made listening difficult and dangerous. The British short-wave service—now the BBC World Service—and the Voice of America broadcast throughout the war and expanded hours and languages after the war.

The U.S. government activity at the end of the war came when occupation forces in Germany and Japan opened information centers so the public, after a heavy dose of anti-U.S. propaganda from their own governments during the war, could learn about the nation that would control their immediate future and influence them permanently. In Germany, each center was known as an "Amerika Haus" and became a combination reading room, lending library, and general gathering point for information about the United States.

In 1953, these activities were brought together into a single agency, the United States Information Agency, or USIA. The agency later took over from the State Department educational exchange programs, such as the well-known Fulbright program established at the end of the war when the then-young senator from Arkansas proposed using the proceeds from the sale of surplus war materiel to promote international educational exchange activities.

The USIA overseas operations retained the name they had acquired, United States Information *Service,* USIS. Now the diplomats and bureaucrats use the term *USIS* to refer to the overseas operations and activities and *USIA* refers to the agency's headquarters in downtown Washington, D.C. Overseas libraries/cultural centers are often named for distinguished Americans or called simply the American Center, American Cultural Center, or American Library. Agency officials take pride in knowing that most cab drivers in major cities overseas know immediately where to take you when you tell them you want the American cultural center or simply USIS (pronounced YOU-sis).

USIA Today

If you could get a tour of a well-guarded U.S. embassy overseas (or any foreign embassy in Washington, D.C.), you would find an umbrella organization. In addition to the ambassador and his or her staff, who belong to the State Department (or Foreign Ministry) and more or less run the place, you would find representatives of a range of other government agencies. These include the Peace Corps, U.S. Agency for International Development (USAID), the military, possibly Drug Enforcement Administration and Treasury agents, Departments of Commerce and Agriculture, and presumably the intelligence services. You would also find USIS whose chief is called the public affairs officer (PAO) for the embassy. He or she both runs the USIS operation and serves as the ambassador's staff adviser on public diplomacy. The operation may consist of a single USIA foreign service officer with a small staff of local employees to nearly a dozen officers with a staff numbering in the hundreds staffing a half dozen branch centers.

Libraries or centers are not intended to serve U.S. tourists but are open to anyone, including homesick travelers who need a fix of familiar newspapers and magazines. A few of the largest libraries are comparable to medium-size university libraries and maintain impressive research and reference collections. The smallest are storefront reading rooms with a few shelves of books and handful of newspapers and magazines. Most are comparable to a small-town library with modest

The United States Information Service (USIS) library in Auckland, New Zealand, is one of nearly 160 libraries and reading rooms in 100 countries maintained by the United States Information Agency (USIA). In addition to normal library services, major activities include English language instruction and advice about study in the United States.

SOURCE: Robert B. Laing.

collections of books, periodicals, basic research and reference sources, and—increasingly—videotapes. Unlike hometown libraries, USIS centers sometimes offer English language lessons, and all supply information about U.S. colleges and universities and advice to the several million students who inquire about study in the United States each year. Most centers also have meeting and classrooms, exhibit areas, and frequently an auditorium that host a stream of speakers, performers, exhibitions, and other activities.

The USIS center is the most visible part of the agency's activities—and an occasional target of protests—but public diplomacy is broader. At larger USIS posts (as they're called overseas), the work is divided into cultural affairs and information. The former is less political and generally noncontroversial and includes operation of the library, educational and cultural exchange programs, and other cultural activities. The information office functions as the public relations/public information for the embassy and is more closely tied to foreign policy.

It's difficult to describe a "typical" USIS operation because they vary by size and location. Imagine, however, a medium-size post that includes a half dozen USIA foreign service officers with 100 local employees running a main library/cultural centers in the national capital and two or three branch facilities in the larger regional cities. In any given week, you will find the cultural affairs officer (CAO) ordering books and magazines for the libraries, overseeing English-language classes and a full-time academic advisor for students interested in study in the United States, and coordinating arrangements for a visiting speaker and jazz concert and workshop. He or she probably is also involved in some aspect of the Fulbright program, which is actually run by a binational commission that sets programs and selects participants.

The information officer (IO) may spend the day responding to reporters' questions and requests for film or photos, making sure that key editors and government officials get the full text of a presidential address (distributed by USIA's wireless file), and planning a seminar to explain the intricacies of a presidential election to local journalists and politicians. The library itself is generally open to the public, including Americans looking for a quiet, air-conditioned respite from the rigors of tourism and exchange professors updating lecture notes.

Criticism

By law, USIA is prohibited from distributing its products within the United States, although an exception was made for a scholarly journal called *Problems of Communism* that perished with communism. The purpose is to keep the agency from becoming a domestic propaganda arm of the president, but it works to USIA's advantage. A large part of the material distributed overseas is reprinted from domestic sources that are willing to authorize further use as long as it does not compete with their own sales at home.

The effect of having a government public diplomacy operation barred from domestic operation is that very few Americans even know that USIA exists. The good side of this is that USIA operates without most of the special interest and congressional influence that plagues most government agencies. The bad side is that the agency has virtually no domestic constituency to protect it from presidents who want to mobilize it for short-term political gain by shoring up unpopular policies overseas or members of Congress looking for an easy way to cut the budget without threatening domestic programs. The Fulbright program is a partial exception. Its tens of thousands of alumni mobilized successfully when the Reagan administration wanted to shift money from educational exchange to more pointed information activities. On the whole, however, USIA goes about its business in Washington and abroad with little public or media attention.

Critics point to a schizophrenic streak in USIA that is inevitable in a government-run propaganda program in a country where separation of government and media is part of the secular theology. Three aspects of USIA operations are especially vulnerable to these complaints. One is lumping both the educational and cultural programs—nonpartisan, long-range, and generally very effective—with the information programs that are, almost by definition, partisan, focused on short-term policies, and inevitably suspect in foreign newsrooms. The handful of other countries that maintain comparable public diplomacy activities tend to separate the two so that the one does not taint the other. At USIS, the question is whether the visiting musician or Fulbright scholarship is at heart a cover for a campaign to win support for U.S. foreign policy. Overseas, it sometimes means that students rally for anti-U.S. demonstrations at the USIS library—a well-known and visible symbol—during the day and then return in the evening for English lessons or advice on getting into graduate school in the United States.

The second issue is the role of the Voice of America, which is accessible to anyone in the United States with a short-wave receiver. Like the rest of USIA, it carries a mandate to deliver news and other programming with the highest professional standards and is generally acknowledged to deal with the dark sides of U.S. life candidly. Official policy under the Reagan and Bush administrations was presented as clearly labeled "editorials." This must have confused listeners in countries where the distinction of information and opinion—even in newspapers—is unknown. Aside from a slower rate of delivery and emphasis on international affairs, a VOA English newscast sounds very much like that of a domestic station.

Because most of the major short-wave broadcasters come from countries where domestic broadcasting is either government controlled or part of a public system subject to varying government influence, the question arises why VOA should not be part of a combined domestic-international service such as the BBC or Deutsche Welle, the German international short-wave service that belongs to the consortium of domestic broadcasters that make up ARD.

A call to change U.S. public diplomacy surfaces every few years, but no president is willing to give up even the cultural side of USIA to a totally independent public body, and a forced marriage of VOA and National Public Radio (NPR) probably would be fought from all sides. From one would come the familiar warnings of a government-run domestic propaganda apparatus, from the other warnings of a weak but respected domestic public broadcast system getting entangled with overseas propaganda. Given the turf wars that accompany any bureaucratic reform and lack of public pressure for change, any change in the U.S. government's public diplomacy apparatus and programs is unlikely.

Finally, there is a small controversy around USIA's second mission. In addition to carrying out public diplomacy abroad, the original legislation mandates USIA to advise the president on overseas response to U.S. policy. To do this, USIS posts monitor overseas media and opinion polls and send reports of media and popular reaction back to Washington. A small research staff in Washington commissions opinion polls overseas and also tries to understand what people abroad think of the United States and why. Presumably foreign opinion is one factor considered in formulating policy. The PAO acting as advisor on public diplomacy has a similar role at the U.S. embassy overseas.

The controversy is over the fine line between public diplomacy and psychological operations—''psyops,'' as the military calls it—that are oriented toward discovering psychological vulnerabilities in a target group and exploiting those vulnerabilities as part of a broader offensive. Even the agency-sponsored public opinion surveys overseas frequently generate controversy, although it is not clear why some people who like to express their opinion of U.S. foreign policy by throwing rocks through the USIS library windows are outraged when the agency surveys opinion on a more systematic basis. Because the agency reports back to Washington, critics charge that it is really an intelligence agency hiding behind cultural and educational exchange. In fact, while USIA is clearly a part of the foreign policy apparatus of the federal government, it keeps itself at arm's length from the spooks.

OTHER PUBLIC DIPLOMACY

Operating a successful public diplomacy service is limited to the handful of Western democracies that have the money, human resources, and credibility to mount an effort something like USIA. Most follow a similar mix of international short wave radio, long-term and apolitical cultural and educational activities, and short-term information programs related to policy. However, most countries separate the functions and organize them differently on the assumption that long-range benefits of programs untainted by suspicions of short-range propaganda goals outweigh the loss of political control.

The British government pays for the BBC World Service and specifies the languages and hours of programming in each, but content is left to the BBC. As we saw in Chapter 6, the BBC maintains a reputation for independence and authority despite severe legal restrictions at home. If anything, its global reputation is even higher. In dozens of countries, events are not taken as real until the BBC reports them. Even more national leaders, while mobilizing their own domestic media under the banner of national development, tune in the crackling, unstable World Service signal to find out what's going on in the world, sometimes even in their own countries.

British cultural and educational activities are handled through the British Council, a government-funded body that operates abroad outside the umbrella of the British embassy. Oversight and policy guidance come indirectly from the government and directly from boards made up of experts in relevant areas of programming such as the arts and teaching of English as a second language. Germany follows a similar pattern with its string of Goethe Institutes around the world. France's Alliance Francaise is part of a cluster of similar libraries and cultural centers that are found in the diplomatic quarter or university area of most national capitals. Canada, Australia, and Japan maintain similar operations, although mostly on a regional scale. Few other countries even try to compete regionally, although most embassies have a press officer and occasionally someone who handles other aspects of public diplomacy along with other duties.

The Soviet Union and some of its richer allies also ran large public diplomacy operations, usually focused on a center with the pretentious name of "palace of culture" or binational "friendship society." In most cases, the palace of culture was noted for ugly architecture and a smattering of programs and materials that were of little interest to their intended audiences. At one point in the 1960s, a Soviet cultural attaché in Latin America discreetly asked his counterpart at USIS about materials for teaching English. Courses in Russian had drawn no response.

The size of a foreign cultural center—even the presence of one—and scope of its activities are a function of history, geography, and current foreign policy of the sponsoring government. Only a few countries can maintain a public presence around the world, and some prefer to expend their public diplomacy budgets on scholarships, junkets for foreign journalists and government officials, or even lobbying abroad. Others prefer to concentrate on promoting tourism and trade, assuming that public understanding abroad will follow.

One activity, however, that is nearly universal is international short-wave broadcasting. It is the one propaganda activity that, in theory, allows any government to reach the world without ever crossing its own borders. An evening with a pocket-size short-wave receiver—late night and early morning are best, daytime the worst for both technical and programming reasons—is a simple armchair tour of the world. Interpretations of the day's events are as varied, jumbled, and cacophonous as the signals themselves.

SHORT-WAVE RADIO

Chapter 13 described the unusual quality of short-wave signals—tucked into the spectrum between the medium wave AM and very high frequency FM and TV sound band—to bounce off the ionosphere to receivers thousands of kilometers from the transmitters. Even with a high-quality receiver, reception can be unreliable and marginal. But if local media are nonexistent or lacking in credibility, people will strain their ears to pick out a signal from London, Washington, D.C., or Moscow. Sometimes, of course, people tune in several stations to get different points of view.

As the Data Base in this chapter indicates, only a half dozen countries are truly global broadcasters according to criteria of broadcast hours and languages. Even these numbers can be misleading because smaller broadcasters typically tape a single 30- to 90-minute program and broadcast it over and over. VOA and BBC, in contrast, repeat some of their programs but do all of their news programs live.

Most broadcast only from transmitters at home, which limits the signal. While in theory the signals will travel around the globe, in practice, reliable reception is possible when transmitter and receiver are separated by no more than a few thousand kilometers. The handful of true global broadcasters (1) have transmitter complexes around the world, (2) broadcast each program on multiple frequencies, and (3) maintain extensive information-gathering networks that allow them to be fast and comprehensive. VOA and BBC are among the very few that operate with the sense of urgency we associate with CNN or other domestic news services. With technology such as the portable satellite phone, it is possible—and no longer uncommon—for a field reporter to broadcast live from a remote part of the world through the global satellite system to London or Washington, then to listeners around the world.

Usually the short-wave services are identified as representing, more or less, the governments that pay for them, but exceptions occur. Radio Free Europe (RFE) and Radio Liberty (RL) were set up by the U.S. government at the end of World War II to broadcast to communist Central Europe and the Soviet Union respectively. Their goal was to function as watchdogs of government, albeit in exile, as media do in the West. RFE and RL were embarrassed in 1971 when the main source of their funding was revealed to be the U.S. government, funneling most of their operating funds through the CIA, rather then contributions from a public dedicated to penetrating the Iron Curtain. Often criticized as relics of the cold war, the two broadcasters were embarrassed again when the Iron Curtain collapsed. It turned out that they were more popular and more successful than even the coldest warrior had claimed. Lech Walesa, Vaclav Havel, and Mikhail Gorbachev were among the voices urging that the services be maintained even after the reasons for their creation had disappeared. President Clinton was unimpressed, however, and called for their disbanding, although some of their resources would be transferred to VOA. A similar exile voice to Cuba, Radio Marti, which was established in response to political pressure from Cuban Americans, was left alone, although less reason existed for its continued existence because Cubans could listen to Spanish-language stations in Miami. In Washington, post–cold war talk focused on establishing a ''Radio Free Asia'' to broadcast to China and several other closed regimes.

Traditional short-wave remained an important piece of the global communication system in the 1990s, but the medium was changing. BBC and VOA led the change, not surprisingly, securing medium wave frequencies in several Central European cities and feeding their services directly or on tape to private stations around the world. In early 1992, VOA Europe—a snappy 24-hour-a-day rock service with news and features interspersed among the top 40—was the most popular station in Sofia, Bulgaria. VOA Europe competed with the BBC for a new generation of listeners in the heart of Europe, including those who practiced their English by listening to the World Service broadcast on the eight FM transmitters the BBC rented in Czechoslovakia. Both services supplied programming to local broadcasters who mixed it with their own to extend the stations' total reach.

Audiences

Based on a mixture of scientific surveys, hunches, and hopes, both BBC and VOA estimated the weekly audiences of their direct broadcasts at about 120 million listeners. BBC had the edge in southern Asia and Anglophone Africa; VOA was probably ahead in China and Central America. Formerly communist nations of Europe were up for grabs, with RFE/RL still ahead of both. The audience jumped dramatically everywhere during moments of crisis. Programs fed directly or on tape to medium wave stations increased the total audience by a factor of several times the direct audience, but neither broadcaster was willing to guesstimate a grand total. Medium-wave relays, placement on local stations, and short-wave via direct broadcast satellites, if the technology emerged, seemed to be global radio's future in the twenty-first century.

Strategies

BBC and VOA operate with somewhat differing broadcast philosophies. The BBC's World Service English broadcasts emanate from studios in central London around the clock and are beamed via satellite and surface transmitters to different parts of the world at different times of the day. Usually you can pick up the signals for several hours in the early morning and again in the evening. Almost every hour begins with the words, "This is London," and a sprightly version of an Irish song, "Lilliburlero." After a news summary, programming usually moves to extended public affairs coverage and various entertainment segments in the second half of the hour. At various times during the day, you will find rock and country music, even an original play of the week. Quarter hours are noted with chimes from Big Ben, picked up by an open microphone in the clock tower of the House of Parliament. Specific programs—the play of the week, several hour-long news programs—may or may not be broadcast when listeners in specific regions want them, a constant headache for those who put together the broadcast schedule.

VOA's English programs, in contrast, are regionalized. A morning program to Africa may be on the air from one of the tiny studios in the basement of the Health and Human Services Building on Independence Avenue at the same time as an evening program is broadcast from a studio across the hall to listeners in Asia. Like BBC, the VOA top-of-the-hour newscast is live and the same for all services. Then the regional services offer a magazine format of pop music, interviews, and extended news features. These are alternated with longer programs of music and public affairs that are timed to preferred listening times in target regions. Services sign on and off with a laid-back version of "Yankee Doodle" and use musical variations on the three letters—V - O - A—as bridges within the programs. Periodically news and special features are broadcast in Special English, an unusual-sounding service using a limited vocabulary (word lists are available at USIS posts) and a *very* slow rate of speaking. It is designed, of course, for English-language beginners and listeners trying to pick out the weak VOA signal from a crowded spectrum.

With high-quality FM stereo broadcasts the standard in most countries and digital radio, perhaps beamed directly from satellites, on the horizon, short-wave radio's crowded, crackling signals seem to be a relic of outmoded technology, but they aren't. In information-poor countries, a search of the medium-wave spectrum often produces at best one or two weak signals. Away from the capital city, it is not unusual to be outside the range of any consistent signal for hours on end. Even when a local signal is available, competent programming, especially news, is limited to nonexistent and often confined to the low-credibility puffery that passes for news in the development and authoritarian media concepts.

With the exception of a handful of religious broadcasters headquartered in the United States, short-wave radio belongs to governments and is noncommercial (unless you consider the entire service an advertisement for the sponsoring government). However, conventional advertising is a large—and growing—component of global persuasive communication. The two fledgling global television news services, CNN International and the BBC World Service Television, are, of course, financed by ads, but most media remain national rather than global. Nevertheless, people around the world learn about Big Macs and the United Colors of Bennetton.

ADVERTISING

Students sometimes sign up for advertising courses on the assumption that the craft resembles an episode of *thirtysomething*. They assume that an advertising career will have them dividing their time, like Michael and Elliott, between personal crises and thinking up clever slogans.

Advertising does include that—thinking up clever slogans, not coping with personal crises—but the field is much broader. Most of the people in it spend most of their time pounding the pavement selling time and space, calculating costs-per-exposure, and planning media buys. Given what we have seen so far on our global tour of global communication, it it is reasonable to learn that (1) advertising is growing rapidly, especially outside of the media-saturated Anglo-American world and (2) Anglo-America dominates global advertising, just as it dominates other parts of the global system. What may not be so obvious is that advertising remains largely a national medium, even though the products and media are increasingly global.

Global Advertising

Modern advertising began more than a century ago when James Walter Thompson began designing advertisements for clients. Before that, the business consisted of buying space in newspapers and magazines on behalf of local clients. Most ads were simple announcements of the availability of local products or services until mass production and distribution made it necessary to tout the advantages of a mass-produced product imported from outside the community over the equivalent made at home.

Now advertising is a multibillion-dollar global industry that includes billboards in Red Square aimed at the international audience of the May Day parade and TV commercials for Boeing jets in China. Everybody in the world, it seems, knows the icons and jingles of a global consumer society. As a result, as *The Economist* notes, "the Coca-Cola can may be better known than the crucifix."[2]

It's hard to get a clear focus on the industry. It overlaps with marketing, public relations, and other forms of promotion. Even statistics can be confusing, but some international comparisons are possible. Agencies usually calculate the total amount of money that moves through their accounts, but most of it goes to produce the advertising and to buy the space and time to get it in front of the consumer. The agency commission is usually 15 percent, not loose change when the annual billings total a billion dollars or more.[3] Twenty agencies around the world billed more than $1 billion in 1990. Six of them had gross incomes—the agency cut of the total billing—of a billion dollars or more.[3] Half of the "big 20 club" are in New York City, two (the largest agencies in the world) are in London, four are in Paris, and four are in Tokyo.

Sliced a different way, the global advertising pie confirms the international traveler's suspicion that advertising is more pervasive in the United States than anywhere else on the planet. At more than $500 per person per year, the per capita advertising expenditure in the United States is twice that of Canada ($248) and almost as far ahead of Finland ($359) and Switzerland ($302), which rank second and third. Translated into a national total, the $130 *billion* spent on advertising in the United States (about equivalent to the national expenditure on higher education) is more than the rest of the world combined. Even the federal government spends more than $300 million a year, most of it on military recruiting.[4]

British Giants

Recall the global trends of Anglo-American dominance in international communication and the emergence of a global culture. Consistent with these trends, international advertising follows the arc of Anglo-American influence. But although the entertainment component of global communication is anchored in Hollywood, global advertising, like news, follows the curve from New York City to London. London—not New York City—is the center, thanks to the presence of the two largest agencies in the world, WPP Group and Saatchi & Saatchi Co. The WPP Group logged billings of more than $18 billion in 1990 (and gross income of more than $2 billion). Second-place Saatchi & Saatchi had billings of nearly $12 billion and gross income of $1.7 billion, slightly ahead of third-place Omnicom Group in New York City.

The first of the British giants was founded in 1970 when two Iraqi-born brothers, Maurice and Charles Saatchi, established a tiny advertising agency in

---

[2] "The Advertising Industry," *The Economist,* June 9, 1990, p. 1.

[3] "World's Top 50 Advertising Organizations," *Advertising Age,* January 8, 1992, p. S6.

[4] Andrew L. Shapiro, *We're Number One: Where America Stands—and Falls—in the New World Order* (New York: Vintage, 1992), p. 174. The figures are from 1988–1990.

a country where advertising was clever but subdued and much less prominent in the popular and media culture. They quickly developed a reputation for creativity, such as the British Airways commercial in which the entire island of Manhattan took off from New York and landed in London. They also operated on two principles that seemed reasonable at the time: one-stop service including public relations and marketing as well as advertising and globalization of services.

For two decades, particularly in the business-friendly atmosphere of Prime Minister Thatcher's regnum, the Saatchis prospered. "To Saatchi" meant to sell aggressively, and the agency was known for clever, creative products, such as the famous billboard for the Conservative party that featured a queue of unemployed with the slogan, "Labour Isn't Working." A global perspective on a global industry kept the money rolling in and allowed the brothers to buy several leading New York agencies. Then in 1985, Saatchi & Saatchi's finance director, Martin Sorrell, decided he could do better alone and left the company to take over a small manufacturing company that originally made wire and plastic products (hence the name WPP).

WPP took after Saatchi & Saatchi and then overtook it in billings to become the largest agency in the world. Both companies were caught up in the corporate takeover frenzy of the late 1980s and were helped by a weak dollar and political environment in both countries that encouraged freewheeling capitalism not seen since the robber barons of the nineteenth century. The sudden shift of the global advertising from Madison Avenue in New York to London was not the result of a growth in the industry itself but of the purchase of major U.S. agencies by the two aggressive British upstarts. The emergence of Saatchi & Saatchi and WPP as the global giants had a lot in common with leveraged buyouts of big, old companies by small, aggressive companies on Wall Street.

Saatchi & Saatchi set the pattern by buying Ted Bates Worldwide in 1986 and then Dancer Fitzgerald Sample, both large, well-established agencies. Then WPP moved ahead by buying the JWT Group, parent of the venerable J. Walter Thompson agency in 1987 and then the Ogilvy Group in 1989, the latter a classic hostile takeover worthy of Gordon Gekko of the film *Wall Street*. Other purchases allowed each giant to operate two separate, often competing global agencies. If your competition's advertising went to one, you could sign with the other. The two competed with each other until the end of the year when the profits flowed back into the parent conglomerate. In the mid-1980s environment of exploding global communication, growing global markets and advertising budgets, and friendly governments in London and Washington, Saatchi & Saatchi and WPP seemed destined to join Murdoch, Bertelsmann, and Sony as the creators of the twenty-first century's information empires.

The two new giants of global advertising barely had time to draw up their organizational charts, however, before their advertising empires began to crumble. Part of the problem was the economic downturn that hit both the United States and Britain. The two media-saturated markets accounted for the giant part of their business, and advertising remained very sensitive to economic conditions. Part was the inevitable risk of high-stakes economic growth that sent a good number of hard-charging tycoons to millionaire-status one day and to bankruptcy (or jail) the next. In 1990 and 1991, ledger sheets changed from multimillion-dollar profits to red ink, and pink slips replaced buyout tenders. In 1992, the dynamic duo's troubles continued. Saatchi & Saatchi's pretax losses increased to $1.05 billion (from $83 million in the previous year). WPP finished in the black with 1992 profits of $13.7 million, an 86 percent drop in a year.

National Campaigns

Both Saatchi & Saatchi and WPP—and most other international agencies that suffered comparable setbacks—survived the great crash at the beginning of the 1990s, but the experience produced a rethinking of the principles behind their rapid growth. Economic conditions and growth policies aside, they asked at the trendy watering holes where account executives still gathered after work, is the future of advertising in the direction of one-stop persuasive communication agencies and global campaigns? Despite the emergence of a global culture and global communication systems, the direction of advertising in the twenty-first century was not clear. Skeptics could cite several reasons why advertising remained essentially a national enterprise.

Absence of Global Media. Despite the nearly universal use of Western (especially Anglo-American) media products around the world, virtually all media are national rather than regional or global. And the handful of global media are tailored to national advertisers. When the TV network in country X buys *Dallas* or a Mexican telenovela, it adapts it for a domestic market. This may be nothing more than dubbing the soundtrack and deciding where to put in the commercials (or editing out the existing breaks). Sometimes, of course, local laws or customs mandate further changes, but in virtually every case, these are decisions made at the national level in preparation for broadcast on national systems.

Even the handful of international print media offer advertisers various advertising editions. Just as an advertiser can buy specific states, regions, or metropolitan areas in the domestic editions of *Time, The Economist,* or the *Wall Street Journal*—always packed around the same editorial content—overseas advertisers can buy single countries, mixes of various countries, or regions. The copy of the European edition of *Newsweek* you buy in London, Paris, or Rome will have the same stories and pictures, but the ads will differ, even to the point that occasionally ads appear in languages other than English.

Time got itself into trouble when it offered an "ex-Israel" advertising edition of its European/Middle East/African editorial edition. The specific advertising edition circulated to all of markets normally receiving that specific editorial edition except Israel. The practice allowed companies honoring an Arab-sponsored boycott to advertise in *Time* without the risk of being thrown out of Arab countries. Jewish groups in the United States and Congress were not amused when existence of the ex-Israel edition became known, and *Time* was forced to cancel it.

Broadcasting is either noncommercial (short-wave services) or national. The one exception to the general pattern of national media is CNN International and the BBC World Service Television, both of which carry advertising. However, at this point, advertising on these channels is minimal—mostly a few commercials for British and U.S. tourists—and the signals are usually fed into cable systems, where local commercials can be inserted, just as they are on domestic U.S. cable systems. The handful of regional TV channels and DBS services in Europe represent a minor exception to the general principle that advertising, even for globally marketed products, reaches out to target audiences on national channels. Even when supranational media are available, legal restrictions can get in the way.

Legal Restrictions.   In special circumstances, the global information system overrides normal national channels and the national gatekeepers who usually decide what gets into the national media and what is kept out. During the Gulf War, a number of countries in the Middle East that maintain tight control of domestic media allowed people who could afford it to install satellite dishes that could receive CNN. After the war, however, the dishes disappeared from Saudi Arabia.

In many countries, CNN was patched into national systems without any effort to control content. Along with the news came commercials, including an occasional spot for alcoholic products that are normally prohibited on Norwegian television. Other countries also carried CNN—and occasionally other sources—live, but in most cases, the exception to national broadcast laws or policies was overlooked in favor of the drama of live coverage. When the war ended, CNN was unplugged, and the national broadcasters went back to normal practice. Norwegians were again spared commercials for beer and wine.

Global events aside, variations in national laws make multinational advertising almost impossible. Even in the United States, where advertising is constitutionally protected "commercial speech," cigarette ads do not appear on TV, and no one is ever seen actually drinking a Bud or Miller Lite. Of course, in most other countries the rules and regulations are more complex. In 1989, two officials of J. Walter Thompson described the problems of promoting a theoretical low-fat diet candy bar, "Jupiter." A pan-European TV commercial would underscore three points: "Your waistline will like it, and you get a free tape measure to prove it"; "It's an after-school treat that won't spoil your evening meal"; and "When your doctor says cut down, reach for Jupiter, with one-third the calories of other chocolate bars." A simple challenge for Michael and Elliott? Even for them, it wouldn't be simple. Here's how the JWT team described the obstacles:

> In Belgium, commercials may not refer to dieting. In France, premiums can't be worth more than one percent of the sale price, which rules out the tape measure, and children can't give endorsements, which means no child eating a Jupiter after school. In West Germany, any comparison with another candy bar would be illegal; in Denmark, ads can't make nutritional claims; in Britain, candy must be presented as only an occasional snack—and no doctors in the commercial.[5]

---

[5] Quoted in Martin Mayer, *Whatever Happened to Madison Avenue? Advertising in the '90s* (Boston: Little, Brown, 1991), p. 204.

Other national rules can also influence advertising. A few countries require some proportion of domestic content or use of domestic labor. Revlon spent an extra $100,000 filming ads in Australia and Colombia after the governments refused the U.S. version. The local versions, of course, were virtually identical to the original. Some companies found it cheaper to fly in a foreign film crew to stand around with their hands in their pockets while the U.S. commercial was shot than to repeat the process abroad. Apparently governments and labor unions were appeased.[6] Even when laws and professional practices permit the same message in different countries, cultural differences become an issue.

Cultural Differences.   Culture, as we have seen, is a powerful countervailing force to the globalization of communication and a complex element of any persuasive communication campaign. When your product hits a cultural barrier overseas, you can change the product or the advertising. Usually the latter is the easier solution, but not always.

U.S. brand catsup is noticeably sweeter in Australia, and Oreo cookies are sold in Japan without the cream center because it is too sweet for Japanese tastes. On the other hand, Hershey chocolate chose to ignore the European market rather than sweeten its distinctly bitter product to European preferences. The usual approach is to look for ways of promoting the same product with different appeals that match the culture of the country. Tang was promoted in France as a general refreshment good for any time of the day after someone noticed that the French rarely drink orange juice and never for breakfast. Canon promoted its cameras in the United States for their simplicity of use but in Japan for their high-tech qualities. Americans, it seems, are afraid of complex technology—consider the millions who never learn to program their VCRs—but Japanese see technological complexity as sophisticated and modern.

What is commonplace in one market is chic in another. In Beijing, a customer visiting the Golden Arches for the first time noted, "I guess for a high-fashion restaurant like this, the prices are OK."[7]

In Chapter 4, we noted one international advertising failure, the "no-go" Spanish name of the Chevrolet Nova. It is hard to imagine Gott ice chests doing well in Germany because the company name means "God" in German (and, of course, Germans seldom use ice). Usually advertising agencies are sensitive enough to avoid most of the obvious gaffes that make up the lore of cross-cultural blunders, but international advertising is still a minefield for anyone who thinks only of global markets and ignores the persistence of culture.

"Think Global, Act Local" is the motto of one global agency as well as the environmental movement. Sometimes it means changing the product, sometimes changing the advertising message, sometimes merely making sure that the details reflect the local culture. This can mean redoing the identical commercial in each country to capture the nuances of language, behavior, and appearance. Check

---

[6] Ronald Alsop and Bill Brams, eds., "Playing by International Rules," *The Wall Street Journal on Marketing* (New York: New American Library, 1986), pp. 246–248.

[7] "Overheard," *Newsweek,* May 4, 1992, p. 21.

similar broadcast or print ads in culturally close countries (Austria and Germany, Colombia and Venezuela, Lebanon and Jordan, Canada and the United States) for subtle differences.

One company that unabashedly uses a global approach in advertising is the Italian clothing retailer, Bennetton. Its "United Colors of Bennetton" slogan and provocative ads are used around the world and seem to have little to do with selling sweaters. Raising controversial social issues and getting into the news, however, may be part of the strategy. Minorities in the United States protested an ad showing a closeup of two men—one black, one white—handcuffed together. Another ad showing a closeup of a black woman nursing a white baby won awards in Europe but was considered too provocative for the United States and Britain. A shot of a U.S. military cemetery with rows of cross-shaped gravestones surrounding a lone Star of David had the misfortune to appear during the Gulf War. In Italy, it was ruled an offense to religion and banned. The government there was not happy either with a photo of a traditionally attired priest and nun locked in a very unplatonic embrace. All in the name of global social consciousness, according to the company. And, of course, selling sweaters.

THE FUTURE

Future Shock

A 1970 book introduced a phrase that has become part of the popular vocabulary. It seems to describe global communication in the twenty-first century. *Future Shock* is a combination of culture shock and time. This is how Alvin Toffler defines it:

> The culture shock phenomenon accounts for much of the bewilderment, frustration, and disorientation that plagues Americans in their dealings with other societies. It causes a breakdown in communication, a misreading of reality, an inability to cope. Yet culture shock is relatively mild in comparison with the much more serious malady, future shock. Future shock is the dizzying disorientation brought on by the premature arrival of the future. It may well be the most important disease of tomorrow.[8]

Early in this book, we talked about culture shock, defined there as problems of understanding and adapting to different languages and cultures. Future shock is tougher to cope with because, as Toffler notes, there is no escape. If unfamiliar languages, unfamiliar foods, and unfamiliar customs are overwhelming, you can usually go back home, where life is familiar and reassuring. The future is different. We have no choice; we all have to live there.

Recall some of the patterns of change described in several chapters and Data Bases: growth of radio and TV sets in the third world, global growth of telecommunication traffic, the capacity of the global communication system, the amount of information that rushes through it, and the speed of information flow. All follow an exponential curve that doubles over each time period. After passing

---

[8] Alvin Toffler, *Future Shock* (New York: Bantam, 1971), p. 10.

the takeoff point, the curve becomes nearly vertical. Change gathers speed, racing toward an inevitable crash.

Older people are right when they complain that everything seems to move faster now. Indeed it does. We have more information and get it faster, and it is harder to avoid. Traditional cultures have the most trouble coping with future shock because they are least capable of absorbing change. But even in our own culture, which has always been oriented more toward the future than toward the past, future shock causes discomfort.

Cultural Squeeze

Toffler documents the acceleration of change with several factors that have figured prominently in our discussion of communication revolutions. Accept his assumption that human civilization has existed about 50,000 years and that a lifetime lasts about 62 years. On that basis, there have been about 800 lifetimes or generations, at least 650 of which were spent in caves. Then change began:

> Only during the last seventy lifetimes has it been possible to communicate effectively from one lifetime to another—as writing made it possible to do so. Only during the last six lifetimes did masses of men ever see a printed word. Only during the last four has it been possible to measure time with any precision. Only in the last two has anyone anywhere used an electric motor. And the overwhelming majority of all the material goods we use in daily life today have been developed within the present, the 800th, lifetime.[9]

Put another way, half of all the collective activities of humankind—half of cultural change—have taken place during the lifetime of an adult living today.[10] No wonder the present seems confused and the future hopelessly chaotic.

It is impossible to avoid the future—and future shock—but it is possible to immunize ourselves and our cultures from part of the disruption that accompanies rapid change. Several of the writers we have encountered on these pages offer sound advice for and a hopeful interpretation of the future: tolerance of differences, flexibility in accommodating change, and willingness to embrace the future rather than fighting it.

Many of the problems that are likely to fill the future are, in fact, a result of progress. People die of cancer and heart disease in their 70s and 80s because they didn't die of smallpox and polio as children. Overpopulation is a product of dramatic improvements in health and food production. Wars are getting smaller, less deadly, and probably less frequent. Reporters in the future won't run out of coups and earthquakes to report, but we need to remind ourselves again that news in the future as now, will be largely the disruptive exceptional event, not what happens to most people most of the time.

---

9 Alvin Toffler, *Future Shock* (New York: Bantam, 1971), p. 14.

10 The idea is from Kenneth Boulding, *The Meaning of the 20th Century* (New York: Harper & Row, 1964), quoted by Toffler.

Change, progress, and the future are likely to be exciting as well as discomforting, full of progress and discovery as well as disruption, and more and more accessible even to the armchair traveler. Best of all, you will be able to watch the global trends woven into these pages create a new tapestry of human achievement that will be as different at the end of the twenty-first century as it is near the beginning.

MAIN POINTS

1. The global communication system offers increasing opportunities for governments, private corporations, and occasionally individuals to reach and influence people around the world. Scholars still debate whether mass media have mass effects or only limited effects on audiences, but efforts to influence audiences around the world continue.

2. All governments engage in public diplomacy—or propaganda—which is an effort to reach people and influence public opinion in other countries. A few countries operate extensive programs of public information, educational and cultural exchange, and international broadcasting.

3. The United States Information Agency, known as United States Information Service abroad, is responsible for U.S. public diplomacy. Activities include public information and cultural centers in most countries, the Fulbright and other educational exchange programs, and the Voice of America (but not Radio Free Europe and Radio Liberty, which are funded by the U.S. government but operated separately).

4. Most countries broadcast internationally on short-wave frequencies. A few services—VOA, the BBC World Service, Radio Beijing, Radio Moscow before the collapse of the Soviet Union—operate global systems and reach audiences around the world. Short-wave is an important source of information in many parts of the world where domestic services are inadequate or lack credibility.

5. International advertising is increasing, but advertising of even globally marketed goods and services is still largely a national activity. A lack of global media, government rules, and cultural factors make global advertising difficult.

6. "Future shock" is the product of accelerating social change and the exponentially increasing global communication system. It is likely to increase in the twenty-first century.

FOR MORE INFORMATION

General information on public diplomacy is hard to come by. Details of USIA are contained in an annual review put by out by the United States Advisory Commission on Public Diplomacy, which has an office at USIA in Washington, D.C., and in congressional budget and oversight hearings. Thomas C. Sorensen's *The Word War: The Story of American Propaganda* (New York: Harper & Row, 1968) takes the agency into the Lyndon Johnson era. Wilson P. Dizard, *The Strategy of Truth: The Story of the U.S. Information Service* (Washington, D.C.: Public Affairs Press, 1961), covers much of the same ground. Both authors were USIA foreign service officers. Holly Cowan Shulman, *The Voice of America: Propaganda and Democracy, 1941–1945* (Madison: University of Wisconsin Press, 1990), covers the founding of VOA.

Current controversies and activities can be researched by searching contemporary news media data bases for USIA, VOA, and other key words.

Garth S. Jowett and Victoria O'Donnell, *Propaganda and Persuasion,* 2nd ed. (Newbury Park, CA: Sage, 1992), is wide ranging and includes an extensive bibliography.

Most advertising texts contain some material on international and global advertising, although less one would expect, given its size and growing importance. Criticisms of U.S. "cultural imperialism" usually contain some references to advertising.

Stephen Fox, *The Mirror Makers: A History of American Advertising and Its Creators* (New York: Vintage, 1985), is a good history with some discussion of international activities. Marti Mayer, *Whatever Happened to Madison Avenue? Advertising in the '90s* (Boston: Little, Brown, 1991), has a good chapter on international advertising.

FOR DISCUSSION

1. Interview international students about their knowledge of and attitudes toward USIA. Inquire about their use of the USIS facility in their home country to find out about studying in the United States and whether they listened to VOA.

2. Find someone in class who has a short wave radio and borrow it for a few days. Experiment to find frequencies and broadcast times of major international broadcasters. Then compare newscasts and other programming for several days and try to determine probable audiences and policy goals. If you can find a regular short-wave radio listener, ask him or her about reasons for listening and evaluations of various stations.

3. Look through popular magazines from different countries for advertisements of the same or similar products. Look for differences in the ads that reflect subtle cultural differences. Identify products that seem to use the same advertising in different countries.

DATA BASE

I. Weekly hours of international short-wave broadcasting:

	1950	1960	1970	1980	1992	Number of Languages in 1992
The West						
United States*	497	1,495	1,907	1,901	2,316	51
Britain	643	589	723	719	817	37
West Germany**	0	315	779	804	673	36
France	198	326	200	125	401	15
Israel	0	91	158	210	388	16
Turkey	40	77	88	199	346	16
Japan	0	203	259	259	336	22
Australia	181	257	350	333	326	8
Holland	127	178	335	289	315	9
Spain	68	202	251	239	263	9

	1950	*1960*	*1970*	*1980*	*1992*	*Number of Languages in 1992*
Communist						
China	66	687	1,267	1,350	1,668	43
Russia	533	1,015	1,908	2,094	1,317	46
North Korea	0	159	330	597	702	10
Bulgaria	30	117	164	297	308	12
Cuba	0	0	320	424	251	9
Albania	26	63	487	560	196	13
Romania	30	159	185	198	170	11
Czechoslovakia	119	196	202	255	143	6
Poland	131	232	334	337	110	8
East Germany	0	185	274	375	0	0
Third World						
Taiwan	NA	NA	NA	NA	1,281	16
South Korea	NA	NA	NA	NA	617	12
Egypt	0	301	540	546	593	30
India	116	157	271	389	541	24
Iran	12	24	155	175	400	18
Nigeria	0	0	62	170	120	5

* Includes VOA, RFE, and RL.
** Deutsche Welle and Deutschlandfunk.

SOURCE: "And Nation Shall Speak Guff unto Nation," *The Economist,* May 2, 1992, p. 21.

II. Languages used by VOA, RFE/RL, and BBC World Service:

BBC World Service

English, Albanian, Bulgarian, Croatian, Czech, Finnish, French, German, Greek, Hungarian, Polish, Portuguese, Romanian, Russian, Serbian, Slovak, Slovene, Turkish, Ukrainian (for Europe)

English, Arabic, French, Hausa, Portuguese, Somali, Swahili (for Africa)

English, Bengali, Burmese, Cantonese, Hindi, Indonesian, Mandarin, Nepali, Pashto, Persian, Sinhala, Tamil, Thai, Urdu, Vietnamese (for Asia)

English, Portuguese, Spanish (for Latin America)

Voice of America

Albanian, Amharic, Arabic, Armenian, Azerbaijani, Bangla, Bulgarian, Burmese, Cantonese, Creole, Croatian, Czech, Dari, English, Estonian, Farsi, French, Georgian, German, Greek, Hausa, Hindi,

Hungarian, Indonesian, Khmer, Korean, Kurdish, Lao, Latvian, Lithuanian, Mandarin, Pashto, Polish, Portuguese, Romanian, Russian, Serbian, Slovak, Slovene, Spanish, Swahili, Tibetan, Turkish, Ukrainian, Urdu, Uzbek, Vietnamese

Radio Free Europe (to Central Europe) and Radio Liberty (to countries of the former Soviet Union)
Armenian, Azerbaijani, Belarus, Bulgarian, Czech-Slovak, Dari, Estonian, Georgian, Hungarian, Kazak, Kyrgyz, Latvian, Lithuanian, Pashto, Polish, Romanian, Russian, Tajik, Tatar-Bashkir, Turkmen, Ukrainian, Uzbek

SOURCE: From information supplied by USIA, BBC, and the Board for International Broadcasting (RFE/RL).

III. The 10 largest advertising agencies in the world (by gross income) in 1990 are listed below. U.S.-based agencies belonging to each are in parentheses. The two figures are the agency's 1990 gross income and 1990 billings.

1. WPP Group, London (Ogilvy & Mather Worldwide; Ogilvy & Mather Direct; J. Walter Thompson Co.; Thompson Recruitment; Brouillard Communications; Scali, McCabe, Sloves; Fallon McElligott; Martin Agency): $2.7 billion income on billings of $18.1 billion.
2. Saatchi & Saatchi, London (Saatchi & Saatchi Advertising Worldwide; AC&R Advertising; Cadwell Davis Partners; Cliff Freeman & Partners; Conill Advertising; Klemtner Advertising; Runrill-Hoyt; Team One; Backer Spielvogel BatesWorldwide; Campbell-Mithun-Esty; Kobs & Draft): $1.7 billion income on billings of $11.9 billion.
3. Interpublic Group of Companies, New York City (McCann-Erickson Worldwide; Lintas Worldwide; Dailey & Associates; Laurence, Charles, Free & Lawson; Lowe & Partners; Fahlgren Martin): $1.6 billion income on billings of $11.2 billion.
4. Omnicom Group, New York City (BBDO Worldwide; Baxter, Gurian & Mazzei; Frank J. Corbett, Inc.; Doremus & Co.; Lavey/Wolff/Swift; Tracy-Locke; Rapp Collins Marcoa; DDB Needham Worldwide; Bernard Hodes Group; Kallir, Philips, Ross: $1.3 billion income on billings of $9.7 billion.
5. Dentsu, Inc., Tokyo (DCA Advertising): $1.3 billion income on billings of $9.7 billion.
6. Young & Rubicam, New York City (Young & Rubicom; Cato, Johnson Worldwide; Chapman Direct; Sudler & Hennessey; Creswel, Munsell, Fultz & Zirbel; Wunderman Worldwide; Dentsu, Young & Rubicom Partnerships): $1.1 billion income on billings of $8 billion.

7. Eurocom Group, Paris (Della Femina, McNamee): $748.5 million income on billings of $5.1 billion.
8. Hakuhodo, Inc., Tokyo (Hakuhodo Advertising America): $586.3 million income on billings of $4.5 billion.
9. Grey Advertising, New York City (Grey Advertising): $585.3 million income on billings of $3.9 billion.
10. Foote, Cone & Belding Communications, Chicago (Foote, Cone & Belding Communications; Albert Frank-Fuenther Law; Impact; Vicom/FCB; Publicis-FCB Communications): $536.2 million income on billings of $3.6 billion.

SOURCE: *Advertising Age,* January 6, 1992, p. S-6.

IV. Total spending on advertising and advertising spending per capita, 1988–1990:

Country	Millions	Per Capita Spending
United States	$128,640	$514
Finland	$1,776	$359
Switzerland	$2,001	$302
Canada	$6,440	$248
Australia	$3,928	$238
Japan	$27,345	$223
United Kingdom	$11,737	$206
Sweden	$1,646	$195
Norway	$759	$181
New Zealand	$569	$173
Germany	$10,326	$169
Denmark	$822	$160
Spain	$5,967	$153
Netherlands	$2,198	$149
France	$8,029	$144
Austria	$872	$115
Belgium	$1,095	$110
Italy	$5,776	$101
Ireland	$272	$77

SOURCE: Andrew L. Shapiro, *We're Number One! Where America Stands—and Falls—in the New World Order* (New York: Vintage, 1992), p. 174.

Index